Organizations

Organizations

Structures, Processes, and Outcomes

Ninth Edition

Richard H. Hall

Distinguished Service Professor
University at Albany
State University of New York

Pamela S. Tolbert

Professor
School of Industrial and Labor Relations
Cornell University

Pearson Education International

Publisher: Nancy Roberts
Executive Editor: Chris DeJohn
Managing Editor (Editorial): Sharon Chambliss
Editorial Assistant: Kristin Haegele
Full Service Production Liaison: Joanne Hakim
Senior Marketing Manager: Marissa Feliberty
Assistant Manufacturing Manager: Mary Ann Gloriande
Cover Art Director: Jayne Conte
Cover Designer: Bruce Kenselaar
Manager, Cover Visual Research & Permissions: Karen Sanatar
Cover Illustration/Photo: Javier Romero/Stock Illustration Source, Inc.
Composition/Full-Service Project Management: Penny Walker/*The GTS Companies*/
    York, PA Campus
Printer/Binder: Phoenix Book Tech Park

Credits and acknowledgments borrowed from other sources and reproduced, with permission, in this textbook appear on appropriate page within text.

Pearson Education Ltd., London
Pearson Education Singapore, Pte. Ltd
Pearson Education Canada, Ltd
Pearson Education—Japan
Pearson Education Australia PTY, Limited

Pearson Education North Asia Ltd
Pearson Educación de Mexico, S.A. de C.V.
Pearson Education Malaysia, Pte. Ltd
Pearson Education, Upper Saddle River, New Jersey

10 9 8 7 6 5 4 3 2 1
ISBN: 0-13-129378-8

For Sherry and for Steve

Brief Contents

Preface   xv

Part I   **The Nature of Organizations**
Chapter 1   The Nature of Organizations   1

Part II   **Organizational Structure**
Chapter 2   Organizational Structure: Forms and Outcomes   27
Chapter 3   Organizational Structure: Explanations   63

Part III   **Organizational Processes**
Chapter 4   Power and Power Outcomes   86
Chapter 5   Leadership   107
Chapter 6   Decision Making   127
Chapter 7   Communication   137
Chapter 8   Change   154

Part IV   **Organizational Environments**
Chapter 9   Organizational Environments and Interorganizational
             Relationships   173

Part V   **Organizational Theory and Organizational Effectiveness**
Chapter 10   Organizational Theory   207
Chapter 11   Organizational Effectiveness   222

References   245

Name Index   275

Subject Index   285

Contents

Preface   xv

Part I   The Nature of Organizations

Chapter 1   The Nature of Organizations   1

Overview   *1*
Why Study Organizations?   *1*
Why Do We Have Organizations?   *4*
The Definition of Organizations   *4*
Organizations and Individuals   *5*
Categories of Individuals   *8*
Organizations and the Community   *9*
Societal Outcomes   *11*
    Some Specific Organizational Impacts   11
    General Societal Outcomes   15
Organizations and Social Change   *17*
    Internal Change and the Social Structure   17
    The Organization as a Change Agent   17
    Organizations as Resisters of Change   21
Multinational Organizations   *23*
The Voluntary Organization   *25*
Why Study Organizations?   *25*
Summary and Conclusions   *26*
Exercises   *26*

Part II   Organizational Structure

Chapter 2   Organizational Structure: Forms and Outcomes   27

Overview   *27*
Defining Organizational Structure   *29*
    Multiple Structures   30
    Structural Forms   31
Complexity   *31*

Communication Problems   *149*
   Omission   149
   Distortion   150
   Overload   150
Communication to and from Outside the Organization   *151*
Possible Solutions   *151*
Summary and Conclusions   *153*
Exercises   *153*

Chapter 8   **Change** **154**

Overview   *154*
The Nature of Organizational Change   *155*
   The Potential for Change   156
The Change Process   *157*
   Organizational Change Cycles   158
Innovation in Organizations   *167*
Summary and Conclusions   *172*
Exercises   *172*

Part IV   **Organizational Environments**

Chapter 9   **Organizational Environments and Interorganizational Relationships   173**

Overview   *173*
The Environment and the Formation of Organizations   *174*
Environmental Dimensions   *176*
   Technological Conditions   176
   Legal Conditions   177
   Political Conditions   178
   Economic Conditions   179
   Demographic Conditions   181
   Ecological Conditions   182
   Cultural Conditions   182
Analytical Dimensions   *183*
   Environmental Capacity   183
   Environmental Homogeneity–Heterogeneity   184
   Environmental Stability–Instability   184
   Environmental Concentration–Dispersion   184
   Domain Consensus–Dissensus   185
   Environmental Turbulence   185
The Perception of the Environment   *186*
The Impact of the Environment on the Organization   *187*
Interorganizational Relationships   *189*
   IOR: Forms and Levels   189

A Framework for IOR Analysis   *193*
  General Environmental Characteristics   193
  Situational Factors   194
  Reasons for Interaction   197
  Resource Flows   200
  Transaction Forms   201
Interlocking Boards of Directors   *202*
Outcomes of IOR   *205*
Summary and Conclusions   *206*
Exercises   *206*

Part V   **Organizational Theory and Organizational Effectiveness**

Chapter 10   **Organizational Theory   207**

Overview   *207*
The Population-Ecology Model   *208*
The Resource-Dependence Model   *211*
The Rational-Contingency Model   *215*
The Institutional Model   *217*
Combining the Perspectives   *221*
Summary and Conclusions   *221*
Exercises   *221*

Chapter 11   **Organizational Effectiveness   222**

Overview   *222*
Toward a Contradiction Model of Effectiveness   *223*
Models of Organizational Effectiveness   *225*
  The Goal Model   226
  Goals and Effectiveness   229
  Participant-Satisfaction Models   232
  Constraints, Goals, and Participants   235
  Effectiveness for Whom?   237
The Contradiction Model   *239*
  Some Applications   241
Summary and Conclusions   *244*
Exercises   *244*

References   245

Name Index   275

Subject Index   285

Preface

———————— • ◆ • ————————

This ninth edition of *Organizations: Structures, Processes, and Outcomes* has undergone a major revision. Pamela S. Tolbert is now a coauthor and has rewritten three of the chapters. A large number of out-of-date references have been removed. We have tried to make each chapter reflect the cutting edge of the field of sociology of organizations, while retaining the insights that previous research has revealed.

Many contemporary organizations are coping with an array of major crises, ranging from terrorism to financial collapse. In the face of these changing conditions, the way in which many organizations continue to function, providing the stability our society needs to persist on its course, is remarkable. This book is intended to help readers understand the sources of both change and stability in modern organizations.

We have retained the overviews at the beginning of each chapter and the exercises at the end of each chapter. These appear to be useful resources for students. We have made strong efforts to make this edition more accessible to beginning students of organizations, while still indicating nuances of theories and research that may be of particular interest to those with a stronger background in the field.

OUR THANKS GO TO OUR REVIEWERS

Yang Cao, University of North Carolina—Charlotte; Louis Hicks, St. Mary's College of Maryland; and Debra Welkley, California State University, Sacramento. We thank Sharon Chambliss of Prentice Hall for her patience and support as our progress was slowed for a while. And of course we thank each of our spouses, Sherry Hall and Steve Carver, for their continued love and support.

Organizations

is filled with them. They are just about impossible to escape. They are as inevitable as death and taxes. They have "absorbed society" (Perrow, 1991:726).

A simple exercise will illustrate the pervasiveness of organizations in our lives. Think of all the activities that we engage in during a day. Which, if any, are not influenced by an organization in one way or another? If you alone are reading this book, it may seem to be an individual matter; however, the book was prepared and published by an organization, Prentice Hall, Inc., and you are reading probably because of some kind of organizational demand from your college or university. We wrote the book in organizational contexts, the University at Albany and Cornell University. Our tastes in food and drink (and the amounts we consume) are shaped by marketing organizations. The food and drinks themselves are processed and distributed by organizations. The products we come into contact with, such as automobiles and desks, are made in organizational settings. The services we rely upon, such as police, banking, and insurance, are clearly organizational. We work in organizations. The world of e-commerce is made up of organizations. Even our leisure activities typically take place in some sort of organizational setting. A favorite leisure activity is alpine skiing. We cannot imagine how we could pursue this sport without a ski area, which, after all, is just another organization.

The great social transformations in history have been essentially organizationally based. The rise of the Roman Empire, the spread of Christianity, and the growth and development of, and the changes in, capitalism and socialism have been accomplished through organizations. Toxic-waste disposal, nuclear energy, terrorism, unemployment, abortion, and all of the issues facing contemporary society cannot be understood without a consideration and an understanding of their organizational contexts.

These simple examples were intended to suggest that the careful analysis of organizations is a serious and important matter. It is not just an academic exercise. Organizations are continually analyzed from a variety of perspectives. The stock market, for example, is an ongoing organizational analysis. Investors constantly assess how business firms are doing and buy and sell stocks accordingly. The major investment decisions are actually made by other organizations. Like other forms of organizational analysis, stock market analysis is not an exact science.

If we are lucky and have the opportunity to choose between potential employers, we are making an organizational analysis. We are attempting to decide which would be a better place to work. To a surprising extent, the election of the President of the United States is an assessment of an organization. A large organization has handled the campaign, and the voters estimate what kind of organization the individual will bring to office.

Organizational analysis also occurs at other levels. The job of organizational management is to assess the state of the organization. Labor unions, themselves organizations, analyze the operations of the companies with which they have contracts. Customers assess the quality of stores and their merchandise. A car buyer wants to be sure that the manufacturer has a reputation for producing high-quality cars and is likely to be in business for a long time, and that the dealer can handle any problems that might arise. The selection of an organization such as a health provider is of even greater concern to each client.

Organizations have the capacity to do great good or great evil. Most are somewhere in between, and that brings us to the second answer to our opening question: We study organizations because organizations have outcomes. They are not benign objects. They can spread hate but also save lives and maybe souls. They can wage war but also bring peace. These outcomes can be intentional or unintentional, recognized or not recognized (Merton, 1957). They can also be surprising. For example, in states that have a large sector of private-school organizations, students in public-school organizations perform better than those in states with smaller private-school populations. The reason is that public schools are provided with more resources (Arum, 1996). The outcome of the presence of private schools is not necessarily harm for public schools. In this first chapter we will analyze the outcomes of organizations for individuals, for categories of individuals, for communities, and for society.

Before we examine these outcomes, however, it is important to note that not everything is organizational. Our feelings and emotions are our own, even though they are in part shaped by our organizational experiences. Our relationships with our spouses and children are also not organizational. This last point becomes a little complicated, however, since couples do things such as attend university events together, attend church together, work at the same ski area, and share other facets of our lives that are shaped by organizations.

There are a number of paradoxes about the organizations that shape our lives. For example, the "typical U.S. employee works in an establishment with 599 full-time workers . . . and 72 part-time workers . . ." (Marsden, Cook, and Knoke, 1996: 49). At the same time, the "median numbers are 50 full-time and 2 part-time employees" (Dun's Census of American Business, 1995:26). One reason for this size paradox is that although most business firms are small, organizations in the not-for-profit and public sectors are larger (Marsden et al., 1996:50).

We will deal with the issue of organizational size more fully in Chapter 3, but two points regarding size are important here. First, goods and services once supplied by solo practitioners or small organizations are increasingly being delivered by large organizations, which are often branches of still-larger organizations (Danet, 1981:382). For example, Prentice Hall, Inc., the publisher of this book, was a subsidiary of Simon & Schuster, which in turn was part of Paramount Communications, which was owned by Viacom, Inc.

Second, this tendency toward consolidation and growth is countered by the fact that many organizations have joined the downsizing movement. It may be the case that the actual heart of the American economy is shifting from large firms to smaller ones (Ritzer, 1989). Ritzer reports that the large Fortune 500 companies laid off more than 3 million workers between 1980 and 1987. During the same period, firms with fewer than 100 employees created 12 million new jobs. When these small organizations are successful, of course, there is a strong tendency for them to become larger and larger through growth or merger.

Small organizations are vitally important as incubators of ideas. They have also been identified as vitally important in developing countries in the form of the "informal economy" or "microenterprises" (Liedholm and Mead, 1993; Rakowski, 1994).

There is another interesting twist here. There are some organizations that have many employees but whose operations seem to be very small. These are "direct selling" or "multilevel" organizations such as Amway, Tupperware, and Mary Kay Cosmetics (Biggart, 1989). One insurance company, for example, has a sales force of 155,000 agents (Biggart, 1989:117), but its home office is small and each agent acts independently.

WHY DO WE HAVE ORGANIZATIONS?

The answer here is simple: to get things done. We have organizations to do things that individuals cannot do by themselves. We will use a very simple personal example to illustrate this point. The example is the National Ski Patrol. This organization did not exist until alpine skiing began to become popular in the United States. The founder of the National Ski Patrol, Charles "Minnie" Dole, came upon an injured skier in Vermont and could not help the injured person by himself. He started the organization, which is now found at almost every alpine and nordic ski area in the United States.

This same process takes place when people want to make a profit, save souls, have fun, or fight drunk driving. Organizations are the answer. Economists have a simplified, and perhaps oversimplified, model to explain why we have organizations. They develop to take the place of markets, where people could barter, trade, or purchase goods and services (Williamson, 1975; 1985). In this framework, markets and organizations are alternative ways to get things done.

Recently, analysts have been studying networks, which are essentially between markets and organizations (Beckman and Haunschild, 2002; Podolny and Page, 1998). Networks are formed by organizations working together in joint ventures in areas such as petroleum exploration, scientific frontiers, and other arenas in which single organizations do not have the resources to proceed on their own. For our purposes here, the key point is that networks are made up of organizations, which, again, are the way things get done.

There is an additional new form that should be noted. This is the "virtual organization." Virtual organizations are formed when organizational members are in contact with each other via the internet or other media. They meet for a specific purpose and are disbanded if the purpose has been accomplished. An example of this was the virtual organizations formed to fight the West Nile virus in the northeastern United States (Zanetich, 2003).

THE DEFINITION OF ORGANIZATIONS

Now that the reasons for studying organizations and the reasons for having organizations have been considered, it is time to define organizations.

An **organization** *is a collectivity with a relatively identifiable boundary, a normative order (rules), ranks of authority (hierarchy), communications systems, and* *membership coordinating systems (procedures); this collectivity exists on a relatively continuous basis, in environments, and engages in activities that are usually related to a set of goals; the activities have outcomes for organizational members, for the organization itself, and for society.*

This is a cumbersome and perhaps unwieldy definition, but then so is the subject matter. Aspects of the definition will be considered in depth in later chapters. At this point, we will consider the crucial topic of organizational outcomes.

ORGANIZATIONS AND INDIVIDUALS

Most analyses of the impact of organizations on individuals focus on work organizations. That is appropriate, of course, since work organizations take up so much of individuals' lives. At the same time, participation in voluntary organizations provides individuals with all kinds of possibilities for growth and development. Having noted this, we will focus here primarily on organizations in which people work. Although some analysts foresee an "end of work" (Rifkin, 1995), the end of work and work organizations has not yet taken place. We will, therefore, proceed as usual, with the awareness that work organizations may well decline in the future.

Many analyses have examined how individuals react to their lives as employees of organizations (Aronowitz, 1973; Hall, 1994; Rosow, 1974; Terkel, 1974; *Work in America,* 1973). These analyses agree that work that is highly routinized, repetitive, and dull is highly alienating for the individual. There is no evidence, of course, that work in preorganizational societies was not alienating. Subsistence farming or hunting and gathering is hardly enlightening. Romanticized imageries of preorganizational systems forget that people starved to death and froze to death. Some people were slaves. Early industrialization, with its exceedingly low pay, child labor, and absence of worker protection, was also alienating but in a truer Marxian sense than the social–psychological alienation felt by today's worker in a routine job.

The studies of individual reactions to work also reveal that work which provides challenge, potential for advancement, and the use of creative or expressive capabilities is enjoyable and even enlightening. People's reactions to their work result from the individuals' own expectations and the characteristics of the employing organization (Lorsch and Morse, 1974). Neither organizations nor individuals can be easily changed to yield consistent positive reactions.

There is another side to working in organizations. In an important study, Kohn (1971) found small but consistent tendencies for people who work in more bureaucratized organizations to be more intellectually flexible, more open to new experiences, and more self-directed than those working in nonbureaucratized settings. Peoples' occupational conditions both affect and are affected by their psychological functioning (Kohn and Schooler, 1978, 1982). In regard to work in a bureaucratized setting, Kohn attributes the findings to the fact that bureaucratized organizations require their workforce to be better educated and also provide more job protection, higher salary, and more complex work. The implication of these studies is that work in organizations is not necessarily deadening to the individual. The work of a secretary or an executive can be challenging and have potential for advancement in one organization but not in another. Some jobs have a strong potential for idiosyncratic behavior, and others do not (Miner, 1987). Here again, organizational characteristics are critical variables as they interact with those of the individual.

Thus far, the discussion of individuals in organizations has been based on studies of full-time, permanent workers. There is a growing trend toward part-time and nonpermanent work. In 1988, for example, one-fourth of all U.S. workers were nonpermanent or part-time workers (Davis-Blake and Uzzi, 1993)—that is, temporary workers, leased workers, or independent contractors. The temporary help industry employment level grew from 184,000 in 1970 to 1.5 million in 1993 (Tilly and Tilly, 1998:152). This form of employment typically offers low pay and few benefits.

Another growing trend is home-based work, or telecommuting, in which people work from their homes and use electronic communications to link with their employers (Lozano, 1989). Clerical work can be done this way, as can the work of some professionals, such as editors and professors. Home workers see themselves as having more freedom than their office-bound counterparts. In some cases, home work entails a loss of employee benefits and diminished opportunities for promotion, so it cannot be seen as desirable for everyone.

People not only work in organizations but also have extensive contacts with them as customers or clients. The growth of consumer and client-advocacy organizations is testimony to the fact that those who come to organizations for products or services are not totally satisfied with what they receive. Advocacy organizations, of course, are every bit as much organizations as the ones they are advocating against.

A survey of people's reactions to their contacts with government agencies in the areas of employment, job training, workers' compensation, unemployment compensation, welfare services, hospital and medical services, and retirement services found that the majority of the clients interviewed were satisfied with the service and treatment they received (Katz et al., 1975). Thus, widespread discontent with the system in this regard appears to be a myth, because common stereotypes about encounters with government bureaucracies are contradicted by the data. Nevertheless, the fact that most people are satisfied does not mean that the organizations are operating as effectively as possible. Katz and his colleagues note:

> A majority of satisfied clients may leave a sizable minority dissatisfied. Even a 75 percent level of satisfaction may be low for some programs in which 90 percent or high is desirable and feasable. In a population of 200 million, small percentages are large numbers. (p. 115)

In a related study of the same phenomenon, this time among juveniles who have had contact with the juvenile justice system, Giordano (1974) found "something less than a seething rage against the professionals who staff the juvenile justice system." Apparently, even in this population, which is thought to have very negative encounters with the establishment, organizations are not viewed with the distaste that is generally believed to be present.

An element in the Giordano research is worth noting: If a client feels close to an individual in an organization, his or her interpretation of the total organization appears to be affected. Individuals coming to an organization do so as individuals. The person in the organization may or may not be able to respond in a personal way. Many organizations prescribe the manner in which their employees are to respond to outsiders. Even if the prescribed manner is warm and friendly, as is the case for airline flight attendants, it is still an organizational prescription (see Hochschild, 1983). In the case of the professional staffs with which Giordano dealt, and which formed the bulk of the services studied by Katz et al. (1975), the professional is granted some latitude in interpersonal interactions. Such latitude is less likely at the clerical or retail sales level, where many individual contacts with organizations are made.

The analysis of individuals in organizations must also consider economic factors. Sociologists have a tendency to ignore the economic, but it is a mistake to do so. Focusing on factors such as morale and satisfaction deflects attention from the fact that economic factors are a major consideration for both management and workers. Hage (1980) notes that "on the one hand managerial elites and owners of capital want to drive costs down by means of policies of low wages and uniform tasks. On the other hand workers want to increase their standard of living and have interesting work. There is an inherent conflict of interest between these two perspectives" (p. 7). Hage goes on to suggest that the inherent conflict can be handled by either fighting or quitting, as suggested by Hirschman (1972). When workers neither fight nor quit, they may neglect their work (Withey and Cooper, 1989).

People have an obvious economic stake in the organizations in which they work. Organizations affect the economic well-being of workers and hence also their dependents. Organizations are the context in which people work. The performances of individuals are shaped by that context. For example, the productivity of scientists is strongly affected by their work context (Allison and Long, 1990; Long and McGinnis, 1981). These studies find that departments encourage scientific productivity through motivation, intellectual stimulation, and good facilities. If the expectations are that an individual be highly productive, behavior tends to conform to those expectations.

The most important outcome of organizations for individuals is the placement or attainment of individuals within the social stratification system. In the 1980s there was a dramatic realization that organizations are key actors in stratification. The division of labor among jobs (the internal labor market) within an organization and differentiation among organizations result in a situation in which unequal opportunities and rewards are attached to organizational positions. These are present before the arrival of any particular incumbent. Organizations also have procedures for filling their positions. Education, skill, or experience of varying levels and intensities is specified in advance. Organizations then match workers with jobs. Organizations are thus the process by which stratification is accomplished (Baron, 1984; Baron and Bielby, 1980; Kalleberg, 1983; Kalleberg and Van Buren, 1996; Pfeffer and Cohen, 1984; Stolzenberg, 1978). This is a dynamic process. When organizations are growing, there are more promotional opportunities (Rosenbaum, 1979). When organizations are in a decline, the opportunity structure also is diminished.

An important consideration in the relationships between organizations and individuals is that some organizations have developed policies that are designed to be more individual and "family friendly." These policies include job sharing, flextime, telecommuting, shortened workweeks, and child and elder care assistance (Glass, 2000). The relationships between organizations and individuals are thus, to some degree, reciprocal.

In addition to being reciprocal, the relationships between organizations and individuals are complicated by other considerations. Organizations vary in their ability to adopt flexible work systems. The variation is based on their age and size, their existing labor–management relationships, and their existing work process arrangements (Uzzi and Barness, 1998). Organizational wealth would be another consideration here. Thus, some organizations might not be able to adopt family- or worker-friendly policies even if they wanted to do so.

CATEGORIES OF INDIVIDUALS

The topic of this section is probably best captured by the phrase "the glass ceiling," through which it is commonly believed that women can't pass. It is also captured in a conversation that was overheard by an acquaintance who worked for a major office-equipment firm. He told me that there was an informal (and probably illegal) company policy not to promote people who were older than 45. The categories of individuals are gender, age, race, religion, and ethnicity.

Organizations can have and have had policies regarding hiring and promotion aimed at specific categories of individuals. For example, "No Irish Need Apply" was frequently seen on signs outside some business firms at the height of Irish immigration to the United States.

The Civil Rights legislation of the 1960s has had an ongoing impact on organizational policies regarding categories of individuals. At the same time, categories of individuals still are differentially affected by the organizations in which they work (and study).

The situation at the beginning of the twenty-first century is one of change. Economic restructuring is happening rapidly; manufacturing work is declining and service work is increasing. This will encourage the growth of jobs in which women and minority group members are concentrated (Reskin and Padevic, 1994:166). For example, nurses' aides and orderlies and food-counter and related workers are job categories that will increase, as will the categories of registered nurses and managers and administrators. These job categories are differentially filled by women and minority group members. This is not an organizational outcome, except that organizations do seek out the least expensive labor that they can find, at least at lower organizational levels. At the same time, organizational hiring practices will maintain pay and promotion differentials between categories of individuals.

Another important trend that has been documented is skill upgrading and simultaneous deskilling (Reskin and Padevic, 1994:167–68). Organizational policies are important here in that work with computers can be reduced to data entry or upgraded to autonomous decision making.

In a similar manner, the contingent workforce of temporary workers, part-time workers, and independent contractors is "largely driven by employer needs, not workers' choices" (Reskin and Padevic, 1994:169). Contingent workers typically receive lower pay and benefits than full-time workers and, again, the impact of this shift affects categories of individuals differentially. A final trend noted by Reskin and Padevic is the very evident increasing diversity of the labor force. Immigration to the United States, particularly from Asia and Latin America, is fueling this diversity.

The basis of discrimination in hiring is moving away from gender and minority group membership and is shifting to educational achievements on the part of individuals. Those without educational credentials will find work in the lower-paying part of the labor force. Since there is differential access to and success in educational achievement among racial, religious, and ethnic groups, differential distributions on those bases will remain. Reskin and Padevic (1994) are pessimistic about changes in promotional opportunities for women and minority group members in the short run, since many in these categories are exactly the ones being forced into the contingent labor force because of downsizing (p. 173). At the same time, in the longer run, employing organizations may select newly trained graduates on the basis of their credentials over gender or minority group status (Acker, 1992).

It is difficult to project what will happen in regard to the age category. There is a dramatic age bulge as the large number of baby boomers born after World War II move into late middle age. Organizational policy is yet to be developed for this group.

This section has discussed categories of individuals in terms of gender, age, race, religion, and ethnicity. Other categories could be added, such as people who smoke, who are overweight, and/or who are homosexual. Certainly, discrimination and even violence take place in and by organizations based on these categories as well.

ORGANIZATIONS AND THE COMMUNITY

Organizations are clearly not benign in their outcomes for individuals and categories of individuals. The same is true for the communities or localities in which they operate. A college or a university can be the dominant institution in the town or city in which it is located. One only has to think of Bloomington,

Indiana; Ann Arbor, Michigan; and Durham, North Carolina, the homes of large universities, or of Granville, Ohio, a small college town, to see this point. The Mayo Clinic dominates Rochester, Minnesota. General Electric once dominated Schenectady, New York.

In the Schenectady case, the outcome can be seen dramatically. When General Electric was running its Schenectady operations at full employment, the city prospered. As GE changed its product mix and downsized its Schenectady operations, the city slid downhill. The downsizing of GE has taken retail stores, hotels, restaurants, and a whole series of other small businesses with it.

This community impact can also be seen clearly in a study reported by Seiler and Summers (1979). They examined the consequences of a large steel manufacturing firm's decision to locate a major new plant in a small town in the middle western United States. This company did not want to be identified in the community power structure as such, but their actions clearly had a major impact on the community.

The steel company, Jones and Laughlin, engaged in unilateral actions, such as buying land for their plant through ghost buyers and hiring workers from surrounding counties rather than in the home county. The company also co-opted the local community leaders by using key bankers and lawyers as their local representatives. No Jones and Laughlin personnel were active in the community, but their operatives were. The company also directly intervened in plans for a new high school in the community, forcing the building of a less expensive and more practical school, thus reducing their tax liability.

Seiler and Summers do not suggest that all the results of the company's actions were bad for the local community. Indeed, some were recognized as positive. The important point is that this organization had a direct and dramatic impact on the local community. The impact of a single powerful organization can thus be great.

Most communities have more than a single dominant organization, but that does not dilute the power of organizations in the community. Local power structures reflect interorganizational competition and thus the interests of powerful organizational actors (Galaskiewicz, 1979; Perrucci and Pilisuk, 1970).

Interorganizational relationships, which will be considered in detail in Chapter 9, can have both positive and negative consequences for a community. For example, Minneapolis, Minnesota, is blessed with an extraordinarily high level of corporate philanthropy (Crittenden, 1978). Much of this is based on the interorganizational linkages among the business firms there. Most other cities are less fortunate. Some, such as Schenectady, have been literally destroyed as businesses move to other areas. Still others receive virtually nothing from their organizational inhabitants. In many ways, communities can be viewed as networks of interorganizational linkages (Galaskiewicz and Krohn, 1984).

There is a more subtle way in which organizations influence the communities in which they are located. One study found that companies vary in the degree to which they encourage their middle managers to participate in community affairs (Christenson et al., 1988). If communities were filled with organizations that encourage such participation, local life would be enriched. This same study also found that those middle managers who did get involved in community life were less likely to opt for transfers to other communities.

SOCIETAL OUTCOMES

If organizations have important outcomes for individuals and communities, it is obvious that they also have important outcomes for the wider society or environment in which they are embedded. At the very outset, it must be recognized that there is a reciprocal relationship between organizations and their environments. Indeed, the dominant contemporary theories regarding organizations stress the central role of environments for the operations of organizations. As we will see in the chapters that follow, the environments of organizations are viewed as a major determinant of the structure and processes of organizations. In this section we are going to turn this line of reasoning around and consider the impacts of organizations on their environment. The analysis will begin with a consideration of some specific organizational impacts and then move into more broadly based conceptualizations.

Some Specific Organizational Impacts

Organizations serve the interests of individuals or groups. These controlling interests shape the directions that organizations take, and this in turn can have an impact on the wider society. Consider the Roman empire as an organization. The Roman administrative organization was controlled by the ruling class, whose orientation was to dominate the masses (Antonio, 1979). The emphasis on domination led to a decline in the production of goods and services and "preserved, and even intensified, conditions which contributed to the erosion and eventual destruction of the socio-economic substructure of the bureaucracy" (Antonio, 1979:906). Short-term success thus contributed to long-term failure— a theme to which we will return later.

The major point of the Antonio study is that the administrative bureaucracy serves the interest of the ruling elite. This has been a point of contention for organizational analysts for some time. Some analysts believe that ownership has become diffused and that control is now in the hands of corporate managers, not specific owners, with boards of directors serving as tools of management rather than of owners and stockholders (Berle and Means, 1932).

This point of view has been severely challenged on several grounds. First, there is evidence that families such as the Mellons of Pittsburgh, who had controlling interests in Gulf Oil, Alcoa, Koppers Company, and Carborundum Company in the manufacturing sector, also had controlling interests in the First Boston Corporation, the General Reinsurance Corporation, and the Mellon National Bank and Trust Company in the financial sector (Zeitlin, 1974). The Mellon National Bank, in turn, owned almost 7 percent of Jones and Laughlin Steel. The

Rockefeller family had similar points of linkage among financial institutions and insurance companies. Patterns of interlock like these have also been found outside the United States. Although there is no direct evidence that such family control has direct economic implications, family ownership has the potential for organizational control, rather than control by organizational management or diffused stockholders (Aldrich, 1979).

There is also a remarkable degree of interlock among the boards of directors of corporations. This means that members of the board of directors of one corporation are likely to serve on the boards of other corporations. Such interlocks are believed to give a corporation access to capital and to co-opt or control sources of pressure in the environment (Pennings, 1980b).

In general, the more interlocks, the more effective was the organization. A specific finding of interest in the Pennings study was that firms that are well interlocked with the financial community enjoyed lower interest rates for their debts than their more poorly interlocked fellow firms. Similar relationships between interlocks and profitability have been found in analyses by Burt and his colleagues (Burt, 1983; Burt et al., 1980).

There are two basic ways to view findings such as these. One way views them as sound management. Interlocks, with or without family ties, are basically a means to achieve a competitive edge. The other view is more conspiratorial. Such interlocks permit a ruling class to maintain its power and wealth at the expense of the rest of the population. Both views undoubtedly contain grains of truth.

There are some additional interpretations of the impact of corporate power in society. According to Useem (1979), an "inner group" of business elites are selected to assist in the governance of other institutions, such as governmental advisory boards, philanthropic organizations, and colleges and universities. The same pattern of interlocking directorates is found in the noncorporate sector of society. Useem concludes that this permits the promotion of the more general interests of the entire capitalist class. This political interpretation could be challenged by the claim that these institutional interlocks are merely a means by which able people are brought to the boards of directors of organizations that provide benefits for society. Whichever interpretation is taken cannot deny the importance or presence of the interlocks.

Organizations are active participants in the development and implementation of governmental or public policy. This takes place through lobbying and other political action. We are using the generic sense of the term "organizations" here, since just about every form of organization is involved in political action. The American Symphony Orchestra League (ASOL) and the National Football League (NFL) are active political players. Organizations must be concerned with all branches of government—the legislative, the executive, and the judicial. Organizations can thus be viewed as one source of laws; they are also vital in the selection of judges (Champagne, Neef, and Nagel, 1981).

Analyses of the U.S. State Department support these conclusions. One analysis of the patterns of interests that were represented in State Department actions for the period 1886–1905 found that core financial and industrial interests became vested interests for the State Department to an increasing degree. American foreign policy came to reflect these organizational interests (Roy, 1981, 1983a; see also Carstensen and Werking, 1983).

Yet another study, in the areas of energy and health, found that corporate entities in the form of trade associations, professional societies, public-interest groups, government bureaus, and congressional committees were the key actors in these state policy domains (Laumann, Knoke, and Kim, 1985). These organizations have a stake in the policies that are enacted and implemented. Individuals, unless they act on behalf of or at the behest of the corporations, have little importance in these policy domains. It is important to note that Laumann and his colleagues also found that government bureaus and congressional committees function as important actors in these policy areas. From the frequent revelations of apparent overspending on defense contracts, it is apparent that there are common interests among defense contractors and government agencies, with some congressional organizations also having common interests.

Harmful Impacts.   Organizations can bring actual and direct physical, social, and mental harm to society. For example, General Electric, discussed earlier in connection with the city of Schenectady, New York, had two factories that released harmful industrial chemicals into the Hudson River (Revkin, 1997). General Electric has stopped the flow of the chemicals, polychlorinated biphenyls (PCBs), that has crippled commercial fishing and harmed wildlife and is thought to pose a danger of cancer and learning problems. The point here is not to castigate GE. The point is that the poisons are in the river, whether GE knew of the dangers or not. The long-term consequences of short-term decisions cannot always be anticipated (Hall, 1981).

Another example of harmful impacts can be seen in a study of the chemical industry and toxic pollution emissions. This study found that larger organizations emitted toxins at a significantly higher rate than smaller organizations (Grant, Jones, and Bergesen, 2002). Perrow (1984) coined the term "normal accidents" to describe actual and potential disasters involving nuclear plants, nuclear weapons systems, recombinant DNA production, ships carrying highly toxic or explosive cargoes, and chemical plants. His analysis was published before the chemical plant disaster in Bhopal, India, in which thousands of individuals were killed, and the Chernobyl nuclear disaster in Russia. Perrow's contention is that highly complex technical systems that are tightly coupled or integrated have a strong potential for catastrophe because it is not individual operator error that is the source of the accident but systemic or organizational problems.

Perrow may not go far enough in his organizational analyses of technologically related disasters, since there are potential organizational solutions to these very real problems (Hirschhorn, 1985). Nonetheless, Perrow's basic point remains valid and frightening—organizational arrangements have the potential to contribute to catastrophes of immense scope.

This point can be underscored by an analysis of the Space Shuttle *Challenger* disaster. Both organizational and technical decisions were faulted in that catastrophe

(Vaughan, 1990, 1996, 1999). The decision to launch the *Challenger* was the result of organizational structure and culture that led to the making of decisions under conditions of great uncertainty. According to Vaughan, the disaster was not a product of amoral calculation.

This line of reasoning has been extended to the AIDS epidemic by the same Charles Perrow and his colleague Mauro Guillen (1990). They find that AIDS is "as much an organizational problem as a biological one" (p. 150). These researchers see the organizations that deal with AIDS as "recalcitrant tools in the service of diverse interest groups" who have "performed very poorly in coping with AIDS" (p. 15). If they are correct, then organizations are having a very harmful impact on the wider society.

When people in organizations make the fatal mistake of bringing bad news (whistle-blowing) about dangerous or life-threatening conditions to their supervisors, they are likely to suffer silence, isolation, or dismissal (Alford, 2001). Organizations do not like whistle-blowers.

In keeping with the theme of reciprocity that was introduced at the beginning of this analysis of organizational–societal relationships, organizations can themselves experience disasters from events outside their own control. An analysis of "corporate tragedies" describes how things happen to organizations (Mitroff and Kilmann, 1984). These tragedies include events such as product tampering, as in the case of Tylenol being laced with cyanide, and the projection in the minds of some people that the logo long used by Procter & Gamble is an occult symbol. Organizations can be affected by events far beyond their control, just as activities that are within organizational control can have effects that are not anticipated by society.

Organizations can cause accidents or can be accident victims. They can also engage in criminal acts (Sutherland, 1949; Clinard and Yeager, 1980). Criminal acts have been identified in a wide array of types of organizations, including the nursing home industry, the stock market ("insider trading" on Wall Street), and the savings and loan industry (Tonry and Reiss, 1994).

Organizations can contribute to crime in two ways. Some organizations are "crime-coercive"; that is, they force their members or customers to engage in illegal activities (Needleman and Needleman, 1979). For example, some franchised automobile dealers are forced into illegal practices such as kickbacks and unrecorded income to survive financially (Farberman, 1975). Needleman and Needleman propose that there are also "crime-facilitative" organizations. For example, fire insurance companies facilitate the "torching" of buildings by arsonists. The arsonist owns the building, which is rundown and unsellable. After it burns, the arsonist collects the insurance on the building. The insurance companies facilitate the arsonist but do not benefit themselves. More vigorous investigations of slum ownership and insurance patterns could be conducted, but apparently insurance companies believe that vigorous background investigation might offend or drive away legitimate customers. Organizations thus contribute to these property crimes. In the case of arson, of course, there is the potential for the loss of life, making it more than a simple financial matter.

The well-documented history of crimes committed by corporations can be interpreted from two basic perspectives. One is that it is simply a case of individual deviance, with people attempting to line their own pockets whether it hurts the organization or not. The alternative perspective brings the organization into the picture. Vaughan (1983), for example, uses the idea of "authority leakage" (p. 74) as a means of indicating that organizational characteristics play a role in crime. Organizational leakages involve long hierarchies and intensive specialization to the extent that subunits cannot be controlled. In Vaughan's view, corporate crimes are more likely to develop in such situations, and this indeed seems to be the case in most instances of such crimes. Seldom is the total organization involved, and seldom do the majority of personnel in organizations participate in such crimes.

Other research has come to the somewhat surprising finding that corporate illegal acts are more likely to be committed in rich or "munificent" environments (Baureus and Near, 1991). There may be less fear of surveillance in such environments, and illegal acts may be seen as less risky.

One further point regarding the harmful effects of organizations must be noted to complete the picture. Although the emphasis has been on private business firms, government or public organizations can also produce harmful outcomes. After all, it is government organizations that wage wars and commit atrocities of the right and the left. Government organizations can have harmful effects of a more subtle nature, for example, by their inactions. Levine's (1982) analysis of the Love Canal situation in Niagara Falls, New York, is an excellent case in point. In this case toxic wastes were placed in an unused canal, which was later covered with landfill. Homes and a school were built on and near the site. When the homeowners became aware of the situation and its consequences, which included miscarriages, birth defects, and illness, they approached local, state, and federal agencies for help. At each level, government organizations, such as departments of health, worked hard to protect their own interests and in so doing prolonged the harmful outcomes for the residents.

Organizations thus do misbehave, engage in misconduct, and create disasters. These are the consequence of the interconnections between organizations and their environments and of the choices made within organizations (Vaughan, 1999). The key point for our purposes here is that these are organizational actions.

General Societal Outcomes

The impact of organizations on the societies in which they are embedded is great. This is a fairly recent historical development, since organizations as corporate actors are actually of relatively recent origins (Kieser, 1989). The unprecedented role of organizations in contemporary society is based on the fact that the modern organization is a legal entity, just like the individual person. In a perceptive set of essays, Coleman (1974) has indicated that organizational legality is granted by the state, itself a legal creation. Whereas the individual is given a set of rights and responsibilities by the state, rights and responsibilities are extended to organizations.

These rights, coupled with the large size of many organizations, give organizations an enormous amount of power within the state. Coleman also points out that the state or government is more comfortable dealing with other organizations than with individual persons and thus tends to provide more preferential treatment to organizations in areas as diverse as taxation and rights to privacy.

We have reached the point where one form of organization, the modern corporation, has become the *dominant institution in our times* (Bowman, 1996; emphasis added). Corporations are so powerful that their impact on law, politics, and social life are unparalleled and unchallenged, according to Bowman's analysis. This is not a new phenomenon, of course. In Western history, the Roman Catholic Church played such a role for many centuries.

The recognition of organizations as legal entities is not a trivial matter. Organizations, rather than individuals, can be held responsible for certain actions. Air New Zealand, for example, was held responsible for a crash that killed 257 people (*New York Times,* 1981). The crew had not been informed that a new flight plan had been put into effect, and the plane crashed into a volcano. The judge in the case also accused airline officials of attempting to conceal their mistakes.

Swigert and Farrell (1980–81) analyzed the case of the Ford Motor Company, which was charged with homicide as a result of deaths that had occurred in crashes of its Pinto models in the 1970s. They found that the mass media shifted its orientation from the recognition of harm based on mechanical defects to an attribution of non-repentance on the part of the offender. Swigert and Farrell concluded that a shift in public attitudes had occurred in which an organization was believed to have engaged in criminality in a form previously reserved for individuals. The fact that Ford was found not guilty does not alter the importance in the shift in public attitude.

Organizations recognize that they can be held accountable for their actions and try to redefine situations so that either their actions do not appear to be criminal or mitigating circumstances relieve them of responsibility (Waegel, Ermann, and Horowitz, 1981; Marcus and Goodman, 1991). Organizations recognize that they can be blamed and thus also recognize their legal status.

The consideration of the legal status of organizations raises an issue that will be considered directly in the next chapter: Can organizations be considered as objects or entities in their own right, apart from the individuals that compose them? This is a complex question that involves more than their legal status.

At the very broadest level, then, organizations are affected by society and affect it. Even in situations in which efforts are made to reduce the impact of organizations, organizational factors intrude. For example, bureaucratic rules and specialization were evident during the extreme periods of the Cultural Revolution in the People's Republic of China (Shenkar, 1984). Organizational outcomes were inevitable in even that totalitarian situation. The specific forms of the Chinese organizations, of course, were affected by the traditional Chinese culture and social system, a point clearly punctuated by the events in Tiananmen Square in June 1989. Organizations are thus systems within the wider social system (Abbott, 1989).

ORGANIZATIONS AND SOCIAL CHANGE

Organizations are active participants in society. This becomes abundantly clear when we consider the issue of social change. Paradoxically, organizations both foster and impede social change. In this section we will first examine the ways in which internal changes in organizations have social-change outcomes. We will then turn to organizations as active change agents. Finally, we will consider organizations as resisters of change.

Internal Change and the Social Structure

Internal organizational changes affect the social structure in two ways. The first is through changing membership patterns. A clear example is the employment of women in the labor force at all levels in organizations. The social structural changes that have resulted include altered family roles for women and men, altered patterns of childbearing and child rearing, and an increase in services, such as food preparation, performed by service organizations. Restaurant food is not home-cooked food.

The second way in which internal changes affect the social structure is through altered patterns of work. Although it is unclear whether people's attitudes toward their work affect their outlooks on life, or vice versa, there certainly is such a relationship (see Hall, 1994). Thus, changes in the manner in which work is performed through programs of participative management and quality circles or through other such mechanisms are related to other important social relationships. The recent waves of downsizing have had societal impacts that will play out for years to come, in ways that we cannot anticipate.

The Organization as a Change Agent

Besides affecting society (intentionally or unintentionally) through their structuring of social life and impacts on members, organizations are also active participants in the social-change process. This can be most readily seen in the political arena, as organizations lobby and fight for legislation and rulings favorable to their own programs. A decision favorable to one organization leads to programs that in turn affect the society. Whenever a government agency is established to carry out a new program, it becomes a social-change agent. We will begin the analysis of change agents with this point, moving from this commonly accepted form of social change to a consideration of organizations as revolutionary agents.

A prime example of the organization as a change agent is provided by Selznick's (1966) now-classic study of the Tennessee Valley Authority (TVA) during its formative years. In addition to its pertinence to the analysis of change, this study is also very important for its contribution to the analysis of the environmental impact on organizations, serving as the forerunner of many subsequent such studies.

The TVA Act was passed by the U.S. Congress in 1933. As Selznick (1966) notes:

> A great public power project was envisioned, mobilizing the by-product of dams built for the purpose of flood control and navigation improvement on the Tennessee River and its tributaries. Control and operation of the nitrate properties, to be used for fertilizer production, was also authorized, although this aspect was subordinated to electricity. . . . A new regional concept—the river basin as an integral unit—was given effect, so that a government agency was created which has a special responsibility neither national nor state-wide in scope. (pp. 4–5)

That the TVA has had an effect on the physical environment is evident. Of greater interest for our purposes is its effect on the social system into which it was placed. An important consideration in understanding the social effects of the TVA is that the organization was designed to be decentralized. Not only were decisions within the organization to be made at the lowest reasonable levels with participation by members, but local organizations and even local citizens were also to be brought into the decision-making process—the grassroots level. For example, the agricultural-extension services of the land-grant colleges were intimately involved with the TVA. This, of course, is one of the prime examples of a co-optation, or "the process of absorbing new elements into the leadership or policy-determining structure of an organization as a means of averting threats to its stability or existence" (Selznick, 1966:13).

Co-optation, however, is a two-way process. The organization itself is affected by the new elements brought into its decision-making process; Selznick documents the manner in which some activities of the TVA were deflected from the original goals because of the new elements in the system. At the same time, the co-optation process affects the system from which the elements were co-opted. The presence of the agricultural-extension element from the land-grant colleges gave this part of the local system much more strength than it had had in the past. The American Farm Bureau Federation was also brought into the process at an early point. In both these cases, the inclusion of one group was associated with the exclusion of another. For example, non–Farm Bureau farm organizations either lost power or did not benefit to the degree that the co-opted organizations did. In addition, the strength of the Farm Bureau in the decision-making process led to the exclusion of other federal government farm programs. Regardless of their merits, those programs were therefore unavailable to the system. Selznick notes, "This resulted in the politically paradoxical situation that the eminently New Deal TVA failed to support agencies with which it shared a political communion, and aligned itself with the enemies of those agencies" (p. 263). This becomes a rather complex analysis when one considers that the other government programs involved were also part of the same larger organization, so that internal politics in one large organization were affected by the external relationships of some of its components. An alternative analysis of the TVA sees the entire process as dominated by New Deal intellectuals, which makes the situation even more complex (Colignon, 1997).

An organization like the TVA affects the surrounding social system. Some elements prosper while others suffer. New social relationships arise as alliances among affected individuals and organizations are formed. Thus, an organization specifically designed to be a change agent can be exactly that, but perhaps in ways that can be most inconsistent with the original intent of the planners. The dynamics of the interactions with the environment affect both the organization and its environment.

In a later reexamination of the same study, Selznick (1966) notes that the TVA has been attacked by conservationists for strip mining. The need for coal in the production of power and the strength of those supporting an expansion of this function within the TVA have led to a further environmental impact. Selznick attributes the current state of the TVA to the internal struggles that occurred in its early history—struggles to obtain environmental support. Since such support is selective, a strong organization such as this rearranges the world around it. If the groups in power in the TVA see the need for a greater capacity to generate electrical power as more important than soil conservation, the internal decision-making process, affected as it is by external pressures, makes a further impact on the social and physical environment.

In another analysis of organizations as change agents, Selznick (1960) studied the Bolshevik revolution in Russia. Here he analyzed the nature and the role of the "organizational weapon." In defining what he means, Selznick states:

> We shall speak of organizations and organizational practices as weapons when they are used by a power-seeking elite in a manner unrestrained by the constitutional order of the arena within which the contest takes place. In this usage, "weapon" is not meant to denote any political tool, but one torn from its normal context and unacceptable to the community as a legitimate mode of action. Thus the partisan practices used in an election campaign—insofar as they adhere to the written and unwritten rules of the context—are not weapons in this sense. On the other hand, when members who join an organization in apparent good faith are in fact the agents of an outside elite, then routine affiliation becomes "infiltration." (p. 2)

An important component of the organizational weapon is the "distinctive competence to turn members of a voluntary association into disciplined and deployable political agents" (Selznick, 1960:xii).

Before we turn to further elements of Selznick's analysis, it should be clear that the organizational weapon cannot be regarded as a tactic of the Bolsheviks alone. Indeed, it is the vital component of most major social changes and of change within the organization itself. In other words, to achieve change, there must be organization. Spontaneous demonstrations or collective emotional responses may be sincere and well intended, but longer-lasting movements toward change must come about through the organizational mode.

The scope of the organization as a weapon is determined by its aims. Even if the change sought is a limited one and one that will not upset the basic system under attack, the change agent still must be viewed as a weapon, although of lesser scope than one that seeks total organizational or societal change. The aim of Bolshevism was total societal change. The basic means of accomplishing the movement's goal was the "combat party." Cadres of dedicated people are a basic component of such parties. This dedication requires that the individuals be totally committed to the cause, insulated from other concerns, and absorbed in the movement. Once a core of dedicated personnel is available, the party must protect itself from internal dissension, banning power centers that might threaten the official leadership. The party must be capable of mobilization and manipulation; it must be protected from possible isolation from the people it hopes to convert and also from possible liquidation at the hands of the existing authorities; and it must struggle for power in every possible area of action. This struggle can take place through seeking official recognition, as well as through conspiratorial or illegal practices. And at all times, the basic ideology must be kept at the forefront of the members' minds (Selznick, 1960:72–73).

The operation of these principles can be seen in the history of the movement that Selznick carefully traces. This manifesto for an organizational weapon is potentially applicable at any point in history, in any social setting, and at either the total societal or more microcosmic levels. Contemporary terrorist groups exhibit many of the same characteristics as the Bolshevik movement, and so does the history of early Christianity. The homeowners in the Love Canal situation described earlier formed an organization as their weapon for their own good. The Holocaust can certainly be viewed as an organizational weapon for evil.

The important lesson from Selznick's analysis is simple: To be successful, an organizational weapon must gain power and support in the society it is attempting to change. The pages of history are filled with abortive efforts that did not gather sufficient support from the society they were trying to change. The basic set of ideas underlying the change effort must therefore be compatible—or become compatible—with the values of the population as a whole. These values of the wider community can be altered during the change process to become more congruent with those of the change agent. At the same time, the change agent itself can become altered as it seeks support from the wider community.

The importance of this form of support can be extrapolated from Joseph Gusfield's (1955, 1963) analysis of the Women's Christian Temperance Union (WCTU). This organization was highly successful in its attempts to change society through the passage of legislation prohibiting the sale of alcoholic beverages. Its tactics were appropriate for the values of the times, and it succeeded in mobilizing support from a sufficiently large segment of the population. But later, as it became evident that Prohibition was not accomplishing what it was intended to do—and indeed had some unintended consequences that have lasted until the present—and as the originally supportive society changed, the WCTU was faced with a decision regarding its future. It could have altered its stance on alcohol to keep it in line with the prevailing opinions or maintained its position in favor of total abstinence. The latter course was selected as the result of decisions made within the organization. The consequences of that decision were to isolate the movement from the population, reducing it to virtual ineffectiveness as a force in the wider society.

The social system around a social-change organization thus affects it as much as it does any other form of organization. Although such organizations can appear to be revolutionary, deviant, or martyred, or to fit any other emotion-laden category, the fact remains that they are organizations. The critical aspect is the acceptance of the organization by society. This is obviously important for any organization, since to survive, it must receive support in one form or another, but for these change-oriented ones it is even more so. Unfortunately (or fortunately in some cases), because organizational analysts, decision makers, and politicians have not figured out exactly how to determine when an idea's time has come, the organization embarking on a change mission is in a precarious position at best.

There are other, more subtle ways in which organizations are change agents. As Perrow (1970b) notes:

> We tend to forget, or neglect, the fact that organizations have an enormous potential for affecting the lives of all who come into contact with them. They control or can activate a multitude of resources, not just land and machinery and employees, but police, governments, communications, art, and other areas, too. That is, an organization, as a legally constituted entity, can ask for police protection and public prosecution, can sue, and can hire a private police force with considerably wider latitude and power than an individual can command. It can ask the courts to respond to requests and make legal rulings. It can petition for changes in other areas of government—zoning laws, fair-trade laws, consumer labeling, and protection and health laws. It determines the content of advertising, the art work in its products and packages, the shape and color of its buildings. It can move out of a community, and it selects the communities in which it will build. It can invest in times of imminent recession or it can retrench; support or fight government economic policies or fair employment practices. In short, organizations generate a great deal of power that may be used in a way not directly related to producing goods and services or to survival. (pp. 170–71)

The power potential of organizations is often used to thwart change, as will be seen in the next section. Even when an organization is an active change agent, it tends to resist further changes once the desired change is accomplished. The labor union movement, which was once considered revolutionary, is now viewed by some as reactionary. National revolutions lead to established governments that, in turn, are attacked as opponents of social progress. We commonly think of the American, French, Russian, Chinese, and Cuban revolutions. Now, many people inside and outside those nations view the present regimes as highly conservative and even reactionary.

Organizations as Resisters of Change

Since our concern in this chapter is with organizational outcomes, it is important to go beyond the basic fact of organizational contributions to social change. Organizations also actively resist change. This resistance is directed toward change introduced from outside the organization.

Organizations by their very nature are conservative. An analysis of populist rural socialism in Saskatchewan, Canada, provides an ironic example of this point (Lipset, 1960). In 1944 the Cooperative Commonwealth Federation (CCF) came to power in that province. Its objective was "the social ownership of all resources and the machinery of wealth production to the end that we may establish a

Cooperative Commonwealth in which the basic principle regulating production, distribution and exchange will be the supplying of human needs instead of the making of profits" (p. 130). That aim was only partially realized. One reason is that there was continued political opposition to the movement; another, consistent with the argument here, is that the movement itself apparently became more conservative as it achieved power. An additional important consideration is that the new socialist government utilized the existing government structures in attempting to carry out its program. In explanation Lipset notes:

> Trained in the traditions of a laissez-faire government and belonging to conservative social groups, the civil service contributes significantly to the social inertia which blunts the changes a new radical government can make. Delay in initiating reforms means that the new government becomes absorbed in the process of operating the old institutions. The longer a new government delays making changes, the more responsible it becomes for the old practices and the harder it is to make the changes it originally desired to institute. (pp. 272–73)

The reason for this blunting is quite simple. The new ruling cabinet had to rely on the system already in operation.

> The administratively insecure cabinet ministers were overjoyed at the friendly response they obtained from the civil servants. To avoid making administrative blunders that would injure them in the eyes of the public and the party, the ministers began to depend on the civil servants. As one cabinet minister stated in an interview, "I would have been lost if not for the old members of my staff. I'm only a beginner in this work. B—— has been at it for twenty years. If I couldn't go to him for advice, I couldn't have done a thing. Why now (after two years in office) I am only beginning to find my legs and make my own decisions. . . . I have not done a thing for two years without advice." (p. 263)

It is important to note that the aims of a movement can be blunted without malice or intent. It is not a personal matter but an organizational one. Certainly, personal motivations may also be important, but the crucial factor is that the new leaders did not understand the organizations they were to head. The organization itself contained rules and procedures that had to be learned along the way, so that the organization became the instrument that deflected the party in power from its goals.

The organization trains its members to follow a system for carrying out its activities. It would require a complete resocialization before the takeover of a new party to prevent this sort of thing. That, of course, is impossible in government organizations. An alternative practice would be to purge the entire system, replacing the original members with ones of the appropriate ideology. That would in essence mean that the organization would have to start de novo and that nothing would be done until the organizational roles were learned and links to the society were established. Since the organization already has clients and customers, as well as a broader constituency in the case of government organizations, the expectations of nonmembers would also have to be altered. For these reasons, the likelihood of success is slim, regardless of the technique selected. The tendency for the organization to operate as it has in the past is very strong.

Most government organizations in Western democracies operate with a civil service system. An extension of Lipset's analysis suggests, therefore, that changes in the party in power will have less impact on the operation of the government agencies than political rhetoric would suggest. In most societies, the same principles seem to hold. The potentiality for major social change through change in government is therefore modified by the organizational realities that exist. Since social systems do change, of course, the organizations must be viewed as entities that do not change overnight but will change with time. The changes that occur may not be in phase with the change in political philosophy of the government in power. A liberal or conservative party in power may over time be able to introduce more of its adherents into the civil service system. Nonetheless, in whatever political direction a state, a county, or a nation is moving, organizational conservatism will remain an important consideration.

MULTINATIONAL ORGANIZATIONS

The analysis of the outcomes of organizations thus far has moved from the individual to the society. Organizations also have important outcomes across societies. This is easily seen in the myriad accounts of international spy rings and terrorist groups and in the case of extractive industries that take natural resources away from developing nations and give little in return, aside from usually low wages to workers.

There have been international organizations for longer than there have been nations. The Roman Empire and the Catholic Church exemplify this, as do the imperialist organizations that were at the heart of the British Empire. Many universities have overseas branches. The University at Albany sociology department had a joint Ph.D. program with Nankai University in the People's Republic of China in which several of us taught (in English) a cadre of Chinese students. The program officially ended in 1989, but the students have been able to complete their degrees in the United States. There are multinational organizations in just about every sphere of life. Most of the research focus has been on the multinational corporation.

Multinational corporations involve much more than simply having branch offices in more than one nation. In the case of the multinational firm, the total operation of things as diverse as the production and sale of automobiles and chocolate candy and banks is in the hands of a subsidiary or equal firm in another nation. German, Dutch, British, French, Swedish, Canadian, U.S., and Japanese firms are all important parts of this international scene.

There are many explanations for the emergence of the multinational corporation, all with strong elements of truth. The first explanation is imperialism, or the attempt to expand corporate markets and reduce costs by exerting economic power over a weaker nation. That nation could have lower pay scales and thus provide cheap labor; it could be politically dependent and thus give corporations of the more powerful nations tax breaks and incentives. Technology is one key to the growth of multinationals. Mass-production systems and computer information handling have pushed all societies to larger and larger units of production (Heilbroner, 1974). An inevitable consequence of this is expansion to markets and production facilities overseas.

Another explanation is that local economic independence is impossible for many nations, particularly those with weak political and economic systems. The multinational firm becomes the dominant economic and political form of organization, superseding the traditional nation-state in weaker parts of the world (Toynbee, 1974).

A more complex explanation is that the multinational corporation is a consequence of corporate choices made to implement product-market strategy: As corporations begin to produce a complex range of products, these are to be sold in different markets through multiple channels of distribution (McMillan, 1973; Egelhoff, 1982). This explanation, which, as will be seen later, is solidly within contemporary organizational theory, suggests that multinational corporations are in essence inevitable. Even in a no-growth economic situation, the desire to cut costs or maintain the share of the market would lead to international expansion.

Each of the preceding points explains part of the international growth of organizations. Each also explains why organizations in general seek to expand their influence over the environment as a means of protecting their flanks and expanding their operations. These explanations all assume that the organization acts in a rational manner, which, as we will see, is a highly questionable assumption. Interestingly, these analyses have all dealt with organizations that produce goods. Relatively little attention has been paid to multinational service organizations, such as international banking, which are of crucial importance. International hotel operations, though perhaps less important, are also very evident as one travels beyond a nation's border.

There are additional consequences of multinational corporations. Considerations of what is best for a national economy are secondary to considerations of what is best for the corporation as a whole. Although the multinational is frequently welcomed in areas of high unemployment, its presence can create extremely high dependence on the firm. Once the local economy is dependent on such a firm, the firm itself has a great deal of power. The multinational is also often able to avoid paying taxes at the rate paid by domestic corporations through reporting profits in countries with lower tax rates and other forms of financial shifts. When a multinational moves some of its production operations overseas, of course, domestic employment is adversely affected (Clegg and Dunkerly, 1980).

There is an aura of inevitability in most discussions of multinational firms. This aura is generally warranted, but there are conditions that could drastically affect the operations of multinational firms. Changes in government policy brought about by revolutions or elections in the host country can result in the nationalization of all industries or the confiscation of all foreign investments. The case of Iran and the United States was a graphic illustration of that. Not all multinational ventures are successful. Nonetheless, the multinational corporation appears to be an increasing part of the international scene and will continue to influence international events.

THE VOLUNTARY ORGANIZATION

Our focus thus far has been primarily on organizations with paid employees or members. Voluntary organizations, another form of organizations, are quite different in many respects. According to Knoke and Prensky (1984), voluntary associations are formally organized named groups, most of whose participants do not derive their livelihoods from the organizations's activities, although a few positions may receive pay as staff or leaders. A substantial proportion of associations consist of organizations or persons with economic interests, such as trade associations, professional societies, and labor unions, while many others promote the noneconomic concerns of their members. Association boundaries are often fuzzy and porous (Aldrich, 1971), since many involve episodic supporters and passively interested constituents who can be mobilized under exceptional circumstances to provide financial or political sustenance (pp. 3–4).

The issue is more complex than Knoke and Prensky portray. The Roman Catholic Church has long been viewed as one of the more complex and comprehensive bureaucratic organizations in the world, with thousands of paid employees. Local parishes, on the other hand, are exactly like the voluntary organizations Knoke and Prensky describe. Professional associations, such as the American Medical Association or the American Nurses' Association, have extensive professional staffs. Of course, there are organizations that are strictly voluntary, such as the Greater Loudonville Association or the Willard Mountain Ski Patrol. The Greater Loudonville Association is an association of homeowners concerned primarily with community beautification. This can be contrasted with the Love Canal Homeowners Association, which was concerned with matters of life and death (Levine, 1982).

Knoke and Prensky believe that traditional organizational theory has limited usefulness for voluntary organizations. They base their conclusion on analyses of incentive systems and participant commitment, formal structures, leadership and authority, environmental conditions, and organizational effectiveness issues.

WHY STUDY ORGANIZATIONS?

This chapter ends with the very question with which it began. It seems obvious that organizations will continue to grow, bureaucratize, and centralize (Child, 1976). In other words, we will have more of the same, which can be a depressing conclusion.

At the same time, there are organizational theorists and social philosophers who see organizations as the only way by which desirable ends such as peace, prosperity, and social justice can be achieved (Etzioni, 1968, 1991, 1993). In a very real sense, we are living in an "organizational state" (Laumann and Knoke, 1987), in which the major actors in national policy events are organizations and interorganizational networks. The second answer to our question, then, is that we must study organizations if we are to understand our society and what is happening in and around it.

One of the major contributions that our organizational analysis can make is to point out the limitations to what is feasible for organizations themselves and for the wider social system. We will also point out that organizations contain some inherent contradictions that limit the impact that individual actors can have.

Jackall (1988) noted that business is a "social and moral terrain" (p. 3). The same point is true for all organizations. Moral and ethical issues are confronted whenever decisions are made. In a book prepared under the auspices of the Business Roundtable, an organization made up of the chief executive officers of many of the largest and most powerful American business firms, Steckmest (1982; see also Burke, 1986) urges corporate social responsibility. The argument of his book is that corporations need to "develop executives and functions (e.g., government relations and consumer affairs staffs) to effectively monitor, and responsibly interact in, an increasingly complex sociopolitical environment" (Yeager, 1982:748). Again, the notion of corporations has to be expanded to all organizations, including those that are part of government itself.

Organizational theory has much to contribute to "clients" of many types, ranging from politicians and journalists in the public-at-large, to workers and managers within organizations, to opponents of organizations who operate inside and outside the organizations themselves (Lammers, 1981). The true relevance of organizational theory lies in the following conclusion: *"The more we are able to create worlds that are morally cogent and politically viable, the more we are able, as workers and as citizens, to manage or resist"* (Brown, 1978:378; italics added).

SUMMARY AND CONCLUSIONS

The purpose of this chapter has been a simple one—to indicate the importance of organizations at every level of human life. Thus, we examined the manner in which organizations have outcomes for the individual, classes of individuals, the community, the society, and the international order. Organizational analysis can be dull until the crucial and central role of organizations is understood. If organizations are understood, then individuals have a tool with which they can deal with the reality that they face.

EXERCISES

1. Write down all of the activities that you do in a day, or in a week. Describe the degree to which each activity is affected by organizations.
2. Think about two organizations with which you are very familiar. They can be places where you worked or are working, athletic teams, fraternities or sororities, clubs, religious organizations, or other organizations that you can describe. What are the outcomes of these organizations? Remember to use the materials in this chapter in your answers.

Chapter 2

Organizational Structure: Forms and Outcomes

‒‒‒‒‒‒‒‒‒‒‒‒‒‒‒ •◆• ‒‒‒‒‒‒‒‒‒‒‒‒‒‒‒

OVERVIEW

The subtitle of this book begins with the word *structure*. This chapter starts out with a definition of what is organizational structure. The first element of structure is complexity. Complexity has three aspects—vertical, horizontal, and geographical. In simple terms, these refer to how deep, how wide, and how spread out an organization is. As might be expected, organizations vary from one another on these complexity aspects. Formalization is the next element of structure. Formalization means the degree to which rules and procedures are spelled out by an organization. This, of course, has outcomes for individuals. The final element of structure is centralization, which refers to where decisions are made in an organization. Structure involves the rules and procedure and the hierarchy noted in the definition of organizations.

Organizational structure is very easy to understand. Just think about your undergraduate college or university. How did all students enter? Through the admissions office. Where do professors send your grades, and from what office are those grades sent at the end of the term? The registrar's office. Both offices are part of the structure of colleges and universities. They can be thought of as parts of those organizations. Organizational structure can be considered as the arrangement of organizational parts. In some ways, organizational structures are analogous to building structures. Buildings have doors through which we enter.

Organizations have "ports of entry" as well, such as the admissions office. Hallways and corridors govern our movements. Organizations have rules and procedures, which serve this purpose for their members. Some buildings are small and simple, such as a garage; others are complex and multilayered, with intricate linkages and passageways to other buildings. Organizations vary in their degree of complexity. They also vary in their degree of centralization. In some buildings the heating and air conditioning are centrally controlled; in others each room is essentially autonomous and its heating and cooling destiny can be controlled by the occupants. Organizations vary in the degree to which people and units are given autonomy in decision making.

This chapter describes the nature of structure. The next chapter considers the reasons structural forms take the shape that they do. At the outset, it is important to realize that the building analogy is not perfect. The structure of my house has not changed a bit since it was built some forty years ago. Organizational structures, however, are continually changing as they are influenced by successive waves of members, interactions among the members, and incessant environmental changes. At the same time, the emergent nature of structure should not blind us to the fact that organizational structures have a strong tendency toward inertia.

What is structure? A formal definition will be given later. Here, some examples are presented to begin to indicate the nature of the topic. The examples are drawn from the State University of New York (SUNY). SUNY itself is quite complex. It has units scattered throughout the state of New York and an office in Washington, D.C. It has a myriad of divisions and departments, both by academic specialty and by administrative division. It has a tall hierarchy, with a chancellor, vice-chancellors, assistant vice-chancellors, and other ranks at the central office and presidents, vice presidents, associate and assistant vice presidents, deans, associate and assistant deans, faculty members of various ranks, and clerical and service personnel arranged along an array of civil service rankings. By almost any standard, it is a very complex organization. Very complex organizations face very complex coordination and control problems, and SUNY is no exception. One way in which coordination and control can be achieved is through effective communication among units. Such communication can be facilitated by the use of a computerized management information systems (MIS). This strategy is not always successful, of course, and the system can be plagued with missing information.

SUNY is formalized to varying degrees. In some areas rules and procedures are spelled out in minute detail; in other areas low formalization exists. High formalization at Albany can be seen in the faculty promotion process. The procedures for documenting faculty members' accomplishments in teaching, research, and service are spelled out in excruciating detail. If the details are not followed to the letter, the promotion can well fail. Low formalization, on the other hand, can be seen in the classroom. Individual faculty are almost totally free to select their texts and their methods of classroom presentation. Only in truly extreme cases would the organization intervene in the classroom.

For students, the registration process is highly formalized, with specific dates and times to register, steps to be taken in the process, and forms to be completed. Again, the classroom is at the opposite extreme, except in the case of laboratories, with no official rules on attendance, methods of taking notes, or hours required for studying for exams.

SUNY is also centralized to varying degrees. Low centralization can be seen in an academic department that is almost totally free to select graduate students and faculty members on the basis of the department's own judgment. There is a minimal amount of power utilized at the campus or central administrative levels, except when senior-level professors are being hired. The potential for the exercise of power is there, but it is seldom invoked. High centralization occurs when decision-making power is retained at or near the top of the organization. When new academic programs are developed, particularly when they involve scarce resources, the central administration is heavily involved in the decision-making process. As a general rule, the higher the quality of the higher educational organization, the lower the level of centralization (Blau, 1973). The important conclusion is that complexity, formalization, and centralization can vary within a single organization. They are multidimensional phenomena.

A great deal of the research to be considered in this chapter and the next is comparative in the sense that data are collected from more than one organization (Heydebrand, 1973). Some of the research is comparative in the sense that there is an attempt to compare organizations in different settings or societies. Comparative research is emphasized in the belief that it permits generalizations beyond a single research setting. As the discussion of typologies suggests, of course, in the absence of a sound typology such generalizations are risky. Most analysts try to make their findings as widely usable as possible, but the problem of crossing "types" should continue to be recognized. Indeed, as will be evident in the discussion, some of the major research projects have included such a limited range of organizations that generalization becomes difficult.

There is an additional problem in the studies to be considered, and this involves measurement (Price and Mueller, 1986). Data can come from organizational documents and records, key organizational informants, samples of members from the whole organization, or published data sets. (See Azumi and McMillan, 1974; Dewar, Whetten, and Boje, 1980; Lincoln and Zeitz, 1980; Pennings, 1973, for more detailed discussions of some of the methodological issues.) The problem has been that measures of different types, which are designed to measure the same phenomena, such as formalization, may not correlate well. Documents may tell us one thing, but informants another. Research is beginning to show us that there are measures that can be used across diverse sets of organizations (Kalleberg et al., 1996; Leicht, Parcel, and Kaufman, 1992), but as yet we do not have universal measures.

DEFINING ORGANIZATIONAL STRUCTURE

By organizational structure we mean "the distributions, along various lines, of people among social positions that influence the role relations among these people" (Blau, 1974:12). This simple definition requires amplification. One implication of the definition is the division of labor; people are given different tasks or jobs within organizations. Another implication is that organizations contain ranks, or a hierarchy; the positions that people fill have rules and regulations that specify, in varying degrees, how incumbents are to behave in those positions.

Other definitions stress the importance of human interactions in the formation of structures as "structures shape people's practices, but it is also people's practices that constitute (and reproduce) structure" (Sewell, 1992:4). In a similar vein, structure is seen as "a complex medium of control which is continually produced and recreated in interaction and yet shapes that interaction: structures are constituted and constitutive" (Ranson, Hinings, and Greenwood, 1980:3). These approaches emphasize that an organization's structure is not fixed for all time. Rather, it shapes what goes on in an organization and is in turn shaped by what goes on in an organization. This point highlights the fact that organizations are by nature conservative. Their structures constitute the interactions that take place within them. Structure does not yield total conformity, but it is intended to prevent random behavior.

A very similar conceptualization of structure is that there is a juxtaposition of technological solutions, political exchanges, and social interpretations in and around organizations, which results in modes of structuring, and that there is a dialectical unfolding of relations among organizational actors. This results in consequences for organizational forms (Fombrun, 1986). Structure is thus continually emergent.

Organizational structures serve three basic functions. First and foremost, structures are intended to produce organizational outputs and to achieve organizational goals—in other words, to be effective. Second, structures are designed to minimize or at least regulate the influence of individual variations on the organization. Structures are imposed to ensure that individuals conform to requirements of organizations and not vice versa. Third, structures are the settings in which power is exercised (structures also set or determine which positions have power in the first place), in which decisions are made (the flow of information into a decision is largely determined by structure), and in which organizations' activities are carried out (structure is the arena for organizational actions).

Multiple Structures

In the discussion that follows, there is an unfortunate problem with much of the literature. The overwhelming majority of studies of organizational structures wittingly or unwittingly make the assumption that there is one structure in an organization, but there is ample evidence that this is just not the case (Hall, 1962; Heydebrand, 1990; Litwak, 1961; Stinchcombe, 1990). There are structural differences between work units, departments, and divisions. There are also structural differences according to the level in the hierarchy. For example, a hospital admissions unit has explicit rules and procedures so that all persons who are admitted are treated the same way and so that employees are guided by a clear set of organizationally prescribed expectations. The physical rehabilitation unit of the same hospital has many fewer specific guidelines concerning what it is to do. Similarly, the behavior of lower-level workers, such as orderlies and kitchen workers, is prescribed to a much higher degree than is that of nurses and physicians. There is intraorganizational variation, both across organizational units and up and down the hierarchy.

This intraorganizational variation is a crucial factor, of course, when multinational organizations are considered. Not only are there variations within an organization in one national location, but also there can be even greater variations within the same organization across national boundaries (Gupta and Govindarajan, 1991).

Structural Forms

Organizational structures take many forms. A brief review of some of the "classic" literature in the area will demonstrate the manner in which variations occur. The seminal work on structure is Weber's (1947) description of the ideal type of bureaucracy. He states that a bureaucracy has a hierarchy of authority, limited authority, division of labor, technically competent participants, procedures for work, rules for incumbents, and differential rewards. If all these components are present to a high degree in a bureaucracy, it is the ideal type. The important implication, of course, is that organizations in practice will vary from this ideal type, as has been demonstrated (Hall, 1963). A bureaucratic organization is designed for efficiency and reliability (Hage, 1980; Perrow, 1979). This point may seem odd, since for many people, the terms *bureaucracy* and *bureaucrat* have negative connotations. Bureaucracies are actually designed to work well.

Burns and Stalker (1961) took a major step forward with their development of a model of multiple organizational forms. They identified the "mechanic" form, which is very close to Weber's ideal type of bureaucracy, and the "organic" form, which is almost a logical opposite. Thus, instead of having hierarchical authority, organic organizations have a network structure of control; instead of task specialization, a continual adjustment and redefinition of tasks; instead of hierarchical supervision, a communication context involving information and advice; and so on. The authors see organizational forms as being closely linked to the environment in which organizations are embedded, particularly in regard to the technology being employed by the organization.

The analysis of organizational forms moved forward again when Hage (1965) noted that structural characteristics, such as complexity, formalization, and centralization, vary in their presence from high to low. This formulation serves as the basis for the analysis that follows.

COMPLEXITY

The term *complex organizations* describes the subject matter of this entire book—and indeed is the title of several important works. In this section we will look carefully at the concept of complexity, noting what it is and what are its sources and its consequences. From this examination it should become clear that the complexity of an organization has major effects on the behavior of its members, on other structural conditions, on processes within the organization, and on relationships between the organization and its environment. It also has particular importance for communication.

Complexity is one of the first things that hits a person entering any organization except the simplest: Division of labor, job titles, multiple divisions, and hierarchical levels are usually immediately evident. Any familiarity with large corporations (and many small ones), the government, the military, or a school system verifies this. Even organizations that seem very simple at first may exhibit interesting forms of complexity. Local voluntary organizations, such as the Rotary Club, labor union locals, and garden clubs usually have committees for programs, publicity, membership, community service, education, finance, and other matters, all with their attendant structures. These kinds of organizations must make provisions for the control and coordination of activities just as their more complex counterparts must.

The issue is itself made more complex by the fact that individual parts of an organization can vary in their degree of complexity. In a study of the regional office of a major oil company, for example, it was found that there were six divisions, as shown on the organization chart, Figure 2–1. The heads of the divisions had

FIGURE 2–1   Regional Office Organization

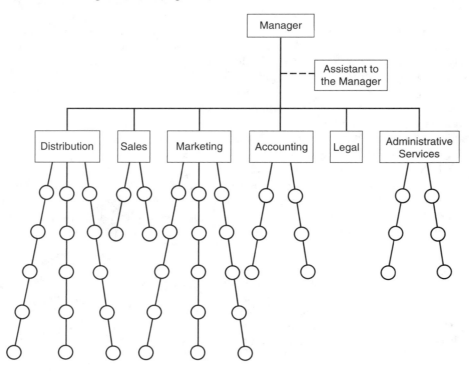

equal rank in the organization, and each was thought to be equally important to the overall success of the organization. When the divisions themselves were examined, it was found that they varied not only in size—from three to one hundred members—but also in complexity. The largest division, distribution, had five hierarchical levels and three important subdivisions, each of which was further specialized by tasks performed by specific work groups. The smallest division, which performed legal services associated with land acquisition and other problems of service station development, was composed of a lawyer and two secretaries.

These intraorganizational variations in complexity can also be seen in manufacturing firms with research and development departments. These departments are likely to be characterized by a shallower hierarchy than that found in other divisions of the organization. Although there may be several levels above them, the research and development workers will be rather loosely supervised and have a wide span of control. In manufacturing departments, the span of control for each supervisor is shorter, and the whole unit looks more like a pyramid. (See Figure 2–2.)

These examples indicate the obvious—complexity is not a simple issue. It has several components, which do not necessarily vary together. At the same time, the concept itself conveys a meaning in organizational literature: Complex organizations contain many subparts requiring coordination and control, and the more complex an organization is, the more difficult it becomes to achieve coordination and control. Since organizations vary widely in their degree of complexity, regardless of the specific component of complexity used, and since wide variations are found within specific organizations, an understanding of complexity is important for the overall understanding of organizations.

To make sense out of the literature on complexity, we will examine the components of the concept. The three elements of complexity most commonly

FIGURE 2–2   The Shape of Two Departments in the Same Organization

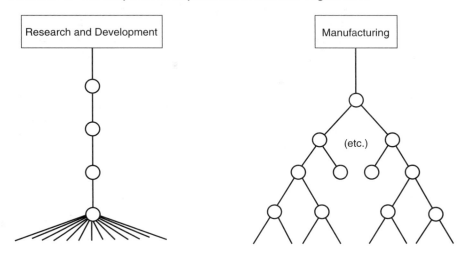

identified are horizontal differentiation; vertical, or hierarchical, differentiation; and geographical dispersion.

Horizontal Differentiation.   Horizontal differentiation refers to the ways the tasks performed by the organization are subdivided. Unfortunately for conceptual clarity, there are two basic ways in which such tasks can be subdivided and two ways by which complexity can be measured.

The first way tasks can be subdivided is to give highly trained specialists a comprehensive range of activities to perform; the second is to minutely subdivide the tasks so that nonspecialists can perform them. The first approach is exemplified by professionals or craft workers in the organizational setting who are solely responsible for complete operations. (For a discussion of craft-organized work, see Stinchcombe, 1959. For a comprehensive discussion of the nature of professionally controlled work, see Ritzer and Walczak, 1986.) They are given the responsibility and the authority to carry out the task to its completion.

The second form of horizontal differentiation is most plainly seen in "McDonaldized" situations, where each worker performs only one or a few repetitive tasks (Ritzer, 2000). The nature of the task itself is important here, since it is the routine and uniform task that is most amenable to the second type of differentiation; nonroutine and quite varied tasks are more commonly subdivided according to the first type.

Several writers have elaborated on the first form of horizontal complexity. Hage (1965) defines complexity as the "specialization in an organization . . . measured by the number of occupational specialties and the length of training required by each. The greater the number of occupations and the longer the period of training required, the more complex the organization" (p. 294). Hage's assumption is that the more training people have, the more they are differentiated from people who might have similar amounts of training but in different specialties. This definition is almost identical in its implications to that of Price (1968), who states: "Complexity may be defined as the degree of knowledge required to produce the output of a system. The degree of complexity of an organization can be measured by the degree of education of its members. The higher the education, the higher the complexity" (p. 26). In some later research, Hage and Aiken (1967a) develop this approach further:

> We interpret complexity to mean at least three things: the number of occupational specialties, the professional activity, and the professional training. Organizations vary in the number of occupational specialties that they utilize in achieving their goals. This variable was measured by asking respondents to report their major duties; each respondent was then classified according to the type of occupational specialty, e.g., psychiatrist, rehabilitation, counselor, teacher, nurse, social worker. The variable, degree of professional activity, reflects the number of professional associations in which the respondents were involved, the number of meetings attended, and the number of offices held or number of papers given at professional meetings. The amount of professional training was based on the amount of college training as well as other professional training. (pp. 79–80)

Hage and Aiken's research was carried out in health and welfare organizations, where the emphasis on professional backgrounds was very appropriate. The first form of horizontal complexity, then, is based on the number of occupational and professional specialties in the organization.

This form of horizontal differentiation introduces additional complications for the organization, in that a high level of specialization requires coordination of the specialists. In many cases, personnel specifically designated as coordinating personnel have to be assigned to ensure that the various efforts do not work at cross-purposes and that the overall organizational tasks are accomplished.

The second form of horizontal complexity is typically based on counts of job titles within an organization. In large offices, for example, one can find a number of job titles for clerical personnel, such as Typist-1, Typist-2, Typist-3. These distinctions frequently are based on salary or seniority, but they also are usually based on the way labor is divided in the organization. The greater the division of labor, the higher the level of horizontal complexity. The division of labor here is into highly specialized work that is repetitive and routine.

There is greater proliferation of job titles when an organization's racial and sexual composition is heterogeneous (Strang and Baron, 1990). This study found that newer and larger organizations are lowering their number of job titles as they attempt to streamline their operations. It is probable, also, that job distinctions based on race and sex are declining in larger, more bureaucratic organizations.

These two approaches to horizontal differentiation appear to have very similar roots, since both are concerned with the division of labor of people within the organization. The critical difference between these forms of horizontal differentiation appears to be the scope of the ultimate tasks of organizations (Dewar and Hage, 1978). Organizations that attempt to carry out a wide variety of activities and that have clients or customers who require a variety of services divide the labor into work performed by specialists. Probably the clearest examples are hospitals, with their medical, dietary, and other specialties. The more minute division of labor occurs when the organization's tasks are not so diffuse and when the organization has grown in size, since such a division of labor provides an economy of scale. Examples are automobile manufacturing firms or state bureaus of motor vehicles. These two forms of complexity are not alternative ways to organize for the same task.

The last two paragraphs contain an apparent contradiction that must be addressed. The Strang and Baron (1990) research found that larger and newer organizations have fewer job titles, whereas Dewar and Hage (1978) found that large organizations have more minute division of labor, which means more job titles. There are two probable explanations for the contradiction. One is that large organizations—either by choice or by force—have eliminated job title distinctions based on race and gender since the 1970s and thus have fewer job titles. The second explanation is that Hage and Dewar might have studied organizations that engaged in more routine work than those studied by Strang and Baron. As the next chapter will show, these explanations are consistent with organizational theorists who emphasize the importance of the environment of organizations and technology, respectively. Finally, there is a generally positive relationship between complexity and size, the Strang and Baron findings notwithstanding.

Horizontal complexity can be measured by the number of different jobs that people have, whether the jobs are in specialized professions or crafts or in routine specialized work, through counting job titles.

Horizontal complexity can also be measured by counting the number of divisions, departments, or units within an organization. This is a completely different unit of analysis, which can be found in the research of Blau and Schoenherr (1971), Hall, Haas, and Johnson (1967b), and Pugh et al. (1968). Using measures of this sort, we would find the U.S. Army to be very complex, with its vast array of commands, battalions, brigades, companies, and so on. Organizations low on the complexity scale would be a local church or an auto dealership.

Even though the unit of analysis is very different, the control and coordination issues would be the same whichever measure is used. At the present time, there have not been sufficient attempts to integrate the measurement levels to permit us to determine whether or not the measures really are alternative approaches to the same phenomena.

Vertical Differentiation.   Vertical, or hierarchical, differentiation is less complicated than horizontal differentiation. Research into the vertical dimension has used straightforward indicators of the depth of the hierarchy. Meyer (1968a) uses the "proliferation of supervisory levels" as his measures of the depth of an organization. Pugh et al. (1968) suggest that the vertical dimension can be measured by a "count of the number of job positions between the chief executive and the employees working on the output" (p. 78). Hall, Haas, and Johnson (1967b) use the "number of levels in the deepest single division and the mean number of levels for the organization as a whole" (total number of levels in all divisions/ number of divisions) as their indicators (p. 906).

These direct indicators of vertical differentiation assume that authority is distributed in accordance with the level in the hierarchy; that is, the higher the level, the greater the authority. Although in the vast majority of cases that would be a valid assumption, there are some situations in which proliferation of levels can represent phenomena other than the distribution of authority. For example, in organizations that utilize professional personnel, arrangements may not have been made to allow advancement within the same job title. Physicists may be hired as physicists, but if the organization's policies do not allow much of a salary range for that job title, some physicists may be "promoted" to a higher position without an actual change in their work or an increase in authority. This is known as the "dual ladder."

Both horizontal and vertical differentiation present organizations with problems of communication, control, and coordination. Subunits along either axis (this would include both aspects of horizontal differentiation) are nuclei that are differentiated from adjacent units and the total organization according to horizontal or vertical factors. The greater the differentiation, the greater the potentiality for difficulties in control, coordination, and communication. Informal social networks are also differentiated vertically (Stevenson, 1990).

Geographical Dispersion.   The final element in complexity, geographical dispersion, can actually be a form of horizontal or vertical differentiation. That is, activities and personnel can be geographically dispersed, according to either horizontal or vertical functions, by the separation of power centers or tasks. Field or branch offices of sales or welfare organizations exemplify horizontal dispersion: The tasks performed by the various field offices are essentially identical (low complexity on the horizontal axis) and the power in the organization is differentiated between the central office and the field offices. Banks frequently have a national headquarters, regional headquarters, and then branches. This is an example of vertical differentiation along with geographical dispersion.

Geographical dispersion becomes a separate element in the complexity concept when it is realized that an organization can perform the same functions with the same division of labor and hierarchical arrangements in multiple locations. A business firm, for example, can have a complex set of sales procedures requiring highly specialized sales personnel in the field. These sales personnel can be dispersed from a central office or through regional or state or local offices, with essentially the same hierarchical arrangements. Complexity is thus increased with the development of geographically dispersed activities, even if the horizontal and vertical differentiation remains the same across the spatially separated units.

Geographical dispersion is relatively simple to measure. One can simply count the number of locations in which an organization has offices or plants. Alternatively, one could simply count the proportion of an organization's personnel who work away from a home headquarters (Hall, Haas, and Johnson, 1967b; Raphael, 1967).

VARIANCE OF COMPLEXITY ELEMENTS

The discussion thus far has suggested that the three major elements of complexity vary, often independently of each other. Before we discuss such independent variance further, we should note that these elements can vary together. Organizations with little horizontal, vertical, or geographical complexity can easily be identified—the small business firm with a single product or service and a single location comes most readily to mind. The same phenomena can occur, however, in large organizations. Crozier's (1964) analysis of two separate government organizations in France graphically demonstrates this.

The first organization, a clerical agency, was characterized by a very simple division of labor; although tasks were highly routine and repetitious, there was little differentiation among them. In addition, considering the size of the organization, there was a very shallow hierarchy. The organization was not complex on the horizontal and vertical axes.

The third axis, spatial dispersion, appeared in Crozier's analysis of a French tobacco company (the Industrial Monopoly). The system comprised thirty geographically dispersed plants. The plants were fairly large, with 350 to 400 employees on the average, but there were only six categories of workers in each plant.

Production workers, who were paid equal wages throughout the system, made up the bulk of the labor force, and there was little differentiation among their tasks. Maintenance workers (electricians, boilermakers, and metalworkers) were more specialized. Shop foremen held supervisory positions in both plant and white-collar office operations. Even there, the tasks performed were quite similar. Administrative jobs, such as personnel, purchasing, or accounting, were few in number and minimally professionalized. There was one technical engineer per plant. The top position was that of the plant director, who usually had an assistant.

This relatively large dispersed organization was structurally very simple. That simplicity did not eliminate severe problems—Crozier documented these in great detail—but the problems were based on external and internal conditions that were not related to its structure. The imposition of civil service personnel regulations, the power of the maintenance personnel—who could actually control the output of the plants by the speed at which they maintained the equipment—and certain characteristics of the French society combined to make these organizations much less efficient and effective than they might have been. It seems clear that increased complexity on the vertical and horizontal axes would do little to improve the performance of these plants. These noncomplex organizations are enormous systems designed to perform simple and unchanging tasks. It can be hypothesized that if the tasks and technology were altered to develop a more effective system, the organizations would become more complex.

In direct contrast to the simple organizations just described, the diversified industrial or government organization serves as an example of the organization that is complex on all three axes. Huge businesses such as Microsoft or multinational banks are characterized by extreme complexity. The same is true for operations of national, state, and some local governments, as well as such diverse organizations as the Roman Catholic Church, the New York City school system, the University of California, and SUNY.

These extreme cases serve as a reminder that organizations can be highly or minimally complex in all facets of complexity. Other commonsense examples suggest that such covariance is not the necessary pattern. A liberal arts college, for example, usually has a low degree of vertical differentiation and usually no geographical dispersion but a high degree of horizontal differentiation. Most manufacturing plants have a greater division of labor along the horizontal axis than those studied by Crozier, although the hierarchical levels may be the same. The offensive unit of a football team is highly specialized but essentially has only two ranks. High vertical differentiation with little horizontal differentiation is exemplified by the army infantry battalion.

An assumption throughout this discussion is that most organizations are complex in one of the various configurations discussed. Another assumption, verifiable from a variety of forms of evidence, is that there is a strong tendency for organizations to become more complex as their own activities and the environment around them become more complex. Organizations that survive tend to grow in size, and size and complexity are related. Increased complexity leads to greater problems of coordination and control. We now turn to this outcome of complexity for organizations.

Coordination and Control

In their landmark study, *Organization and Environment,* Lawrence and Lorsch (1967) examined the sources and consequences of complexity. (They used the term "differentiation" instead of "complexity.") They found major differences between departments in the same organization. They also found that structural differentiation contributes to differences in attitudes and behaviors on the part of members of the differentiated departments. These differences include orientations toward the particular goals of the department, emphases on interpersonal skills, and time perspectives. Departments, therefore, vary not only in the specific tasks they perform but also in the underlying behavior and outlooks of their members.

The data for the analysis of differentiation came from firms in three industries in the United States. The first set of industries comprised firms making and selling plastics in the form of powder, pellets, and sheets.

> Their products went to industrial customers of all sizes, from the large automobile, appliance, furniture, paint, textile, and paper companies to the smaller firms making toys, containers, and household items. The organizations studied emphasized specialty plastics tailored to specific uses rather than standardized commodity plastics. They all built their product-development work on the science of polymer chemistry. Production was continuous, with relatively few workers needed to monitor the automatic and semiautomatic processing equipment. (p. 24)

These organizations were in a highly competitive market. According to the executives interviewed, the primary competitive issue was the development of new and revised products and processes. The life cycle of any product was likely to be short, since competitors were all engaged in intensive research and could make even a very successful product quickly obsolete. The executives noted that "the most hazardous aspect of the industrial environment revolved around the relevant scientific knowledge" (p. 25). These organizations were in a changing and "turbulent" environment, with both input—in the form of scientific knowledge— and the consumption of output—in the form of customer satisfaction after purchasing the product—highly uncertain. On the other hand, the production process itself was characterized by its certainty. Once the original technical specifications for a particular product were developed, the production process could proceed automatically, since the mix between such production variables as pressure, temperature, and chemical composition could be easily measured, and monitoring was a part of the production process itself.

The six organizations studied within the plastics industry each had four basic functional departments—sales, production, applied research, and fundamental research—that differed in their own structures. The production departments were the most formalized, the fundamental research units the least. Sales department personnel were the most concerned with interpersonal relationships, and production departments were the least, with the two research units falling in between. The interesting dimension of the time perspective taken by the personnel shows the departments falling into a predictable pattern—from shortest to longest time perspective, with sales, production, applied research, and fundamental research fitting the time perspective framework in that order. In practice, this means that sales personnel wanted to have orders filled immediately, whereas the scientists in the fundamental research department were looking two or three years down the road in their time frame. The members of the various departments also differed in personal goals; sales personnel were concerned with customer problems and the marketplace, production personnel with cost reduction and efficiency, and research personnel with scientific matters, as well as the more immediate practical issues of process improvement and modification. The scientific personnel were not as concerned with purely scientific matters as the authors had anticipated, but they did have clearly different goals from those of the members of other departments.

These differences in task, behavior, and attitude are directly related to the kind of environment that various departments must work with in their short- and long-run activities. A high degree of differentiation (complexity) is, therefore, related to a highly complex and differentiated environment (Burns and Stalker, 1961). In this case the complexity refers to the competitive situation in which the organizations find themselves (this degree of competition is not limited to profit-making organizations) and to the rapidly changing and complicated technological world in which they must survive.

To provide contrasts to the plastics firms, Lawrence and Lorsch (1967) studied two other industries; the primary factor in their selection was the rate of environmental change. The second industry they chose was the standardized container industry. The standardized containers were beer bottles. The rate of sales increase in this industry was at about the level of the rate of population growth and the growth of the gross national product, so the organizations in the industry were approximately keeping even with the environment in these respects. More important for the purposes of the study, no significant new products had been introduced in two decades—in the 1960s beer bottles were almost all brown and held 12 ounces. The major competitive factors were "operational issues of maintaining customer service through prompt delivery and consistent product quality while minimizing operating costs" (p. 86). Although these are not easy or simple tasks to perform, they are stable; and the problems and prospects for the future are much more certain than in the plastics field.

The third set of organizations studied was in the packaged foods industry. The environmental conditions of these organizations were in between those of the plastics and container firms. Although the organizations engaged heavily in innovations, the rate of new-product introduction and the growth of sales were less than in the plastics industry but more than in the container field.

When the differentiation within the organizations in these three industries was examined, the findings were as predicted—the plastics firms were the most differentiated, followed by the food firms, and then by the container firms. Lawrence and Lorsch did not stop their analysis with differentiation, however.

They extended their analysis to the concept of integration, which they define as "the quality of the state of collaboration that exists among departments that are required to achieve unity of effort by the demands of the environment" (p. 47). The authors were also concerned with the effectiveness of the organizations. Here they used standard and appropriate market and economic measures, such as profit. Organizations are also more effective when they meet environmental pressures and when they allow their members to achieve their individual goals.

The results of the analysis of integration and effectiveness are in some ways surprising. In the plastics industry, the most effective organizations were those with the greatest degree of differentiation, and they also faced the most severe integration problems. Their effectiveness in the face of high differentiation was explained by their successful conflict resolution. It is not the idea of successful conflict resolution that is surprising; it is the fact that the effective organizations were characterized by a high degree of conflict in the first place—that they were not totally harmonious, with all personnel working as members of one happy team. From the data discussed earlier, it is apparent that the differentiation in departmental and individual attitudes and behavior would lead inevitably to conflict. In these organizations, such conflict contributed to effectiveness.

Conflict per se, of course, would be detrimental to the organization if it were not resolved. So another important contribution of this research is its analysis of conflict resolution. The authors do not suggest that there is one best form of such resolution. Rather, they provide evidence that conflict-resolution processes varied according to the specific conflict situations in a particular form of organization. In the case of the highly differentiated plastics organizations, integration was achieved by departments or individuals who were in a position, and had the knowledge available, to work with the departments involved in conflict situations. In this case, the position was relatively low in the managerial hierarchy rather than at the top. The lower position was necessary because of the specific knowledge required to deal with the departments and issues involved. The highly differentiated and effective organization thus anticipated conflict and established integrating (conflict-resolving) departments and individuals whose primary purpose was to work with the departments in (inherent) conflict. Another important consideration was that the integrating departments or individuals were equidistant between the conflicting departments in their time, goal, interpersonal, and structural orientations. This middle position led to effective resolution not through simple compromise but through direct confrontations between the conflicting parties. Conflict resolution in this setting thus became a process whereby the parties thrashed out their differences in the open with the assistance of integrators who understood both positions.

In the container corporations, with their lesser degree of differentiation, conflicts also arose, but not to the extent found in the plastics firms, owing to less differentiation. In the container industry, conflicts were resolved at the top of the organization, because those at the top had greater knowledge, made possible by the stable environment and the lack of differentiation between organizational segments. With less differentiation, knowledge was not as specialized, and a top executive could have a good grasp of what was going on in all the major divisions. Lawrence and Lorsch suggest that in this case, and in others like it, decentralization of influence would be harmful. The food-processing firms generally fell between the plastics and the container firms in the extent of their differentiation and in the integration problems faced.

A major conclusion from this analysis is that effectiveness is not achieved by following one organizational model. This conclusion is vitally important for understanding organizations. In other words, there is no one best way to organize for the purpose of achieving the highly varied goals of organizations within highly varied environments. This is a contingency approach to organizational structure, which says that under some conditions one form of structure is more effective or efficient, whereas under other conditions alternative forms are more effective or efficient. The contingency model continues to be a dominant force in organizational theory.

Research in a very different setting—hospital emergency units—reached a very similar sort of conclusion (Argote, 1982). Argote found that in situations of low uncertainty, programmed coordination contributed to greater effectiveness, whereas in situations of high uncertainty, nonprogrammed modes of coordination were more effective. The structural arrangements are contingent upon the situation being faced.

This conclusion is further strengthened by a consideration of Blau and Schoenherr's (1971) findings, which were based on research into government finance and public personnel agencies. Blau and Schoenherr also found that increased complexity engenders problems of communication and coordination. Personnel in the managerial hierarchy spend more time in dealing with these problems than in direct supervision in a highly complex organization. There is also pressure in complex organizations to add personnel to handle the increased difficulties with control and coordination, increasing the proportion of the total personnel devoted to such activities. This is known as administrative intensity.

This last finding introduces an interesting paradox into the analysis of organizations. Although large organizations can experience savings through economies of large size, the complexity that is related to large size creates cross-pressures to add managerial personnel to reduce the problems associated with control, coordination, and conflict. Decisions to physically disperse, add divisions, or add hierarchical levels may be made in the interests of economy. Paradoxically, the economies realized may be counterbalanced by the added burdens of keeping the organization together. There is yet another paradox. Although there is a positive relationship between technical and structural complexity and administrative intensity when an organization is growing, the relationship weakens when organizations are in a period of decline (McKinley, 1987).

Complex organizations are thus complex in more ways than just their structure. The processes within such organizations are also complex. The techniques that are effective and efficient within a simple structure just may not be effective or efficient in a more complex one. Also, within a complex organization, different departments deal with different degrees of uncertainty and are structured differently, as Lawrence and Lorsch's research so strongly demonstrated.

Some Additional Correlates of Complexity

Complexity is related to additional characteristics of organizations. An analysis of program change in sixteen welfare organizations illustrates this point well.

Program change in these agencies involves the adoption of new services and techniques designed to increase the quality of the services rendered. When this study was being conducted, a great number of new social programs were being introduced (Hage and Aiken, 1967b).

This study found that both vertical and horizontal differentiation are related to higher rates of program change. This finding suggests that when such forms of differentiation are present, much information will be flowing in the system—information that contains conflicting ideas and proposals. Organizations that are complex in this way face the problem of integrating the diverse occupations and ideas deriving from the different organizational members. Later studies confirm that such conflict is present and must be dealt with by the organization. The proper method of handling such conflict is not by suppression; we have already seen that that would represent the exact opposite of the effective utilization of highly trained personnel. We will see later that such conflicts actually work to the organization's advantage.

Hage and Aiken's work on program change implies that organizational change is related to organizational characteristics. This implication is supported in later research, which compared the effects of structural characteristics (such as size and complexity), together with environmental conditions (changing or heterogeneous), with individual characteristics (age, attitudes, and education) on organizational innovation (Baldridge and Burnham, 1975). Organizational characteristics were more strongly related to innovation in organizations than the other factors. This does not negate the role of the individual but suggests that factors such as complexity are crucial in understanding how and why processes such as innovation occur.

Aiken and Hage (1968) continued their investigation of the sixteen welfare agencies three years after their initial study. The dependent variable in their second study was organizational interdependence, as indicated by the number of joint programs in which the agencies participated. The findings from this analysis are not surprising in light of the earlier findings and discussion. *"Organizations with many joint programs are more complex organizations, that is they are more highly professionalized and have more diverse occupational structure"* (p. 920; italics in original). The interpretation given to these findings is that a decision to engage in joint programs leads to the importation of new specialties into the organization, since joint programs are likely to be highly specialized and the personnel in the agency would not have the skills necessary for participation. A recent analysis in this same tradition finds that creative capacities in organizations are linked to complexity (Hage, 1999). Complexity is thus one of the most critical organizational characteristics.

These findings have major implications for organizations and for the society of which they are a part. There is a tendency for organizations to become more complex because of internal and external pressures. Joint programs and other interorganizational relationships will continue to develop, probably at an increasing rate. In the long run, this would lead to a society in which the web of interrelationships between organizations would become extremely intricate and the total society more organizationally "dense." This in turn implies a condition in which both individuals and the society as a whole are dependent upon fewer and more complex organizations. The nature of these organizations and their orientation toward the good of the few or the many is thus a major social issue. The 2000 U.S. government case against Microsoft is based on just these considerations. Decisions regarding organizational futures become decisions about society.

The short-run implication of these findings seems to be that the more complex an organization is, the more complex it will become, since the development of new programs and interorganizational relationships both lead to additional complexity. These relationships remain true, but in the thirty years since the Hage and Aiken studies, there have been changes that have altered considerations of complexity. Both downsizing and the improvement of management information systems have contributed to the potential for less complexity in many organizations. Organizations thus contain cross-pressures that push toward both greater and lesser complexity.

There is one more twist to the complexity issue that is interesting. Vaughan (1983, 1999) found that corporate crimes are related to complexity. In this formulation, organizations may become so diversified and complex that top management may not be able to control subunits. The same argument is frequently made in regard to intercollegiate athletics and the illegal recruitment and payment of college athletes.

Complexity is a basic structural characteristic. It is linked to the fate of the organization and to the fates of individuals within the organization. There appears to be strong evidence that particular degrees of vertical, horizontal, or spatial complexity are related to organizational survival and continuity in particular situations. If an organization chooses an inappropriate form or is unable or unwilling, for whatever reason—economic, personnel, tradition, leadership—to adapt its structure to changed situations, it will likely soon be in trouble.

FORMALIZATION

We have already alluded to formalization several times. In this section the exact nature of this important aspect of organizational structure will be explicitly defined. The antecedents and outcomes of formalization will also be spelled out. In addition, the reactions of individuals to the degree of formalization will be analyzed. In many ways, formalization is the key structural variable for the individual, because a person's behavior is vitally affected by the degree of such formalization. The amount of individual discretion is inversely related to the amount of preprogramming of behavior by the organization.

Formalization is not just an abstract concept. Indeed, the degree to which an organization is formalized is an indication of the perspectives of its decision makers in regard to organizational members. If the members are thought to be capable of exercising excellent judgment and self-control, formalization will be low; if they are viewed as being incapable of making their own decisions and requiring a large number of rules to guide their behavior, formalization will be high. Formalization involves organizational control over the individual (Clegg and Dunkerley, 1980) and thus has an ethical and a political meaning in addition to being a structural component.

The introduction of the individual does not mean a shift away from the organizational level of analysis. Formalization has important consequences for the organization and its subunits in regard to such processes as communications and innovation.

The rules and procedures designed to handle contingencies faced by the organization are part of what is called formalization. The extent of rules and procedures varies. The simple matter of when people get to work can vary widely among and within organizations in regard to the degree to which this act is formally specified. At the high end of the formalization continuum are organizations that specify that people must be at their desks or workstations at 8 A.M. or they will be "docked" a half-hour's pay. At the other end of the continuum are organizations that have no rules about being in the office or shop at a particular time, just as long as the work gets done. This is typified by many academic institutions and by telecommuting.

Formalization can also be enabling for individuals, since formalized procedures assist people in accomplishing their work. At the same time, it is also coercive as people are forced into compliance (Adler and Borys, 1996). It is hardly a neutral concept.

Maximal Formalization.   Rules and procedures can vary from highly stringent to extremely lax. These variations exist on the whole range of behaviors covered by organizational rules. An example of highly formalized procedures is the assembly line, where a piece of material is always passed in the same direction and the same work is always performed on it. Similarly, in an office, letters requesting a certain type of information are always processed in the same way, and the same type of information is returned to the requester. Much telemarketing also represents a high level of formalization, since telemarketers have a script from which they cannot deviate.

Minimal Formalization.   At the other end of the formalization-of-procedures continuum are unique cases, for which no procedures have been developed. In these cases, members of the organization must use their own discretion in deciding what to do. At the extreme are situations that call for intuition, and even perhaps inspiration, to be solved—unique situations with no preprogrammed answers (Perrow, 1967). Organizations that have low formalization are those that deal constantly with new situations for which precedents do not exist—for example, organizations engaging in frontier areas of scientific research. Organizations dealing with human problems, such as mental health clinics, are in a similar situation.

Most organizations are somewhere between the extremes of the continuum of formalization, as research on measuring formalization has found.

Measuring Formalization.   It usually doesn't matter whether procedures or rules are formalized in writing, since unwritten norms and standards can frequently be just as binding as written ones. Nevertheless, most research utilizes the written systems of rules and procedures as the basis for assessment and analysis.

In some familiar research, Hage and Aiken (1967a) provide the following definition of formalization:

> Formalization represents the use of rules in an organization. Job codification is a measure of how many rules define what the occupants of positions are to do, while rule observation is a measure of whether or not the rules are employed. In other words, the variable of job codification represents the degree to which the job descriptions are specified, and the variable, rule observation, refers to the degree to which job occupants are supervised in conforming to the standards established by job codification. Job codification represents the degree of work standardization while rule observation is a measure of the latitude of behavior that is tolerated from standards. (p. 79)

These variables are measured by asking the members of organizations to respond to a series of questions bearing directly on these issues. Measures of their perceptions of their own organization are thus used to determine the extent to which the organizations are formalized.

The British Aston Group (Pugh et al., 1968), working in the same era, used essentially the same conceptualization of formalization but based their measurement on official written records and documents from the organizations they studied. For example, if workers were provided with an official handbook describing their tasks and duties, the organization got a high score on formalization. In highly formalized situations, there is very little discretion available for members to operate on their own.

The similarities between these definitions point up the general consensus about the meaning of formalization. Even when quite different measures of this variable are used in research, the same meaning is utilized, an all-too-rare occurrence in organizational analysis. Unfortunately, research (Dewar, Whetten, and Boje, 1980; Pennings, 1973) has indicated that these different measures are themselves only weakly related. Thus, although there is conceptual closure in regard to formalization, measurement problems are not fully resolved.

Formalization and Other Organizational Properties

Centralization of Power.   Power is an important component of all organizations. The distribution of power in organizations is conceptualized as the degree of centralization, which is the topic of the last major section of this chapter. Here we consider the relationships between formalization and centralization.

In their study of the social welfare agencies, Hage and Aiken (1967a) found that formalization was weakly associated with a centralized decision-making system. Organizations in which the decisions were made by only a few people at the top relied on rules and close supervision as a means of ensuring consistent performance by the workers. These organizations were also characterized by a less professionalized staff. Thus, the presence of a well-trained staff is related to a reduced need for extensive rules and policies.

This interpretation is supported in an analysis of public personnel agencies (Blau, 1970). In organizations with highly formalized personnel procedures and rigid conformity to those procedures, there was decentralization of authority. At first glance this is contradictory, since the evidence seems to say that formalization and decentralization are related. A closer examination reveals strong compatibility with the Hage and Aiken findings. In this case, adherence to merit-based personnel procedures ensures the presence of highly qualified personnel at the local (decentralized) level. These people are then entrusted with more power than are personnel with fewer qualifications. Formalization in one area of operations may thus be associated with flexibility in another.

On this point Blau states:

> Rigidity in some respects may breed flexibility in others. Not all aspects of bureaucratization are concomitant. The bureaucratic elaboration of formalized personnel procedures and rigid conformity with these personnel standards do not necessarily occur together, and neither aspect of bureaucratization of procedures gives rise to a more rigid authority structure, at least not in employment security agencies. Indeed, both strict conformity with civil service standards and the elaboration of these formalized standards have the opposite effect of fostering decentralization, which permits greater flexibility. (p. 160)

This relatively simple set of findings reinforces a notion expressed earlier: Complex organizations are complex. Formalization in one area brings pressure to decrease formalization in another area. Organizations are thus constantly in conflict, not only between individuals or subunits, but also between and within the processes and structures that make up the organization. Formalization is not just a matter of internal adjustment.

It is important to note that the research of Hage and Aiken and of Blau deals with relatively professionalized workforces. One of the hallmarks of professionalization is the ability and willingness to make decisions based upon professional training and experience. It is not surprising to find lower levels of formalization in such situations. When the workforce under consideration does not or is assumed not to have this decision-making capacity, the implications of the Blau findings have to be reexamined. In that case, formalized personnel procedures would probably be associated with a more centralized decision-making system, with the formalization level probably more consistent in all phases of the operation. The organization retains control over the individual in both cases. By selecting highly qualified or indoctrinated individuals, it assures itself that the individuals will act according to organizational demands (Blau and Schoenherr, 1971:347–67).

Program Change.   Further research by Hage and Aiken (1967b) into the rate of program change in the agencies reveals that formalization is also related to the number of new programs added in the organizations. In this case, formalization is negatively associated with the adoption of new programs. The reduction of individual initiative in the more formalized setting is suggested as the primary reason for this relationship. In organizations that establish highly specific routines for the members to follow, there is likely to be little time, support, or reward for involvement in new ideas and new programs.

Technology.   In their continuing research in these sixteen agencies, Hage and Aiken (1969) divide the organizations into "routine" and "nonroutine" categories of technology. Even though these are all social agencies, there is a marked difference in the degree of routineness.

> The highest on routineness is a family agency in which the case-workers use a standard client interview that takes less than fifteen minutes. The purpose of the interview is to ascertain the eligibility of clients for county, federal, or state medical aid. An interviewee said:
>   " . . . somewhat routine—even though each patient is individual, the type of thing you do with them is the same. . . ." The organization at the other extreme is an elite psychiatric family agency in which each member is an experienced therapist and allowed to work with no supervision at all. (Hage and Aiken, 1969:369)

The relationship between routinization and formalization is in the expected direction. *"Organizations with routine work are more likely to have greater formalization of organizational roles"* (Hage and Aiken, 1969:371; italics in original). Since these organizations tend to be on the nonroutine end of an overall continuum of routineness, the findings are even more striking. Had organizations more toward the routine end of the continuum been included, the differences observed would probably have been greater. Hage and Aiken's research, one of the most thorough and systematic programs of research available in the literature, is based on data from a limited number of organizations of relatively similar characteristics. The limitations inherent in using this type of database are difficult to avoid, given the intrinsic difficulties in organizational research. But despite these limitations, the findings are generally consistent with those of the Aston Group (Pugh's research team), which proceeded independently and with very different measures.

It will be remembered that the Pugh research was carried out on a sample of English work organizations. These researchers were interested in obtaining indicators of the organizations and the contexts in which they operated. Their major indicator of technology was workflow integration.

> Among organizations scoring high, with very integrated, automated, and rather rigid technologies, were an automobile factory, a food manufacturer, and a swimming baths department. Among those scoring low, with diverse, non-automated, flexible technologies, were retail stores, an education department, and a building firm. (Pugh et al., 1968:103)

Although they contain more diversity than those in the Aiken and Hage study, these organizations are clustered toward the routine end of the routine–nonroutine continuum. As would be expected from the previous discussion, technology emerges as an important predictor of the degree to which activities are structured in these organizations.

Another study that examined the technology linkage found strong evidence in favor of the high routinization–high formalization conclusion. Dornbusch and Scott (1975) studied an electronics assembly line, a physics research team, a university faculty, a major teaching hospital, a football team, schools, a student newspaper, and a Roman Catholic archdiocese. Their evidence, from that diverse set of organizations, is consistent with the technological argument that has been presented.

Lest it appear that the relationship between technology and formalization is settled because of the weight of the evidence presented, Glisson (1978) essentially reverses the causal ordering. He finds that procedural specifications (formalization) determine the degree of routinization in service delivery. In the Glisson study, a decision made in regard to how to structure the organization led to the utilization of a particular service delivery technology. Although the high correlation between routinization and formalization remains, the reason for the correlation is reversed in this case.

Tradition and Culture.   One more component must be added to these considerations. Organizations emerge in different historical eras (Meyer and Brown, 1977), face varying contingencies, and develop different traditions. These differences in turn influence how factors such as technology affect the degree of formalization. For example, if for some reason—such as the belief system of an important early top executive—an organization became highly formalized in its codification of job descriptions in writing, it would probably continue to be more formalized over time than other factors would predict. Organizations develop characteristics that are embedded in the formal and informal systems of the organization. They are constrained by the structure and knowledge that are built up in their history (Zhou, 1993). This point is well recognized by scholars who study organizational culture (see Frost et al., 1985). Organizational culture will be considered in more detail in the next chapter.

By its very nature, formalization is central to the life of and in organizations. The specification of rules, procedures, penalties, and so on predetermines much of what goes on in an organization. Indeed, formalization is a major defining characteristic of organizations, since behavior is not random and is directed by some degree of formalization toward a goal.

We have examined the relationships between formalization and other organizational properties. We now shift the focus to the individual in the organization. Like formalization, individuals must be treated as variables, since they bring different abilities and habits and other behaviors with them into the organization. Again, formalization is designed to be a control mechanism over individuals (Clegg and Dunkerley, 1980).

FORMALIZATION AND OUTCOMES FOR INDIVIDUALS

An extreme example of formalization can be found in Crozier's (1964) analysis of the two French organizations. He notes: "Impersonal rules delimit, in great detail, all the functions of every individual within the organization. They prescribe the behavior to be followed in all possible events. Equally impersonal rules determine who shall be chosen for each job and the career patterns that can be followed" (pp. 187–88). This extremely high degree of formalization, plus several other characteristics of the organizations, create a "vicious circle" in which the workers follow the rules for the sake of the rules themselves, since that is the basis on which they are evaluated. The rules become more important than the goals they were designed to help accomplish. The organization becomes very rigid and has difficulties dealing with customers and other aspects of the environment. Since the rules prescribe the kinds of decisions to be made, those in decision-making positions tend to create more rules when situations arise for which there are no precedents. Rules become security for the employee. There is no drive for greater autonomy, since that would be threatening. There is a strong desire to build safeguards through increased rigidity. The personnel in such a system become increasingly unable to operate on their own initiative and, in fact, seek to reduce the amount of freedom to which they are subject. To one who values individual freedom, this is a tragedy. It would be presumptuous to say that it is such for the individuals involved, even though the argument could be made that the long-run consequences for them and for the total social system may indeed be tragic from several moral and ethical perspectives. For the organization, the consequences are clear; it becomes maladaptive to changes of any sort.

These personal and organizational dysfunctions were recognized in Robert Merton's (1957) seminal discussion of the "bureaucratic personality." Merton notes that a trained incapacity can develop in the kind of situation under discussion. Actions and decisions based on past training and experience may be very inappropriate under new or different conditions. Merton suggests that the process whereby these conditions develop is part of the system itself.

> The bureaucrat's official life is planned for him in terms of a graded career, through the organization devices of promotion by seniority, pensions, incremental salaries, etc., all of which are designed to provide incentives for disciplined action and conformity to the official regulations. The official is tacitly expected to and largely does adapt his thoughts, feelings, and actions to the prospect of this career. *But these very devices* which increase the probability of conformance also lead to an overconcern with strict adherence to regulations which induces timidity, conservatism, and technicism. Displacement of sentiments from goals onto means is fostered by the tremendous symbolic significance of the means (rules). (pp. 200–201; italics in original)

Organizations are concerned primarily with the work behavior of their members. They also can extend their control into other areas of life. Even though it is politically incorrect to discuss sexual attraction, it does take place, even in organizations, and organizations actually do attempt to control romance in the workplace (Quinn, 1977). Although Quinn does not claim that organizations are hotbeds of romance, he documents the obvious point that sexual attraction does occur. When a romance develops, actions are taken to terminate the relationship, since it is typically seen as disruptive for the organization. Punitive actions, such as dismissals, are one course of action and are much more likely be taken against the women involved than against the men. Less drastic measures, such as transfers, reprimands, or simple efforts to persuade people to stop the romance, were also found. The point is that even in areas of intimacy, organizations attempt to control behavior.

Reactions to Formalization

Formalization is frequently seen as some form of evil, leading to such reactions as "bureaupathic" or "bureautic" (Thompson, 1961) in which people are consumed by organizational rules and regulations. There is another side to the issue, of course. In Chapter 1, we noted that some research (Kohn, 1971) actually sees formalization, in the form of bureaucracy, as one mechanism by which individuals can experience personal growth and development. So the question really is, How do people react to formalization?

Some insights can be found in the literature on professionals in organizations. There has been a strong interest in this topic, since increasing numbers of professionals of all sorts are working in organizations, and many occupations are attempting to professionalize. Analyses of the relationships between professionals and their employing organizations formerly proceeded from the premise that there are built-in strains between professional and organizational principles and values (see, for example, Blau and Scott, 1962; Kornhauser, 1963). More recent research has challenged that assumption. It is now viewed as quite possible that there can be situations in which professionals are able to carry out their work with a minimum amount of interference from the organization, and the organization is able to integrate the work of the professionals for its own benefit.

This approach is followed in a study of the degree of alienation experienced by scientists and engineers employed in a large corporation in the aerospace industry (Miller, 1967). These professionals reported that they felt more alienation when their supervisor used directive, rather than participative or laissez-faire, supervisory practices and less alienation in situations in which they themselves had some control over the decisions affecting their work. The same general pattern was found in regard to other incentives that the organization provided professionals. There was less alienation when the scientists and the engineers had some part in deciding the nature of their own research efforts, when the company provided opportunities and a climate for the pursuit of their own professional careers, and when the company encouraged purely professional activities, such as the publication of papers or pursuit of additional training.

Miller also found that the length of professional training was associated with the extent of alienation felt. The more training people have, the more they are likely to feel alienation under those conditions that produce it for the group of professionals as a whole. That is, for a Ph.D. scientist, the absence of encouragement of professional activities is more likely to produce alienation than it is for an M.A. scientist.

Utilizing the idea of intraorganizational variations in structure, Miller also examined the extent of alienation felt by the professionals when the specific work location was considered. Some of the professionals worked in a basic research-and-development laboratory in the company, but most were employed in research and development in one of the major production units. The personnel in the basic research laboratory experienced much less alienation than those in the production-oriented unit.

This study is most relevant for the analysis here. Professionals were examined because they bring to the organization a set of externally (professionally) derived standards by which they can guide their own behavior. The presence of organizational guidelines (formalization) is thus a duplication of norms that are probably perceived as less valid than are the norms of the profession involved. For professionals, therefore, the greater the degree of formalization in the organization, the greater the likelihood of alienation from work. This point is supported further when two additional research reports are considered. Part of the research of Aiken and Hage (1966) was concerned with the degree of alienation felt by the professionals in the sixteen social welfare agencies they examined. They, too, were concerned with alienation from work, but they also looked at alienation from expressive relations. This was measured by responses to questions asking the degree of satisfaction felt about superiors and co-workers. The less satisfaction felt, the more the individual is alienated from expressive relations.

As would be expected from the direction of this discussion, the greater the degree of formalization of the organization, the more alienated were the workers in both areas of alienation. Alienation was much more strongly felt in regard to the job itself. "This means that there is great dissatisfaction with work in those organizations in which jobs are rigidly structured; rigidity may lead to strong feelings of work dissatisfaction but does not appear to have such a deleterious impact on social relations in the organization" (p. 504). Strict enforcement of rules was strongly related to both forms of alienation; social relations are also disturbed when rules are strictly enforced. It was also found that both forms of alienation were high when authority in the organizations was centralized and the members had little opportunity to participate in decision making.

A different approach was taken in Hall's analysis of the relationships between professionalization and bureaucratization (Hall, 1968). Bureaucratization is a broader concept than formalization, but it contains many of the same implications, as indicated in earlier discussions of the topic. Hall attempted to demonstrate that professionalization, like formalization, is a continuous variable, with some occupations being more professionalized than others. The study included physicians, nurses, accountants, teachers, lawyers, social workers, stockbrokers, librarians, engineers, personnel managers, and advertising account executives. After the occupations were ranked according to their attitudes toward several professional values, the average scores for each occupation were matched with the scores on bureaucratization measures for the organizational units in which these people worked. The results indicated that, in general, bureaucratization is inversely related to professionalization. This is consistent with the argument in this section. Examined more closely, these findings reveal some interesting patterns.

A weak relationship was found on the bureaucratic dimension involving the presence of rules. The kinds of rules the organizations developed in these cases apparently did not interfere with the work of the professionals. There was a stronger negative relationship on the procedural-specifications dimension. As more procedures were specified by the organization, the burden on the professionals apparently was stronger. In this case, the professionals were likely to want to utilize procedures that they themselves developed on the job or through their professional training.

Most of the studies that have been discussed have concluded that professionalization and formalization are incompatible. The more professionalized the workforce, the more likely that formalization will lead to conflict and alienation. A major implication of these findings is that formalization and professionalization are actually designed to do the same thing—organize and regularize the behavior of the members of the organization. Formalization is a process in which the organization sets the rules and procedures and the means of ensuring that they are followed. Professionalization, on the other hand, is a nonorganizationally based means of doing the same thing. From the organization's point of view, either technique would be appropriate, as long as the work gets done.

It is exactly at this point that the organization faces a major internal dilemma. If it allows too little freedom for its members, they are likely to feel oppressed, alienated, and "bureaucratic," and to engage in rule following for its own sake. If, on the other hand, it allows more freedom, behavior could become erratic and organizationally irrelevant. The basic factor here appears to be the kinds of guidelines for behavior that the individuals themselves bring to the organization. The more work standards they bring with them, the less the need for organizationally based standards.

Before moving to some additional implications of formalization for the individual and the organization, we must draw another conclusion from the analysis of professionals in organizations. The emphasis in much of the research in this area is on conflict between the professional and the employing organization. Evidence from the Hall research suggests that such conflict is not inevitable and should not be assumed without demonstration. This research found, for example, that the legal departments of large organizations are not necessarily more bureaucratized than law firms of comparable size. Lawyers working in the trust department of a bank may actually be working in an organizational environment similar, and perhaps even identical, to the one they would find in a law firm. This suggests that it is very possible to find organizational structures that are compatible with the degree of professionalization of their members. The finding that legal departments in organizations may not be more bureaucratized or formalized than autonomous law firms raises another issue. The legal department of a bank is clearly less formalized than the division in charge of handling, sorting, and verifying checks. As is true of complexity, there are degrees of formalization within the organization. This can be most easily seen between departments, but it also occurs between levels in the organization. In general, the higher the level, the less the formalization (Child, 1973; Hall, 1962).

We have been treating formalization as rules and procedures, with an assumption that these are usually written. Formalization can also be present in unwritten ways. A study of the "Big Six" accounting firms found that mentoring programs and financial management paradigms imposed interpersonally by superiors led to resistance among knowledge workers and entrepreneurs in the organizations (Covaleski et al., 1998). Similarly, imposing demands by setting meetings, reviews and internal deadlines, controlling vacations and requesting extra work were mechanisms found in a study of software firms (Perlow, 1998). These are control mechanisms just as much as written rules and procedures.

How much should organizations control their professionals and entrepreneurs? How much should they control their clerical workers? These questions are at the heart of our analysis of formalization. Obviously, there is not a single answer here, from the standpoint of the individual and of the organization.

CENTRALIZATION

Centralization refers to the distribution of power within organizations. Centralization is thus one of the best ways to summarize the whole notion of structure. As was noted earlier, structure can be viewed as constituted and constitutive (Ranson, Hinings, and Greenwood, 1980). In the case of centralization, a given distribution of power is constitutive in that it generates other actions—people comply with organizational rules and decisions. Centralization is also constituted in that power distributions are subject to change as groups and individuals gain or lose power over time. Power itself will be considered in detail in Chapter 4. Here we will consider the nature and correlates of the structural aspect of power in organizations.

Centralization has been defined in several ways, the emphasis always being on the distribution of power. Hage (1980) defines centralization as "the level and variety of participation in strategic decisions by groups relative to the number of groups in the organization" (p. 65). The greater the level of participation by a greater number of groups in an organization, the less the centralization. Hage's approach emphasizes that power is exercised in a variety of ways and in a variety of locations in an organization. For example, at most good universities (see Blau, 1973) the decision of whom to hire for a faculty position lies with the hiring department. The decision here is decentralized. Whether a particular department will be able to hire someone, however, is decided by the central administration, which reviews faculty vacancies and determines whether or not there needs to be a redistribution of vacancies; departments with declining enrollments and weaker programs are likely to lose positions to departments with high enrollment demands and strong programs. This is a centralized decision.

Van de Ven and Ferry (1980) define centralization as the "locus of decision making authority within an organization. When most decisions are made hierarchically, an organizational unit is considered to be centralized; a decentralized unit generally implies that the major source of decision making has been delegated by line managers to subordinate personnel" (p. 399). Van de Ven and Ferry go on to note that the substance of the decisions is an important consideration. In a highly professionalized organization, for example, decisions in regard to areas of professional competence are left to the professionals involved. Areas that are considered to be outside the limits of professional competence are likely to be more centralized.

What Is Centralized or Decentralized?

Of the several elements of centralization, the most obvious is the right to make decisions. Who or what office has the right to make which kinds of decisions and when can they be very specifically spelled out? If most decision making occurs at the top, the organization is centralized. The matter is not that simple, however. Centralization is not only a matter of who makes decisions. If personnel at lower levels in the organization are making many decisions but the decisions are "programmed" by organizational policies, a high degree of centralization remains. A low degree of centralization is found in situations of democratic, collective decision making (Rothschild and Whitt, 1986).

Another element of centralization is the evaluation of activities (Dornbusch and Scott, 1975:82). The evaluation process involves the determination of whether work was done properly, well, or promptly. If evaluation is carried out by people at the top of the organization, there is centralization, regardless of the level at which decisions are made. A situation in which there is centralized evaluation would probably—but not necessarily always—also be one in which policies are centralized.

For the sake of clarity, it is important to distinguish centralization from centrality. Centrality refers to a person's or a social role's position in workflow, communications, or friendship networks. It is related to people's being perceived as influential by both supervisors and nonsupervisors (Brass, 1984).

Centralization and Other Organizational Properties

In this section we will examine the relationships between size, technology, and environmental factors as they relate to centralization. These factors will be considered in detail in the next chapter in the discussion of explanations of structure. Here, the purpose is to develop an understanding of centralization.

Size.   Research evidence in regard to the relationships between organizational size and centralization is paradoxical. From their study of state employment security offices, Blau and Schoenherr (1971) conclude that "the large size of an agency produces conflicting pressures on top management, as it heightens the importance of managerial decisions, which discourages delegating them, and simultaneously expands the volume of managerial responsibilities, which exerts pressure to delegate some of them" (p. 130). The net result of increasing size is increased delegation or decentralization. The risk of delegation is lessened if personnel have expert qualifications. A centralized policy in regard to employee qualifications thus appears to contribute to delegated or decentralized power.

One problem with this line of reasoning (a variation of the chicken–egg debate) is important: It is impossible to determine if increased size leads to pressures to delegate and thus to utilize experts, or if the hiring of experts leads to pressures to delegate, with size not really being a factor. The question cannot be answered with the kinds of data now available, but probably a combination of the two types of answers is most appropriate.

Blau's (1973) further research on colleges and universities revealed basically the same findings. Large universities were more decentralized than smaller ones. Academic institutions and government agencies show a major difference in the qualifications of their personnel. In the government agencies, qualified personnel were utilized to carry out the organization's policies; in the academic organizations, the highly qualified personnel were able to gain power for themselves and to exercise a great deal of power over educational policies.

In a study using the Aston data and their measures on a second set of data, Mansfield (1973) reached conclusions essentially the same as those of the Blau research. Mansfield found that increasing size is related to the increasing use of rules. This leads to the decentralization of decision making but not to loss of control for the organization. In smaller organizations, specialists report directly to the top of the organization, whereas in larger ones, problems are handled at a decentralized level, but under the guidance of organizationally based rules. A study of large corporate medical practices found that important decisions shifted from clinicians to administrators. In such medical practices, decisions have ramifications for the total organization (Kralewski, Pitt, and Shatin, 1985).

The relationship between size and centralization is thus complex, with increasing size leading to delegation in some circumstances. But delegation usually takes place within a framework of rules, so larger size generally is related to greater centralization.

Technology.   The technological factor has already been implied in this discussion. Some work is delegated, with the control remaining at the top of the organization by the use of rules governing the work. Other work is delegated to specialists who make their own decisions at lower levels in the organization. Work that is delegated with controls is routine in its technology (Child, 1973). In a bank, for example, each teller can handle thousands of dollars if the transactions are routine, small cash deposits and withdrawals, but if a customer presents a check for $2,000 and asks for cash, that is a different matter. The handling of thousands of dollars is not delegated; rather, the decision moves back up the organization to the teller's supervisor. The routine nature of the technology, of course, is reflected in the rapid spread of ATMs, which have taken over much of the routine work of tellers.

Organizations deal with tasks that vary in the certainty with which they can be accomplished (Dornbusch and Scott, 1975). The variety of tasks performed in an organization means in essence that it has multiple technologies and thus must structure itself according to the task being performed. In a hospital, administering clinical treatment is more uncertain than processing insurance forms. Decision making in regard to which clinical treatment to provide is decentralized to the nurse, the physician's assistant, or the physician involved with a particular case. The processing of insurance forms is centralized (and formalized) by organizational procedures. These conclusions coincide with our earlier comments on intraorganizational structural variations. Variations in centralization are linked to different tasks with varied technologies.

Technology also permits organizations to monitor members' behavior. The amount of data entered, the number of telemarketing calls made, or the number of units produced are work output measures that can be monitored (Ouchi, 1977). Ouchi notes that organizations can monitor people's behavior or their work outputs. A combination of large size and homogeneous tasks contributes to the utilization of such output controls.

Another aspect of technology adds some slight confusion to the discussion. Participative management, in the form of consultation with subordinates in regard to decisions that affect them, is more likely to be successful in situations involving advanced technology (Taylor, 1971). Advanced technology here refers specifically to that concentrated at the workflow level; thus, participative management is most effective in the more automated kinds of situations.

Hage and Aiken's (1967a) work has shown that participation in decision making—a different aspect of centralization—is related to the absence of rules, thus suggesting that centralization by rules and centralization by nonparticipative decision making tend to operate together. In routine situations, rules govern the actions of the organizational members and there is likely to be little delegation of power through participation. In less routine situations, where there is task uncertainty, activities such as group meetings are likely to be held to try to resolve problems (Van de Ven, Delbecq, and Koenig, 1976).

The issue of routinization and uncertainty and their relationship to centralization is closely linked to the level of professionalization of the personnel in the organization. Lincoln and Zeitz (1980) report that individual professionals desire and achieve participation in decision making. They also find that the overall level of professionalization of an organization results in all employees experiencing an increase in influence.

There are two cautions in regard to participation in decision making. First, the fact that there is participation by organizational members may not mean that power is actually delegated. If the final decision still rests in the hands of the superiors in the organization, little power is actually delegated and participation is advisory at best. Although participation may help in the implementation of a decision, there is no decentralization or delegation of power unless it contributes to the actual decision.

The other caution regards something that is too seldom considered by sociologists and other organizational researchers—budgetary controls, such as internal audits. Although Hofstede (1972) and Ouchi and Maguire (1975) have dealt with this issue, it has tended not to be considered, which is a loss for organizational theory. Budgetary controls have the potential for retaining a great deal of control at the top of the organization. Most of the studies that have been cited here have not included budgetary control mechanisms. It would certainly appear that budgetary matters could be centralized in ways other than the allocation of tasks or decision making on other issues.

Environmental Relations.   The relationships among size, technology, and centralization have not been straightforward. The same pattern is found when studies of the relationships between organizations and their environments are considered. As we know from the Lawrence and Lorsch (1967) study, environments are critical for organizations.

A basic consideration is how much competition an organization faces in its environment. From their study of thirty business firms in India, Negandhi and Reimann (1972) suggest that competitive market conditions make decentralization more important for organizational success than do less competitive situations. This study was a successful replication of the Lawrence and Lorsch (1967) contingency theory. Further analysis of these data indicated that the degree of dependence on other organizations was actually more strongly associated with decentralization than were the factors of size, technology, and market competitiveness. The perceptions of the organizational decision makers are a critical mediating variable between the organization and the environment. It is those decision makers who make the strategic choices about the environment and about how the organization will respond to it. In this set of findings, the competitiveness of the environment affects the degree of decentralization (Negandhi and Reimann, 1973a,b).

A very different conclusion was reached in a study of thirty-eight small manufacturing firms in the United States (Pfeffer and Leblebici, 1973). This study found that a more competitive environment led to a greater demand for control and coordination. There was a greater frequency of reporting, more emphasis on written communications, and a greater specification of decision-making procedures—in short, a much greater degree of centralization. The study also found that in less competitive environments, there were more changes in product design, production processes, and number of products.

The contradictory findings seem to offer few conclusions about the effects of competition on centralization. A good part of the difficulty may lie in the fact that the more general characteristics of the organizational environments were not specified. For example, in an expanding economy in which the competing organizations are all gaining, decentralization may occur. In a contracting economy, where one organization's gain is the other's loss, the tightening up and centralization that Pfeffer and Leblebici found would occur (Khandwalla, 1972).

Another aspect of organizational environments is their degree of stability. Research on this topic reaches contradictory findings, as did that on competition (Whetten, 1980). Authors such as Burns and Stalker (1961) and Aldrich (1979) have argued that decentralization is more appropriate for conditions of turbulence or nonstability in the environment, whereas others (Hawley and Rogers, 1974; Rubin, 1979; Yarmolinsky, 1975) have argued in favor of centralization in such situations. Again, a resolution of the differences in these findings might be possible if it were possible to determine if the environment was expanding or contracting, as was suggested in the case of competition. In a situation of growth, decentralization might be the more appropriate response to turbulence, whereas centralization might be necessary in periods of contraction.

Competition and stability are important general environmental characteristics. Another important component of the environment is the degree of uncertainty experienced. When the environment is quite uncertain, organizations are likely to decentralize (Alexander, 1991). This same study also found that spatial dispersion and previous practices (historical precedent) were related to decentralization.

Closely related to centralization is the notion of "loose coupling" (Aldrich, 1979; Orton and Weick, 1990; Weick, 1976). This idea was developed to describe situations in which organizational units have low levels of interdependence. There is agreement that loosely coupled organizations tend to be more flexible and responsive to environmental pressures (Whetten, 1980). The degree of coupling can be misleading. For example, school organizations are commonly considered to be loosely coupled. In actuality, administrators can retain control through the allocation of resources such as curricular materials (Gamoran and Dreeben, 1986).

Loose coupling is not the same as decentralization, since the degree of coupling refers to the level of interdependence among units rather than to the distribution of power. In general, a loosely coupled organization would also be decentralized. An example of a loosely coupled organization is the business conglomerate. If the consumer products division is having a difficult time because of high interest rates, that will not affect the heavy-machinery division whose market is growing. Such an organization is loosely coupled. Each division may be more or less centralized in such a situation.

Centralization and Macropolitical Considerations

The overriding importance of organizations for the social order is underscored by considering some examples of their use for political purposes. Organizations can be shaped to be part of the process of political change and development. We have already seen how the Bolsheviks used their "organizational weapon" (Selznick, 1960). During the Cultural Revolution, the People's Republic of China used its organizations as a means of continuing political indoctrination and involvement. This was high centralization of both government and enterprise. The former Yugoslavia developed a program of "self-management" in which the workers in an enterprise elected a workers' council that in turn elected the management of the enterprise. This is not participative management of the sort discussed earlier but, rather, management by participation. Enterprises in the Israeli kibbutz system (composed of small organizations) have a socialist ideology that is promoted by a system of rotation of all people through all positions. These ideological purposes are not always met. In Yugoslavia, participation was lower and alienation was higher than the ideology indicated or political leaders desired (see Rus, 1972).

A major study of differing patterns of centralization in ten nations has been conducted by Tannenbaum and his colleagues (1974, 1986). The original research was carried out in manufacturing plants in Austria, Italy, Israel, Yugoslavia, and the United States. Austria and Italy are basically capitalist, like the United States; the Israeli kibbutz is socialist, and the Yugoslav economy was socialist. Israel and the United States contained the plants that were most successful, as defined not only by the standards used in the country in question but also by such universal factors as efficiency and morale. The kibbutz plants are highly decentralized, and the effects of hierarchy are virtually eliminated. In the United States, hierarchy is present, but its effects are mitigated by several factors. There is a limited potential for upward worker mobility in the American plants, but it is greater than in the Italian plants. There is also greater participativeness in the American plants. Workers are consulted and treated more as equals, even though they are not equal in power, and the rewards are higher.

Some of the Tannenbaum researchers believed that American workers had a form of "false consciousness," since they did not have opportunities for advancement, and that they were being duped by human relations efforts of the American managers.

This Marxist approach gets at the very heart of the macropolitical issues involved in centralization. Management by participation, as in the case of Israel and Yugoslavia, is a direct attempt to alter traditional power arrangements within a society.

China offers a different picture of macropolitical conditions and organizational centralization. Chinese policies were not at all participative but, rather, were designed to strengthen the power of the regime and emphasized political indoctrination and loyalty. The country was highly centralized. In China today, there is a move to decentralize the social system. Here also, there has been rapid growth in small, local enterprises (Hall et al., 1993; Nee, 1992). In the Hall et al. study, the small Chinese enterprises were found to be much more centralized than a sample of small firms in the United States. This could be a carryover from the earlier, highly centralized era or even perhaps a reflection of Confucian family values.

The American approach, which increasingly features some degree of participation in decision making, does not attempt to redistribute power. It does, however, minimize the perceptible effects of power differences. Those of the Tannenbaum et al. researchers who judge this as immoral and misleading miss an important consideration. Even if it is agreed that workers are exploited to even a small degree, the end result remains in question. What is better—a situation such as that in Italy, where the exploitation is definitely experienced and verbalized, or a situation such as that in the United States, where it is experienced more blandly and scarcely verbalized? This would be up to each reader to decide.

It is possible, for example, that at some time in the future, American workers, having experienced at least symbolic participation, would press very hard for actual participation. Those who had never experienced participation might not necessarily want to move in this direction.

The final consideration, developed by the Dutch sociologist Cornelius Lammers (1975), is that participative management involves taking part in decision making, whereas both management by participation and self-management involve workers taking over organizational management. Participative management is a functional form of decentralization that may lead to greater efficiency and effectiveness, and the other two forms are structural forms of decentralization that lead to power equalization. True power equalization in organizations is extremely unlikely. The very nature of organizations requires some form of hierarchy, once organizations move beyond very small size, simple technologies, and low levels of complexity. As in the wider society, power differences are ubiquitous. The effects of such power differences can perhaps be minimized by making them less abrasive through participative schemes.

Centralization and Micropolitical Considerations

Organizations are part of the political system. They also contain their own internal political system, which is an important consideration for centralization. There are contradictions between traditional control structures and new forms of organizing, such as along the lines of professional organizations (Heydebrand, 1977). As noted earlier, the presence of professionals increases the level of participation in the organization. The increased participation is not accomplished benignly. Instead, it is fought for and over, since those who had decision-making power are not likely to give it up easily to the professionals coming into the organization.

Some authors view the internal politics of an organization as a reflection of the external political system. One view is that the technology employed in many factories is there not so much for technical efficiency as to be a means by which maximal control over labor can be achieved (Marglin, 1974). Ongoing labor management negotiations and battles over the prerogatives of management and workers can reflect wider political schisms. This is true particularly in Europe. Power can be delegated to lower participants, and power can be taken by these same lower participants (Bacharach and Lawler, 1980). Universities in the late 1960s and early 1970s exemplified the give-and-take of power as students gained in power and thus had the right to make decisions that previously had been made by faculty or administrators. This internal organizational power struggle was a reflection of the larger political context.

The exercise of power within organizations will be considered in a later chapter. In regard to centralization, it is critical to note that the micropolitics of organizations involves the continuing power struggles that occur within organizations, whether among departments, hierarchical levels, or individuals (Pfeffer, 1978). Although the micropolitical approach emphasizes power struggles, the fact that power is distributed at one point in time (the pattern of centralization) will have a crucial impact on the distribution of power at succeeding points in time.

The Outcomes of Centralization

The degree of centralization in organizations says a great deal about the society in which they are found. A society in which the majority of organizations are highly centralized is one in which the workers have little say about their work. The same would probably be true of their participation in the society. The degree of centralization of organizations is also an indication of what the organization assumes about its members: High centralization implies an assumption that the members need tight control, of whatever form; low centralization suggests that the members can govern themselves. In both cases, it should be remembered, the control is on behalf of the organization. Professionals and other expert personnel in organizations do not work on behalf of their professions. Their expertise is intended to be on behalf of their organization.

A major outcome of varying degrees of centralization is for the organization itself. High levels of centralization mean greater coordination, but less flexibility; consistent organization-wide policies, but possibly inappropriate policies for local conditions; and the potential for rapid decision making during emergencies, but overloaded communications channels during normal operations as communications flow up and down the hierarchy.

SUMMARY AND CONCLUSIONS

This chapter has considered the basic organizational characteristics of complexity, formalization, and centralization. These characteristics have outcomes for the individuals who are in the organizations and who have contacts with it. They also have outcomes for the organizations themselves and for the wider society of which they are a part.

We have already begun an examination of the topic of the next chapter—the explanations of structure. Issues such as size, technology, and relationships with the environment have loomed large in analyses of structure. We will examine these issues and also pay attention to some broader explanations that have been recently introduced.

EXERCISES

1. Compare the degree of the three forms of complexity of your two organizations.
2. Compare the levels of formalization and centralization of your two organizations.

Chapter 3

Organizational Structure: Explanations

◆•

The purpose of this chapter is to explain why varying degrees of complexity, formalization, and centralization are found in organizations. The chapter will also contain elements of organizational theory as it has developed to explain organizational structure. The first set of explanations involve the context in which an organization operates. Contextual factors include organizational size, technology(ies), and internal culture(s). Additional contextual factors are the environment (social and physical) and national culture in which an organization is operating. The second set of explanations turns the focus onto organizational actions in regard to structure. Organizations can design their structure on their own or they can borrow ideas about structure from other sources, including other organizations. This last explanation is known as institutional theory.

In this chapter we will attempt to explain the forms of organizations that were described in the last chapter. Obviously, degrees of complexity, formalization, and centralization are neither random nor accidental. We have already developed the points that size, technology, and environment play roles in determining organizational forms. We will return to those factors here and then add some other important considerations. Our conclusion will be that organizational structures are a consequence of the simultaneous impact of multiple factors.

The idea of structure is basically simple, and we will return to our building analogy to illustrate this. Buildings have structures, in the form of beams, interior walls, passageways, roofs, and so on. The structure of a building is a major determinant of the movements and activities of the people within it. Buildings are supposed to have structures that fit the activities that go on within them. An office building is different from a factory. Factories where automobiles are made are different from those where computers are made. Buildings are designed to fit the needs of the activities that are to be carried out within them. They are designed to accommodate populations of various sizes—no sane architect would design a huge cathedral for a small congregation—and to withstand the environment in which they are located. Buildings in upstate New York are different from those in Arizona. Just as the size, the major activity or technology to be used, and the environment are important in building design, so is the element of choice—of style, color, and so on. Buildings also reflect the values and ideologies of the persons in control; corporate headquarters and state capitols do not take the form they do by accident.

The analogy of organizational structures to those of buildings is not perfect, since organizations are not built by architects but by the people within them. Those people are not necessarily in agreement about how the organization should be arranged. Just as one building can be a copy of another, organizational structures can be copies of other organizations. Like buildings, they can also reflect the particular fads or fashions popular at the time of their construction. And, just as buildings can be renovated, organizations can be redesigned.

The present chapter is an attempt to explain the variations in organizational structures or forms. There is no single explanation for the forms of organizations. Rather, multiple explanations are needed to understand organizational structure. This is not a simple matter. Some factors operate together in a positively correlated manner, as when large size and routine technology combine to yield a highly formalized situation. In another situation size and technology might operate in a negatively correlated fashion, as when large size and nonroutine technology are present. These relationships could themselves be affected by differences in national cultures or by historical events.

Explanations of factors affecting structure fall into two major categories. The first is the *context* in which organizations operate. Contextual explanations include organizational size, technology, internal culture (or organizational climate), the environment, and national cultural factors. Context here means the situation in which an organization is currently operating. This situation is simultaneously within and beyond an organization's control. For example, an organization can decide to expand its operations and in so doing expand its size. Once the size is expanded, it is part of the context of the organization, since the sheer factor of size has an influence on structure. The same process operates in the technologies employed by an organization, the environments with which it deals, its internal culture, and the national culture in which it is embedded. These contextual conditions are a result of earlier decisions that were made in and for an organization. In keeping with the theme of our analysis, the decisions were made to move the organization toward a higher level of effectiveness. Whether this worked or not is another matter.

The second category of explanations of structure is design. By design we mean the choices made in an organization about how the organization is to be structured. The major approaches here are strategic choice and institutional models of structure. Any study of design must consider that not all actors within an organization will have the same judgment in regard to the design of structure. Organizational design is by definition a political issue but, again, a political issue linked to our notion of effectiveness.

CONTEXTUAL EXPLANATIONS

Size

At first glance, organizational size appears to be a simple variable—the number of people in an organization. The size issue is much more complicated than that, however. The discussion of organizational boundaries suggested that it sometimes is problematic who is in or out of an organization. In a penetrating article, Kimberly (1976) demonstrated that size actually has four components.

The first component of size is the physical capacity of the organization. Hospitals have a fixed number of beds. Hotels have a fixed number of rooms. Airlines have a relatively fixed number of airplanes. Universities have capacities in regard to classroom or dormitory space.

The second component of size is the personnel available to the organization. This is the most commonly used measure and conceptualization of size, having been used in 80 percent of the studies reviewed by Kimberly. The basic problem with using this component is that the meaning of the number of personnel is ambiguous. For some religious organizations and universities, size in this form is sometimes a goal. Larger size can mean an increased budget. For other organizations, the goal is to keep the size at a minimum to reduce costs.

The third component of size is organizational inputs or outputs. Inputs can be such factors as the number of clients or students served and the number of inmates housed in a prison. A college or university's graduation rate is an output and an important one when intercollegiate athletic programs are considered. Sales volume is an important output measure for many businesses. Kimberly correctly suggests that this measure is limited in its usage to comparisons between organizations of a similar type.

The final component of size is the discretionary resources available to an organization, in the form of wealth or net assets. For a college or a university, the size of its endowment is an important consideration. This is conceptually distinct from the other aspects of size.

The components of size may be highly intercorrelated in some instances, and indeed they are, but the conceptual distinctions among them are so great that each should be treated separately. These structural characteristics may be a consequence, a covariant, or a determinant of size, making the utility of the size variable even more uncertain.

Much of the work relating size to organizational structure was conducted before Kimberly's analysis. We will review some of that literature now, with the realization that these studies are based almost exclusively on the number of personnel available. These studies do indicate the directions that have been taken in research on size; some authors argue that size is the determinant of structure, and others argue the opposite.

The major proponents of the importance of size as a determinant of structure have been Peter M. Blau and his associates (see Blau, 1968, 1970, 1973; Blau, Heydebrand, and Stauffer, 1966; Blau and Schoenherr, 1971; Meyer, 1968a, 1968b, 1971; also Blau, 1972; and Klatzky, 1970a). Their data were collected primarily from studies of government agencies, such as state employment services and municipal finance divisions, with supplementary data from universities and department stores. The data reveal some fascinating anomalies in organizations and also some important considerations about the role of organizations in contemporary society.

Blau's studies are concerned primarily with organizational size and vertical and horizontal complexity, as discussed in Chapter 3. The research findings indicate that increasing size is related to increasing complexity. The rate of complexity decreases, however, with increasing size. Administrative overhead is lower in larger organizations, and the span of control for supervisors is greater. Since administrative overhead is inversely related to size, and the span of control is directly, or positively, related to size, larger organizations are able to achieve an economy of scale. It is here that the first anomaly is demonstrated. Size is related to complexity, which leads to increased need for control and coordination, which in turn is related to increased requirements for administrative overhead. Size and complexity thus work at cross-purposes. Blau concludes that the size factor is the more critical and that economy of scale still results from large size.

The second major set of studies that find size to be the major determinant of organizational structure are those of the Aston group in England (see Pugh et al., 1963, 1968; Hickson, Pugh, and Pheysey, 1969; Inkson, Pugh, and Hickson, 1970; Child and Mansfield, 1972; Donaldson and Warner, 1974; and Hickson et al., 1974). These works represent the original Aston studies. The major conclusion of these studies is that increased size is related to increased formalization and decreased centralization. Most of the data come from manufacturing organizations, but some are based on studies in government agencies and labor unions.

The evidence presented thus far has emphasized the strong positive relationship between size and structure. Other researchers question that emphasis. Hall's research, for example, has not found such strong relationships. In one study, which used a subjective approach, they found only a modest relationship between size and perceived degree of bureaucratization (Hall and Tittle, 1966). In another study, utilizing an approach similar to that of Blau and the Aston group, they came up with mixed findings in regard to size and structure. Using data from a set of seventy-five organizations of highly varied types, they concluded:

In general, the findings of this study in regard to size are similar to those of previous research which utilized size as a major variable; that is, the relationships between size and other structural components are inconsistent. . . . There is a slight tendency for larger organizations to be both more complex and more formalized, but only on a few variables does this relationship prove to be strong. On others, there is little, if any, established relationship. (Hall, Haas, and Johnson, 1967b:908–09)

These findings do not suggest that size is unimportant but, rather, that factors other than size must be taken into account to understand structure. These additional factors will be discussed in the sections that follow.

Research on size has met with additional criticisms. Argyris (1972) has analyzed Blau's research and found it wanting in several regards. He first questions the reliance on official descriptions of organizational structures. Citing several studies that have found that organization charts are nonexistent or inaccurate, and that members of top management cannot always accurately describe their own organization, Argyris wonders if the approach that Blau has taken might not invalidate the results. He also suggests that size may be correlated with, but not generate or cause, differentiation.

Another major criticism of the view that size is the determinant of structure comes from a reanalysis of the Aston data (Aldrich, 1972a, b). Aldrich suggests that size is actually a dependent variable: ". . . the more highly structured firms, with their greater degree of specialization, formalization, and monitoring of role performance, simply need to employ a larger work force than less structured firms" (Aldrich, 1972a:38). In Aldrich's reanalysis, technology emerges as the major determinant of structure.

Before turning to technology, we should note some additional matters related to size. First, as we saw in Chapter 1, most organizations are small. Within small organizations, the effects of organizational design efforts are likely to have more direct consequences for the organization. Geeraerts (1984) found that the heads of small organizations who were professional managers were more likely to adopt bureaucratic practices than were heads of small organizations who were owner–managers. Geeraerts attributes this to the education and professional careers of the professional managers. A study of airlines found that small airlines are more active in initiating competitive challenges in the airline industry than are the big carriers (Chen and Hambrick, 1995). Small organizations can be nimble.

At the same time, small organizations are highly vulnerable. Most new organizations are small. Research has consistently shown (see Starbuck and Nystrom, 1981) that new organizations have a low survival rate. Starbuck and Nystrom note that "nearly all small organizations disappear within a few years" (p. xiv). Interestingly, they provide data that support this conclusion for both governmental agencies and corporations. Apparently, governmental organizations are not as protected as many people think. The corollary of this research, of course, is that large organizations are more likely to survive and are less vulnerable than small ones.

Large organizations are also more likely to have more resources. This would permit them to enter new markets. At the same time, large organizations do tend to be more bureaucratic, and this would operate against entering new markets (Haveman, 1993). Large organizations are also more likely to have more highly developed internal labor markets. Paradoxically, rapid growth may hinder the development of internal labor markets as growing organizations bring in personnel from outside the organization (Van Buren, 1992). Larger organizations do provide better pay and fringe benefits (Kalleberg and Van Buren, 1996)—these are not aspects of structure, but they certainly are important.

Organizational size is a crucial factor for much of what goes on in and around organizations. It is just one of the contextual factors that are important, however, as we move to a consideration of technology.

Technology

The relationship between technology and organizational structure is not easy to understand. It may seem easy if you consider something like the routine processing of checks in a bank. This is usually done in a situation of high division of labor, high formalization, and high centralization. Technology is much less easy to understand, however, in more complex situations.

For example, at the University at Albany there is the Intercollegiate Athletics Advisory Board (IAAB). This is the body that oversees the intercollegiate athletics program. All colleges and universities that are National Collegiate Athletic Association (NCAA) members have IAABs or their equivalents. The IAAB dealt with the issue of gender equity in our athletic programs a few years ago. After some months of deliberation, it recommended a program in which the proportion of women and men participating in intercollegiate athletics is very close to the proportion of men and women in the student body.

Where is technology in this example? Well, it is in the processing of the issue of gender equity. Technology involves "acting on and/or changing an object from one state to another. . . . The object can be a living being, a symbol, or an inanimate object" (Goodman, Griffith, and Fenner, 1990:48). The IAAB was dealing with complex symbols. Our technology involved discussion, consultation, looking at our own values, thinking about the coaches and players involved, and considering the ramifications for the future. This was a very imprecise technology. Organizationally, it was high on complexity and low on formalization and centralization.

Interest in technology as a major component of organizational analysis was sparked by the work of Woodward (1958, 1965) and Perrow (1967). Woodward's work is particularly interesting because she stumbled onto the importance of technology during the course of a research project in the United Kingdom. She found that several critical structural variables were directly linked to the nature of the technology of the industrial firms being studied. The organizations were categorized into three types: first, the small-batch or unit-production system, as exemplified by a shipbuilding or aircraft-manufacturing firm; second, the large-batch or mass-production organization; third, the organization that utilizes continuous production, as do chemical or petroleum manufacturers.

Woodward's findings show that the nature of the technology vitally affected the management structures of the firms studied. The number of levels in the management hierarchy, the span of control of first-line supervisors, and the ratio of managers and supervisors to other personnel were all affected by the technology employed. Not only was structure affected, but also the success or effectiveness of the organizations was related to the "fit" between technology and structure. The successful firms of each type were those that had the appropriately structured technical systems.

"Raw materials" are central to Perrow's (1967) approach to technology. This raw material

> may be a living being, human or otherwise, a symbol or an inanimate object. People are raw materials in people-changing or people-processing organizations; symbols are materials in banks, advertising agencies and some research organizations; the interactions of people are raw materials to be manipulated by administrators in organizations; boards of directors, committees and councils are usually involved with the changing or processing of symbols and human interactions, and so on. (p. 195)

The nature of the raw material affects how the organization is structured and operated. According to Perrow, the critical factors in the nature of the raw material, and hence the nature of the technology employed to work on it, are the number of "exceptional cases encountered in the work" and the nature of the "search process" that is utilized when exceptional cases are found (pp. 195–96). Few exceptional cases are found when the raw material is some object or objects that do not vary in their consistency or malleability over time. Many exceptions are found in the obvious cases of human beings and their interactions, or the less obvious cases of many craft specialties or frontier areas within the sciences. Search processes range from those that are logical and analytical to those that must rely upon intuition, inspiration, chance, guesswork, or some other such nonstandardized procedure. The first form of search may be found in the engineering process in many industries. The second form of search may be found in some activities in the software industry. Thus, within "industry" we have a wide array of technologies and organizational forms.

Perrow's framework has been tested several times with mixed results. Most studies find that routineness is related to high formalization and centralization (Hage and Aiken, 1967a; Lawrence and Lorsch, 1967; Comstock and Scott, 1977; Mohr, 1971). An interesting twist is reported by Miller et al. (1991). They found that the routineness–centralization relationship operates in small organizations but not in large ones. It would seem that large organizations are probably dispersed, and thus decentralization would be necessary. Interestingly, the original Aston studies did not find a strong relationship between technology and organizational structure.

The mixed results in regard to technology appear to be based on several factors. In the first place, there has been uncertainty about the level at which technology is operative in the organization. The Aston group sheds some light on the subject. Hickson, Pugh, and Pheysey (1969) break down the general concept of technology into three components: operations technology—the techniques used in the workflow activities of the organization; materials technology—the materials used in the workflow (a highly sophisticated technique can conceivably be applied to relatively simple materials); and knowledge technology—the varying complexities in the knowledge system used in the workflow. In their own research, these authors have been concerned with operations technology.

In the English organizations they studied, operations technology had a secondary effect in relationship to size. They conclude:

> Structural variables will be associated with operations technology only where they are centered on the workflow. The smaller the organization, the more its structure will be pervaded by such technological effects; the larger the organization, the more these effects will be confined to variables such as job-counts of employees on activities linked with the workflow itself, and will not be detectable invariables of the more remote administrative and hierarchical structure. (pp. 394–95)

These findings mean that operations technology will intervene before the effects of size in these work organizations. They also imply that the administrative element in large organizations will be relatively unaffected by the operations technology. It is here that the form of the knowledge technology, which was not examined, becomes important.

The importance of knowledge technology can be seen in Meyer's (1968a) examination of the introduction of automated procedures into the administrative structures of state and local departments of finance. This resulted in more levels of hierarchy, a wider span of control for first-line supervisors, fewer employees under the direction of higher supervisors, and fewer responsibilities—but more communications responsibilities—for members who are nominally in supervisory positions. In these particular organizations, the knowledge technology changed from simple to relatively complex.

In the second place a basic problem with the studies on technology has been the kinds of organizations studied. The Aston group is most confident of its data when service and administrative units are removed from the sample. The type of industry and its technology are related—for example, the steel industry versus the book publishing industry—so that sampling differences between studies could increase or decrease the relationship between technology and structure (Child and Mansfield, 1972).

The technology-structure issue has been approached in a diametrically different manner by Glisson (1978). He found that the structural attributes of division of labor and procedural specifications determined the degree of routinization and thus the nature of service delivery among a set of human-service organizations. Glisson thus reverses the causal argument. The issue, then, may be one of those chicken-versus-egg phenomena. Additional research, particularly longitudinal studies, is needed to begin to resolve this particular issue.

A good part of the literature on size and technology has been presented in an either-or fashion, with either technology or size being proposed as the key structural determinant. This was, in fact, a major debate in the early 1970s. Fortunately, researchers dropped the debate and began to examine size and technology together.

A study of a large state employment security agency examined task uncertainty, task interdependence (technological variables), and work-unit size as they related to coordination mechanisms (Van de Ven, Delbecq, and Koenig, 1976). As tasks increased in uncertainty, mutual work adjustments through horizontal communications channels and group meetings were used instead of hierarchical and impersonal forms of control. As task interdependence increased, impersonal coordination decreased and more personalized and interactive modes of coordination, in the form of meetings, increased. Increasing size, on the other hand, was related to an increased use of impersonal modes of coordination, such as policies and procedures and predetermined work plans. In a related study, Ouchi (1977) found that both size and homogeneous tasks were related to output controls on workers.

A study of architectural firms revealed that structural complexity and task diversity were dependent upon size when there were uniform tasks, but the cognitive ideas and a professional orientation were more important in nonuniform tasks (Blau and McKinley, 1979). Thus, size is important under one technological condition but not under another.

In the last section on size, the work of Peter Blau and his associates was prominent in the discussion of the importance of size. Beyer and Trice (1979) reexamined the original Blau and Schoenherr (1971) study and suggest that the earlier findings, with their strong emphasis on size, were probably a result of the type of organizations studied—state employment agencies that had very routine technologies. Beyer and Trice's own data show that in nonroutine organizations, personnel specialization generates horizontal differentiation. They correctly suggest that a search for a single or primary cause of organizational complexity is doomed to failure. They also suggest that there should be a focus on the strategic choices that decision makers select, which may be an important step forward in the analysis of structure. We will consider this issue at a later point.

The final study to be considered in regard to the size-technology issue is that of Daft and Bradshaw (1980). In a study of universities, they found that growth in administrative departments was related to large size, whereas growth in academic departments had more of a technological base. Daft and Bradshaw go on to consider some additional explanations. They suggest that factors in an organization's environment, such as pressures from the community or the government, contribute to differentiation among the academic departments. They also suggest that the decision-making process is critical and offer the interesting notion that there are two levels of decisions—the formal decision to add a department or a program and an earlier decision by someone who senses a problem and becomes an idea champion—who pushes for the formal decision. They are correct in this regard, of course, since the idea to make some kind of structural change has to begin somewhere. They do miss the fact that decisions in organizations are highly political and that many ideas that are developed never see the light of day in the sense that there is no formal action on them because they died in some committee. A final suggestion of Daft and Bradshaw's is that financial resources affect decisions about structural change. This is almost never considered by organizational analysts (economists aside, of course), but it would appear to be of great importance.

We have been treating technology as some sort of impersonal force. In many ways it is, even with interacting computers. At the same time, people certainly do react to technology and technological change (Weick, 1990; Barley, 1990). Some people show fear and loathing toward computers (or committees), and others literally fall in love with their computers (or committees). These individual reactions cannot be ignored, but they are not central to our concerns here.

We have also been treating technology only at the organizational level. Obviously, technology and technological change affect entire industries, nations, and the world itself. "It is increasingly apparent that the causal influences flow in both directions. Organization at the level of the firm, the industry, and the nation affect technological advance. In turn, technical advance affects organizational structure at all three of these levels and at the level of the world economy" (Tushman and Nelson, 1990:2). For our purposes here, of course, technology is just one of the factors affecting organizational structure.

Internal Culture

The importance of the internal culture factor has received varying degrees of attention by organizational scholars and practitioners. At one time it was referred to as "informal structure." It received prominence in Barnard's (1938) important analysis of the functions of the executive. One of the major functions of the executive was to "set the tone" for the entire organization.

The emphasis returned with a vengeance in the 1980s as organizations sought a culture of "excellence" (Peters and Waterman, 1982). Culture became a buzzword in much of the management literature.

According to Smircich (1985), organizational culture "is a possession—a fairly stable set of taken-for-granted assumptions, shared meanings, and values that form a kind of backdrop for action" (p. 58). Another formulation considers culture to be "shared values and beliefs, assumptions, perceptions, norms, artifacts, and patterns of behavior" (Ott, 1989; p. 1). Culture includes jargon and slang, humor and jokes, and other such forms (Trice and Beyer, 1993). Culture also includes preferences of employees, as a study of male employees in Thailand revealed. These preferences led to lowered opportunities for female employees (Appold, Siengthai, and Kasarda, 1998). Culture can also include strong ideologies, as Hyde's (1992) analysis of feminist health centers indicates. Strong ideologies make an organization conservative, since actions and decisions are made within a particular ideological framework.

Internal organizational cultures are relatively stable. People come and go, but the culture remains robust. The stability and robustness of internal cultures make it puzzling that culture became such a theoretical and managerial buzzword in the 1980s and early 1990s. After all, if culture is stable, it is hard to change and thus not a real management tool.

Internal cultures are an organizational context in which structures are formed. Along with size and technology, it is part of the configuration of internal organizational factors that have been formed in interaction to yield structure and that compose the context in which future structural arrangements are developed. Like size and technology, culture is an internal contingency variable. It is a factor that affects preferences, such as one for centralization or decentralization, and interacts with other contextual factors. We will turn now to a consideration of external contextual factors.

The Environment

In later chapters we will deal with organizational environments in detail; here our concern is simply to trace some of the implications of organizational environments for organizational structure. Of primary interest is the social environment of organizations; but the physical environment, such as climate or geography, can also be important, particularly for organizations that utilize or affect that physical environment.

One way of looking at environments is to determine whether they are "hostile" or "friendly" (Khandwalla, 1972). A friendly environment is supportive, providing funds and value support. In a hostile environment the very underpinnings of the organization are threatened. The grave doubts raised about the nuclear energy industry in the wake of the Three Mile Island accident in Pennsylvania, plus other assorted problems with the industry, made the environment hostile for organizations in that industry in the United States. Colleges and universities had friendly environments during the 1960s and early 1970s. Money poured in for new facilities and personnel, and there was a general belief that education was the key to solving social and international problems. Obviously, that environment has moved from one of friendliness to one of neutrality, if not hostility.

Khandwalla suggested that in a friendly environment, organizations will be structurally differentiated. The environment will be monitored by differentiated personnel who are then integrated by a series of mechanisms, such as committees and ad hoc coordinating groups. If the environment turns hostile, the organization will "tighten up" by centralizing and standardizing its operations.

In a slightly different approach to the same issue, Pfeffer and Leblebici (1973) analyzed the effects of competition on structure. They found that in more competitive situations, there is a greater demand for control and coordination. Reports are more frequent, and there are more written communications and a greater specification of decision procedures. When competition is less intense, there are more frequent changes in product design, production processes, and number of products. Less competition provides some "slack," so that the organization can afford to do more than its routine competitive activities.

Competition is an interesting phenomenon. It occurs in the public and private sectors. It also has ramifications above and beyond economic factors. A study of a set of newspaper companies found that in a competitive environment—for example, where there was more than a single newspaper in a city—the structure of the newspaper reflected the complexity of the community. If there was no competition, the newspaper did not mirror the community as closely. Thus, in the competitive situation, attention would be paid to all components of the community, such as minority groups. Without competition, those groups could be ignored (DuBick, 1978).

A study of competition among hospitals shows an additional side of the noneconomic aspects of competition (Fennell, 1980). Fennell found that hospital services increased in competitive situations. She attributes the increase in services to the competition rather than to service needs. Thus, competition here is counter to economic rationality, raising the costs of medical services as each hospital in a competitive situation adds more and more expensive equipment and services that are not actually needed.

When environmental demands are conflicting, as in the case of community mental health programs that move into drug abuse treatment, organizations can develop structures that have conflicting goals and inconsistent structures and practices (D'Aunno, Sutton, and Price, 1991).

Another approach to the analysis of environment on organizational structure is represented by those who have attempted to compare organizations in different social settings. Meyer and Brown (1977) made a historical analysis of government organizations in the United States. They found that the era of origin and subsequent environmental shifts was related to the degree of formalization, which was in turn related to multiple levels of hierarchy and the delegation of personnel decisions to lower levels in the organization. Although the era-of-origin effects are pervasive, the environmental shifts force the organization to continually adjust to the context in which it is found.

National Culture

National cultures affect how organizations are structured in many ways. For example, in the United States, all airline passengers must pass through an elaborate set of security procedures prior to boarding their flights. In New Zealand, on "internal flights" (trips within New Zealand), there are no such security procedures. You simply walk out the gate and get on the airplane. Everything else about airline organizations is the same—the airplanes, the flight attendants, the ticketing, etc.—but national culture makes the difference in terms of using structured security procedures.

Organizational decision makers and boundary spanners therefore consider their environments in terms of their national culture. The perception of the environment is then enacted in the organization through decision making. Managers in South Africa and the United States perceive different amounts and kinds of environmental turbulence (Malan, 1994). Interestingly, the decisions made in these two settings were not found to be very different.

The importance of national cultures for organizations can be examined most clearly, perhaps, in cases of multinational organizations. The use of the multinational organization permits an examination of the effects of the country of origin compared with the effects of the host country. Schollhammer (1971) suggested that the multinational firm is affected by its country of origin so that a Dutch-based firm would exhibit different characteristics from those of a Japanese-based firm in their American operations.

In an analysis of Japanese companies in the United States, Ouchi and Jaeger (1978) and Ouchi and Johnson (1978) found the following general differences between Japanese and American firms:

American	Japanese
Short-term employment	Lifetime employment
Individual decision making	Consensual decision making
Individual responsibility	Collective responsibility
Rapid evaluation and promotion	Slow evaluation and promotion
Explicit, formalized control	Implicit, informal control
Specialized career path	Nonspecialized career path

The Ouchi analyses found that the Japanese firms with operations in the United States resembled the Japanese model more than the American model, again suggesting that the country of origin is of critical importance.

Interest in national cultural differences and their impacts on organizations has risen dramatically in recent years. The easiest imagery here is the multinational enterprise, with manufacturing, distribution, sales, and administrative operations spread around the globe. But there are other imageries as well. Many international religious organizations have long had multinational operations. One only need think about the well-publicized policy differences between American Roman Catholics and the Vatican to get a glimpse of national cultural factors in operation.

How does national culture interface with internal organizational culture? One answer is provided by Geert Hofstede (1993), who is a leading scholar of multinational organizations. He sees culture as "mental programming or software" (p. 1) and believes national and organizational cultures overlap. For some issues, such as dealing with authority, national culture is most important. For other issues, such as dealing with innovations, organizational cultures are more important.

Perhaps the easiest way to frame the national culture issue is to look at the juxtaposed arguments of "culture free" versus "culture bound." The culture-free view is that organizational characteristics are based on factors other than national cultures. These other factors could be size, technology, internal culture, or factors not yet considered. The culture-bound argument is that national cultures are the dominant force in operation. As we will see, neither extreme argument can be sustained.

In their study of multinational banks in Hong Kong, Birnbaum and Wong (1985) found support for a "culture-free" determination of structure. Centralization, vertical and horizontal differentiation, and formalization were not related to the cultures in which the multinational banks studied had operations. Marsh and

Mannari (1980) also report that structural relationships found in the West tend to have the same form in Japan, rather than varying with culture. Conaty, Mahmoudi, and Miller (1983) found that organizations in pre-Revolutionary Iran were modeled on Western organizations.

These findings are in contrast to the arguments of the "culture-bound" analysts. A study of manufacturing plants in France, West Germany, and Great Britain found that the education, training, recruitment, and promotion processes lead to a situation in which the organizational processes of differentiation and integration are carried out by logics that are particular to a society and result in nationally different organizational shapes (Maurice, Sorge, and Warner, 1980). Differences have also been found in studies of Saudi Arabia and the United States (At-Twarjri and Montansani, 1987), in multinational firms in India (Rosenweig and Singh, 1991; Gupta and Govindarajan, 1991), in business organizations in East Asia (Japan, South Korea, Taiwan, and Hong Kong), small businesses in China and the United States (Hall et al., 1993), newspapers in Finland (Dalin, 1997), and breweries in Germany and the United States (Carroll, Preisendoerfer, Swaninathan, and Wiedenmayer, 1993).

There are thus contrasting findings and interpretations in regard to the importance of cultural differences for organizational structure. There are several possible explanations for these differences. Quite obviously different research methodologies were used in the various studies (Tayeb, 1987). Different conceptual frameworks were also in evidence. The most intriguing explanation for these differences is that of Birnbaum and Wong (1985). They suggest that cultural differences themselves might be the source of the different findings. Where particular organizational forms are acceptable, as in the case of Western forms in pre-Revolutionary Iran, one would expect to find such forms. In post-revolutionary Iran, on the other hand, one would be surprised to find a preponderance of such Western forms.

Organizations are affected by the culture and environment in which they are located, just as they are affected by size and technology. These factors interact with one another, with no single factor dominating. Lincoln, Hanada, and McBride (1986) suggest that national culture effects are additive in the sense that they are added to the variations in structure introduced by operations technology, size, and market constraints. These authors go on to note that there may be situations in which cultural factors could override technology.

Whereas Lincoln and colleagues believe that the effects of culture are additive, Hamilton and Biggart (1988) argue, in their analysis of South Korean, Japanese, and Taiwanese organizations, that cultural effects and market factors explain organizational growth but that authority patterns and legitimation strategies best explain organizational structure. This is the first suggestion of a theme that will be developed in later pages: that explanations of organizations must be used together rather than in opposition.

Hall and Xu (1990) disagree with Hamilton and Biggart in regard to Chinese and Japanese differences They believe that differences in family and Confucian values in the two countries contribute to crucial differences in structure between the two countries. They do not disagree in regard to using explanations in combination.

The research we have been reviewing has two important characteristics. First, national culture is being moved to the forefront of explanations of organizational structure and organizations more generally. Second, the attention being paid to culture is being given with the realization that other factors affecting structure, such as size, technology, and other environmental conditions, are not diminished in importance. They are retained in the explanatory equations.

Our attention now shifts to the ways in which organizational design affects structure, but there is a final point to be made in regard to our contextual factors. Organizational design strategies are themselves affected by the cultures in which the design efforts are made (Schneider, 1989; Schreyogg, 1980). American, British, Japanese, and Chinese organizations would all have their own techniques of formulating their strategies.

ORGANIZATIONAL DESIGN

The notion of organizational design has a very rational ring to it. We simply design organizations to attain their goals and be effective. Fortunately or unfortunately, the matter is not that simple. Rationality itself is hard to accomplish, regardless of what is being planned. At the same time, events in organizations are not entirely random, since the very intent of structure is to provide some degree of certainty of action. In the sections that follow, alternative approaches to organizational design will be presented and evaluated.

The complicated nature of organizational design is well captured by Starbuck and Nystrom (1981):

> Evidently, people and organizations solve problems by processes that operate quite separately from the processes by which they characterize and perceive problems. . . . This separation is probably beneficial, for people and organizations misperceive problems and they characterize problems in ways that grossly distort what they do perceive. When people and organizations generate solutions, the productive solution attempts combine multiple, simultaneous attacks on the components of problems. Solution attempts produce both predicted and unpredicted effects and both good and bad ones. Consequently, solution attempts become components of the problems they address. The initial problems, if they are solved, are ultimately solved through iterative sequences of solution attempts, and these sequences succeed because the people and organizations have observed and reacted to intermediate effects. Usually, of course, environmental changes render the initial problems and early solution attempts obsolete before the initial problems are actually solved. (pp. xix–xx)

Starbuck and Nystrom's comments suggest that organizational design is problematic and uncertain. Other observers are more sanguine and offer prescriptions such as Caplow's (1976) book *How to Run Any Organization*. The very title smacks of rational organizational design. Peters and Waterman's (1982) long-running best seller, *In Search of Excellence,* contains the kinds of prescriptions that are typical of the view that organizations can be the object of rational organizational design. They prescribe the following:

1. A bias for action—do it, try it, don't analyze the problem to death.
2. Stay close to the customer and understand the service or product needs.
3. Engage in entrepreneurship and promote autonomy within the organization.
4. Productivity is through people and not technology.
5. Have high values and demand excellence.
6. Stick to the knitting—do what you do best.
7. Keep the staff lean and simple.
8. Have simultaneous looseness and tightness—allow people to be autonomous, but at the same time be disciplined. (This summary is from Van de Ven, 1983.)

From the perspective of Starbuck and Nystrom and that taken here, these prescriptions are far too simplistic. They ignore the perceptual and judgmental difficulties that Starbuck and Nystrom stress and the weight of several bodies of literature. Organizational design does affect structure, but not in the simple, overly rational manner suggested by the authors of prescriptive solutions for organizations. In the sections that follow, we will consider alternative perspectives on organizational design, beginning with the idea that organizations make strategic choices in regard to how they are structured.

Strategic Choice

The idea of strategic choice is not a new one. Chandler (1962) emphasized the importance of strategic choices for business firms such as Sears, Roebuck and General Motors as they attempted to take advantage of perceived markets in their environment. The establishment of General Motors as a multidivisional form with Chevrolet, Pontiac, and the other automotive divisions was seen as a consequence of strategic choices.

Child (1972) advanced this argument by noting that the internal politics of organizations determine the structural forms, the manipulation of environmental features, and the choice of relevant performance standards that are selected by organizations. The internal politics are themselves dependent upon the existing power arrangements in the organization. Again, structure begets structure.

Strategic choices are made on the basis of "bounded rationality" (Simon, 1957). The nature of rationality as a component of the decision-making process will be considered in detail in Chapter 6, but it is important here to note that the bounded-rationality idea means that the strategic choices are not necessarily the optimal choices. Rather, they appear to be optimal as a consequence of decisions made through the political process within organizations. The concept of "equifinality" is useful here. Equifinality refers to the presence of several means (structures) available to reach a given end (goal) (Katz and Kahn, 1966). Organizations are faced with both equifinality of means to ends and the presence of multiple ends. That is why the notion of choice is important. An organization is faced with multiple environmental pressures and must choose one path among many options toward one of many objectives.

Organizations are faced with environments that differ in their rates of change and degree of uncertainty. Specific parts of organizations are affected by specific environmental elements (Miles, Snow, and Pfeffer, 1974). The legal department of an organization has different environmental interactions from those of the public relations department and would thus choose a different form.

The political context of the decision-making process has an important relationship with structure. For example, people carrying out nonroutine tasks are likely to have power because of their expertise; those doing routine tasks do not have that power source. People with expertise can claim and receive more discretion, or decentralization on a broader basis, as something won from a position of power, rather than something delegated from above (Pfeffer, 1978; Pfeffer and Salancik, 1978).

The power holders in organizations decide what are issues and what are not issues. Thus, the decision to make a strategic choice or not is based on power arrangements (Ranson, Hinings, and Greenwood, 1980). The term that is most commonly used to describe power arrangements in organizations is the dominant coalition (Thompson, 1967). The "dominant coalition comprises a direct and indirect 'representation' or cross-section of horizontal constituencies (that is, subunits) and vertical constituencies (such as employees, management, owners, or stockholders) with different and possibly competing expectations" (Pennings and Goodman, 1977:152).

This approach does not see the dominant coalition as representative democracy. Rather, the dominant coalition is the outcome of the power held by the various parties in the coalition. Thus, some units are more powerful among the horizontal constituencies, and there is obvious power differentiation among the vertical constituencies. The dominant coalition, then, comprises the power center in the organization. This power center or coalition is that which makes the strategic choices in regard to the organization and its structure. In some cases, there is no dominant coalition, with a single individual or set of individuals dominating all others. In those cases, personality characteristics of powerful chief executive officers may be a key determinant of structure (Miller and Droge, 1986).

Decision makers in the dominant coalition select those parts of the environment with which they will be concerned. This selection is done within a political framework in which membership in the dominant coalition can shift, as can the distribution of power within it. On the basis of selective perception of the environment, appropriate strategies can be selected for dealing with this environment. This decision making includes utilizing the appropriate technology for implementing the strategy. In the strategic choice perspective, technology is thus brought into the organization. The decisions also involve strategies for arranging roles and relationships to control and coordinate the technologies being employed. This is done to ensure continuity of the organization, its survival, and its growth (Chandler, 1962).

Strategic choices take place within contexts. For example, a study of the multidivisional form, such as that employed by General Motors, found that industrial diversity and geographical dispersion were strongly related to the presence of the multidivisional form, with organizational size having an indirect effect by contributing to diversity and dispersion (Palmer et al., 1987). Conversely, the absence of diversity would limit the extent to which the multidivisional form would be used. The industrial limits to choice are evident in the fact that the petroleum and agricultural industries were less diverse than other industries. Also, firms dominated by banks or by family members were less diverse and dispersed and had fewer multidivisional forms. The industrial context in which firms operated thus had a major impact on the form adopted.

In recent years a new element has been added to strategic choice. Many organizations are choosing the path of downsizing. This can involve laying off employees at all levels (except the very top, of course) and "outsourcing" activities—purchasing products and services outside the organization's boundaries, employing cheaper labor in a location "offshore," or buying janitorial or payroll services from an outside vendor.

Government organizations engage in a form of downsizing when they "privatize" some of their activities. Privatization is a volatile issue, particularly for government employee unions who make an interesting linkage between privatization and privateers. In any event, the privatizing of schools or prisons is another example of the downsizing approach to organizational design.

Most of the analyses of strategic choice that have been considered make the implicit assumption that choices are made to increase organizational efficiency. The downsizing argument turns this around and sees "structures as outcomes of efficiency constraints" (Meyer, 1990:209). According to this point of view, financial control has become paramount.

Strategic Choice: A Summary.   The consideration of downsizing must not blind us to the fact that choices are made about organizational structures. Strategic choices are made on an ongoing basis. As Chapter 6 will demonstrate, whether or not such choices can be rational is truly problematic. Decision makers continue to make choices. A key factor here is that these choices are made within a system of constraints. The constraints are exactly the factors we have been considering in this chapter.

We will use an example to illustrate this. The example is the "gender equity" decision discussed earlier. The decision was announced to the local news media that our intercollegiate athletic program was making major structural changes to achieve gender equity. This choice involved dropping some men's teams and adding some women's teams. At that point another part of the environment came into the picture. Students, coaches, alumni, and parents of players on the affected teams protested the decision and successfully blocked it in court. After a year of additional deliberations, the original recommendation was upheld. Decision making is not a simple process.

Our operating constraints were size, in the form of the amount of resources (money) available for intercollegiate athletics; the internal organizational culture, in the form of tradition and strong emotional support for maintaining some of the men's teams; and the environment, in the form of federal and NCAA mandates for gender equity.

Decisions made under constraints are at the core of what has come to be known as structural contingency theory (Donaldson, 1995, 1996). This theory is built on the work of Lawrence and Lorsch, which was considered in the last chapter. Organizational structures are based on decisions made in the contexts in which the organizations are operating. This means, simply, that there is no one best form of structure.

The Institutional Explanation

The final explanation of organizational structure to be considered is the institutional model. This model has become a major contributor to our understanding of organizational phenomena. It is another attempt to answer the question, Why do organizations take the forms that they do? Much of the research here has been carried out in not-for-profit organizations with somewhat indeterminate technologies. DiMaggio and Powell (1983) argue that "institutional isomorphism" is now the dominant reason that such organizations assume the forms that they do. According to DiMaggio and Powell, Weber's (1952, 1968) original analysis of the driving force behind the move toward rationalization and bureaucratization was based on a capitalist market economy, with bureaucratization an "iron cage" in which humanity was bound since the process of bureaucratization was irreversible.

DiMaggio and Powell believe that major social changes have altered that situation to such a large extent that an alternative explanation is needed. Their analysis is based on the assumption that organizations exist in "fields" of other, similar organizations. They define an organizational field as follows:

> By organizational field, we mean those organizations that, in the aggregate, constitute a recognized area of institutional life: key suppliers, resource and product consumers, regulatory agencies and other organizations that produce similar services and products. The virtue of this unit of analysis is that it directs our attention not simply to competing firms, as does the population approach of Hannan and Freeman (1977b), or to networks of organizations that actually interact, as does the interorganizational network approach of Laumann et al. (1978), but to the totality of relevant actors. (p. 148)

According to this perspective, organizations are increasingly homogeneous within fields. Thus, public universities acquire a sameness, as do department stores, airlines, professional football teams, motor vehicle bureaus, and so on. DiMaggio and Powell cite three reasons for this isomorphism among organizations in a field. First, there are coercive forces from the environment, such as government regulations and cultural expectations, which can impose standardization on organizations. Government regulations, for example, force restaurants (it is hoped) to maintain minimum health standards. There is strong evidence in support of the coercive force of government mandates. Both the adoption of disciplinary and grievance processes and the formation of internal labor markets have been traced to the development of government mandates for equal employment opportunities (Dobbin et al., 1993; Sutton et al., 1994).

Second, DiMaggio and Powell note that organizations mimic or model each other. This occurs as organizations face uncertainty and look for answers to their uncertainty in the ways in which other organizations in their field have faced similar uncertainties. Rowan (1982) argues, for example, that public schools add and subtract administrative positions in order to come into isomorphism with prevailing norms, values, and technical lore in their institutional environment. DiMaggio and Powell argue that large organizations tend to use a relatively small number of consulting firms, which "like Johnny Appleseeds, spread a few organizational models throughout the land" (p. 152). A concrete example, noted by DiMaggio and Powell, is Japan's conscious modeling of its courts, postal system, military, banking, and art education programs on Western models in the late nineteenth century. As DiMaggio and Powell note:

> American corporations are now returning the compliment by implementing (their perceptions of) Japanese models to cope with thorny productivity and personnel problems in their own firms. The rapid proliferation of quality circles and quality-of-work-life issues in American firms is, at least in part, an attempt to model Japanese and European successes. (1983:151)

A *New York Times* article reports that business firms are establishing formal intelligence departments to keep tabs on competitors from home and abroad. One source is quoted as saying that "understanding your competitors' positions and how they might evolve is the essence of the strategic game" (Prokesh, 1985). In DiMaggio and Powell's conceptualization, the field is more than simply competitors. The establishment of intelligence departments reflects the strong mimetic tendencies within organizations. The mimetic explanation has received disproportionate attention in recent years (Mizruchi and Fein, 1999). It has become a popular explanation of isomorphism in structure.

A third source of institutional isomorphism is normative pressure as the workforce, and especially management, becomes more professionalized. Both professional training and the growth and elaboration of professional networks within organizational fields leads to a situation in which the managerial personnel in organizations in the same field are barely distinguishable from one another. As people participate in trade and professional associations, their ideas tend to homogenize. This normative factor was found to be important in the Dobbin et al. (1993) and Sutton et al. (1994) studies cited earlier. Here, along with the importance of government mandates, professional personnel managers were instrumental in bringing about employment reforms. Additional support is found in research on the financial reporting practices in Fortune 200 business firms. This research found that financial reporting practices were based on the professionalization in the environment of the firms studied (Mezias, 1990).

The institutional perspective thus views organizational design not as a rational process based on organizational goals but as one of both external and internal pressures that lead organizations in a field to resemble each other over time. This perspective sees strategic choices as coming from the institutional order in which an organization is embedded.

The institutional perspective itself has become institutionalized (Tolbert and Zucker, 1996) and perhaps even "authoritarian" within the field of organizational theory (Hirsch, 1997:1703). Indeed, it is being applied, some would say misapplied, in fields far beyond the indeterminate technologies that were the focus of DiMaggio and Powell's original formulation. Sometimes it appears that structural characteristics that cannot be explained by any other reason are attributed to institutional forces.

At the same time, institutional theory is providing insights into important things that have happened in and around organizations. For example, the growing proportion of women in management and an increased awareness of work–family issues have been attributed to both normative and coercive institutional processes (Blum, Fields, and Goodman, 1994; Goodstein, 1994).

EXPLAINING ORGANIZATIONAL STRUCTURE

We have been considering a series of explanations of organizational structure. These have ranged from contextual factors such as size and technology to the design factors of strategic choice and institutional isomorphism. Which is the correct explanation? It should be obvious by now that neither "all of the above" nor "none of the above" is the appropriate answer. The explanations of structure must be considered in combination.

This has become well recognized among sociologists. For example, Tolbert (1985) combined the environmental pressure and institutional perspectives in explaining aspects of the administrative structures of universities. Fligstein (1985) studied the spread of the multidivisional form among large corporations and found support for the strategic choice, member control, and institutional perspectives. Fligstein also suggests that in a different set of organizations, other explanations might be valid. Fligstein concludes (and we concur):

> . . . [E]ach school of thought has tended to view its theory as a total causal explanation of organizational phenomena. This suggests that one of the central tasks in organizational theory is to reorient the field in such a way as to view competing theories as contributing to an understanding of organizational phenomena. (p. 377)

The healthy and informed eclecticism that Fligstein calls for has essentially become the norm in organizational analyses. Hamilton and Biggart's (1988) study of the importance of national culture for organizations in the Far East is another example of this multiple-theory approach, as is Drazin and Van de Ven's (1985) analysis of the structures of a set of employment security units.

Further examples of this move toward multiple theoretical explanations are found in Kraatz and Zajac's (1996) study of private colleges and universities, where local economic and demographic conditions (environmental conditions) were more important than institutional factors in explaining structural changes.

Similarly, a study of the development of the thrift industry in California found that environmental pressures operated in tandem with institutional forces (Haveman and Rao, 1997). There is a growing recognition that market and task contingencies operate along with institutional pressures (Bugùra and Üsdiken, 1997; Gupta et al., 1994; Sutton and Dobbin, 1996). National cultural differences have been found to explain differences in formalization among organizations in the Nordic countries, the United States, and Canada, along with institutionalized patterns (Dobbin and Boychuk, 1999). In a similar fashion, centralization was found to vary by national culture. Decision-making patterns become institutionalized differently in different countries (Gooderham, Nordhaug, and Ringdal, 1999).

Organizations are structured in a context. Van Houton (1987) analyzed the various approaches to organizational design that were attempted in Sweden in the 1970s and 1980s. He concludes that these cannot be understood out of their historical context. Organizations are thus complex structures-in-motion that are best conceptualized as historically constituted entities (Clegg, 1981:545). There are, then, multiple explanations of structure. When these explanations are taken singly, in opposition to one another, and outside their historical and cultural context, they have little to offer. When combined and in context, they enable us to understand why organizations take the forms that they do.

Organizations do not take form automatically. They do so because of decisions that are made, and that brings us back to the factor of strategic choice. But our move back is informed by the theoretical inclusiveness that we have just considered. Thus, organizations may diversify or reorganize to better fit their environments (Donaldson, 1987). They adapt their forms to fit the national culture in which they are operating (Sorge, 1991). They may also seek to differentiate themselves from other organizations and thus not conform to institutional pressures (Han, 1994). When they face multiple and conflicting environmental contingencies, they may respond with "misfits" (Gresov, 1989). Strategic choices are also made in light of the technologies available and appropriate for the organization involved.

As we turn now to a consideration of organizational processes, it should be made clear that organizational structures affect these processes and vice versa (Miller, 1987). Structure affects the flow of information and the power arrangements in organizations. Decisions made in regard to attempted strategies affect structure. Unlike the buildings in our analogy at the outset of this chapter, structures are in motion.

SUMMARY AND CONCLUSIONS

We have considered the various explanations that have been developed to explain the forms that organizational structures take. Organizational structure is dynamic. Organizations change in size, adopt new technologies, face changing environments and internal and national cultures, adopt new strategies or find old ones, and adjust to other organizations in their field.

Before turning to organizational processes, we must repeat that organizational structures are there for a purpose and that the purpose is to be as effective as possible. There are many sources of deflection from the structure–effectiveness linkage—some intentional and some accidental, some humorous and some tragic—but the linkage remains.

It has been implicit in the discussion that the structure of an organization has important outcomes—for its members and for the social system of which it is a part. It is within structure that the processes of power, conflict, leadership, decision making, communication, and change operate. We now turn to a consideration of those processes.

EXERCISES

1. How well do the contextual explanations of organizational structure fit your two organizations?
2. Explain how well the organizational design explanations do or do not fit your two organizations.

Chapter 4

Power and Power Outcomes

—•◆•—

OVERVIEW

One important component of organizational structure is centralization, or the distribution of power. Organizations have been defined as systems of power—an interconnected series of order-givers and order-followers. In this light, organizations can be viewed as tools by which those people with power can use other people to achieve particular goals. But individuals who are not formally designated as order-givers in an organization may also wield power, that is, be able to get others to carry out their wishes. Even individuals who are not official members of the organization may influence others in the organization to do as they wish. Where does power come from in organizations, and what factors influence its distribution as well as changes in this distribution? In this chapter we focus on these questions. We begin by examining authority as a particular type of power relationship, and consider different types and bases of authority. Authority is an important aspect of power in organizations, but authority can be buttressed by or undercut by other kinds of power. Thus, we also look at other types of power that are often found in organizations and the things that affect such power. The exercise of power in organizations has outcomes that are important for the parties involved, and for the organization as a whole. The most common outcome is compliance—power works. But power can also lead to the more dramatic outcome of conflict. We examine the nature and consequences of conflict in organizations. Finally, we consider how organizations exercise power within the larger society.

In many ways, power is a most puzzling phenomenon. On the one hand, power is often stable and self-perpetuating, partly because those in power have the resources to maintain that power (Hardy and Clegg, 1996). On the other hand, as the events in Eastern Europe and the USSR in 1989 and 1990 demonstrated, long-entrenched systems of power can be overthrown with startling quickness. Different members of an organization, as well as actors outside the organization, can at different points in time exert critical influence in decision-making processes, and thus affect what organizations actually do. In Mintzberg's (1983) terms, we can think of power "in and around" organizations. Understanding both the perpetuation of power relations in organizations and how and when shifts in these relations may occur requires consideration of the variety of bases of power in organizations, factors that affect when individuals and groups may be able to use these bases, and different responses to the exercise of power. These are the topics that we focus on in the following discussion.

THE NATURE OF POWER IN ORGANIZATIONS

Power can be rather simply defined. There is general agreement that it has to do with relationships between two or more actors in which the behavior of one is affected by the behavior of the other. Robert Dahl (1957), a political scientist, defines power thus: "A has power over B to the extent that he can get B to do something B would not otherwise do" (pp. 202–3). (For other general discussions of power, see Bierstedt, 1950; Blau, 1964; Kaplan, 1964; and Weber, 1947:152–93.) If we remember that the *he* in the definition can also be a *she* and that A and B are not necessarily individuals, this simple definition captures the essence of the power concept. It implies an important point that is often neglected: The power variable is a relational one. A person or a group cannot have power in isolation; rather, the concept describes a relationship between a given individual or collectivity and another specified person or collectivity (Pfeffer, 1992).

Power relationships involve much more than interpersonal power. In the case of organizations, interunit power relationships are an important determinant of organizational outcomes. The units here can be hierarchical levels, such as labor and management, or they can be departments or divisions at the same hierarchical level, such as sales and manufacturing. We will examine interorganizational relationships from the power standpoint at a later phase of the analysis. We have already considered the power of organizations in society. Power is thus a crucial feature of organizations at every level of analysis.

AUTHORITY AND POWER

There are many different bases of power, and hence, different types of power. In this context, a key distinction that is commonly drawn is between authority and other forms of power. Weber (1947), in his classic analysis of bureaucratic organization, emphasized this distinction. Authority is a type of power that is based on the acceptance by others of a given individual's legitimate right to issue orders or directives. Thus, orders are followed because it is believed that they *ought* to be followed; recipients are expected to "suspend judgment" and comply voluntarily. The exercise of this type of power requires a common value system among members of a collectivity, one that defines who has the right to give orders to whom, and under what conditions.

As part of his effort to understand the nature of modern organizations, Weber (1947) developed a widely known typology of authority, one that distinguished among rational-legal, charismatic, and traditional authority. Rational-legal authority characterizes most power relationships in contemporary organizations. It is based on a value system that holds that relations in social groups should be governed by a set of general laws and rules that are created purposively, to deal efficiently and effectively with common problems and questions that people encounter. It is also believed that those laws and rules should be subject to change, if there is a reason to believe that they are not effective or efficient. Consistent with this value system, it is accepted that people with particular knowledge and skills that are relevant to dealing with some set of problems should be assigned to positions or offices that handle those problems. We accept orders that come from those persons and the offices because we assume that they are rational, that is, designed to effectively accomplish some ends (Zucker, 1977). We are not always, and perhaps not even typically, conscious of this assumption, but if pressed to explain our behavior, it is usually reflected in our explanations. For example, at the start of every semester, an instructor hands out a course syllabus to each student. When the students read the assignments, write the papers, and take the exams, rational-legal authority has operated. They have accepted the professor's right to tell them what to read and what they must do as students in the class, in part because they assume that the professor holds her position because of her relevant knowledge about the topics addressed in the class.

This emphasis on positions takes the person out of the equation—we will put the person back in now. Charismatic authority stems from devotion to a particular power holder and is based on his or her personal characteristics. Members of a collective view these characteristics as being extraordinary, indicating special gifts, talents and abilities; they accept the person's right to give orders because they believe in the person's superiority. Although this type of authority is not the main form in most modern organizations, it occurs occasionally, and it can help or hinder the regular operations of the organization. If a person with rational-legal authority (gained by virtue of the position that he holds) can extend this through the exercise of charismatic authority, he has more power over subordinates than that prescribed by the organization. This additional power may be harnessed to enhance the performance of the organization. If, on the other hand, charismatic authority is held by persons outside the formal authority system, they may use this to contravene rational-legal authority, and the system itself can be threatened.

The third form, traditional authority, is based on the belief that an established set of social relations is divinely intended. Within this social system, some individuals were destined to hold power, or "born to rule." This was the main basis of political authority in many societies for much of history; western feudal societies and eastern dynasties both provide good examples. The Roman Catholic Church serves as at least a partial example of this form of authority in contemporary organizations: The system of pope, cardinals, archbishops, and so on reflects the belief in a divinely ordained set of relations.

Dornbusch and Scott (1975) offer an additional distinction that is useful to thinking about authority in organizations, between endorsed and authorized power. This distinction addresses an old debate over the locus of authority in organizations. On one hand, Chester Barnard (1938) argued that authority resides in the individual who complies with an order; in this "bottom up" view of authority, if one individual does not accept another's right to give an order and fails to comply, the order-giver cannot be said to have authority over that person. On the other hand, Weber's analysis is predicated on the notion that authority resides in a social collectivity, and more specifically, in shared normative beliefs about who has the right to give orders. Weber's "top down" approach is based on the assumption that noncompliance with an order given by a person with normatively approved authority will result in the application of sanctions by the larger group. By distinguishing between endorsed and authoritative power, Dornbusch and Scott recognized that authority has both bottom-up *and* top-down aspects. Endorsed power is said to exist when subordinates accept and comply with the orders given by their superiors. Authorized power exists when an individual's orders are supported and enforced by higher-level members of an organization, and ultimately, by the larger society. This distinction is useful in thinking about situations involving different types of organizational conflicts over authority—mutinies, coup d'etats, revolutions, and so forth.

OTHER TYPES OF POWER

As noted, although authority is an important type of power in organizations, it is not the only type. Other types of power relationships entail dependency, one party's need or desire for something that another party can provide (Emerson, 1962). When two parties need each other equally, their dependence is mutual— for example, managers need workers to produce goods and services, and workers need managers to provide their pay. But when dependence is *not* balanced, then one actor may have more power over another than vice versa. Or to put it another way, when A wants or needs things that B has more than B wants things from A, this can provide B with power over A.

The things that actors may possess or control that can be sources of power are usually referred to as resources. David Mechanic (1962), analyzing the factors that affected how much power people at lower levels of an organization had, identified three general types of resources in organizations that such members might have access to: persons, information, and "instrumentalities." The last refers to physical or tangible resources, such as machinery, office supplies, and money. If we broaden this list to include nontangible, social factors, such as status and friendship, this constitutes a useful list of basic resources that may provide organizational members with power above and beyond the formal authority they hold.

Access to Resources

Bacharach and Lawler (1980) identify a number of different ways in which actors come to control such power resources. Access to resources can be affected by the official or formal organizational position an individual holds (see also Brass and Burkhardt, 1993; Finkelstein, 1992; Fligstein and Brantley, 1992). Clearly, this is an important source of power for persons who hold high-level positions in organizations and whose jobs involve such tasks as assigning compensation, making decisions about promotions and awards in the organization, and setting working conditions. These are the kinds of key resources that Etzioni (1975) used in his typology of organizations that we discussed in Chapter 2; he referred to these as involving remunerative rewards, normative rewards, and coercion, respectively, and argued that you could classify organizations in terms of which kinds of resources the top level members primarily relied on to secure compliance by lower level members. Remunerative rewards involve material, often financial incentives (e.g., salaries and bonuses); normative rewards involve satisfying social or psychological needs (e.g., status, friendship); coercion involves affecting physical conditions (e.g., opportunities to eat, rest breaks).

But lower-level positions can also provide people with access to resources that others need, and thus potentially give them power. For example, Crozier's (1964) study of relations in a French cigarette-manufacturing firm found that, although the maintenance personnel were not in high-level positions in the firm, they held the most power of any group because of their role in repairing the equipment necessary to the production process. Only the maintenance men were allowed to work on the machines when they broke down, and production workers and their supervisors were essentially helpless unless the maintenance personnel performed their work. Thus, their formal job responsibilities provided them with control of the machines, and this gave them a great deal of power.

> With machine stoppages, a general uncertainty about what will happen next develops in a world totally dominated by the value of security. It is not surprising, therefore, that the behavior of the maintenance man—the man who alone can handle the situation, and who by preventing these unpleasant consequences gives workers the necessary security—has a tremendous importance for production workers, and that they try to please him and he to influence them. (p. 109)

Similarly, think of an administrative assistant or aide whose job involves making appointments for a high-ranking executive in an organization. This job allows him to determine who gets to see the executive, a resource that others are apt to desire highly; thus, although the position may be relatively low-level, it provides him with control of an important resource (a person, the executive) that can make others willing to do much to secure his favor.

Bacharach and Lawler (1980) discuss structural position as a determinant of access to resources of power. In this usage, structural position can be thought of in terms of network relations. An actor's position in a network, defined by which other actors are linked to the focal actor, is commonly seen as a key determinant of power (Ansell and Padgett, 1993; Burt, 1992; Gould and Fernandez, 1994; Stevenson and Greenberg, 2000). Links to others are assumed to provide access to two basic resources, information and people; thus, members of a network who have high centrality—are connected to many others, either directly or indirectly—should find it easier to get information and to control people (i.e., affect what others do through their social connections). Some have suggested *whom* an actor is linked to also needs to be considered in understanding the impact of network position on power (Lin, 1999); links to a few high-status people may have the same, or even more, impact on power as links to many low-status people. This approach is consistent with Allen and Panian's (1982) finding of the role of "family ties" in influencing choice of top-level executives in organizations.

Finally, personal characteristics have been suggested to have an effect on access to power resources (Bacharach and Lawler, 1980; Etzioni, 1975; French and Raven, 1968; Mechanic, 1962). Such characteristics include social attractiveness, intelligence, and willingness to invest effort in getting such resources. When others find a person attractive, they are likely to value her friendship and esteem (Blau, 1964); as noted, insofar as others find such non-tangible, social resources desirable, they can serve as a source of power. Thus, for example, if someone asks a favor of you, you are more likely to comply if you want her to like you than if you are indifferent to her opinion of you. Whether attractive individuals are willing to use this as a source of power may depend on personality characteristics that affect their interest in gaining and using power. Likewise, individuals are apt to vary in their willingness to put in the time to acquire information, cultivate others' good-will and favorable recognition, and to make other efforts to acquire resources that can serve as a source of power (Kanter, 1979).

Resources and Strategic Contingencies

Having access to resources that others desire isn't sufficient, by itself, to provide individuals with power. Rather, power rests on how much those resources are highly valued or considered to be important, whether their acquisition is difficult or uncertain, and whether other resources can be substituted for them or not. When resources are viewed as important, when there is high uncertainty surrounding their acquisition, and when they are nonsubstitutable, they represent what's referred to as a "strategic contingency" for the organization. Control of strategic contingencies is fundamental to power in organizations (Hickson et al., 1971; Pfeffer and Salancik, 1974).

The value attached to a resource, or its importance, is affected by whether it's seen as central to the organization's workflow and ability to carry out main production functions. The importance of a resource may also be affected by environmental demands. Thus, a study by Hambrick (1981) showed that if executives coped with the dominant requirements imposed by the environment of their industry, they had high power. This finding is consistent with other studies that have examined who attains top-level positions in organizations. One study, for example, found that lawyers (coming from legal departments) were disproportionately represented among corporate chief executives. In organizations that face complex legal problems, lawyers move to the top of the organization as they appear to have the information, or knowledge, needed to solve key problems for the organization (Priest and Rothman, 1985).

Similarly, another study, a historical analysis of prominent corporations in the United States from 1919 to 1979, reported that people with manufacturing backgrounds dominated corporate presidencies in the early decades of the century. Knowledge of manufacturing processes was key to the success of these organizations. In the middle decades, changes in the kinds of problems facing the corporations led people with backgrounds in sales and marketing to dominate in executive offices. In the more recent decades, personnel from finance tended to occupy presidential positions in the corporations (Fligstein, 1990). The difference in the findings reported here (lawyers versus finance) is undoubtedly due to differences in samples of organizations studied. These findings also indicate an important point: If the environment changes, or the organization develops new markets and concerns, different types of knowledge and other resources can come to be seen as more or less important to the organization's survival and success, and power can shift from one individual or group to another.

It's not only the importance of a resource in an organization that affects whether it provides power to the individual or group that holds it; its scarcity and the relative uncertainty surrounding it affect this as well. The ability to cope with uncertainty has been found to make an important contribution to power differentials (Hickson, Pugh, and Pheysey, 1969). If an organization needs additional financial support (e.g., because it wants to expand), and if its ability to secure funding from banks or other sources is in doubt, the finance department or unit that handles this task will have more power (Salancik and Pfeffer, 1974). In this context, Perrow (1970a) used data from twelve industrial firms to examine the question, "Which group has the most power?" He found that most of the firms were overwhelmingly dominated by their sales departments. This domination is shown in Figure 4–1.

Perrow argued that the power of the sales department stemmed from the fact that this was the least predictable area of resource flows for most organizations in his study; thus, the departments' ability to cope with uncertainty increased their relative power within the organization. His findings amplify those of Crozier (1964), described earlier. Part of the reason the maintenance workers had such power in the cigarette-manufacturing firm was because the rest of the organization

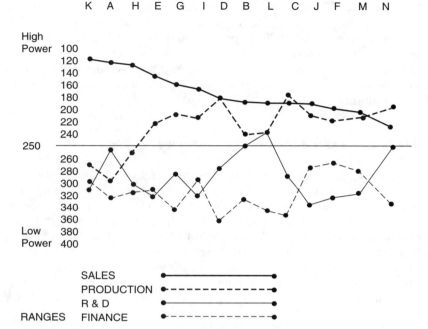

**FIGURE 4–1   Overview Power of Departments in Industrial Firms
(Means of Departmental Means)**

*Each letter represents a company or separate unit.

Source: Charles Perrow, "Departmental Power and Perspective in Industrial Firms," in Mayer N. Zald, ed.,
Power in Organizations (Nashville, TN: Vanderbilt University Press, 1970), p. 64.

was highly predictable. The organization was a state-owned monopoly; thus, ensuring sales was not an issue, nor was securing financing. Only the machinery,
which was old and apt to break down unexpectedly, was a key source of uncertainty in the organization. Consequently, controlling this uncertainty provided the
maintenance men with power.

Finally, whether there are alternative ways of obtaining needed resources,
or whether there are other, substitutable resources is important in determining the
relevance of a given resource for power. In a hospital, for example, the application of medical knowledge that physicians hold is central to the organization's
work processes; this potentially provides physicians with a great deal of power in
these organizations. When there is a shortage of physicians in an area, and the organizations' ability to obtain enough physicians is uncertain, this increases physicians' power. However, if there is an oversupply of physicians, there is less
uncertainty surrounding organizations' ability to get the needed resource, medical knowledge, and this should decrease physicians' power. Moreover, insofar as

other personnel, such as nurses, physicians' assistants, and others, have relevant knowledge and are allowed to use it (which may depend on state regulations), they represent a potential substitute for physicians. This also can lessen physicians' power (Scott et al., 2000). If the production workers in Crozier's study had been allowed to fix their own machines when they broke down, the power of the maintenance men would have declined considerably; however, the organization's rules forbade anyone but the maintenance men from doing this task, thus ensuring their nonsubstitutability.

Social Definitions and Strategic Contingencies

It's important to note that the value, uncertainty, and lack of substitutability of resources are not necessarily objectively given; these qualities can be socially constructed, or manipulated (Alvesson and Willmott, 2002). A study by Kanter (1968), for example, documented ways in which leaders of an organization can increase the value of social resources controlled by the organization (status, friendship, etc.) for members, and thus secure their compliance. Similarly, Kunda's (1992) research on an engineering firm described the creation of an organizational culture that encouraged employees to set high value on rewards controlled by management, which enhanced managers' power. It is also possible for groups and individuals to persuade others that the resources they control are unique, and thus not substitutable, or to influence perceptions of the uncertainty of resource flows. To understand changes in power in organizations, then, it is important to pay attention to the way in which various resources are defined and evaluated by members of the organization (Enz, 1988).

Similarly, the use of authority may be affected by the emergence of new social definitions of who *should* be in charge of certain situations and problems. An interesting example of an opportunity for this sort of redefinition is provided by Bucher's (1970) anecdotal account of a confrontation between students and university administration during the 1960s.

> According to the students' statements, the dean asserted that "nobody in the university has the authority to negotiate with the students. . . ." "Obviously somebody in the university makes policy decisions," the students said, "and until an official body comes forward, we consider the present situation a refusal to negotiate our demands." (p. 3)

In the situation described, neither the students nor the university administration in question could locate an office or an individual who had the authority to negotiate with students. The students' perception that this constituted a refusal to negotiate is only partially accurate. Such a situation simply had not arisen before, and it really was unclear who had the knowledge and skills relevant for the assignment of authority. In campus situations such as these student–administration confrontations, issues and relationships are explored that have not really been part of the preexisting power system. Individuals or groups that are able to define it as part of their domain can increase their power.

SHIFTS IN POWER

Because more power is introduced into the system as arrangements are made to handle incidents such as the one described previously, we see that there is not a fixed amount of power in the system for all time; the amount of power can contract or expand. Thus, Lammers (1967:204), discussing research on increasing workers' participation in organizational decision-making, concludes, "To sum up, managers and the managed in organizations at the same time come to influence each other more effectively and thereby generate joint power as the outcome of a better command by the organization over its technological, economic, and human resources in the service of certain objectives." This suggests that the introduction of more cooperative decision-making systems can result in greater power for both managers and workers alike, and thus, overall increases in power.

In addition, power may shift among individuals and groups in organizations over time, as noted above. However, changes in power, either overall or in distribution, do not occur quickly—except perhaps in rare cases, such as a disaster, where dramatic changes in power in an organization may take place in a very short period. There are a number of factors that normally limit such power shifts. First, once an individual or organizational unit gains power, it tries very hard to maintain this power (Michels, 1949). This can account for the observation that an organizational unit's previous power position is the main predictor of its current power (Lachman, 1989). It also explains Boeker's finding (1989b) that environmental conditions at the time an organization is formed, along with the background of the founding entrepreneur, determine which departments are regarded as most important in organizations long after the founding period. Likewise, powerful CEOs are less apt to be dismissed than their weaker subordinates when their organizations are doing poorly (Boeker, 1992).

Second, since the allocation of organizational resources is affected by the existing power system, it tends to perpetuate the system (Pondy, 1970; Zald, 1970), even in the absence of active efforts by power-holders. For example, an analysis of United Fund agencies found that community organizations that were successful in raising funds themselves received greater allocations from the United Fund. These community organizations were less dependent upon the United Fund, and the United Fund feared that the successful community organizations might attempt their own fund-raising efforts (Pfeffer and Long, 1977). Similarly, studies of university budget allocation decisions have found that the more powerful units and departments receive more resources—the rich get richer and the poor get poorer. This pattern is particularly evident in times of financial adversity (Hills and Mahoney, 1978; Pfeffer and Salancik, 1974).

Despite these strong inertial forces, shifts in power systems of the organization *do* occur. External forces often play a key role in such shifts (Zald, 1970). Relationships with similar organizations (e.g., trade associations or baseball leagues), suppliers and customers of the organization's output, regulatory agencies, and others can all affect the amount and distribution of power within the organization. For example, the National Labor Relations Board, after its establishment in the 1930s, facilitated the growth in power of labor unions (Peterson, 1970). At the same time, the increasing complexity of labor laws and regulations led to the development of specialists in labor relations, and these personnel also gained in power in the organization, largely as a consequence of these external factors (Jacoby, 2004). External economic conditions also affect the power system in organizations as markets for labor, raw materials, and outputs shift. The external world thus invades the power structure of these organizations: Power, like other organizational phenomena, does not exist in isolation within the organization itself.

POWER OUTCOMES: COMPLIANCE AND INVOLVEMENT

The most frequent consequence of the exercise of power is compliance. This outcome is so common that it is almost boring. People come to work on time, do what their bosses desire, and produce their goods or deliver their services. Organizational units generally also comply with demands of their superiors. This is frequently overlooked in analyses of power, as the resistance to power—conflict—is more dramatic and exciting. Actually, the less dramatic phenomenon of compliance is much more frequent; despite the importance of conflict for organizations, compliance is really their heart.

It was this reasoning that led Etzioni (1975) to make compliance a key component of the typology of organizations that he proposed. It may be remembered from the discussion of typologies in Chapter 2 that Etzioni argued that lower-level members of organizations could be characterized in terms of the dominant type of involvement they experienced. He also argued that these types of involvement tended to be associated with the dominant types of rewards that top-level members used to induce compliance. The use of coercion should be associated with alienative involvement, remunerative rewards with calculative involvement, and normative (or symbolic) rewards with moral involvement.

Research associated with Etzioni's approach suggests that when organizations are able to develop moral involvement on the part of their members, their commitment to the organization is higher. For some organizations, such as voluntary organizations, moral involvement is crucial to ensuring members' continued participation, and hence the survival of the organization (Kanter, 1968). Consequently, providing opportunities for democratic participation by members is often especially important in such organizations because moral involvement is often increased when members are encouraged to participate and actually do participate (Craig and Gross, 1970; Hougland and Wood, 1980; Hougland, Shepard, and Wood, 1979; Wood, 1975). However, this can sometimes create a dilemma for higher-level, full-time staff members of voluntary organizations, since they have more information and skills that are relevant to making core organizational decisions than most members do (Valcour, 2002).

Compliance is clearly not the only response to power, however. The recipient of exercised power has other options, such as withdrawing from the situation or attempting to persuade the power holder to act otherwise (Blau, 1964;

Hirschman, 1972). Withdrawal can entail complete departure from an organization, or simply psychological disengagement—making only the barest efforts required to remain in the organization. Persuasion can entail direct discussion with the person who has issued an order, or it may involve "going over the boss's head," which is a risky move but certainly not infrequent. Another example of the latter response would be going to a department chair or college dean to appeal the acts of a professor. The power outcome of greatest interest, however, is conflict.

POWER OUTCOMES: CONFLICT

As will be discussed in Chapter 7, decision making is a critical organizational process. Power is obviously important in decision making. Conflict arises whenever individuals or groups perceive differences in their preferences involving decision outcomes, and they use power to try to promote their own preferences over others. There is a strong tendency to view conflicts as necessarily harmful, or "bad" for organizations. Likewise, most people are at least initially inclined to interpret conflict as a problem of individuals, reflecting personality problems, personal rivalries, natural antagonisms, or some combination of these. However, research indicates that conflict can serve positive functions in organizations (Lawrence and Lorsch, 1967). Moreover, the propensity to attribute conflict to individual failings is called into question by the very pervasiveness and constancy of conflict in organizations (Sabel, 1982).

> . . . [C]onflict is *always present* in organizations. Conflict may be personal, interpersonal, or between rival groups and coalitions. It may be built into organizational structures, roles, attitudes, and stereotypes, or arise over a scarcity of resources. It may be explicit or covert. Whatever the reason, or whatever the form it takes, its source rests in some perceived or real divergence of interests. (Morgan, 1986:155; emphasis added)

This pervasiveness suggests that organizational conflict is likely to have systemic, rather than individual sources, and in more recent years, researchers have begun to focus on common organizational bases and forms of conflict. As psychologist R. Nevitt Sanford (1964:95) states: "Twenty years ago, it seemed easy to account for organizational conflict by blaming the problem behavior of individuals. But the simple formula, 'trouble is due to trouble-makers,' is unfortunately inadequate in the light of our present knowledge of the social process."

Bases of Conflict

Katz (1964) and others have identified several common bases of organizational conflict. One is "functional conflict induced by various subsystems within the organizations" (p. 105). This form of conflict stems from differentiation, as discussed in Chapter 3, which leads people and units to have different and often opposing interests. The study by Lawrence and Lorsch (1967) described in that earlier chapter documented the way in which the specialization of organizational departments in different types of tasks led them to have different views of what key organizational problems were, different ideas about what kinds of solutions could best address those problems, even differing orientation toward time—whether to focus on long-term organizational objectives or short-term ones. When this kind of differentiation is coupled with interdependence—the need for different units to coordinate for work flows, decision making, and so forth—it is likely to result in persistent conflict. This factor is key to explaining one common axis of conflict in many business organizations, between sales and production departments. Members of the sales department typically place very high priority on keeping customers happy, and thus are apt to make promises for delivery of goods or for innovations that are difficult for the production department to meet. The production department places more emphasis on minimizing scrap (products that have problems and have to be discarded), and this makes increasing the rate of production and changing production processes to suit new innovations in product design very undesirable. Thus, the two departments have fundamentally different goals as a consequence of the different functions they serve in the organization.

A second basis of conflict suggested by Katz (1964) is the opposite of differentiation; it involves overlap or similarity in the functions of two units. Conflict here can take the form of "hostile rivalry or good-natured competition" (p. 106). For example, members of the HR department and the legal department of an organization both have some responsibility for ensuring that the organization conforms to key labor laws; conflict sometimes arises between these areas because of the overlap in responsibility. Such competition can be beneficial, but it can also be destructive. This kind of conflict was reflected in Dalton's (1959) observations of staff–line relations in manufacturing organizations. The staff, trained in engineering and other areas related to production processes, was supposed to provide advice and support to line personnel, to help improve production processes. However, the line managers were concerned that accepting the staff's input would make them seem incompetent or unimaginative, unable to handle the production processes in their charge. The outcome of this competition was a series of conflicts between line and staff that, viewed from outside the organization, were costly to it. This conflict resulted in relatively high levels of turnover among staff personnel, who were frustrated by the line's lack of attention to their recommendations. It also encouraged the staff to moderate proposals for changes, overlook line practices that didn't conform to technical standards, and generally be subservient to the line, all of which reduced the effectiveness of the staff. Dalton's study of staff–line relations provides an example of a general form of conflict that often takes place in organizations that have professional employees. We will discuss this at more length following.

A third basis of conflict that Katz (1964) made note of is "hierarchical conflict stemming from interest-group struggles over the organizational rewards of status, prestige, and monetary reward" (p. 106). In thinking about this aspect of conflict, it is important to keep in mind that organizations are the means by which societal resources are distributed among social groups (Baron, 1984; Hall, 1994).

In allocating people to different positions, and defining the extrinsic rewards attached to these positions, organizations play a key role in reproducing or changing social inequality. Employing organizations affect inequality not only directly, via their hiring, promotion, and compensation practices, but indirectly as well, since parents' employment experiences are a major determinant of the educational attainment of their children. Thus, it is not very surprising that lower-level personnel "try to improve their lot by joining forces as an interest group against the more privileged members of the organization" (Katz, 1964:106).

Although one typically thinks of blue-collar workers and unions in this regard, such conflict can also involve white-collar workers and subgroups in the management hierarchy. In the latter case, workers may use lawsuits and public relations pressures in conflicts that are defined in terms of equity issues, involving the distribution of rewards, or equality issues, involving the allocation of people to different organizational statuses (Kabanoff, 1991). Equity issues have been the focus of various lawsuits and protest actions involving comparable worth, or ensuring that female-dominated jobs that require levels of skills, training, and effort similar to those of male-dominated jobs are similarly compensated. This inequity is a common, and much-debated issue for organizational policy (Boraas and Rodgers, 2003; England, 1992). Another organizational policy addressing issues of equality, affirmative action, has also been the source of much recent conflict in contemporary organizations; affirmative action claims are brought by women and minorities when they believe that they have been denied access to positions based on their gender or race (Reskin, 1998).

Since these key bases of conflict—differentiation, duplication of functions, and hierarchy—are more or less inevitable features of modern organizational life, the potential for conflict is inherent in all organizations. This does not mean, however, that conflict will necessarily take place. Before conflict can arise, the parties involved must perceive that they are in a position to interfere with the other party (Kochan, Huber, and Cummings, 1975; Schmidt and Kochan, 1972). A decision must be made to engage in conflict. Whether the decision is based on rational calculation or fervid emotion, or is individual or collective, it does not occur automatically.

Professional–Organizational Relationships

One of the bases of conflict in organizations noted above is overlapping functions, instances where two different groups or individuals in an organization have responsibility for handling the same set of tasks. Often, this entails a problem of ambiguity in authority; it is not absolutely clear who has the "right" to make organizational decisions in a given case. This is a classic problem in organizations whose members are professionals, that is, who belong to occupational groups that society recognizes as having specific knowledge and skills necessary for handling certain tasks or dealing with certain problems (Abbott, 1988).

In organizations with professionals, there are two, potentially competing bases of authority. Freidson (1994) discusses this as the difference between the occupational principle and the administrative principle (see also Parsons, 1960). Both principles are consistent with the logic of rational-legal authority, that is, with the belief that individuals who have relevant knowledge and skills for handling problems in particular areas are best able to choose the appropriate means for achieving given ends, and therefore have the "right" to give orders in these areas (Satow, 1975). According to the administrative principle, however, authority is tied to the official, hierarchical position a person holds. This is based on the assumption that people are allocated to different hierarchical levels because of their organizational knowledge and expertise. Thus, people at higher hierarchical levels are expected to have more knowledge of the operating processes and requirements of an organization, and therefore to be better able than people at lower hierarchical levels to make effective decisions. According to the occupational principle, on the other hand, authority is tied to occupational certification that an individual possesses specialized knowledge that is deemed relevant and necessary for managing some set of tasks or problems. People with such occupationally based knowledge are expected to be better able than those lacking such knowledge to make effective decisions.

The administrative and occupational principles, then, point to two very different types of knowledge and skills, both of which may be relevant to rational decision making in organizations, but which may lead to different conclusions about preferred actions (Tolbert, 2004). Ambiguity about which principle should dominate, administrative or occupational, can lead to enduring and sometimes dramatic conflict within organizations with professional members. For example, one of the most visible instances of changing power relationships between professionals and their employing organizations can be seen in analyses of health maintenance organizations (HMOs). HMOs attempt to control costs, sometimes by limiting referrals to other physicians, limiting the length of hospital stays, and placing other restrictions that infringe on physicians' decision making. When physicians believe that a patient needs more care than the HMO permits, the likelihood of conflict erupting is evident (Hoff, 1998; Hoff and McCaffrey, 1996).

Such conflict is difficult to manage, but it is not inevitable. Its occurrence depends in part on the degree to which the knowledge base of the professional is apt to lead to decisions that are inconsistent with those of management. For some professions, such as accounting and engineering, there is a very close alignment in professional and organizational points of view (Barley, 2004), and conflict is less apt to be a problem. In other instances, organizations may avoid such conflict by allowing professionals to control themselves, to a large degree, with a fellow professional held accountable for the work of that unit (e.g., a research administrator). This allows professionals to work in a situation where there is less direct administrative scrutiny of their day-to-day decision making, but provides the organization with a system of accountability. The reward system in organizations with such arrangements is even altered sometimes to reflect recognition of the importance of using professional criteria in decision making. Instead of promoting professionals by moving them into higher positions in the administrative system, organizations develop "dual ladders" for their promotion system, whereby professionals can advance either by being promoted into purely managerial positions or by staying in their technical position unit but at increasingly higher salaries, based on recognition of their achievements by the larger profession (Hall, 1968). A more extreme version of this approach, perhaps, is represented by the increasing use of professionals as independent contractors in many contemporary organizations. Some research suggests that working as an independent contractor can provide professionals with a sense of freedom that they do not have traditional employment relations, and thus alleviate some of the conflict associated with such arrangements. The degree to which contractors experience such freedom depends, however, on the labor market; when it is tight, and jobs are plentiful, they can easily move across employing organizations if they have problems with one employer (Kunda, Barley, and Evans, 2002).

Not all organizational conflicts involving professionals stem from the question of whether to follow administrative or occupational principles in a given decision-making situation. Conflict can also grow out of the presence of a number of different professional groups in organizations. Members of different professions are apt to take differing views on what is good, rational, legal, or effective for the organization. This can happen even in situations of professional dominance, where a clear status hierarchy exists among professional groups, such as physicians, nurses, and nurses' aides (Freidson, 1970). It is even more likely in multidisciplinary partnerships (MDPs), formed from the merger of two or more firms, each composed of the members of one profession, such as the merger of a law firm and an accounting firm (Cooper et al., 1996). Although these are new forms of organization and little is known about how they actually function, one may surmise that when the perspectives of accountants, lawyers, research scientists, management consultants, and executives are combined, it is extremely unlikely that a common viewpoint will emerge even after serious discussions. Rather, each set of professionals is apt to vie with the others to make their point of view dominant (Hage, 1980).

This discussion has emphasized ways in which conflicts involving professionals and organizations may be resolved. But obviously, in many cases the issues are not resolved, and professional–organizational relations remain an important element of conflict in many organizations.

THE COMPONENTS OF CONFLICT SITUATIONS

We have been looking at the bases of conflict situations and the parties engaged in them. We now examine the conflict situation itself and then turn to the outcomes of conflict. There are four components of the conflict process (Boulding, 1964). The first is the parties involved. Conflict must involve at least two parties—individuals, groups, or organizations. Hypothetically, therefore, there can be nine types of conflict—person–person, person–group, and so on. Boulding suggests that there is a tendency toward symmetry in these relationships, such that person–organizational or group–organizational conflict tends to move toward organizational–organizational conflict. This is based on the power differentials that are likely to exist between these different levels in the organization.

The next component in this framework is the field of conflict, defined as "the whole set of relevant possible states of the social system" (p. 138). What Boulding is referring to here are the alternative outcomes toward which a conflict could move. Thus, the field of conflict includes a continuation of the present state, plus all the alternative conditions (e.g., both parties gain or both lose power, one gains at the expense of the other). This concept highlights conflict as a process, in that the parties in the situation will seldom have the same position in relation to each other after the conflict is resolved or continued.

The third component is the dynamics of the conflict situation. This refers to the perceptions that the parties have of each other, and the responses that they make to the other on this basis. That is, each party in a conflict will adjust its position to one that it feels is congruent with that of its opponent. If one of the parties becomes more militant, the other will probably do the same. This assumes, of course, that the power available to the two parties is at least moderately comparable. An interesting aspect of the dynamics of conflict is that conflict can "move around" in an organization (Smith, 1989). Parties in a conflict can "take it out on others" as they engage in their conflict.

The field of conflict can thus expand or contract as the dynamics of the conflict situation unfold. The conflict can move around, allies can be sought or bought, and coalitions can be formed. An example of these dynamics can be found in international relations, where national governments intensify their own conflict efforts in anticipation of or reaction to their opponents' moves. This can escalate into all-out war and eventual destruction, or it can stabilize at some point along the way, but the conflict will seldom be limited in its scope to the parties involved. The same phenomenon occurs in business organizations, with the equivalent of all-out war in the case of labor–management conflicts that end in the dissolution of the company involved. The dynamic nature of conflict can also be seen in the fact that there is an increase and decrease in the intensity of a conflict during its course. Although the field of conflict may remain the same, the energies devoted to it vary over time.

The final element in Boulding's model is the management, control, or resolution of conflict (p. 142). The terms used suggest that conflict situations are generally not discrete situations with a clear beginning and a clear end. They obviously emerge from preexisting situations and often continue to simmer, even if there is a temporary cessation in overt conflict activities. Boulding notes that organizations attempt to prevent conflict from becoming "pathological" and thus destructive of the parties involved and the larger system. One form of conflict resolution is a unilateral move; according to Boulding, a good deal of conflict is resolved through the relatively simple mechanism of the "peaceableness" of one of the participants. Although it relates primarily to interpersonal conflict, this idea can be utilized in the organizational setting. Peaceableness simply involves one of the parties backing off or withdrawing from the conflict. In most cases, the other party reacts by also backing off, even if it would prefer to continue, and the conflict is at least temporarily resolved. This kind of resolution is seen in labor–management disputes when one of the parties finally decides to concede on some points that were formerly "nonnegotiable."

Relying on some or all parties to make concessions is potentially danger-ous, however, because the parties may not exhibit this kind of behavior. For the peaceable party itself, the strategy is hazardous if the opponent is operating pathologically or irrationally to any degree. For that reason, organizations de-velop mechanisms to resolve or control conflict. One technique is to placate the parties involved by offering them some form of "side payment" as an inducement to stop the conflict. For example, in professional–organizational conflict, the pro-fessionals may be given concessions in the form of the relaxing of some organi-zational rules they believe to be excessively burdensome.

Conflicts in organizations can also be resolved through the offices of a third party. The third party may be a larger organization that simply orders the conflict behavior to cease under the threat of penalties (as when the government prohibits strikes and lockouts in a labor dispute that threatens the national interest), or it may be a mediator. Since intraorganizational conflict takes place within a larger context, the organization can simply prohibit the conflicting behavior. This does not resolve the issues, but it reduces the intensity of the conflict behavior. Mediation can do the same and can even lead to a complete resolution of the con-flict by presenting new methods of solution that may not have occurred to the par-ties involved or by presenting a solution that would not be acceptable unless it were presented by a third party.

THE OUTCOMES OF CONFLICT

The resolution of a conflict leads to a stage that is known as the aftermath (Pondy, 1967, 1969). This is a useful concept because conflict resolution does not lead to a condition of total settlement. If the basic issues are not resolved, the potential for future, and perhaps more serious, conflicts is part of the aftermath. If the con-flict resolution leads to more open communications and cooperation among the participants, that, too, is part of the aftermath (see Coser, 1956, 1967). Since an organization does not operate in a vacuum, any successful conflict resolution in which the former combatants are now close allies is not guaranteed to last for-ever. Changes in the environment and altered conditions in the organization can lead to new conflict situations among the same parties or with others.

Conflict is not inherently good or bad for the participants, the organization, or the wider society. Power and conflict are major shapers of the state of an or-ganization. A given organizational state sets the stage for the continuing power and conflict processes, thus continually reshaping the organization. In this way, conflict plays an important role in the development of variations between organ-izations. This may contribute to or detract from their survival (Aldrich, 1979).

Any analysis of conflict would be incomplete without noting that conflict can be viewed as a means by which organizational management can manipulate situations to its advantage (Rahim, 1986, 1989). As with any management tool, the morality of using conflict in this manner is in the eye of the beholder and the activities of the managers and the managed.

SUMMARY AND CONCLUSIONS

This chapter has attempted to identify and trace the sources and the outcomes of power in organizations. Common sense suggests that the forms and distribution of power critically affect the operations of any organization, and that the lives and behavior of organizational members are vitally affected by their relative power positions. In our analysis, we noted that power involves reciprocal relationships between two or more actors. These relationships can be specified in advance, as lines of authority usually are, or can develop over time, as a result of the acquisition and use of resources by groups and individuals. This point reemphasizes the close connection between organizational structure and processes, since it is the structure that defines the relationship between individuals and subunits initially, and that can determine who has access to certain resources. Studies of power in organizations reiterate the dominant theme of this book—that organizational structure and processes are in constant and reciprocal interaction. Power relationships develop out of and then alter existing structural arrangements.

We discussed authority as a prominent aspect of power in organizations, and the nature of rational-legal authority as a type that characterizes most modern organizations. Authority involves vertical (or hierarchical) relations, but other kinds of power often operate along the lateral or horizontal axis in organizations. Whereas authority rests on social definitions and understandings of who has the legitimate right to give orders and make decisions, other types of power rest on dependencies between actors—the need or desire of one actor for resources that are controlled by another. Such resources can take a variety of forms—people, information (including expertise and knowledge), equipment, and even social or psychological outcomes that people value, such as friendship, status, and sense of belonging. We considered some of the factors that affect people's access to such resources, ranging from the job responsibilities that are associated with a formal position or office, to network connections, to individual characteristics. We noted that the control of resources, in and of itself, is not sufficient to provide individuals or groups with power; rather, power depends on how highly others value the resources or view them as important, whether the resources are scarce or can easily be obtained from other sources, and whether other things can be substituted for a given resource.

If all these conditions are met, an actor controlling resources is likely to be able to get others to do what she or he wishes—but not necessarily in perpetuity. Although there are a number of factors that contribute to the stability of power relations, such as power holders' active efforts to protect their power, and systems of resource allocation that typically favor power holders, changes in the environment and/or changes in social definitions of the value of certain resources can lead to shifts in the amount and distribution of power in organizations over time. Thus, a full understanding of power relations requires close attention to the social processes through which resources are defined as valuable and scarce, and authority for various decisions is assigned to particular people and positions.

Compliance is one outcome of the exercise of power, perhaps the least spectacular but probably the most common. The way in which compliance is secured, however, has important consequences for the manner in which individuals attach themselves to organizations and for the more general issue of organizational effectiveness. If inappropriate power forms are used, the organization is likely to be less effective than it might otherwise be. We focused on one particular type of compliance suggested by Etzioni's scheme, moral involvement, and its important role in voluntary organizations.

A much more spectacular, and hence often more interesting, outcome of the exercise of power is conflict. Although compliance is probably the most common response to power, conflict—the mobilization of resources to resist attempts to exercise power—is far from unusual, and thus is reasonably viewed as a normal state of an organization. We discussed a number of different types of conflict that commonly occur in organizations, reflecting different bases (differentiation, overlapping functions or responsibilities, hierarchical relations). One of the most frequently studied types of conflict in organizations involves relations between professionals and their nonprofessional, hierarchical superiors. This can be seen as a special case of overlapping functions, fundamentally due to the ambiguity in relative authority of managers and professionals. As organizations rely more and more on workers with socially legitimated expertise (sometimes referred to as "knowledge workers"), this is apt to be an increasingly important issue for both researchers and practitioners.

Although there is a tendency to view conflict as "bad," its prevalence in organizations makes this conclusion rather dubious; conflict can yield both positive and negative outcomes for individuals and for organizations. On the one hand, interdepartmental conflict can enhance organizational performance in some situations (Lawrence and Lorsch, 1967). It can also enhance individual performance as attention is focused and more energy is used. As noted earlier, some writers such as Rahim (1986, 1989) see conflict management as a sound management tool.

Unfortunately, there is a darker side to all of this. As Clark (1988) notes:

> With unabashed commitment to the goals of negotiation, out-of-court settlements of enormous variety, and the powers of information, flexibility, and limited liability . . . risk and conflict management have become enablers of the transformation of many organizational actions from rule-guided competition to a more adventuresome conflict posture. The spirit of deregulation, the calls for improved organizational productivity, and the corporate drive to become "lean and mean," the frantic search for excellence and improved ratings all may be feeding the fires of organizational conflict at the expense of the rules of competition. (p. 154)

Like conflict, conflict management can get out of hand. Conflict becomes a tool by which the powerful can manipulate situations to the detriment of the less powerful, even without their cognizance of being manipulated. To make matters even worse, the civility with which conflict management was accomplished until recently has disappeared. Now, with restructuring and hostile takeovers, honor and dignity have been replaced by a bottom-line mentality that can take the form of vengeance (Morrill, 1991).

Power and its outcomes are central organizational processes. They can contribute to and detract from organizational effectiveness. In the next chapter, we turn to another organizational process—leadership—which also has a relationship to effectiveness, but as we will see, the relationship is much more problematic than is commonly believed.

EXERCISES

1. Describe two resources that provide people with power (not authority) in your two organizations. What allows them to control these resources?
2. Describe three instances of the exercise of power in your organizations, and discuss the outcomes in terms of compliance and conflict.

Chapter 5

Leadership

───────────◆•───────────

OVERVIEW

Leadership in organizations is a popular topic. In this chapter we consider leadership as just one component in understanding organizations. We begin (and conclude) by noting that leadership is not the easy answer for all that is good or bad in organizations. The first step is to define leadership and consider its functions. Next, we review efforts to define what qualities or conditions determine who is apt to be defined as a leader. We then consider some of the outcomes of leadership. The difference between leadership at the top of organizations and at other levels is an important consideration in evaluating the impact of leadership. Studies of top leadership succession or change are analyzed to help determine the importance of leadership. Finally, leadership in voluntary organizations is considered. Here, leadership can play an important role, but may require different skills and abilities than leadership in traditional work organizations.

Probably more has been written and spoken about leadership than about any other topic considered in this book. Whether the concern is with a local school district, a business corporation, an athletic team, or the nation, there seems to be a persistent assumption that new leadership can produce dramatic changes in the organization. Anyone who follows sports is aware of the air of expectation surrounding the appointment of a new coach or manager. University presidents are selected by blue-ribbon committees with extensive inputs from many different parties, and all members of the search committee are acutely conscious of the potential importance of the outcome. The impact on the organization of the appointment of a new chief executive officer at a large corporation is often the subject of several weeks' worth of lengthy speculation and analysis by the business press.

The phenomenal changes in Eastern Europe and South Africa in 1989 and 1990 were frequently viewed from the perspective of leadership. Interestingly, from the point of view of this analysis, the changes were not attributed only to leadership but also to sweeping historical events. Those sweeping historical events are labeled environmental changes in this analysis.

At election time in labor unions and other political organizations, the assumption is always made that the reelection of the old or the election of the new leaders will make an important difference in the continuing operation of the organization. In short, leadership would seem to be the crucial concept to understand about organizations.

The perspective presented in this chapter is quite different. The research and theory to be examined indicates that leadership is heavily constrained by many of the factors discussed in previous chapters—organizational structure, power coalitions, and environmental conditions. This is not an "anti-leadership" position. Rather, it is an examination of leadership in the contexts in which leadership takes place.

WHAT IS LEADERSHIP?

Part of the general fascination with leadership probably is due to the belief that leadership is an easy solution to whatever problems are ailing an organization. Of course, it takes only a little thought to realize that whether new leadership can mask inappropriate structural arrangements, power distributions that block effective actions, lack of resources, archaic procedures, and other, more basic organizational problems is very problematic. Despite these common constraints on leaders, leadership is a topic that continues to capture the imagination of people from all walks of life, including academic scholars. As Gary Yukl (2002) notes:

> Leadership is a subject that has long excited interest among people. The term connotes images of powerful, dynamic individuals who command victorious armies, direct corporate empires from atop gleaming skyscrapers, or shape the course of nations. The exploits of brave and clever leaders are the essence of many legends and myths. Much of our description of history is the story of military, political, religious, and social leaders who are credited or blamed for important historical events, even though we do not understand very well how the events were caused or how much influence the leader really had. The widespread fascination with leadership may be because it is such a mysterious process, as well as one that touches everyone's life. (p. 1)

What is leadership? Leadership is a special form of power, one that involves "the ability, based on the personal qualities of the leader, to elicit the followers' voluntary compliance in a broad range of matters. Leadership is distinguished from the concept of power in that it entails influence, that is, change of preferences, while power implies only that subjects' preferences are held in abeyance" (Etzioni, 1965:690–91). For our purposes, Etzioni's general definition is a useful one. That followers do in fact alter their preferences to coincide with those of the leader is an important consideration. Leadership entails motivating followers to achieve the outcomes that the leader seeks, and effectively, this requires them to adopt preferences for those outcomes. Katz and Kahn (1978) follow this same line of reasoning when they note: "We consider the essence of organizational leadership to be the influential increment over and above mechanical compliance with the routine directions of the organization" (p. 528). Thus, leadership involves more than simply the normal exercise of authority that is based on a position in the organization or claimed by a member or members of organizations because of the formal requirements of their jobs. It often involves attributions of particular traits and abilities to people by their followers (Meindl, Ehrlich, and Dukerich, 1985).

Functions of Leadership

What do leaders do? Over the years, a variety of efforts to catalogue the main tasks and functions of leaders have been made (e.g., Borman and Brush, 1993). The list by Yukl and his colleagues (1990), which identifies fourteen separate functions, is one of the most comprehensive. Included on their list are planning and organizing, problem solving, clarifying, informing, monitoring, motivating, consulting, recognizing, supporting, managing conflict and team building, networking, delegating, developing and mentoring, and rewarding. While it may be the case that all leaders must carry out these tasks to some extent, their relative importance for the leadership role is apt to depend on the leader's position in the organization, a point that is sometimes recognized in principle, but too often neglected by researchers involved in empirical research on leadership.

As indicated above, leadership is not confined to any particular group or any level within an organization, and at least in theory, does not necessarily involve formal authority. Nonetheless, the vast majority of studies of leadership have focused on persons who have been assigned "a leadership position," that is, who have some authority by virtue of their position. Many of the early leadership studies were concerned, in particular, with first-line supervisors—lower-level military officers, manufacturing foremen, and so forth. This is worth noting because the hierarchical level occupied by a person and, especially, whether a person *has* formal authority or not are apt to be importantly related to the kinds of responsibilities and tasks that are required of him or her as leader.

For example, Selznick (1957) specified four major functions of formal leaders. The first is to define the institutional (organizational) mission and role. This is not a one-time issue, but must be viewed as a dynamic process, since the mission must evolve as the world changes. The second task entails the "institutional embodiment of purpose," which involves choosing the means to achieve the ends desired, or ensuring that the structure reflects and is designed to accomplish the mission effectively. The third task is to defend the organization's integrity. Here values and public relations intermix: Leaders must secure support for the organization from both the public and their own members, without allowing either external or internal constituents to fundamentally reshape the organization's mission. Both constituencies must be persuaded of the value of the organization's defined mission. The final leadership task is the ordering of internal conflict (pp. 62–63). Clearly, these functions are very relevant to leaders at the highest level of an organization.

On the other hand, they are generally much less relevant to the jobs of lower-level managers and supervisors. At this level, the functions of transmitting information, clarifying job expectations, and monitoring individuals' behavior to ensure that it is in compliance with formal structure are likely to be more critical aspects of leadership. Thus, actions that might contribute to effective leadership at one level may be much less appropriate or useful at another level. Leadership at the top level in the organization has the greatest impact on the organization but involves behaviors and actions very different from those taken by leaders in the first-line supervisor position.

As noted, the impact of differences in the organizational level or position a leader occupies has not always been given close attention in research and theories of leadership. This is an important caveat to keep in mind when considering different theories and interpreting findings of various studies that we describe below.

Components of Leadership

Trying to sort through and distill the main findings from the profusion of research on what determines who becomes defined as a leader is a daunting task. We start with the observation that there are three general types of factors that have been the focus of researchers' attention: more or less permanent characteristics and traits of individuals; behaviors and styles that individuals may exhibit (that are, presumably, more subject to conscious alteration by individuals); and characteristics of followers and/or particular situations. Most contemporary theories suggest that leadership is a complex mix of all of these factors (Yukl, 2002), but for ease of presentation we will begin by considering them separately.

Individual Characteristics.   The ideas expressed thus far have implied strongly that individual characteristics are crucial for the leadership role. This notion can easily lead to the conclusion that leadership is an innate quality of individuals, that some people are just "born leaders," while others are not. Indeed, much of the earliest work on leadership was characterized by this notion, and researchers following this tradition spent many years trying to identify the key leadership traits.

However, this effort was largely abandoned by the 1950s because no limited set of common leadership traits could be consistently identified (Gouldner, 1950). A huge set of traits were examined by different researchers, ranging from physical characteristics (e.g., height) to cognitive characteristics (e.g., intelligence) to social psychological characteristics (e.g., extraversion). But studies produced mixed and ambiguous results, and overall, the findings raised serious questions about whether any particular individual characteristics could be found that clearly distinguished leaders from followers.

Within the past decade or so, however, there has been some revival of interest in the link between personality traits and leadership. This revival has been sparked, in part, by focused attention by psychologists on what are referred to as "the big five" personality characteristics: "surgency" (or extraversion), conscientiousness, emotional stability, agreeableness or cooperativeness, and intellect (Digman, 1990). Personality theorists argue that these five dimensions capture critical aspects of personality (more or less permanent psychological orientations of individuals) that importantly distinguish among individuals in terms of behavior. Based on Stogdill's (1974) review of previous work on personality and leadership, Hogan, Curphy, and Hogan (1994) claim that leaders are distinguished by higher levels of extraversion, conscientiousness, emotional stability, agreeableness, and intellect. They argue that studies of emergent leaders, in particular, suggest the importance of such characteristics in distinguishing leaders from followers. "Emergent leaders" are individuals who are identified as leaders by members of groups in which no one was formally appointed to be leader ("leaderless groups"). It may be that individual characteristics play a more important role in influencing definitions of leadership when individuals lack formal positions of authority than when they have such authority.

Leader Behavior and Styles.   Researchers' discouragement with trait approaches to leadership led to increased attention to particular kinds of *behaviors* that might characterize leaders. A number of early studies with this focus provided evidence that leadership often involved two very different types of behaviors, one emphasizing the accomplishment of specific tasks, and the other emphasizing expressive activities and interpersonal relations. This distinction was confirmed by both laboratory studies (see, for example, Bales, 1953; Bales and Slater, 1955), and field studies, including two sets of well-known leadership studies conducted at Ohio State and University of Michigan in the late 1940s. Slightly different terms for these two types of behaviors were used by different researchers. In the Ohio State research, for example, task-oriented behaviors were referred to as "initiating structure," while the Michigan researchers referred to them as "production-oriented." Behavior focused on maintaining good interpersonal relations among group members was labeled "consideration" by the Ohio State group, and "employee-oriented" by the Michigan group.

This distinction provided the basis for a number of theorizing efforts. For example, Etzioni (1965) developed a "dual leadership" approach to organizations, suggesting that, because a task orientation was apt to conflict with an interpersonal orientation, in most cases leadership will rest in the hands of more than one person. He also argued that organizational demands determine which behaviors are most important to effective leadership, with interpersonally oriented behavior more critical in normative organizations and task-oriented behavior in instrumental organizations. On the other hand, others argued that it is possible for leaders to exhibit both types of behavior, and that this combined orientation is necessary for truly effective leadership (Blake and Mouton, 1964).

Other lines of work further elaborated on behavioral aspects of leadership by focusing specifically on decision-making behavior, or leadership style. For example, Vroom and Yetton (1973) identified four styles of decision-making: authoritarian (or autocratic); consultative; delegative; and group-based (or participative). The first, as it sounds, involves making decisions independently, without seeking input from the group; consultative decision-making entails gathering information and suggestions from group members and then making an independent decision; delegative involves providing relevant information and decision criteria to one or more group members and then allowing them to make decisions; and participative entails involving the group in formulating a problem and possible solutions, as well as in selecting among those options. This typology of decision-making styles is similar to that proposed by House (1971), who also identified four types of leaders based on their decision-making styles. Both approaches assume that a given individual is capable of exercising different styles of leadership, and each suggests particular conditions under which a given style is most effective for leaders.

It is important to reiterate that leadership at the top of an organization is vastly different from leadership at the first-line supervisory level, and that different behaviors and decision styles may be more or less appropriate to a given level. For example, the distinction between task-oriented and interpersonally oriented behaviors is most applicable at the first-line supervisory level and is less relevant at top levels because the people at such levels do not engage as much in direct supervisory behavior. By the same token, the use of a delegative or participative style by first-line supervisors is likely to be severely limited by the definitions of their responsibilities. And which kinds of behaviors and styles are more likely to enhance the leadership of individuals who lack formal authority remains to be studied.

Follower/Situational Characteristics.   The recognition that the importance of particular behaviors for being a leader may depend on particular situations that a group or organization is facing led to a number of studies focusing on the conditions that affect leadership. This work rests on the assumption that in one situation, an individual who exhibits certain behaviors and styles is more likely to be defined as a leader, whereas in other situations, different individuals, exhibiting different behaviors and styles, are more likely to be seen as leaders. This focus on situational factors is characteristic of a sociological approach to leadership. Situational approaches draw attention not only to the characteristics of the group and the environment in determining who is defined as a leader, but to the nature of interactions between leader and followers as well. The leader influences the behaviors of followers, of course, but their reactions, in turn, have an impact on the leader's own behavior (Hollander and Julian, 1969). Maintaining a leadership role requires the leader to behave in such a way that the expectations of the followers are fulfilled, or to modify those expectations in some way.

One situational characteristic that has been suggested as an important determinant of leadership is the degree to which tasks are structured, or there are generally agreed-upon solutions to handling problems facing the group. The importance of this factor has been highlighted in work by a variety of researchers, including Fiedler (1967), House (1971), Vroom and Yetton (1973), and others. These studies suggest that individuals who are more task-oriented and use more directive decision-making approaches are more likely to be accepted as leaders when the tasks and problems are highly structured. Interestingly, there is also some indication that this also holds at the other extreme: When tasks and problems are not at all well-defined, task-oriented, less participative styles may be more accepted by followers as well (House, 1971).

Other work suggests that intergroup relations—e.g., the degree of consensus among members on a given goal, and the extent to which conflict is likely—is an important determinant of leadership. When consensus is low and the likelihood of conflict is high, individuals with more participative decision styles (and presumably, a greater orientation to interpersonal relations) are more likely to be accepted as leaders (Vroom and Yetton, 1973).

One interesting determinant of leadership that has begun to be explored relatively recently emphasizes social expectations. Work by sociologists has demonstrated that individuals' perceptions and evaluations of others' behavior are shaped by the expectations those individuals hold initially. These initial expectations, in turn, are based on the others' observable status characteristics—sex, race, age, and so forth. As members of society, we acquire social definitions of those characteristics; for example, we expect men to act in certain ways and to have certain traits, and women to act in different ways and to have different traits. These definitions and expectations, then, shape our perceptions of and reactions to others, and can affect who we see as leaders (Berger et al., 1986). Similar ideas have been expressed by psychologists as implicit theories of leadership (e.g., Lord, DeVader, and Alliger, 1986). The importance of such expectations, or implicit theories, is indicated by many studies of the impact of gender on leadership and, more recently, by some cross-cultural studies of leadership as well.

The limited number of women in high-level leadership positions in organizations strongly suggests that gender affects individuals' ability to assume leadership roles. By the late 1990s, approximately 5 percent of the countries in the world were led by a woman (Adler, 1996), and the number of women at the helms of major corporations in the United States was slightly less—around 3 percent (Ragins, Townsend, and Mattis, 1998). One explanation for such low levels of women's representation in leadership positions is that, according to general social expectations, leaders will be men (Walker et al., 1996). In a classic study by Schein (1973), when individuals were asked to choose adjectives describing "good managers," they chose many of the same words that others had chosen to describe "typical men"; there was very little overlap in the adjectives chosen to describe "typical women" and "good managers." Similar results have been documented in a variety of other studies since this original research (see Carli and Eagly, 1999, for a review). Thus, there is considerable evidence that social expectations make it more likely that men will be assigned leadership roles, and make it easier for men to play these roles.

However, as a caveat to this general conclusion, it should be noted that some work suggests that women are more likely to emerge as leaders when group tasks require relatively complex social interaction and sharing of ideas and information (Eagly and Karau, 1991); this is consistent with common expectations that women will demonstrate stronger skills in managing interpersonal relations. Moreover, a study by Filardo (1996) comparing patterns of interaction in mixed-sex groups of African Americans and European Americans found that the propensity of men to assume leadership roles held only for the latter; among African Americans, men and women did not differ in the behaviors that are usually identified with leadership. This finding of subcultural differences within the United States is consistent with international, comparative studies of leadership indicating that *which* characteristics and behaviors are identified with leadership depend on culturally learned values and understandings (see, for example, Fu and Yukl, 2000).

As this partial review of leadership research suggests, a very wide range of possible determinants of leadership have been studied. Most current researchers believe that, in practice, individual, behavioral, and situational factors interact to affect definitions of leadership. Figure 5–1, from work by Yukl (1981), provides an idea of the types and range of factors that have been investigated or theorized to affect leadership, as well as leadership outcomes, such as group performance and organizational goal attainment (effectiveness in this conceptualization). It is to these latter outcome variables that we now turn.

THE OUTCOMES OF LEADERSHIP FOR ORGANIZATIONS

Many different variables have been examined as outcomes of variations in leadership approaches, but by and large, they reflect two main concerns, as suggested in Yukl's model: group morale and satisfaction, on one hand, and performance/productivity, on the other. The focus on these outcomes again reflects the emphasis of much of the research on first-line supervisors. They are much better suited to assessments of leadership in small groups than to leadership of large, complex organizations. However, there is a literature that may address issues of top-level leadership outcomes—studies of leadership turnover, or executive succession. Below, we will consider work on group-level outcomes as well as on leader turnover.

Satisfaction and Productivity

In general, research suggests that leaders who are more interpersonally oriented and those who use more participative styles in particular have followers with higher levels of satisfaction and morale. For example, Filley and House (1969),

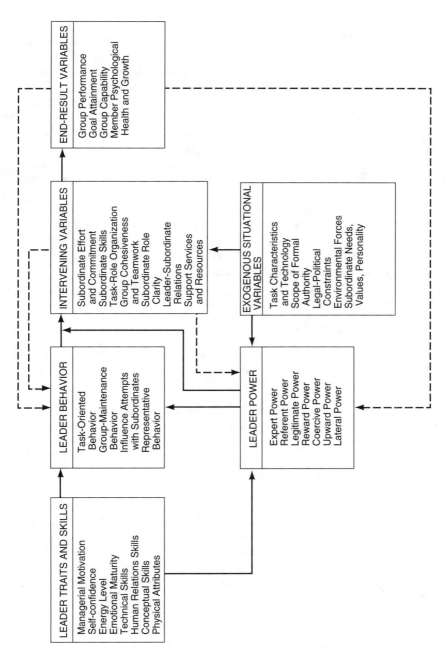

FIGURE 5–1 Leadership Variables

Source: Gary A. Yukl, *Leadership in Organizations* (Upper Saddle River, NJ: Prentice Hall, 1981), p. 270.

reviewing several studies, found supportive and participative leadership to be commonly related to several indicators of subordinate satisfaction and productivity, including: less intragroup stress and more cooperation; lower turnover and grievance rates; and widespread views of the leader as desirable.

The evidence here is confounded, unfortunately, by the possibility that the workers themselves may contribute to their greater satisfaction and productivity by their own attitudes and behavior, independent of those of the leader. They may be high-producing, positively oriented employees who do not require close supervision and direction, and thus permit their supervisors to engage in more participative behaviors. Despite this possibility, the evidence is consistent with the argument that supportive leadership does lead to more positive attitudinal responses among subordinates.

The impact of leadership approaches on productivity issue is not as clear. Filley and House's review (1969) indicated that the majority of research showed a positive relation between participative leadership and productivity, though others raise questions about this. For example, Hamner and Organ (1978), based on their own review of a different number of studies, noted:

> Generally speaking, we find that participative leadership is associated with greater satisfaction on the part of subordinates than is nonparticipative leadership, or, at worst, that participation does not lower satisfaction. We cannot summarize so easily the findings with respect to productivity. Some studies find participative groups to be more productive, some find nonparticipative groups to be more effective, and quite a few studied show no appreciable differences in productivity between autocratically versus democratically managed work groups (pp. 396–97).

Again, issues of causality can be raised: Does higher productivity result in leaders' relaxation of close supervision and direction, or does participative leadership lead to higher productivity? It is well established in the literature that there is no direct relationship between employee satisfaction and productivity. Thus, in considering leadership outcomes, one obvious question here is: What does the organization want? Another obvious question is: What do the workers want? If satisfied employees are desired, then the supportive approach has clearly been shown to be more effective. But what if the managers want high productivity, while the workers want a satisfying work environment? Short-run output gains may well be more easily achieved under an autocratic system, but this may lessen worker satisfaction and lower morale. To complicate matters further, there is evidence that when workers expect to be supervised in an autocratic style, supportive supervision can be counterproductive and threatening to satisfaction. The complexity of leadership choices is also pointed up by Fiedler's studies of the leadership process (Fiedler, 1967, 1972; Fiedler and Chemers, 1982; Fiedler and Garcia, 1987). Fiedler and colleagues found that in stable, structured situations, a stricter, more autocratic form of leadership is more likely to be successful, whereas in a situation of change, external threat, and ambiguity, more lenient, participative forms of leadership work better. Of course, in many organizations conditions will change in one direction or another. Whether shifting from a participative leadership style to a more autocratic one and back again will enhance employee satisfaction and performance or simply alienate employees is debatable.

Most of the studies just cited have relied on data about personnel who are at relatively low echelons in the organization. The general conclusion of this research, the demonstration that leadership at this level can and often does make a difference in objective performance indicators and the attitudes of the personnel involved, is important. Increased output or rapid acceptance of a new mode of organization are not inconsequential matters for organizations. The extrapolation of the conclusions from these studies to top leadership seems straightforward, but should be made with a good deal of caution because of lack of direct evidence. Whereas the range of behaviors affected by first- or second-line supervisors is rather small, if the jump is made to the range of behaviors affected by those at the top of the organization, the potential for a real impact of leadership can be readily seen. Even in performance and attitudes, the high-level subordinates of top administrators can be affected, and their performance in turn has an impact right down through the organization.

Whether these findings can be generalized to or are relevant to higher levels of an organization is, however, open to question. The nature of the limits on leadership and the leadership process itself can be further understood by evidence from studies of changes in personnel at the *top* of the organization.

Leadership Succession

Leadership or managerial succession takes place when a person in a leadership position is replaced. Replacement can occur for many reasons—transfer, resignation, firing, death, and so on. Succession provides a "test case" for the impact of leadership, since there are seemingly clear before-and-after conditions. Two early case studies of leadership succession provided evidence that leadership could make a huge difference in the functioning of the organization. Later studies, however, raised questions about the direction of causality in the relation of leadership change and organizational performance.

Probably the best known case study of managerial succession is Gouldner's *Patterns of Industrial Bureaucracy* (1954), an analysis of a gypsum plant and mine that underwent a major and dramatic change in top personnel. The old manager was very casual and indulgent, inclined to overlook company rules and official standards when these were inconvenient. He was well loved by the plant's employees, but productivity often suffered. The parent organization, concerned about the production record of the plant, replaced this manager with a new manager, who was brought in with the specific mandate of increasing production levels. The new manager faced two choices in accomplishing this mandate; he could either try to ingratiate himself with workers by continuing the established pattern of relations—a procedure that probably would not have worked in any event, since he did not have the personal ties of his predecessor—or he could try to change behaviors by enforcing the existing rules of conduct and performance. He chose the latter course, and as a result the organization shifted from an indulgency

pattern to one that was "punishment centered." This change led to a severe increase in internal tension and stress among employees, and ultimately, to a strike
(described in a later book by Gouldner).

The impact of leadership change in Gouldner's study is in direct contrast to
that found in another classic case described by Guest (1962), based on observations in a large automobile factory. Guest compares the studies:

> Both studies [his and Gouldner's] examine the process by which organizational ten-
> sions are exacerbated or reduced following the succession of a new leader at the top
> of the hierarchy. Succession in Gouldner's case resulted in a sharp increase in ten-
> sion and stress and, by inference, a lowering of overall performance. The succes-
> sion of a new manager had the opposite results in the present case. Plant Y, as we
> chose to call it, was one of six identical plants of a large corporation. At one period
> in time the plant was poorest in virtually all indexes of performance—direct and
> indirect labor costs, quality of output, absenteeism and turnover, ability to meet
> schedule changes, labor grievances and in several other measures. Interpersonal re-
> lationships were marked by sharp antagonisms within and between all levels.
>
> Three years later, following the succession of a new manager, and with no
> changes in the formal organizational structure, in the product, in the personnel, or in
> its basic technology, not only was there a substantial reduction of interpersonal con-
> flict, but Plant Y became the outstanding performer among all of the plants. (p. 48)

The dramatic differences between these two cases might lead one to some
sort of "great person" theory of leadership, with Gouldner's successor *not* a great
person and Guest's a great one. Guest correctly rejects that simple conclusion and
instead attributes the differences to the actions each manager took when confronted with an existing social structure. Although both new managers were expected to improve the situation, the new manager at the gypsum plant described
by Gouldner believed that he was expected to get rid of the personnel who were
not performing properly by enforcing rules to the letter—dismissing men, for example, for offenses that had previously been largely ignored. He felt that he
was—and probably this was true—under severe pressure to turn the organization
around in a short period of time. In Guest's study, the new manager at the auto
plant followed a manager who had tried to improve operations through close and
punitive supervision. Consequently, the new manager decided to take a different
path by using more informal contacts with his subordinates and bringing them
into the decision-making process and by relegating "rule enforcement to a second level of importance." This manager also worked through the existing organizational hierarchy, whereas the new manager at the gypsum plant, after some
failures with the established subordinates, brought in some of his own supporting
staff, thus setting up a formal hierarchy that was in a sense superimposed on the
existing social structure. Thus, Gouldner's new manager and Guest's new manager exhibited very different styles and behaviors.

There were some other important differences in the organizations that may
have also affected the consequences of managerial change, and indeed, may have
affected the styles the managers "chose." In the gypsum plant, top managers traditionally came from "inside," but the parent company broke with this tradition

by sending in an "outsider." In addition, the former manager of the gypsum plant had been active in the small, rural community surrounding the plant and was seen as "one of us." The former manager also had a cadre of subordinates tied to him through personal loyalty, who evinced little inclination to support the successor. The new manager thus had little recourse but to use the more formal bureaucratic mechanisms of control. At the automobile factory, on the other hand, the social setting was radically different. The factory was in a large metropolitan area, and the previous managers had not become involved in the community. The old manager was not particularly well liked within the factory. In addition, the factory had a history of relatively rapid turnover among top managers (the average tenure was three to five years), and it was common for new managers to come from outside the plant itself. Thus, unlike the gypsum plant personnel, the auto plant personnel were used to the kind of succession they experienced.

Guest moves beyond his data and draws a conclusion from the comparison of his and Gouldner's cases. He suggests that the success of the auto plant manager was due in large part to gaining the consent of the governed, or democratization of the leadership process. Gouldner, in a comment regarding Guest's research, emphasizes differences in the total situations in which the successions occurred. The gypsum plant event occurred during a period of recession, with labor relatively plentiful, but with the pressures for improvement probably more intense. He suggests that when the total situation is viewed, it is incorrect to conclude that one or another approach to the leadership process is always the correct one, even though in both of these cases the autocratic approach was less successful.

Both studies, however, indicate that top management has the potential for drastic impacts on the operations and performance of the organization. While not directly contradicting this, a later line of studies of succession called into question the direction of causality in this change: Does leadership change directly affect performance, or is it more a reflection of performance?

A number of the studies focusing on this question use a rather offbeat research site to investigate it—baseball and other sports teams. Baseball managers stand in an unusual organizational position. In relation to the total baseball organization, their role is similar to that of the first-line supervisor; but in relation to the playing team only, their role is similar to that of the top executive. Grusky (1963) was one of the first researchers to use sports teams to examine the relationship between managerial succession and organizational effectiveness. He noted that baseball teams are convenient units for analysis, because of their similarity in "official goals, size, and authority structure" (p. 21). They also offer a ready measure of effectiveness in wins–losses statistics.

His analysis showed that teams with the poorest records had the highest rates of succession. Although this may not be surprising, Grusky rejected the commonsense notion built around succession as the dependent variable—that low effectiveness leads to a vote of no-confidence from the owner, then a firing. Instead, he developed a more complicated analysis, arguing that poor team performance leads to managerial role strain which impairs the manager's performance, and that managerial changes disrupt existing relations among team members and the coaches, thereby further impairing team performance:

> . . . The availability of objective performance standards decreases managerial con-
> trol and thereby contributes to role strain. The greater the managerial role strain,
> the higher the rates of succession. Moreover, the higher the rates of succession,
> the stronger the expectations of replacement when team performance declines.
> Frequent managerial change can produce important dysfunctional consequences
> within the team by affecting style of supervision and disturbing the informal net-
> work of interpersonal relationships. The resulting low primary-group stability pro-
> duces low morale and may thereby contribute to team ineffectiveness. Declining
> clientele support may encourage a greater decline in team morale and performance.
> The consequent continued drop in profitability induces pressures for further mana-
> gerial changes. Such changes, in turn, produce additional disruptive effects on the
> organization, and the vicious circle continues. (p. 30)

This rather complicated explanation was challenged by Gamson and Scotch (1964). Based on a different approach to baseball teams' won–lost records, Gamson and Scotch advanced a "ritual scapegoating no-way casualty theory" (p. 70). This theory essentially suggests that the manager makes no difference:

> In the long run, the policies of the general manager and other front-office per-
> sonnel are far more important. While judicious trades are helpful (here the field
> manager may be consulted but does not have the main responsibility), the pro-
> duction of talent through a well-organized scouting and farm system is the most
> important long-run determinant. The field manager, who is concerned with
> day-to-day tactical decisions, has minimal responsibility for such management
> functions. (p. 70)

Gamson and Scotch note that the players are a critical factor, suggesting that at one point in baseball history, regardless of who was manager, the Yankees would have done as well and the Mets would have (or more accurately, could have) done no worse. When the team is doing poorly, the firing of the field manager is ritual scapegoating. "It is a convenient, anxiety-reducing act which the participants of the ceremony regard as a way of improving performance, even though (as some participants may themselves admit in less stressful moments) real improvements can come only through long-range organizational decisions" (pp. 70–71). Gamson and Scotch add that there does seem to be at least a short-run improvement in team performance in cases when the manager is changed in midseason. They suggest that this might be attributable to the ritual itself.

Grusky (1964), in a reply to the Gamson-Scotch criticism, further analyzes the data regarding midseason changes. Adding the variable of whether the new manager came from inside or outside the organization, he finds that the inside manager is more successful. He takes this as partial evidence that his theory of the dysfunctional consequences of disruption in internal relations is more rea-sonable, since the inside manager is likely to be aware of the interpersonal arrangements and the performance of his predecessor and thus less likely to make the same mistakes again.

Although these analyses were carried out many years ago, when major league baseball was a kinder and gentler business, without expansion and franchise shifts, free agency, and huge player salaries, the analyses of managerial succession in sports teams remain interesting and timely and provide a unique opportunity for analyzing leadership effects. Further studies of college basketball teams and major-league baseball teams concluded that managerial succession does not really change things—poor performance in the past leads to poor performance after succession (Allen, Panian, and Lotz, 1979; Eitzen and Yetman, 1972). A study of succession among coaches in the National Football League concluded that succession is cosmetic, which is consistent with the ritual scapegoating approach. The head coach is fired and replaced by a successor with little opportunity to change policies, procedures, or personnel in the short run (Brown, 1982).

This may seem at first glance to be a lot of words spilled over a relatively minor matter in the larger scheme of things, but the points that these authors are addressing are very relevant for the present analysis. Understanding whether changes in top leadership produce significant changes in the performance of the organization overall, or whether such changes merely reflect performance, is important to understanding the nature and function of leadership.

Studies of leadership turnover in other contexts also suggest that turnover may be as much of a product of organizational conditions and performance as a determinant of performance. Studies of business corporations indicate that political influences often determine leadership turnover. For example, Allen and Panian (1982) studied the effects of the locus of control in business firms on succession. In their study, direct family control of firms was defined as existing when the chief executive was a member of the family controlling the organization. Indirect family control characterized firms when the chief executive was not a family member, but the family had significant representation on the board of directors. A firm was defined as having managerial control when management dominated the board of directors. On the basis of data regarding 242 large industrial firms in the United States, Allen and Panian conclude:

> To begin with, there was a direct relationship between managerial power and corporate performance, on the one hand, and managerial tenure and longevity, on the other. Chief executives of more profitable firms and those who were members of controlling families usually had longer tenures and were usually older at the time of their succession than the chief executive officers of less profitable firms and those who were not members of controlling families. Similarly, there was an inverse relationship between managerial power and the probability of managerial succession during periods of poor corporate performance. Chief executive officers who were members of controlling families were somewhat less likely to experience succession during unprofitable or only marginally profitable years than chief executives who were not members of controlling families. (pp. 545–46)

What is notable about this piece of research is finding that family ties made top leadership succession less sensitive to performance variation than was the case when a chief executive officer did not have these family ties. Similar results were also documented in research by Boeker and Karichalil (2002).

Political influences are also indicated in research showing that chief executive officers tend to be succeeded by individuals with the same career specialization, such as finance, sales, or legal (Fligstein and Freeland, 1995). This succession process is based on previous strategies and power coalitions within the organization. This process can involve poor strategy following poor strategy, so that the process is not necessarily beneficial. It is based on the notion of strategic contingencies developed in Chapter 4.

Likewise, work on "insider" versus "outsider" succession to leadership positions suggests some of the ways in which organizational politics may moderate the impact of leadership change. As noted earlier, Grusky believes that whether the successor is an insider or an outsider (to the organization) makes a difference, suggesting that, for baseball teams at least, the insider is more successful. In regard to overall change in the organization, however, it appears that the person brought in from the outside will be more able to institute greater changes. The outsider is able to replace subordinates with selected lieutenants of his or her own choice. The constellation of immediate personnel around the outsider can be changed more easily than the insider's could be (Boeker and Karichalil, 2002; Helmich and Brown, 1972). A choice between an insider and an outsider is not always available, of course. Political considerations within an organization, its financial situation, and a dearth of outsiders may force an organization to go with insiders, thus limiting the amount of change possible.

The operation of political processes in leadership behavior can be seen in yet another light. Managers of unstable firms strategically manipulate causal attributions to manage the impression of the degree to which they are in control of the situation, even though they may not have any real control over organizational outcomes. They go so far as to claim responsibility for positive and negative outcomes, indicating their awareness and attempts at controlling the situation. These strategies are designed to maintain their positions (Salancik and Mindl, 1984).

Research also suggests that environmental and organizational conditions determine or moderate the impact of leadership on organizational outcomes. One study examining the length of tenure of academic department heads or chairs found that an important influence was the "paradigm development" of the various disciplines. This refers to the extent to which there is agreement on and use of a common theoretical basis. With higher paradigm development, the tenure of the head was longer. Larger size operated against long tenure. The effects of both size and paradigm development were found to be more pronounced in periods of environmental scarcity (Pfeffer and Moore, 1980). This is in line with the conclusion that the situation in which leadership is embedded needs study. In periods of uncertainty, in regard to both the environment and the nature of the organization itself (low-paradigm-development departments), there is likely to be a greater rate of leadership succession. This, in turn, is likely to have strong effects on leaders' ability to produce significant or enduring changes in the organization.

Other studies have indicated that size affects not only the likelihood of leadership turnover, but its impact as well. A study of the relationship between executive succession and stock-price changes related to the succession found significant positive effects of succession, in the form of stock-price increases, but only for external appointments in small firms. These stock-price increases were found when the departure of the former officeholder was announced along with the appointment of the successor (Reinganum, 1985). In a study of newspaper organizations, size was also found to have a significant effect on the likelihood of organizational failure following the succession of a newspaper's founder (Carroll, 1984b). Since most of these newspaper organizations were small organizations, they were more vulnerable to high failure rates to begin with, and the succession of the publisher would make the situation even more risky.

Another set of constraints on what the top leadership of an organization can do consists of the external environment of the organization. This is dramatically seen in an analysis of 167 major U.S. corporations by Lieberson and O'Connor (1972), who were concerned with the sales, earnings, and profit margins of the corporations over a twenty-year period. Their ingenious research considered the issue of executive succession and its impact on these performance criteria. The authors analyzed the effects of succession over one-, two-, and three-year periods to permit the maximum impact of leadership change to demonstrate itself. They also considered the economic behavior of the industry (for example, steel versus air transportation), the position of the corporation within the industry, and the state of the economy as a whole. Their findings are startling to those who really believe in leadership: *"All three performance variables are affected by forces beyond a leader's immediate control"* (p. 124; italics added). For sales and net earnings, the general economic conditions, the industry, and the corporation's position within it were more important than leadership. Leadership was important for profit margins but still heavily constrained by the environmental conditions. These findings were replicated (with slight modification) by Weiner (1977) and Salancik and Pfeffer (1977).

Lieberson and O'Connor's findings have created a great deal of controversy, since they fly in the face of much conventional wisdom and in the face of scholars who believe in leadership. Thomas (1988) reexamined the evidence of the sort that Lieberson and O'Connor used and developed an interesting interpretation. Thomas notes that changes in the order in which variables are entered into the regression equation regarding performance can essentially reverse the findings. Rather than reversing Lieberson and O'Connor's findings, which Thomas believes would be implausible, he suggests that the effects of leadership may not be visible at the aggregate level but such changes can still produce a substantial impact at the *level of the individual firm*. This is because, in the aggregate, the impact of cases of effective leadership cancel out cases of ineffective leadership, and thus there is no obvious impact of leadership change overall.

Another criticism of Lieberson and O'Connor concludes that the impact of organizational size and some contextual effects were not considered sufficiently (Day and Lord, 1988). Like Thomas, this analysis also argues that leadership ability was not considered, which, unfortunately, brings us back to a "great person" perspective.

Lieberson and O'Connor do not claim that leadership is unimportant, nor is that claim made here. Leadership is clearly important in changing organizational directions, developing new activities, considering mergers or acquisitions, and setting long-run policies and objectives. At the same time, from all of the evidence that has been presented, it must be realized that organizational and environmental constraints drastically limit the likelihood of significant change on the basis of leadership alone. The implications of such findings are crucial for organizational analysis. In established organizations, the impact of leadership is heavily constrained, and leadership change may not make much of a difference. For the new organization, leadership is likely to be much more important in determining organizational outcomes. Leadership is also crucially important in times of organizational crisis.

A heroic view of leadership can be contrasted with one that sees leadership as helpless to do anything about the events happening to the organization. Neither view of leadership, heroic or helpless, is typically very accurate, or very helpful to thinking about leadership. What is helpful is to realize that, statistically, half of all leaders are below average. Leadership is neither the solution nor the problem. Leadership is an important, even crucial, activity in some situations; in others there is little that a leader can do. Most situations, of course, fall between these extremes.

This discussion of leadership has ignored an important consideration—the motivations of the leaders. More than two generations ago, Berle and Means (1932) argued that corporate executives have become technical managers, separated from the concerns of capitalist owners. Others have argued that corporate leadership represents the modern capitalist class with phenomenal power and wealth in their organizations and in society as a whole (Allen, 1976; Zeitlin, 1974, 1976). From this perspective, organizational decisions are made on the basis of continued acquisition of power and wealth for owners. Spectacular cases of corporate misconduct and managerial greed, such as those at Enron and World Crossing, where corporate leaders intentionally concealed information about organizational performance and received enormous personal compensation and benefits from the corporation even while it was bordering on financial ruin, are consistent with this view (Huffington, 2003). However, whether such cases represent typical patterns of organizational behavior and relations is not clear.

One analysis of corporate presidents found that they are fired on the basis of poor profit performance, regardless of whether they are owners or managers, thus disconfirming the Berle and Means hypothesis about the separation of ownership and management (James and Soref, 1981). We have already noted that such changes in top leadership may be little more than cosmetic. It may not matter if the top leaders are interested in their own power or wealth, if they are really controlled by owners, or if they are simply technocratic managers, because their organizational roles and impacts would not differ. The question of the organization's outcomes for society remains an important one, however, because what is good for the organization may not be good for society. This is true whether the organizations are corporations, school systems, or churches.

LEADERSHIP IN THE VOLUNTARY ORGANIZATION

The discussion thus far has primarily concerned persons who have been formally appointed to positions of authority in work organizations. The situation is somewhat different in the voluntary organization, in which formal leaders are elected to office, or in which members have at least some official input into who is chosen for leadership roles. It has long been noted that in voluntary organizations there is a tendency toward oligarchy, that is, the emergence of a relatively small set of top-level officials who run the organization and who perpetuate themselves in office (Michels, 1949). Tendencies toward oligarchy exist in business organizations as well, of course. But because democratic representation of the members is a key goal or value in many voluntary organizations, its occurrence in these organizations is especially problematic.

Michels identified a number of factors that contribute to the formation of oligarchy. First, holding office often allows leaders to develop the kinds of skills and knowledge required for leadership—persuasive techniques, an understanding of organizational rules and procedures, and so on. Those who have not held office are apt to lack such inside information and thus are at a disadvantage when they compete for office. Second, existing leaders can reinforce their political power within the organization through patronage and other favors. In addition, over time, leaders become aware that they have a common interest in maintaining their positions, and thus help protect each other from challenges by rank-and-file members. Michels believed that because of these processes, the formation of oligarchies in organizations, even those founded on the principle of democratic representation, was inevitable; he referred to this as the "Iron Law of Oligarchy." However, other work suggests conditions that may mitigate such tendencies. A now-classic analysis of the International Typographical Union (Lipset, Trow, and Coleman, 1956) suggests a number of such conditions, including minimizing differences in the compensation and benefits received by leaders and other members, and encouraging the high levels of social interaction and a strong sense of community among the membership.

Even when oligarchy is unlikely to be a problem (e.g., in smaller social service organizations, cooperatives, or social clubs), leaders of such organizations face unique challenges because their roles are multiplex—they may be responsible for directing the activities of volunteers, but at the same time, they are often viewed as being in the employ of those same volunteers, as well as being expected to provide services to the volunteers, in terms of making their participation enjoyable. Valcour (2002), in an insightful analysis, considers how leaders of such organizations manage these multiplex roles. Her analysis is based on an ethnographic study of a cooperative nursery school, where teachers were responsible for using parent volunteers as classroom aides. In general, her analysis suggests that, to be effective, the leaders in such organizations need to get members to adopt and emphasize a conception of role relations in which leader-as-director is most prominent. Strategies for achieving this include using formal training sessions to convey and emphasize desired role relations to volunteers; spending extra time explaining the rationale for behaviors they ask of volunteers; and providing public recognition to volunteers who exhibit the kinds of behaviors (and thus demonstrate appropriate role orientation) that are desired. Overall, her study suggests that the key to leadership rests on detecting the role orientations that volunteers bring with them, and carefully reshaping those orientations as needed.

SUMMARY AND CONCLUSIONS

In this chapter we emphasized the need to consider leadership behavior within the context of a larger framework, the structure of the organization and the environment in which it was set. Leadership is contingent on a combination of factors: individuals' position in the organization; the specific task demands and environmental conditions that are confronted; the abilities and behaviors of those serving in leadership roles—all of these affect the outcomes of efforts to exercise leadership. Perhaps one useful conclusion from our review of studies of leadership is that it *is* a complex phenomenon. Thus, no single approach or style or set of prescriptions can be counted on to produce desired outcomes. Rather, a nuanced understanding of different approaches and styles, as well as some general idea of the conditions that *may* make one or the other more useful, may be most helpful for practice.

We noted that the impact of leadership may be clearest at the small group level. Whether leadership normally has an independent effect on the outcomes of large, complex organizations is more problematic. Many factors influence the overall performance of organizations—past performance, changing environmental conditions, and so forth. Studies of leadership succession suggest that these factors may typically be much more important in determining the fate of an organization than the policies and choices of the top leader. However, it may still be asked: Even if these factors are very important, perhaps most important in shaping organizational outcomes, do the top-level leaders' behaviors and decisions have an independent effect? Our intuitive answer to this question is "yes." We believe that the decisions that leaders make often set in motion forces that fundamentally reshape organizations (in unintended as well as intended ways) and determine their fates. But these forces are apt to take time to play out in an organization; hence, the ultimate impact of these decisions is apt to be extremely difficult to evaluate in the short run. This suggests, though, that part of understanding leadership involves understanding decision-making processes in organizations, and it is to that topic that we now turn.

EXERCISES

1. Descibe the leadership styles that are present in your two organizations.
2. What has leadership accomplished (or not accomplished) in your two organizations?

Chapter 6

Decision Making

———————————— ◆•————————————

OVERVIEW

In this chapter we consider the decision-making processes that lie behind changes in organizational structure, first discussed in Chapter 4, and other aspects of organizations. We begin by describing a line of work that has emphasized a view of organizations as systems of decision making. In this context, we consider research that has identified some of the organizational and environmental factors that shape decision making. We focus in particular on strategic decisions, those made at the top of organizations, since these decisions usually have the most profound effects on organizations. Decision making is not easy, nor is predicting the outcomes of decision-making efforts.

The aspect of organizations dealt with in this chapter can perhaps be illustrated best with two cases—that of the tragic *Challenger* Space Shuttle, which exploded so dramatically in 1986, killing all on board, and the similar deadly explosion of a second shuttle, the *Columbia,* seventeen years later. Both launches were the result of complex organizational decision-making processes that were purposively designed to prevent such tragedies, but which were affected by important biasing factors: different units' struggle to obtain scarce resources in a competitive environment; an organizational culture in NASA that contributed to the censoring of information; and a regulatory environment that was insufficient for the task (Vaughan, 1996, 1999). No one intended for these tragedies to occur. The launch decisions were not made by stupid or uncaring people. They were made by people like you and me, who were trying to do the best they could. To understand how these decisions were made and why, we need first to understand generally the nature of decision making in organizations.

ORGANIZATIONS AS SYSTEMS OF DECISIONS

The broadest and most systematic efforts to analyze how decisions get made in organizations are represented in work by Herbert Simon and his students and colleagues. This tradition is sometimes referred to as "the Carnegie School" because much of the work was done at Carnegie-Mellon University, where Simon was a long-time faculty member.

Bounded Rationality and Organizations as Hierarchies of Decisions

Simon's early efforts to conceptualize decision making in organizations (1957) grew, in part, from his skepticism toward prescriptive models of decision-making processes offered by economists. He argued that such models rested on a conception of "homo economicus" (or economic man) that had little basis in reality. "Homo economicus is characterized by the following: acting only in his self-interest, possessing full information about the decision problem, knowing all the possible solutions from which he has to choose as well as the consequences of each solution, seeking to maximize utility, having the ability to rank alternatives in order of likelihood of maximizing outcomes" (Zey, 1992:11). As Simon pointed out (1957), in contrast to these assumptions, real individuals have a very constrained cognitive capacity—that is, a limited ability to think of the range of possible options in a decision-making situation, to accurately anticipate what the consequences of those options will be, and to know how much they'll actually value one consequence versus another. Thus, rather than being fully rational, as economic models assumed, Simon argued that individuals were characterized by "bounded rationality." This concept implies that individuals typically are able to consider only a limited number of options in making decisions, and often select the first one that meets some minimal criterion, that's "good enough," rather than searching for the very best option. Simon labeled this approach to decision making as "satisficing," in contrast with the economic notion of optimizing. His explication of this view of decision making contributed to his winning the Nobel Prize in economics in 1998.

Given bounded rationality, Simon also argued that individuals could achieve a greater degree of rationality in decision making in an organization than they could if they acted on their own. This argument rests on a conception of organizations as a hierarchy of means-and-ends decisions. Individuals at the top of the hierarchy make broad decisions about general courses of action to be taken; these decisions define the ends that individuals at the next level will seek to achieve by making their own decisions about actions to be taken, actions that will become the means to achieving higher-level ends. Suppose, for example, a person decides to try to make a profit by manufacturing widgets, and that there are two units that need to be created for this, manufacturing and marketing. The person recruits two others to be the heads of these two units and charges them with making decisions about how to efficiently manufacture the widgets and market them, respectively. The head of manufacturing decides that there are three tasks that need to be taken care of for efficient manufacturing: obtaining supplies, carrying out production, and inspecting for quality. Thus, she gives three individuals under her command responsibility for making decisions about how to carry out each of these tasks. Her decision has defined the ends that her subordinates will concentrate on in making their decisions, and their decisions will provide the means for accomplishing her objective.

Because of this type of division of labor in decision making, Simon believed that the decisions made in organizations are likely to reflect a broader and more thoughtful consideration of factors than if a single individual had to think through these alone—that is, to be more rational. Note that this conclusion rests on the assumption that all members of the organization share the general aim of making a profit through the manufacture and marketing of widgets. When one refers to rationality, it's necessary to specify the referent—that is, for whom or what something is rational (Storing, 1962).

Organizational Structure and Decision Making

Simon followed Chester Barnard's (1938) arguments that when individuals join an organization, they agree to accept the inducements that the organization offers them in exchange for which they will make contributions to the organization. This includes allowing the organization to dictate their behavior within some broad limits, or within their "zone of indifference," and using the criteria and standards set by the organization in making decisions on behalf of the organization. In this context, the aspects of formal structure discussed in Chapter 4 are important because they provide the mechanisms through which organizations shape and control individuals' decision making (Perrow, 1986). In a series of analyses, Simon and his colleagues (Cohen, March, and Olsen, 1972; Cyert and March, 1963; March and Simon, 1958) elaborated on the impact of formal structure on decision-making processes in organizations.

Thus, they note that the formal division of labor defines the relevant issues that an individual is expected to attend to in making decisions. For example, when the head of manufacturing makes decisions, she focuses on their impact on the production of widgets, rather than on their impact for marketing and distribution. This suggests that as horizontal complexity increases, individuals generally will take a narrower, more specific set of issues into account in decision making. This may allow them to be more efficient in making decisions, or more thorough in terms of considering specific factors, but it is likely to lead them to neglect other issues that may bear on the ultimate decision. Hence, there is a need for persons at higher hierarchical levels to review and to coordinate among the decisions made at lower levels.

Likewise, rules and regulations are important because they direct individuals' attention to certain criteria and considerations in making decisions. March and Simon (1958) discuss "performance programs," collections of rules that guide decision making in particular areas. For example, a performance program for inventory decisions might contain the following rules: When inventory reaches a certain point, more stock should be ordered; to decide how much to order, the rate of sales over the past 30 days should be checked and used as a guide; at least three suppliers should be contacted to get competitive prices; and so forth. Higher levels of formalization thus allow individuals at lower levels of the organization to "make" decisions, leading to a greater degree of decentralization, because the criteria to be used are clear and help ensure standard outcomes. Similarly, the hierarchy of the organization is relevant to decision making because it defines which decisions are directly related to other decisions.

Politics, Conflict, and Decision Making

Resting on more realistic notions of individuals' cognitive capabilities than economic models that assume full rationality, this portrayal of organizational decision making provides an important and useful way of thinking about the connection between individual-level choices and actions, on one hand, and organizational-level characteristics, on the other (Perrow, 1986). One drawback, though, is that it does not give much attention to the possibility that different members of the organization may, in fact, have different aims, and that an agreement to allow the organization to define the premises of their decisions does not imply that they completely ignore their particular aims and interests. Recognition of this point has led scholars interested in organizational decision making to give more attention to the role of politics and conflict in decision making.

Consistent with the notion that decision making in organizations is affected by individuals' bounded rationality, political considerations are assumed to come into play because there is often uncertainty surrounding decision-making processes—uncertainty about which objectives are most important to an organization, and what means should be used to pursue a given objective. These core types of uncertainty were highlighted in the framework for thinking about different types of organizational decisions presented by Thompson (1967). As he noted, "decision issues always involve two major dimensions: (1) beliefs about cause/effect relationships and (2) preferences regarding possible outcomes" (p. 134). "Beliefs about cause and effect" refers to whether there is certainty about the outcome of an action choice. If we decide A, we are sure that B and only B will be the result—this is high certainty about cause and effect. "Preferences regarding outcomes" refers to the degree to which there is consensus about what the organization is or should be trying to achieve.

These basic variables in the decision-making process can operate at the conscious or the unconscious level. As an aid in understanding the process, Thompson suggests that each variable can be (artificially) dichotomized as indicated in Figure 6–1. In the cell with certainty on both variables, a "computational" strategy can be used. In that case the decision is obvious. For example, in simple inventorying, when the supply of a particular item dwindles to a particular level,

Preferences Regarding Possible Outcomes

		Certainty	Uncertainty
Beliefs About Cause/Effect Relations	Certain		
	Uncertain		

FIGURE 6–1   Decision Processes
Source: James D. Thompson, *Organizations in Action* (New York: McGraw-Hill, 1967), p. 134.

it is automatically reordered by a computer. Obviously, there is not likely to be conflict surrounding these decisions. The other cells present more problems and are thus more crucial for the organization.

When outcome preferences are clear, but cause and effect relationships are uncertain, Thompson suggests that organizational decisions require what he calls a judgmental strategy. Where the situation is reversed and there is certainty regarding cause and effect but uncertainty regarding outcome preferences, decision making requires a compromise strategy. Finally, when there is uncertainty on both dimensions, Thompson argued that an inspirational strategy for decision making is needed, if indeed any decision is forthcoming. Although Thompson doesn't precisely specify what is involved in an inspirational strategy, it presumably entails a significant effort to forge agreements between parties with different views—that is, political negotiations (Thompson, 1967:134–35).

STRATEGIC DECISION MAKING

The higher one goes in an organizational decision-making hierarchy, the greater the uncertainty surrounding both cause and effect relations and preference outcomes. As Cyert and March (1963) and Perrow (1968) point out, high-level goals of an organization are usually so broadly stated—"providing the highest quality education for students," "enhancing community health and well-being," even "maximizing profits"—that it is difficult to get consensus on what they entail, let alone how best to achieve them. Consequently, decisions that would be described as strategic—big, high-risk decisions made at high levels of organizations that significantly affect organizational outcomes—are often fraught with uncertainty, and hence, potential conflict.

Uncertainty and Strategic Decisions

Although we have a tendency to assume that decisions at high levels of organizations reflect high levels of rationality, or careful consideration of the best means to achieve some given end, evidence suggests that this assumption is very problematic. A good example of this comes from an analysis of General Motors (GM) in the United States. GM was one of the first organizations to adopt a formal structure known as the "M-Form" (for multidivisional); in this form, separate divisions are created for different product lines, and divisional heads are given responsibility for running these, much like independent organizations. Classic accounts suggested that this form was chosen for its high level of efficiency (Chandler, 1962). Instead, a more recent analysis suggests that, for most of its history, decisions about structure in GM were driven not so much by efficiency concerns as by efforts to obtain consensus among its managers (Freeland, 1997). This and other detailed accounts of strategic decision making in organizations (Beamish, 2000; Clarke, 1989; Tickner, 2002) suggest that considerations other than efficiency and effectiveness often influence strategic decisions.

One approach to thinking about how such decisions are made is provided by the "garbage can" model of decision making (Cohen, March, and Olsen, 1972). This model begins with the points noted by Thompson, that preferences and technology (cause and effect relations) are often unclear. In this context, Cohen and his colleagues argue that decisions are shaped by four more or less independent factors: perceptions of current problems facing the organization; potential "solutions," ideas or actions that individual members of an organization wish to champion (e.g., the adoption of a new computer system, creation of a new office or function, etc.); decision-making opportunities, meetings or committees that are assigned to make a recommendation for action; and participants, individuals who are present at decision-making opportunities. The model suggests that decisions result from random combinations of these factors in an organization—conceived of as a large garbage can in which the factors are mixed. That is, decisions are made in the context of particular decision-making opportunities (e.g., meetings) that may have been called to address a particular problem (which is nevertheless subject to redefinition), which are attended by certain individuals (but not others because of scheduling difficulties), and the members may or may not bring current pet projects with them. Needless to say, this approach suggests that decision outcomes are very unpredictable. Other research, though, suggests some structural constraints that "put a lid on the garbage can" (Levitt and Nuss, 1989) and make decision making somewhat more predictable than the image of garbage-can decision making suggests.

Constraints on Decision Making

One constraint on decisions, and thus on potential conflict surrounding decisions, is the existence of previous decisions that commit organizational resources to certain courses of action (Cyert and March, 1963). Such decisions are often embodied in organizational budgets and are psychologically as well as legally binding. By limiting options, these commitments serve to limit conflict over choices of action.

While having the benefit of reducing conflict, commitments can have negative consequences for organizational decision making as well. Organizations committed to losing courses of action are apt to continue to make decisions that make matters even worse. These are called escalation situations. Escalation situations occur when organizational projects have little salvage value, when decision makers want to justify their own past behavior, when people in a project are bound to each other, and when organizational inertia and internal politics combine to prevent a project from being shut down (Staw and Ross, 1989). A classic example is the process by which a power company on Long Island, New York, persisted in a decision to construct a nuclear power plant in the face of fierce opposition. The power company "stuck to its guns," or escalated, for twenty-three years. The cost of the project went from $75 million in 1966 to $5 billion when the project was abandoned in 1989 (Ross and Staw, 1993).

The concept of social embeddedness (Granovetter, 1985) suggests another factor that often constrains organizational decisions and thus limits conflict. The concept calls attention to the fact that organizations (as well as individuals) have enduring relationships with other actors and are part of ongoing social networks. These relations shape decisions both because they are an important source of information about different choices that may be made, and because in order to maintain the relations, organizations may have to take certain actions.

There are a number of studies that document the ways in which network ties shape the flow of ideas between organizations and thus affect organizational decisions (e.g., Beckman and Haunschild, 2002; Budros, 2002; Guler, Guillen, and MacPherson, 2002; Westphal, Seidel, and Stewart, 2001). For example, a study by Davis (1991) of business firms' adoption of poison pills (legal arrangements that make it difficult for other firms to acquire a given firm without the consent of its board) indicated that such adoptions were strongly affected by whether members of the board of a firm considering adoption were also on boards of other firms that had already adopted this arrangement. Davis (1991) concludes:

> Part of the impact of ties to adopters can be explained with reference to the nature of boards as decision-making groups. When the board is faced with a decision, such as whether to adopt a poison pill, the opinions of those with relevant previous experience naturally will be given more weight. . . . Yet the evidence presented here indicates that the more a firm was tied to others that had adopted a poison pill, the more likely it was to adopt a pill itself (up to a point), a finding that suggests a normative element: The knowledge that several interlock partners had adopted poison pills provides information above and beyond the simple pros and cons of adoption that having one or two directors with prior poison pill experience would give. (pp. 607–08)

As this last point indicates, apart from their informational influence, social ties may affect organizational decisions because they make organizations more responsive to interorganizational norms. A study of the semiconductor industry examined the formation of a research-and-development consortium among highly competitive firms and found that individuals and firms in this consortium developed a "moral community" in which both made contributions to the industry without regard for immediate and specific paybacks (Browning, Beyer, and Shetler, 1995:113). Similarly, research on alliances between firms shows that repeated alliances lead to trust between organizations, which then becomes the basis for additional alliances (Gulati, 1995).

Although such decisions may or may not be based strictly on economic calculations, they may yield positive economic outcomes. Thus, research on the garment industry in New York City found that embeddedness, in the form of trust between and networks among garment firms, was related to higher survival rates;

firms that relied solely on "arm's-length" economic transactions were more likely to fail (Uzzi, 1996, 1997). On the other hand, a study of the migration of manufacturing plants from New York State between 1969 and 1985 (and there was a lot of migration) found that firms that had links to local communities in the form of material, social, and political ties were less able to make such moves, even when production costs could be considerably reduced. Not surprisingly, the less mobile firms were in more peripheral industries. Firms in core industries were more able to move (Romo and Schwartz, 1995).

Although strategic decisions in organizations may be constrained by the considerations described above, this is not to suggest that decision makers are purely passive, or that these factors necessarily make decision outcomes predictable. As the garbage-can model of decision making suggests, *who* participates in decision-making processes is a critical factor that affects outcomes; this is not only because different participants see problems differently and bring different "solutions" with them to the table, but because they also have differing amounts of power. Thus, we need to consider how the distribution of power influences decision-making processes.

STRATEGIES OF POWER AND DECISION MAKING

In Chapter 5, we discussed the nature of power in organizations and some of the factors that influence its distribution in organizations. Authority, typically reflected by the positions individuals hold in an organizational hierarchy, is an important aspect of power. Thus, the opinions and aims of those with more authority often carry more weight in decision making. But there are potential costs to making decisions under conditions of high uncertainty: Decisions that turn out badly may affect decision makers' credibility and their ability to exercise influence in later decision-making situations. "Well, it seemed like a good idea at the time." That phrase, which we have all used in our personal lives, also characterizes organizational decisions. The quality of decisions is judged over time. The forty-plus years of Soviet rule in Eastern Europe appeared to be successful decision making on the part of the Soviets. The Ford Motor Company produced both the Mustang and the Edsel. Junk bonds appeared to be a good investment strategy in the 1980s for many pension funds. What appear to be successful, rational decisions at time 1 are often problematic at time 2. Because of this, those with authority to make strategic decisions, such as CEOs and high-level administrators, may resist making the decisions by themselves and leave such decisions to groups or committees (Jackall, 1988). Nonetheless, those in positions of authority have a number of ways to influence decision outcomes in ways that reflect their preferences.

Agenda Setting

One key influence mechanism is through control of the agenda—defining what issues will be discussed, and in what order (Bachrach and Baratz, 1962). Defining an agenda shapes not only what issues will be discussed, but what issues will *not* be discussed. Thus, in a meeting held to make decisions about a company's financial situation, workers' compensation levels may be included as an item for discussion, but compensation levels and pension packages for high-ranking managers omitted.

Moreover, research suggests that the order in which items and issues are discussed can have strong effects on decision outcomes. This is partly because, given a fixed amount of time for a meeting, items that are placed earlier on the agenda are likely to receive more time and attention; decisions made near the end of the meeting may be made more quickly and participants may have less inclination to debate them. Thus, in setting the agenda, individuals may put the issues that they wish to push through quickly toward the end. In addition, since decisions are made in a sequence, decisions that are made earlier may entail commitments that affect subsequent decisions, resulting in an escalation of commitment to a course of action (Pfeffer, 1981). For example, suppose in a college faculty meeting there are two issues to be discussed: changing required courses, and staffing. If a department can persuade the rest of the college that a particular course should be required, then it is in a position to argue for additional faculty lines (for faculty to teach this course) in the subsequent discussion of staffing.

Controlling Information

Information is part of the communication process within organizations. As will be seen in the next chapter, the communication process itself is almost guaranteed to withhold, expand, or distort information. And as noted in Chapter 5, control of information can be an important source of power and have clear effects on decision-making outcomes. Although top-level members of an organization usually have access to more information than lower-level members, which can provide them with more influence in decision making, this is not always the case. As pointed out in Chapter 5, individuals or units that have more contact with organizations, groups, and individuals outside the organization that provide it with critical resources often exercise relatively high levels of power within an organization. By selectively providing information about these resource providers, those individuals or units determine what organizational actions are deemed appropriate and necessary for the continuation of resource support. March and Simon (1958) discuss this in terms of the "absorption of uncertainty." Since securing resources from the environment is a major source of uncertainty in most organizations, those who broker information about key aspects of the environment "absorb" the uncertainty—and accrue influence within the organization.

Control of information from *within* the organization may also be becoming increasingly important, as more and more organizations employ sophisticated tools, including complex, electronically accessible databases containing data compiled by organizational members, as sources of information to be used in decision-making. Research suggests that organizational members who limit the amount of information that they make available through such databases, providing an appearance of quality and selectivity, are apt to be more influential (because the data they make available are given more attention) than those who provide a lot of information. This less-is-more strategy is particularly effective when many individuals are entering information in the database. Under these conditions, users of the database pay more attention to sources that appear to offer information more selectively (Hansen and Haas, 2001).

Forming Coalitions

Another way in which decision-making outcomes are influenced is through the selection of individuals to participate in a decision-making group (Padgett, 1980). Selecting organizational members who are likely to form a coalition that will support a particular choice allows top-level managers to ensure that the decision they favor is likely to be recommended. In addition, inclusion of expert outsiders, such as consultants, who may become part of the coalition, can increase the probabilities of this outcome (Bacharach and Lawler, 1980; Pfeffer, 1981).

Most strategic decisions are centered at the top of organizations, since that is where the power lies. At the same time, there are instances in which lower-level subordinates are brought into the process. As we have seen previously, participation by subordinates has mixed consequences for the organization and the participants. The same is true of decision making. Greater participation can actually be dysfunctional if the participants already feel satisfied or even saturated with their role in decision making (Alutto and Belasco, 1972). Typically, though, bringing them into the decision-making process increases their acceptance of the decision that is made. A useful insight on participation in decision making is that if a decision is important for the organization, a nonparticipative style is likely to be used; if the decisions are important for the subordinates in regard to their own work, a more participative approach will be taken (Heller, 1973). If the organizational decision makers believe that the subordinates have something to contribute to the decision or its implementation, then participation is more likely.

SUMMARY AND CONCLUSIONS

Decision making involves both substance and politics and both economic and socially embedded rationality. It also involves limited rationality in all issues. Nonetheless, we plunge ahead. When and if we are participants in decision making, we do try to do the best we can. To return to our theme, decisions rarely, if ever, provide perfect solutions and they never last over time, but we continue to make them.

Since information is central to decision making, and since communications allow information to flow, we will now examine this process in organizations.

EXERCISES

1. Describe the decision-making processes in your two organizations. What are the issues? Who participates?
2. Describe the forms of rationality present in decision making in your two organizations.

Chapter 7

Communication

—•—

OVERVIEW

This chapter deals with a topic that has been implicit and explicit throughout the preceding chapters. Power is exercised, leadership is attempted, and decisions are made on the basis of communication. Organizational structure shapes communication. This chapter starts with the obvious fact that individuals are at the core of the communication process. Individuals perceive or misperceive. Organizational factors are then introduced. These include the vertical dimension and the horizontal dimension, as discussed in Chapter 3. Both individual and organizational factors contribute to communication problems, such as omission, distortion, and overload. The chapter concludes with a consideration of possible solutions for communication problems.

Organizations are information-processing systems. A vivid metaphor sees the organization as a brain (Morgan, 1986). This imagery captures the idea that organizations receive and filter information, process it in light of what they have already learned, interpret it, change it, and finally act on it. Organizations also have memory lapses. To take the imagery even further, there are mind-altering stimulants and depressants—organizational highs and lows.

The communication process in organizations contains elements that are strongly organizational and strongly individual. At the individual level, consider the simple example of classroom examinations. If there were not individual differences in cognition and interpretation, everyone would give the same answer to an essay question. That obviously does not happen, as every student and faculty member knows. The organizational input into the communication process comes from the structured communication channels and the positions that people occupy. Organizational positions strongly influence the interpretation of communications by individuals. In this chapter the factors that affect the sending, receiving, perception, and interpretation of communications will be examined.

THE IMPORTANCE OF COMMUNICATION

Organizational structures, with their varying sizes, technological sophistication, and degrees of complexity and formalization, are designed to be or evolve into information-handling systems. The very establishment of an organizational structure is a sign that communications are supposed to follow a particular path. Power, leadership, and decision making rely upon the communication process, either explicitly or implicitly, since they would be meaningless in the absence of information.

Organizational analysts have ascribed varying degrees of importance to the communication process. Barnard (1938), for example, states: "In an exhaustive theory of organization, communication would occupy a central place, because the structure, extensiveness, and scope of the organization are almost entirely determined by communication techniques" (p. 91). This approach essentially places communication at the heart of the organization. More recently, Stinchcombe (1990) also made communication the essence of his analysis. Other theorists, however, pay scant attention to the topic (for example, see Aldrich, 1979; Clegg and Dunkerley, 1980). Instead of declaring that communication is either at the heart or at the periphery of organizational analysis, a more reasonable view is that communication varies in importance according to where one is looking in an organization and what kind of organization is being studied.

Communication is crucial for organizational managers and their work. Managers spend an overwhelming proportion of their time in communications (Kanter, 1977). These communications usually involve face-to-face interactions with subordinates, superiors, peers, and customers. There are also meetings of one kind or another. Mail and phone messages have to be answered. In short, the business of the managers is communication. It is estimated that 80 percent of managers' time is spent on interpersonal communications (Klauss and Bass, 1982). The work of clerical personnel is overwhelmingly concerned with information processing. Changing information technology is having a major and unfinished impact on managerial and clerical work, and thus on organizations, as we will see later in this chapter.

These intraorganizational differences are important. Equally important are interorganizational differences. Communication is most important in organizations and organizational segments that must deal with uncertainty, that are complex, and that have a technology that does not permit easy routinization. Both external and internal characteristics affect the centrality of communication. The more an organization is people and idea oriented, the more important communication becomes.

Even in a highly mechanized system, of course, communications underlie the development and use of machines. Workers are instructed on usage, orders are delivered, and so on. At the same time, the routineness of such operations leads to a lack of variability in the communication process. Once procedures are set, few additional communications are required. Although communications occur almost continuously in such settings, their organizational importance is more limited unless they lead to severe distortions in the operations.

The communication process is by definition a relational one; one party is the sender and the other the receiver at a particular time. The relational aspect of communication obviously affects the process. The social relations occurring in the communication process involve the sender and the receiver and their reciprocal effects on each other as they are communicating. If a sender is intimidated by a receiver during the process of sending a message, the message itself and the interpretation of it will be affected. Intimidation is just one of a myriad of factors that have the potential to disrupt the simple sender–receiver relationship. Status differences, different perceptual models, sexual attraction, and so on can enter the picture and lead to distortions of what is being sent and received.

These sources of distortion and their consequences will occupy a good deal of attention in the subsequent discussion. Ignorance of the potentiality for distortion has been responsible for the failure of many organizational attempts to improve operations simply by utilizing more communications. Once the importance of communications was recognized, many organizations jumped on a communications bandwagon, believing that if sufficient communications were available to all members of the organization, everyone would know and understand what was going on and most organizational problems would disappear (Katz and Kahn, 1978:430). This communications bandwagon was at the heart of the flurry of interest in organizational "culture" as the cure-all for organizational problems that appeared in the 1980s (Mohan, 1993). Unfortunately, organizational life is not that simple, and mere reliance on more and better communications cannot bring about major, positive changes for an organization.

Before we turn to a more comprehensive examination of communication problems and their consequences in organizations, a simple view of optimal communications will be presented. The view is simple because it is complementary to the earlier discussion of rationality and decision making.

Communications in organizations should provide accurate information with the appropriate emotional overtones to all members who need the communication content. This assumes that neither too much nor too little information is in the system and that it is clear from the outset who can utilize what is available.

It should be evident that this is an impossible condition to achieve in a complex organization. Indeed, organizations gather more information than they use but also continue to ask for more (Feldman and March, 1981). This is attributed to decision makers' needs for legitimacy. In addition, the communication process is inherently paradoxical and contradictory (Brunsson, 1989; Manning, 1992). Paradoxes and contradictions permeate organizational life.

In the sections that follow, the factors contributing to the impossibility of perfect communication systems will be examined. These factors range from those that are apparently inherent (through learning) in any social grouping to those that are peculiarly organizational. The focus will be primarily on communication within organizations. Communication with the environments of organizations will be considered later.

INDIVIDUAL FACTORS

Since communication involves something being sent to a receiver, what the receiver does with or to the communicated message is perhaps the most vital part of the whole system. Therefore, the perceptual process becomes a key element in our understanding of communications in organizations.

The perceptual process is subject to many factors that can lead to important differences in the way any two people perceive the same person or message. Even physical objects can be perceived differently. Perceivers may respond to cues they are not aware of, be influenced by emotional factors, use irrelevant cues, weigh evidence in an unbalanced way, or fail to identify all the factors on which their judgments are based. People's personal needs, values, and interests enter the perceptual process. Most communications take place in interaction with others, and how one person perceives the "other" in the interaction process vitally affects how a person will perceive the communication, since other people are more emotion-inducing than physical objects are. For example, research has shown that a person's interactions, and thus perceptions, are affected even by the expectations of what the other person will look like (Zalkind and Costello, 1962).

These factors are common to all perceptual situations. For the analysis of perceptions in organizations, they must be taken as basic conditions in the communication process. So it is obvious that perfect perception—that is, perception uniform across all information recipients—is impossible in any social situation. The addition of organizational factors makes the whole situation that much more complex.

Communications in organizations are basically transactions between individuals. Even when written or broadcast forms are used, the communicator is identified as an individual. The impression that the communication receiver has of the communicator is thus crucial in the interpretation of the communication. Impressions in these instances are not created de novo; the receiver utilizes his or her own learned response set to the individual and the situation. The individual's motives and values enter the situation. In addition, the setting or surroundings of the act of communication affect the impression. A neat, orderly, and luxuriously furnished office contributes to a reaction different from the one given by an office that looks and smells like a locker room. Since the perceptual process itself requires putting ideas and people into categories, the interaction between communicators is also subject to "instant categorization," that is, you cannot understand other people unless they are placed in some relevant part of your learned perceptual repertoire. This is often done on the basis of a very limited amount of evidence—or even wrong evidence, as when the receiver notes cues that are wrong or irrelevant to the situation in question (Zalkind and Costello, 1962:221).

Organizational position affects how communications are perceived or sent. In almost all organizations, people can be superordinates in one situation and subordinates in another. The assistant superintendent of a school system is superordinate to a set of principals but subordinate to the superintendent and the school board. Communications behavior differs according to one's position in a role set. If the individual is in a role in which he or she is or has been or feels discriminated against, communications are affected. A study found that women who had suffered discrimination in their roles had a lower feeling of autonomy than others in the same role. This in turn was related to distortions in the information that they communicated upward in the organization (Athanassaides, 1974).

All of these factors are further complicated by the well-known phenomenon of stereotyping. This predisposition to judge can occur before any interaction at all has taken place. It can involve the labels "labor," "management," "minority group," and any other group membership. The individuals involved are assumed to have the characteristics of the group of which they are members; in probably the vast majority of cases, however, the characteristics attributed to the group as a whole are distortions of reality. In the sense being used here, stereotyping is the imposition of negative characteristics on the members of the communication system. The reverse situation—attributing socially approved characteristics—can also occur, of course, with an equally strong potential for damage to the communication process.

Other factors that enter the communication process in somewhat the same manner are the use of the "halo effect," or the use of only one or a few indicators to generalize about a total situation; "projection," or a person's assuming that the other members of a communication system have the same characteristics as the person's own; and "perceptual defense," or altering inconsistent information to put it in line with the conceptual framework already developed. All the factors that have been mentioned here are part of the general literature on perception and must be assumed to be present in any communication system. They are not peculiar to organizations.

The characteristics of the perceived person affect what is perceived. Here are four conclusions from research regarding the perceiver:

1. Knowing oneself makes it easier to see others accurately.
2. One's own characteristics affect the characteristics that one is likely to see in others.
3. The person who is self-accepting is more likely to be able to see favorable aspects of other people.
4. Accuracy in perceiving others is not a single skill. (Zalkind and Costello, 1962:227–29)

These findings are linked to the more general considerations, such as tendencies to stereotype or project. It is when the characteristics of the perceived are brought into the discussion that organizational conditions become important. Factors such as age affect how a person is perceived (Zenger and Lawrence, 1989). The person may be labeled a sales manager (accurately or not) by a production worker, and the entire communication system is affected until additional information is permitted into the system. The situation in which the communication takes place also has a profound impact on what is perceived. This is particularly vital in organizations, since in most cases the situation is easily labeled and identified by the physical location.

Organizations are full of all kinds of information, including gossip. There is a great deal of variance in the degree to which people are in social networks and receive information, whether it is gossip or not. Thus, information itself and individuals are part of the paradoxical communication process.

ORGANIZATIONAL FACTORS

It has already been noted that organizations develop their own cultures, with language, rituals, and styles of communications. It is clear that organizations attempt to socialize their personnel so that communication problems are minimized (Pascale, 1985). Despite the presence of a common culture and socialization efforts, however, organizations contain the seeds of communication problems when their vertical and horizontal components are considered.

VERTICAL COMMUNICATION

Patterns of vertical communication have received a lot of attention, primarily because they are so vital in organizational operations. From our discussions of organizational structure, power, and leadership, it should be evident that the vertical element is a crucial organizational fact of life. Since communication is also crucial, the vertical element intersects in a most important way. Vertical communications in organizations involve both downward and upward flows.

Downward Communication.   There are five elements of downward communication (Katz and Kahn, 1978:440–43). The first is the simple and common job instruction, in which a subordinate is told what to do through direct orders, training sessions, job descriptions, or other such mechanisms. The intent of job instructions is to ensure reliable and consistent job performance. The more complex and uncertain the task, the more generalized the instructions. As a rule, the more highly trained the subordinates, the less specific the instructions are, because it is assumed that those individuals will bring with them an internalized knowledge of how to do the job, along with other job-related knowledge and attitudes.

The second element is more subtle and less often stressed. It involves the rationale for a task and its relationships to the rest of the organization. It is here that different philosophies of life affect how much this sort of information is communicated. If the philosophy is to keep the organizational members dumb and happy, little such information will be communicated. The organization may feel either that the subordinates are unable to comprehend the information or that they would misuse it by introducing variations into their performance based on their own best judgment of how the task should be accomplished. Even apart from the philosophy-of-life issue, this is a delicate matter. All organizations, even those most interested in the human qualities of their members, have hidden agendas of some sort at some time. If the total rationale for all actions were known to all members, the potential for chaos would be high, since communication overload would quickly occur. The danger of too much communication is matched by the opposite danger—too little communication—which also has strong potential for organizational malfunctioning. If the members are given too little information, and do not and cannot know how their work is related to any larger whole, there is a strong possibility that they will feel alienated from the work and the organization. Obviously, the selection of the best path between these extremes is important in the establishment of communications.

The third element of downward communication is information regarding procedures and practices within the organization. Like the first element (job instruction), it is relatively straightforward and noncontroversial. Here again, whether or not this is linked to the second element is problematic.

Feedback to individuals regarding their performance is the fourth element of the downward communication system. This is almost by definition a sticky issue, particularly when the feedback is negative. If the superior has attempted at all to utilize socioemotional ties to his or her subordinates, the issue becomes even more difficult. It becomes almost impossible when the work roles are so thoroughly set in advance by the organization that the worker has no discretion on the job at all. In these cases, only a totally conscious deviation would result in feedback. In the absence of deviation, there will probably be no feedback other than the paycheck and other routine rewards. Where discretion is part of the picture, the problem of assessment deepens, because feedback is more difficult to accomplish if there are no clear criteria on which to base it. Despite these evident problems, feedback is a consistent part of downward communications.

The final element of downward communication involves attempts to indoctrinate subordinates into accepting and believing in the organization's (or the subunit's) goals. The intent here, of course, is to get the personnel emotionally involved in their work and add this to the motivational system.

Downward communication takes place at all levels, from the top down. At each level it is interpreted by individuals, so that individual factors reenter our picture as information flows and is interpreted downward.

Upward Communication.   Contrary to the law of gravity, communication in organizations must also go up, even when nothing is going down. According to Katz and Kahn (1978):

> Communication up the line takes many forms. It can be reduced, however, to what people say (1) about themselves, their performance, and their problems, (2) about others and their problems, (3) about organizational practices and policies, and (4) about what needs to be done and how it can be done. (p. 446)

The content of these messages can obviously range from the most personal gripe to the most high-minded suggestion for the improvement of the organization or the world; and the messages can have positive or negative consequences for the subordinate, from a promotion or a bonus to dismissal. Whistleblowers are constantly in fear of dismissal. The most obvious problem in upward communication is again the hierarchy.

People are unlikely to pass information up if it will be harmful to themselves or their peers. Thus, the amount and kind of information that is likely to be passed upward is affected by hierarchy. Anyone who has been in any kind of organization knows that discussions with the boss, department head, president, supervisor, or other superior are, at least initially, filled with something approaching terror, regardless of the source of the superior's power in the organization.

Another facet of upward communication is important: Whereas communications downward become more detailed and specific, those going up the hierarchy must become condensed and summarized. Indeed, a major function of those in the middle of a hierarchy is the filtering and editing of information. Only crucial pieces of information are supposed to reach the top. This can be seen in clear relief at the national level, where the president of the United States receives highly condensed accounts of the huge number of issues of national and international concern. Regardless of the party in power, the filtering and editing process is vital in the hierarchy, since the basis on which things are "edited out" can have enormous repercussions by the time the information reaches the top. Here, as well as in downward communication, the perceptual limitations we noted earlier are in operation, so there is a very real potential for distorted communications and, more important, for decisions different from those that would have been made if some other editing process were in force (Halberstam, 1972; Wilensky, 1967).

There is an interesting technological twist here. Computer-based information technology is increasingly important in the organizational communication process. The twist is that top executives may not have computers in their own offices. They leave the handling of computer-based information to their staff and subordinates (March and Sproul, 1990). Only time will tell if this situation will change.

Dysfunctions of Hierarchy and Some Positive Outcomes

There are several specific dysfunctions of hierarchy for the communication process. In the first place, hierarchical divisions inhibit communications. There is a common tendency for people at the same status level to interact more with one another than with those at different levels. At the same time, there is a tendency for those in lower-status positions to look up to and direct friendship overtures toward those in higher-status positions. This increases the flow of socioemotional communications upward, but at the same time it leaves those at the bottom of the hierarchy in the position of receiving little of this type of input. This situation is further complicated by the fact that those in higher-status positions also direct such communications upward rather than reciprocating to their subordinates, thus reducing the amount of satisfaction derived for all parties.

A second dysfunction is that approval is sought from superiors rather than from peers in such situations. Nonperformance criteria enter the communication system, in that respect from peers, which can be earned on the basis of performance, can become secondary to approval-gaining devices that may not be central to the tasks at hand. The plethora of terms ranging from apple-polishing to more obscene expressions is indicative of this.

A third dysfunction has to do with the error-correcting function of normal social interaction. Interaction among peers tends to sort out errors and at least provides a common denominator through the interaction process. This is much less likely to happen in upward communication. Subordinates are unlikely to tell a superior that they think an order or an explanation is wrong, fearing for their own positions. Criticism of one's superior is clearly not the most popular form of communication in organizations (Blau and Scott, 1962:121–24).

These problems associated with upward communication in organizations are compounded by the factors affecting individual perception, which we discussed earlier. Since rank in an organization is a structural fact, it carries with it a strong tendency toward stereotyping. The very terms *management, worker, student, general,* and so on are indicative of the value loadings associated with rank. Status differences are necessary and do have their positive side; but the negative connotations attached to many of the stereotypes, and the likelihood that communications will be distorted because of real or assumed differences between statuses, build in difficulties for organizational communications.

In keeping with the earlier discussion in which it was noted that complex organizations contain paradoxes and contradictions, there are also beneficial aspects to hierarchical patterns for the communication process. The studies by Blau and his associates (1966, 1968), cited earlier, are a case in point. It will be recalled that in organizations with highly trained or professionalized personnel, a tall or deep hierarchy was associated with effectiveness. The explanation was that the hierarchy provided a continuous source of error detection and correction. The presence of experts in an organization also increases the extent of horizontal communications (Hage, Aiken, and Marrett, 1971). These can take the form of scheduled or unscheduled committee meetings or more spontaneous interactions. Communications are a vital source of coordination when organizations are staffed with a diverse set of personnel offering different forms of expertise (Brewer, 1971). If a tall hierarchy is found in an organization with a low level of differentiation in expertise, it is apparently due to the need for extensive downward communications. There is an additional aspect of hierarchy that is important. Unless one assumes that people always rise to a level just above that of their competence (Peter and Hull, 1969), the superiors may in fact be superior. That is, they may actually have more ability than their subordinates since they have more experience. If this is recognized and legitimated by the subordinates, some of the hierarchical problems are again minimized.

The most obvious contribution of a hierarchy is coordination (Hage, 1980). If one accepts the common model of communications spreading out in more detail as they move down the hierarchy, then the role of the hierarchy becomes clear. It is up to the superior to decide who gets what kind of communication and when. The superior becomes the distribution and filtering center. Given the vast amount of information that is potentially available for the total organization, this role is crucial.

HORIZONTAL COMMUNICATION

Communications in organizations go in more directions than up and down. Horizontal or lateral communication is a regular and important facet of organizational life. The focus of most analyses of communication has been the vertical axis. The horizontal component has received less attention, even though a greater proportion of the communication in an organization appears to be of this type. A study of a textile factory indicates that the lower the level in the hierarchy, the greater the proportion of horizontal communication (Simpson, 1969). This is not surprising, if for no other reason than that in most organizations there are simply more people at each descending level. This fact and the already noted tendency for communication to be affected by hierarchical differences make it natural for people to communicate with those at about the same level in the organization. And those at the same level are more apt to share common characteristics, making horizontal communication even more likely.

Communication within an organizational subunit is quite different from communication between subunits. Within-unit communication is "critical for effective system functioning" (Katz and Kahn, 1978:444). In most cases, it is impossible for an organization to work out in advance every conceivable facet of every task assigned throughout the organization. At some point, there will have to be coordination and discussion among a set of peers as the work proceeds. The interplay between individuals is vital in the coordination process, since the organization cannot anticipate every possible contingency. Communication within subunits contains much richer content than organizational task coordination materials. Katz and Kahn state:

> The mutual understanding of colleagues is one reason for the power of the peer group. Experimental findings are clear and convincing about the importance of socio-emotional support for people in both organized and unorganized groups. Psychological forces always push people toward communication with peers: people in the same boat share the same problems. *Hence, if there are no problems of task coordination left to a group of peers, the content of their communication can take forms which are irrelevant to or destructive of organizational functioning.* (p. 445; italics in original)

The implication here is clear. It is beneficial to leave some task-oriented communications to work groups at every level of the organization so that the potentially counterproductive communications do not arise to fill the void. This implication must be modified, however, by a reference back to the general model that is being followed here. Organizational, interpersonal, and individual factors are all part of the way people behave in organizations. If the organizational arrangements are such that horizontal communications are next to impossible, then there is little likelihood of any communication. Work in extremely noisy circumstances or in isolated work locales would preclude much interaction. (These situations, of course, contain their own problems for the individual and the organization.) On the other side of the coin, too much coordination and communications responsibility left to those who, through lack of training or ability, are unable to come to a reasonable joint decision about some matter would also be individually and organizationally disruptive.

Although it is relatively easy, in abstract terms, to describe the optimal mix of vertical and horizontal communications, another element of communications among peers is important. Since the communications among peers tend to be based on common understandings, and since continued communications build up the solidarity of the group, work groups develop collective responses to the world around them. These collective responses are likely to be accompanied by collective perceptions of communications passed to or through the work groups. These collective perceptions can be collective distortions. It is clear that work groups (as well as other interest groups) can perceive communications in a totally different light from what was intended. A relatively simple piece of information, such as a memo about possible reorganization, can be interpreted to mean that an entire workforce will be eliminated. Work groups can develop complete sets of meanings that are entirely different from what was intended.

Interaction among peers is only one form of horizontal communication. Another form, obviously vital, occurs between members of different organizational subunits. There is little research on this subject. The principal reason seems to be that such communications are not supposed to occur. In almost every conceivable form of organization, communications are supposed to go through the hierarchy until they reach the "appropriate" office, at the point where the hierarchies of the two units involved come together. That is, the communications are designed to flow through the office that is above the two departments or units involved, so that the hierarchy is familiar with the intent and content of the communications. In a simple example, problems between production and sales are supposed to be resolved through either the office or the individual in charge of both activities.

In reality, such a procedure occurs in only a minority of such lateral communications. There is a great deal more face-to-face and memo-to-memo communication throughout the ranks of the subunits involved, primarily because the communication system would be totally clogged if all information regarding subunit interaction had to flow all the way up one of the subunits and then all the way back down another. The clogging of the system would result in either painfully slow communications or none at all.

Therefore, the parties involved generally communicate directly with each other. This saves time and can often mean a very reasonable solution worked out at a lower level with good cooperation. However, it may also mean that those further up the hierarchy are unaware of what has happened, and that can be harmful in the long run. A solution to this problem is to record and pass along the information about what has been done, but that may be neglected; even if it is not neglected, it may not be noticed.

Although the emphasis in this discussion has been on coordination between subunits, much of the communication of this sort is actually based on conflict. Professional departments are a good example. When professionals or experts make up divisions of an organization, their areas of expertise are likely to lead them to different conclusions about the same matter (Hage, 1974:101–24). For example, in a petroleum company it is quite conceivable that the geological, engineering, legal, and public relations divisions could all come to different conclusions about the desirability of starting new oil-well drilling in various locations. Each would be correct in its own area of expertise, and the coordination of top officials would obviously be required when a final decision had to be made. During the period of planning or development, however, communications between these divisions would probably be characterized as nonproductive, since the specialists involved would be talking in their own language, one that is unfamiliar to those not in the same profession. From the evidence at hand, each division would also be correct in its assessments of the situation and would view the other divisions as not understanding the "true" meanings of the situation.

This type of communication problem is not limited to professionalized divisions. Communications between subunits inevitably contain elements of conflict. The conflict will be greater if the units involved invest values in their understanding and conceptualizations. Horizontal communications across organizational lines thus contain both the seeds and the flowers of conflict. Such conflict, by definition, will contribute to distortion of communications in one form or another. At the same time, passing each message up the line to eliminate such distortion through coordination at the top has the dangers of diluting the message in attempts to avoid conflict and of taking so much time that the message becomes meaningless. Here again, the endemic complexities of an organization preclude a totally rational operation.

Both horizontal and vertical aspects of organizations create complications for communication. At the same time, there are situations in which these obstacles are overcome. An excellent example is an analysis of aircraft carrier flight decks (Weick and Roberts, 1993). When aircraft are landing, the work pace is furious, the noise is overwhelming, and the possibility for tragic error is great. Despite these conditions, flight decks operate very effectively. Communication works across ranks and organizational divisions. Weick and Roberts believe that this is based on "heedful interrelating" and a "collective mind" (p. 357). Everyone is extremely focused. Everyone is well trained. Similar situations certainly exist with successful sports teams and in other spheres of life. At the same time, the flight-deck example is striking because it is so different. In the more mundane spheres of organizational life, the vertical and horizontal factors intrude on communication.

Communication Networks

Before we turn to a more systematic examination of the consequences of all these communication problems in organizations, there is a final bit of evidence regarding the manner in which communications evolve. The communication process can be studied in laboratory situations; among organizational characteristics, it is perhaps the most amenable to such experimentation. There has been a long history (Bavelas, 1950; Leavitt, 1951) of attempting to isolate the communication system that is most efficient under a variety of circumstances. These laboratory studies are applicable to both the vertical and the horizontal aspects of communications, since the manner in which the communication tasks are coordinated is the major focus. Three primary communication networks between members of work groups have been studied. The "wheel" pattern requires all persons at the periphery of the wheel to send their communications to the hub. This is an imposed hierarchy, since those at the periphery cannot send messages to each other; it is the task of the hub to do the coordinating. The "circle" pattern permits each member of the group to talk to those on either side, with no priorities. The "all-channel" system allows everyone to communicate with everyone else.

Using success in arriving at a correct solution as the criterion of efficiency, repeated investigations have found the wheel pattern to be superior. The other patterns can become equally efficient if they develop a hierarchy, but that takes time, and meanwhile efficiency is reduced. The more complex the task, the more time is required for the communication network to become structured. The importance of these findings for our purposes is that whether the communications are vertical or horizontal, hierarchical patterns emerge. In the vertical situation, the hierarchy is already there, although the formal hierarchy can be modified through the power considerations of expertise or personal attraction. In the horizontal situation, a hierarchy will emerge. Communication takes place on the basis of organizational structure; it also contributes to the development of structuring.

COMMUNICATION PROBLEMS

It should be clear that communications in organizations are not perfect. The basic consequence of existing communication systems is that messages are transformed or altered as they pass through the system. The fact that they are transformed means that the ultimate recipient of the message receives something different from what was originally sent, thus destroying the intent of the communication process.

Omission

There are two major forms of transformation—omission and distortion (Guetzkow, 1965). Omission involves the "deletion of aspects of messages" (p. 551), and it occurs because the recipients may not be able to grasp the entire content of the message and receive or pass on only what they are able to grasp. Communication overload can also lead to the omission of materials, since some messages may not be handled because of the overload. Omission may be intentional, as when certain classes of information are deleted from the information passed through particular segments of the organization. Omission is most evident in upward communications, since more messages are generated by the large number of people and units lower in the hierarchy. As the communications are filtered on the way up, the omissions occur. As noted earlier, when omissions are intentional, it is vital to know the criteria for omitting some kinds of information. Omission can occur simply as a removal of details, with the heart of the message still transmitted upward. This is the ideal, of course, but is not usually achieved, since part of the content of the message is usually omitted also.

Distortion

Distortion refers to altered meanings of messages as they pass through the organization. From the earlier discussion of perceptions, it is clear that people are selective, intentionally or unintentionally, about what they receive as messages. Guetzkow (1965) states:

> [B]ecause different persons man different points of initiation and reception of messages, there is much assimilation of meanings to the context within which transmission occurs. Frames of reference at a multitude of nodes differ because of variety in personal and occupational background, as well as because of difference in viewpoint induced by the communicator's position in the organization. (p. 555)

Distortion is as likely to occur in horizontal communications as in vertical, given the differences between organizational units in objectives and values. Selective omission and distortion, or "coding," are not unique properties of organizations. They occur in all communication systems, from the family to the total society. They are crucial for organizations, however, since organizations depend upon accurate communications as a basis for decision making.

Overload

The communication problem that is perhaps more characteristic of organizations than of other social entities is communication overload. Overload leads to omission and contributes to distortion. It also leads to other coping and adjustment mechanisms on the part of the organization. There are adaptive and maladaptive adjustments to the overload situation. Omission and distortion are maladaptive. They are also normal.

Another device used when overload occurs is queuing. This technique lines up the messages by time of receipt or by some other such criterion. Queuing can have positive or negative consequences. If the wrong priority system is used, less important messages may be acted upon before those that are really crucial reach the recipient. At the same time, queuing does allow recipients to act on messages as they come in without putting them in a state of inaction because of total overload. An example of this is an anecdote from a disaster following a major earthquake. Organizations dealing with the earthquake were besieged with messages. Some organizations allowed victims to plead for help face-to-face, letting them crowd into an office and all talk at once; this quickly brought the organizations involved to a halt. The overload was so great that the communications could not be filtered in any way. Another organization received its messages by telephone, a device providing an arbitrary queuing mechanism based on an operating phone and the luck of finding an open line. This organization was able to keep functioning, because the messages came in one at a time. In such a queuing situation, of course, there are no real criteria to determine which messages get through and which do not, other than time phasing and luck in getting a phone line.

A useful modification of queuing is the previously mentioned filtering process, which involves setting priorities for messages. The critical factor here is the nature of the priorities. Many organizations utilize a modified triage system in which the most important messages are permitted to come into the system if it is perceived that the organization can take relevant actions. Less important messages are then taken in as time permits. This sort of filtering system must be set up in advance. The question always is, what is the principle on which filtering takes place?

All the communication problems discussed derive from the fact that communications in organizations require interpretation. If there is a case of extreme overload, the interpretive process becomes inundated with so much material that it becomes inoperative. Queuing and filtering are techniques designed to sort messages into priorities. Any priority system established in advance means that an interpretation of messages has already been made, with some deemed more important than others. Thus, interpretation occurs regardless of whether priorities are set in advance or simply as messages are received.

Organizations generate and receive a vast amount of material. If we think of an organization as a pyramid, the huge mass at the base is the information entering an organization's communication system. As information moves up and through the organization, it is filtered and condensed. It arrives at the top in the form of an "executive summary." The amount of information, like the pyramid, keeps getting smaller as it rises in the organization. Here the pyramid analogy must be abandoned, since the determination of which information moves up is subject to the types of human and organizationally based interpretations we have been considering.

COMMUNICATION TO AND FROM OUTSIDE THE ORGANIZATION

The focus thus far has been internal organizational communication. The complications and problems that have been identified appear even more severe when we realize that so much of what is really important for an organization comes into it from its environment—competitors, creditors, customers, regulators, taxers, constituents, and so on. In addition, there are the more general environmental messages that are sent to and from an organization, such as changes in prime interest rates, demographic shifts, or petroleum price increases. Communications with the environment greatly compound the communication problems that have already been identified.

POSSIBLE SOLUTIONS

With all the problems, potential and real, in the communication process, it is obvious that a "perfect" communication system is unlikely. But although perfection, like rationality, will not be achieved, organizations do have mechanisms by which they attempt to keep the communication system as clear as they can. There are several devices that are available to reduce the distortions and other complications in the communication process (Downs, 1967). Redundancy, or the duplication of reports for verification, though adding to the flow of messages and paper in an organization, allows more people to see or hear a particular piece of information and respond to it. This is a correction device. There are several ways to create redundancy, including the use of information sources external to the situation—such as reports that are generated outside the organization itself—thus ensuring that reporting units and individuals coordinate their communications.

A common solution to at least some communication problems is the ubiquitous meeting. Meetings have the potential for yielding common meanings among participants, particularly when the intent of the meetings is to achieve consensus. Although meetings are quite valuable, it is obvious that time spent in meetings is time not spent on other activities. When I have a day filled with meetings, I have a day when I will not get any research, writing, or preparation for classes accomplished.

Another way in which communication problems can be reduced is through matrix-like systems. A study of a psychiatric hospital found committees or teams that were composed of personnel from the various occupational specialties in the hospital and from the established departments in the hospital (Blau and Alba, 1982). The teams were designed to deal with various issues and programs of the hospital, and hospital personnel served on multiple teams. In addition, traditional ranks were eliminated. For example, a team could have a nurse as the team leader and psychiatrists as team members. Blau and Alba report that these overlapping circles of weak ties inhibited segmentation and sustained participation because participants were rewarded for participating. Their data indicate that there was extensive interunit communication. There are limitations to this approach, of course. Its applicability in other forms of organizations is uncertain, and the approach requires the commitment of all the participants up through the head of the organization.

Some organizations have turned to "project groups" as a means of solving communication problems. These groups, or task forces as they are sometimes called, are typically composed of personnel from a variety of organizational units. Their usual purpose is to develop a new product or service for the organization. They may be isolated from the rest of the organization in the hope that this will enable them to think and work together. One analysis of research and development project groups composed of scientists and engineers found that such groups became increasingly isolated from key information sources within and outside their own organizations (Katz, 1982). Over time, their productivity decreased, with the communication process increasingly focused inward. Such project groups or task forces are probably better off with a short span of existence and a sunset clause specifying a termination date.

A major mechanism for achieving consensus about the meaning of communication is putting things in writing, such as contracts. Even though communication in writing is subject to interpretation, lawyers and accountants make much of their living by negotiating consensus in meanings between parties. This is not the answer for all problems, of course, but it is one way to avoid communication chaos.

The nature of, problems in, and suggested solutions for communications all point to the centrality of this process in much of what happens in an organization. But it is evident that the communication system is vitally affected by other structural and process factors. Communications do not exist outside the total organizational framework. They cannot be over- or underemphasized. More and more accurate communications do not lead inevitably to greater effectiveness for the organization. The key to the communication process in organizations is to ensure that the correct people get the correct information (in amount and quality) at the correct time. All of these factors can be anticipated to some degree. If organizations, their members, and their environments were all in a steady state, communication tasks would be easier. Since obviously they are not, the communication process must be viewed as a dynamic one, with new actors, new media, and new definitions constantly entering the scene. As noted at the beginning of this chapter, ambiguities and paradoxes are to be anticipated.

The media of communication in organizations have received little attention in our analysis here. Breakthroughs in the forms of information and word processing, faxing, electronic message sending and receiving, and the internet continue to be developed. Advanced communication technology itself is not the cure for organizational communication problems. The problems are rooted in the nature of organizations, their participants, and their interactions with their environments.

SUMMARY AND CONCLUSIONS

The communication process in organizations is a complicated one due to individual idiosyncrasies, biases, and abilities and complicated by organizational characteristics such as hierarchy or specialization. Nonetheless, communications within organizations are central for the other processes of power, leadership, and decision making. Communications are shaped by organizational structure and continue to reshape structure.

The "perfect" communication system is yet to be devised and probably never will be. Technological changes in various forms have contributed to more rapid processing of information, but the issues and problems considered in this chapter are not erased by advanced technology; in fact, in some instances they are exacerbated.

Less-than-perfect communication systems and the search for improvements contribute to both changes and innovations in organizations. Change and innovation are related to more than communications, however, and it is to this topic that we now turn.

EXERCISES

1. Describe the extent to which communication omission, distortion, and overload take place in your two organizations. Why does this happen?
2. When communications take place in your two organizations, how are they affected by vertical and horizontal factors?

Chapter 8

Change

---•◆•---

OVERVIEW

We all know that organizations change. The media are filled with news of firms going out of business, new ventures starting, and new alliances forming. In this chapter we examine the organizational change process. We begin with a consideration of the extent to which organizations are able to change—Do they resist change, or does change come easily?

We then examine the change process itself. This process includes the formation of organizations or their births, their transitions, and their declines and deaths. This last change is not inevitable, of course, but it does happen.

An important type of change is the innovation. Here we look at individual, organizational, and environmental factors that contribute to innovations in organizations. As usual, we conclude that all three factors operate together.

The analyses of power, leadership, decision making, and communication have shown that organizations are dynamic. In this chapter we will analyze the ways in which organizations change and the reasons that change does and does not take place. At times change is virtually forced on an unwilling organization, and at other times change is openly embraced and sought. Change can be beneficial or detrimental to organizations. Change can bring growth or decline or an alteration in form. The analysis of change has become a dominant focus in organizational research and theorizing. Change can lead to greater effectiveness, or just the opposite. Several alternative and competing views of change will be considered in the analyses that follow.

THE NATURE OF ORGANIZATIONAL CHANGE

Organizational change can be approached from a number of directions. It can be seen from an internal political perspective, with constantly shifting coalitions and factions (Kanter, Stein, and Jick, 1992). It can also be viewed from a historical or developmental perspective, with markets entered and controlled and with owner-ship shifting over time (Kochan and Useem, 1992).

Another approach is to examine the "life cycle" of organizations (Kimberly and Miles, 1980). The use of this biological metaphor, though imperfect, sensi-tizes us to the fact that organizations do not go along in the same state for eter-nity. "Organizations are born, grow, and decline. Sometimes they reawaken, and sometimes they disappear" (Kimberly and Miles, 1980:ix).

This fact, of course, is well recognized in the stock market, as investors try to determine which organizations are in a growth phase and which are in a de-cline phase. Although organizational analysts are now turning to an analysis of phenomena such as the organizational life cycle, we have not yet developed the tools by which we can ascertain exactly where an organization is in the cycle at a particular time. If we could, of course, we should probably stop being academic organizational analysts and become full-time stock market investors. That con-sideration aside, growth and decline are important components of organizational change. A modified life-cycle approach will be used in this chapter.

Organizational change can be defined as "the alteration and transformation of the form so as to survive better in the environment" (Hage, 1980:262). This is a good definition of organizational change, with the major exception that Hage does not consider organizational goals in this formulation of change. As will be ar-gued in detail at a later point, analyses of organizations that do not include goals are shortsighted, since organizations engage in many activities and make many de-cisions that are not related to survival in the environment but are related to goals.

Organizational survival, or the avoidance of death, is, of course, the ulti-mate test of an organization, but at any time, unless death is imminent, what goes on in an organization is based on both environmental pressures and goals. Changes are made to make more profit or to secure more members. These have both an environmental and a goal relationship.

The distinction between environmentally and goal-based change is at the heart of the major theoretical arguments currently being waged in organiza-tional theory. We will address and comment on these debates but will not re-solve them. We will begin with a consideration of the potential for change within organizations.

The Potential for Change

Some analysts view organizations as being in constant flux. Child and Kieser (1981) state:

> Organizations are constantly changing. Movements in external conditions such as competition, innovation, public demand, and governmental policy require that new strategies, methods of working, and outputs be devised for an organization merely to continue at its present level of operations. Internal factors also promote change in that managers and other members of an organization may seek not just its maintenance but also its growth, in order to secure improved benefits and satisfactions for themselves. (p. 28)

Although we may agree or disagree in regard to the attribution of managerial motivation, Child and Kieser's conclusion is that organizations are constantly in motion. An alternative and highly individualized approach to the potential for change sees individuals as constantly learning and unlearning from their actions. It views the organization as the stage on which that learning takes place; consequently, it views the organization as learning and unlearning (Hedberg, 1981).

The individual can also be taken as the point of departure for the diametrically opposed position that organizations have limited potential for change. For example, individuals can get locked into courses of action. Their commitment to courses of action can escalate when they have already invested previous efforts. They defend their turf and their previous behaviors by continuing to act in the same manner (Staw, 1982). At the organizational level, Staw notes that standard operating procedures are difficult to change and that powerful coalitions exist that will block change if it is not in their interests. Programs can be in motion that have the backing of key figures in the organization ("it's the president's baby"). In Staw's view there are thus individual and collective or organizational counterforces to change.

Organizational personnel are a potential source of inertia in another way. When personnel are selected on the basis of reliability and accountability, organizational structures become "reproducible." This means that the same organizational forms will remain in place because there is no differentiation among the personnel. This tendency toward inertia because of commonalities in personnel is more likely in larger, older, and more complex organizations (Hannan and Freeman, 1984).

The matter is not that simple, however. We have stressed that paradoxes and contradictions are inherent in organizations. That is borne out in the case of change. Consider large organizations. On the one hand, they are likely to have the resources necessary for changes such as entering new markets. On the other hand, they are likely to be more bureaucratic and thus resistant to change (Haveman, 1993).

Another important consideration for the potential for change is the personnel composition or organizational demography within an organization (Carroll and Hannan, 2000; Pfeffer, 1983). Organizational demography is affected both by organizational policies on compensation, promotion, and the like and by environmental factors such as the rate of growth of the industry in which an organization operates.

Organizational demographic characteristics in turn affect the patterns of change, since they will have an impact on succession and power differences among age cohorts. One of the premier analysts of organizational change has been Herbert Kaufman (1971), who states:

> In short, I am not saying that organizational change is invariably good or bad, progressive or conservative, beneficial or injurious. It may run either way in any given instance. But it is always confronted by strong forces holding it in check and sharply circumscribing the capacity of organizations to react to new conditions—sometimes with grave results. (p. 8)

Kaufman goes on to describe the factors within organizations that resist change. These include the "collective benefits of stability" or familiarity with existing patterns, "calculated opposition to change" by groups within the organization who may have altruistic or selfish motivations, and a simple "inability to change" (p. 3). The last point refers to the fact that organizations develop "mental blinders" that preclude change capability. This happens as personnel are selected and trained to do what was done in the past in the manner in which it was done in the past. Some people attribute the earlier difficulties of American automobile manufacturers to just this factor. People were hired and trained into executive positions from only one mold. Change is resisted because it is uncomfortable and threatening.

The basic point is that organizations by their very nature are conservative. Even organizations that try to have a radical impact on society demonstrate this conservatism. The history of the Christian religion or Communist regimes is one of conservatism, with deviants subject to inquisitions, purges, or exile in Siberia.

There are additional factors that contribute to resistance to change. Kaufman (1971:23–39) calls them "systemic obstacles" to change. These are obstacles within the overall system in which organizations operate. They include such factors as "sunk costs," or investments in the status quo; the accumulation of official constraints on behavior, such as laws and regulations; unofficial and unplanned constraints on behavior in the form of informal customs; and interorganizational agreements, such as labor–management contracts.

Another systemic obstacle to change is that organizations may not have the financial or personnel resources to engage in change efforts even if the need is identified. Despite all these obstacles, of course, organizations do change. They sustain pressures that lead to both inertia and adaptability (Gersick, 1994). These dialectical pressures for and against change are not counterbalanced.

THE CHANGE PROCESS

There are multiple explanations for change in organizations. Kaufman (1971) concludes that change takes place through personnel turnover. Despite careful selection and training, successive generations of organizational personnel are not clones of one another.

At other times change is literally forced on an organization by the environment. The requirements of affirmative action have drastically altered many organizations, as have pollution control regulations. Organizations are sometimes driven to incorporate policies and practices that are a part of the prevailing ethos in the society in which they are embedded (Meyer and Rowan, 1977). The environment has institutionalized concepts of how organizations should operate, and this leads organizations to incorporate the institutionalized practices. An empirical extension of this line of reasoning analyzed the adoption of civil service reforms in city governments for the time period 1880 to 1935. This research found that the speed of the adoption of a policy or programs is to a great extent determined by the extent to which the change is institutionalized by law, which leads to quicker change, or by legitimation, which is a more gradual process (Tolbert and Zucker, 1983).

Although there may be a legal mandate to make a change, it does not simply happen. This was documented in an analysis of the enormous power struggles that took place within the U.S. Postal Service in 1970 and 1971 (Biggart, 1977). Biggart concludes: "The reorganization of the U.S. Postal Service unleashed incredible forces both in and out of the organization; the forces were aimed at protecting or consolidating the power of interest groups" (p. 423). This conclusion is in line with analyses that emphasize the importance of interest groups within organizations.

The idea of "punctuated equilibrium" is a useful way to conceptualize the dialectical play of forces operating for and against change in organizations (Romanelli and Tushman, 1994). Organizations go through relatively long periods of stability. These are punctuated by short periods or bursts of fundamental change, which are in turn followed by another period of stability.

Organizational Change Cycles

This section will closely follow the idea of organizational life cycles that was noted earlier. The life-cycle approach of births (formations), transformations, and deaths has informed a great deal of organizational theory, but the biological analogy is potentially confusing. The human species, for example, has a largely predictable life span, whereas organizations do not. The life expectancy of humans can be threatened or extended by their own actions or inactions. This is also true for organizations, but they have the potential to last much longer than individuals—indeed, this is one of the predominant characteristics of organizations. Hypothetically, organizations could last indefinitely. There is only one method of human conception, but organizations can be created by entrepreneurs and by legislatures. Organizations can also be created by other organizations, as when subsidiaries are founded by a parent organization. Subsidiaries are often used to try out a new product or service. We will thus utilize the life-cycle terminology, without completely accepting the analogy.

Births, Foundings, and Formations.   An organizational birth is the "creation of an operating entity that acquires inputs from suppliers and provides outputs to a given public (customers, clients, patients, etc.)" (Delacroix and Carroll, 1983:276). Births also take place through legislative actions as government organizations are born. Research has documented the fact that environmental conditions, such as the characteristics of metropolitan areas for industrial firms (Pennings, 1982), state policies for railroads (Dobbin and Dowd, 1997), the existing density of organizations for women's medical societies (Marrett, 1980), and for life insurance companies (Budros, 1993), and political turbulence for newspapers (Delacroix and Carroll, 1983), have been closely related to the birth frequencies for the organizations studied.

The terms "founding" or "formation" have now replaced "birth" in the literature, apparently as a reaction to the biological analogy. A later study of the data on newspapers suggests that political turbulence serves as part of the institutional environment or value system in which the newspapers are embedded (Carroll and Huo, 1986). This institutional environment affects both organizational formation and organizational failures. Preexisting organizations in an environment provide important resources for similar new organizations—the preexisting organizations serve as sources of legitimation and domain definition (Wiewel and Hunter, 1985). This line of reasoning is taken a few steps further by Hannan and Freeman (1987). In a study of American labor unions, they found that the formation rate varies with the number of other recent union formation in a curvilinear manner. A surge of recent formations leads to imitation and more formations and then a competition for scarce resources. The irony is that a big surge in formations exhausts resources and thus limits future formations.

The social environments of organizations thus affect their rates of formation. Environments also have long-lasting effects into the futures of organizations. It must be reiterated that this is also true for organizations created by an arm of government. For example, the Morrill Act of 1862, which established land-grant colleges, has had a continuing effect on those particular colleges and on higher education in general.

Organizational analysts agree that a combination of available resources, supportive government policies, and legitimation in the form of cultural values is necessary for organizational formations. This combination of explanations brings together organizational theories (population ecology, resource dependence, and institutional theory) in a more powerful explanation than a single theory.

There is another important step in understanding organizational foundings. The environment at the time of founding and the characteristics of the founder had important implications for the structure of a medical school (Kimberly, 1979). Bringing the founder back into the equation is necessary for a complete understanding of the process. Founders must adopt strategies that are appropriate for the environment that is faced (Boeker, 1989; Romanelli, 1989).

Finally, there is another, quite distinct, type of organizational formation. This is the "breakaway" organization (Dyck and Starke, 1999). "A breakaway organization forms when a group of organizational members, frustrated by their inability to implement change in their parent organization, leave it and start up a new organization in which they are free to implement their ideas" (Dyck and Starke, 1999:792). For a breakaway organization to succeed, of course, the other conditions necessary for organizational formation must be present.

Transformations.   Once formed, organizations change. The most likely change is death, since new organizations have exceptionally high death rates (Carroll and Delacroix, 1982; Freeman, Carroll, and Hannan, 1983; Starbuck and Nystrom, 1981). New organizations are usually small and suffer a liability of newness—just think of all the new restaurants that come and go (Freeman, Carroll, and Hannan, 1983). Contrary to popular opinion, a high mortality rate is also found among new government organizations (Starbuck and Nystrom, 1981). Population ecology theorists ascribe the high death rate among new organizations to their inability to find or carve a niche in their environment.

Ecological theory also has a great deal to say about subsequent transformations that take place among the organizations that do survive. A basic premise of ecological theory is that organizations adapt to their environments.

The ecological perspective has a second basic premise: that organizations and organizational forms are selected by the environment for survival. Again, the analogy is that of biological systems, with a heavy emphasis on evolution and "natural selection." In the discussion that follows, we will utilize McKelvey and Aldrich's (1983) summary of the ecological framework.

McKelvey and Aldrich present four principles that operate in the ecological process. These principles determine which organizations will survive and which will not. The first principle is that of variation. Any sort of change is a variation. Variations can be purposeful or blind.

> Purposeful variations occur as an intentional response, when environmental pressures cause selection of adaptations. Blind variations are those that occur independent of environmental or selection pressures; they are not the result of an intentional response to adaptation pressures but rather occur by accident or chance. (p. 114)

Organizational analysts are essentially split on the extent to which variations are blind or purposeful. Any consideration of purposefulness would have to consider the problems of decision making that were specified in Chapter 6. Despite the problems surrounding decision making, I believe that the evidence favors at least a moderate degree of purposefulness, as will be documented in a later section.

The second principle is that of natural selection. Variations differ in the degree to which they enable organizations to acquire resources from the environment. Useless or harmful variations are likely to bring in fewer resources and thus reduce the chances of survival. With the passage of time, organizations that survive are likely to have beneficial variations. Resource acquisition involves much more than financial resources, although they are of crucial importance. Other resources include personnel, power, political support, and legitimation.

The third principle is that of retention and diffusion. This involves the passing of competencies (knowledge and skills) on to succeeding members of organizations over generations. Competencies are those that have enabled organizations to survive in the first place. Competencies are diffused to other organizations as skilled and knowledgeable people change jobs and work for new and different organizations. Competencies are retained by the information flows within organizations and involve formal and informal training. In a study of the microcomputer, cement, and airline industries, Tushman and Anderson (1986) found that technological break-throughs can enhance or destroy organizational competencies. Knowledge and skills can become highly valuable or obsolete on the basis of technological change.

The final principle is that of the struggle for existence. This involves compet-ing with other organizations for scarce resources. As McKelvey and Aldrich note, there are periods in which resources are unusually rich for some organizations. They cite the example of solar energy companies before the Reagan administration. These organizations had tax credit and government subsidies to the extent that almost any organization could enter the field and survive. With the Reagan administration cutbacks, there was a greatly increased mortality rate among these firms.

Another concept from the ecological perspective is the niche in which or-ganizations survive. Organizations enter niches in the environment. The niche contains the resources for the organization and is likely to contain other organi-zations fighting for the same resources. The organization that survives is the one that can make the adaptations that enable it to overcome or at least coexist with its competitors. These adaptations are organizational change.

The ecological perspective on change is a powerful explanation of the change process. Few would argue that resource acquisition within a competitive environment is not crucial for all organizations. The key aspect of this approach, for our purposes, involves variation. We have already argued that variation is more purposeful than some ecological theorists believe. An organization can take steps to safeguard or enhance its position in its environment (Baum and Singh, 1996). These steps include the following:

> (a) securing the benefits of growth, (b) enhancing competitive power or public ap-proval through efficiency and rationalization or through the incorporation of tech-nological progress, (c) establishing a secure domain in the environment through the negotiation of agreement as to the legitimate field of activity for the organization to occupy or through the finding of ecological niches—areas of activity that are rela-tively protected and which suit an organization's specific competences, and (d) the creation of the capacity to respond flexibly to external change through the im-provement of management techniques. (Child and Kieser, 1981:32)

These suggestions contain an element that weakens the ecological argu-ment. This is the point that an organization can develop agreements with other or-ganizations that lessen competition. Although antitrust legislation diminishes the ability to establish monopolies, organizations do reach agreements to minimize survival-threatening competition. The presence of trade associations, which are designed to cope with forces and demands that firms within an industry face, is an example of that (Staber and Aldrich, 1983). Another example is intercollegiate athletic conferences, such as the Big 10 or the Ivy League. Long-term contracts are another device for reducing environmental effects. Singh, Tucker, and House (1986) found that voluntary social service organizations could enhance their likeli-hood of surviving by obtaining legitimation from the environment. They interpreted this finding as support for both the population ecology and the institutional per-spectives. There is additional research that points to bringing potential threatening forces into boards of directors and other such interorganizational linkages as techniques that can buffer an organization against its environment (Goodstein and Boeker, 1991; Miner, Amburgey, and Steams, 1990).

In addition to agreements with other organizations, organizations have constituents who work for organizational survival. In their interestingly titled book *Permanently Failing Organizations,* Meyer and Zucker (1989) document how workers, customers, and communities can fight to keep an organization going in the face of evidence that it is about to die. Examples here would include employees buying out a failing firm, church members fighting an archdiocese and keeping a parish church open, and communities fighting to prevent plant closings.

There is yet another component of organizational transformation that a totally ecological perspective misses. This is the movement into new areas of activity. Kimberly and Quinn (1984) capture this idea well in their comments on transitions:

> A transition is a major change in organizational strategy, structure, or process. Transitions can be precipitated by a variety of factors, such as declines in performance, perceptions of new opportunities, changes in legislation, or the development of new technologies. They may take a variety of forms, such as increasing formalization of structure, redefining principal operating units, broadening or narrowing market definitions, or engineering a shift in culture. (p. 1)

According to Kimberly and Quinn, transitions can take the form of restructuring the organization, repositioning the organization in its marketplace or environment, and revitalizing an organization that is slipping. Although our interest is not in management, as is Kimberly and Quinn's, their point that organizations can take actions that are not necessarily related to environmental pressures is vital for our consideration. This involves a form of entrepreneurism within the organization. Entrepreneurism involves the process of unprogrammed recombinations of preexisting elements of reality (Peterson, 1981:65). It is also possible to conceive of programmed recombinations. Peterson correctly notes that such entrepreneurship can take place outside business firms. Government agencies and universities can be quite entrepreneurial, for example, in their contracting arrangements. These new forms can again develop without environmental pressures.

There is an additional element that has been missing in this discussion of change: the role of decision makers (managers) as they monitor and interpret the environment (Isabella, 1990; Rao and Neilsen, 1992). Organizations that are doing poorly often change management teams. New management teams bring strategies with them and thus contribute to organizational change (Boeker, 1997a,b).

These last few paragraphs have been arguing against a totally environmentally based perspective on change. This is not meant to downplay the importance of the environment but, rather, to emphasize that the environment is only one source of change. Two leading population ecologists (Carroll and Hannan, 1989) have recognized this point by noting that environments differ in their degree of density. In highly dense and competitive situations, environmental pressures are greatest. Later research on breweries sheds some additional light on the density issue (Carroll and Wade, 1991). At one time breweries were more likely to be founded in more dense urban areas than in less dense rural areas. The development of refrigeration changed that and led to more founding of breweries in rural areas and more mortality (deaths) in urban areas.

In less dense situations, there is less competition and more emphasis on achieving legitimation from sources in the environment. This argument is a key component of the institutional model. Organizational change takes place as sources of legitimation shift.

Organizational transformation thus takes place for a variety of reasons. Contemporary research now overwhelmingly supports the view that ecological processes (particularly competition), governmental policies (see Prechel, 1997, 2000), and the institutional processes of legitimization of new organizational forms work together to produce organizational change. These external sources of change are brought into the organization and change takes place, primarily by decisions made at the management level. The chapter on decision making documented the fact that decisions are not necessarily "rational." As is the case in decision making in general, the embeddedness of managers in social networks contributes to both the content of change decisions and the orientations of managers toward change itself (Bacharach, Bamberger, and Sonnenstuhl, 1996; Davis and Greve, 1997; Fligstein, 1995; Palmer, Barber, and Zhou, 1995; Palmer et al., 1995).

There is a final element of the transformation process. Organizational change can happen by accident (March, 1981). Things happen by accident, disaster, or opportunity.

Once again, the theoretical conclusion is that our theories must be considered as working together, rather than oppositionally. They must be combined, rather than be treated individually (Baum and Haveman, 1997).

Once organizations do transform or change, an interesting question arises: Does the new organizational form "set back the clock" and make the organization vulnerable because of a new liability of newness (Amburgey, Kelly, and Barnett, 1993; Delacroix and Swaminathan, 1991; Haveman, 1992)? Although the evidence is inconclusive, it appears that factors such as organizational size and resources overcome this threat of "new newness." At the same time, older organizations might become obsolete or senile, thus raising their vulnerability (Hannan, 1998).

Deaths.   The idea of organizational death or mortality is important in the organizational literature (Baum and Singh, 1994).

> What is an organizational death? The question may seem trivial because all agree on the unproblematic case: an organizational death occurs when an organization fails, closes down its operations, and disbands its constituent elements. But what about mergers? When two organizations combine, at least one ceases to exist and this must be considered a death. If the merger involves a dominant partner that has absorbed the resources of the other partner, then the subordinate organization dies and the dominant organization experiences a change in structure. If, however, neither merger partner assumes a dominant position, it is difficult to assign a death to one organization and a structural alteration to the other. Instead, it is useful to consider the resulting organization as new and the two merger partners as dead. (Carroll and Delacroix, 1982:170)

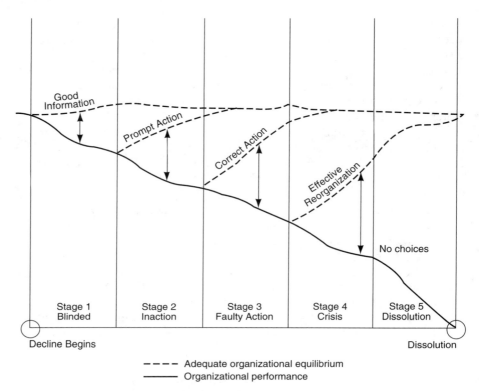

FIGURE 8–1   Widening Performance Gap as Decline Deepens
Source: Reprinted from "Decline in Organizations: A Literature Integration and Extension" by William Weitzel and Ellen Jonsson, published in *Administrative Science Quarterly*, 34, no. 1 (March, 1989), 102. By permission of *Administrative Science Quarterly*, © 1989.

Organizational death is the ultimate outcome of organizational decline, a process which itself has received a great deal of attention. Cameron, Kim, and Whetten (1987) define organizational decline as "a condition in which a substantial, absolute decrease in an organization's resource base occurs over a specified period of time" (p. 224). Weitzel and Jonsson (1989) suggest that there are five stages in the decline process. These are illustrated in Figure 8–1.

In this portrayal of the decline process, the first stage of decline occurs when the organization is blind to the signs of decline. The second stage occurs when the organization recognizes the need for change but takes no action. In the third stage, actions are taken, but they are inappropriate. The fourth stage is the crisis, and the final stage is dissolution.

Another highly graphic depiction of the decline process has been presented by Hambrick and D'Aveni (1988). They picture decline into failure as a downward spiral, as seen in Figure 8–2.

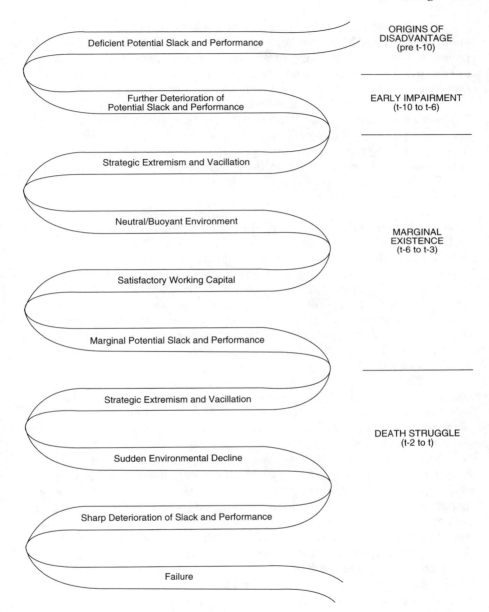

FIGURE 8–2 Organizational Decline as a Downward Spiral

Source: Reprinted from "Large Corporate Failures and Downward Spirals" by Donald C. Hambrick and Richard A. D'Aveni, published in *Administrative Science Quarterly,* 33, no. 1 (March, 1988), 14. By permission of *Administrative Science Quarterly,* © 1988.

Here the decline process is seen as weaknesses in organizational slack and performance, followed by extreme and vacillating strategies that lead to further problems. Lest these last two studies be taken as proof that all organizations are in a decline phase, it should be noted that Hambrick and D'Aveni's study matched fifty-seven firms that went bankrupt with another fifty-seven firms that survived.

Organizational deaths are usually seen as the outcome of the decline process. This is only partially accurate (Carroll and Delacroix, 1982). Many merger partners are actually highly successful—who would want to merge with a failing organization? The many hostile corporate takeovers of recent years indicate the attractiveness of some organizations to others for the sake of merger (Morrill, 1991). Death is thus not necessarily the outcome of failure, but it is the end of the organizational change cycle.

The process of death itself is not simple. An examination of dying organizations in both the private and the public sectors found that there were repeated social occasions, such as parties and picnics, that accompanied the deaths (Harris and Sutton, 1986). The organizations included academic units, stores, manufacturing firms, and a hospital. Some were free-standing, independent organizations, and others were part of larger organizations. In all cases, organizational deaths were traumatic for the people involved. A further analysis of the same cases revealed that death has widespread repercussions (Sutton, 1987). For some organizations, debts were not paid, thus affecting other organizations. In other instances, the personnel from the dead organizations reconnected in new organizations. Organizational death is painful and complicated.

In this discussion of organizational change cycles, and now with a consideration of organizational deaths, we should not lose sight of the fact that many large and powerful organizations persist. The Roman Catholic Church is the best example of that. Organizational longevity has not received as much attention as decline and death, but it would be well worth study.

There have been studies of organizational survival in the face of strong threats. These studies suggest that the presence of institutional linkages with powerful organizations for day care centers (Baum and Oliver, 1991, 1992), a focus on outputs and customer needs in business firms (D'Aveni and MacMillan, 1990), and prior records of success in Irish and Argentinean newspapers (Leventhal, 1991) contribute to survival. To make matters more confusing, Wholey, Christianson, and Sanchez (1992) report that midsized health maintenance organizations are more at risk than small or large HMOs because the midsized organizations cannot compete. This maze of rather confusing findings is reported to suggest that our research evidence does not really have an answer for why organizations survive. Survival is not random, but what works for one type of organization might not work for another, which brings us back to the idea that a useful typology of organizations is sorely needed.

The same array of considerations that were discussed in the section on transformations is operative in organizational deaths. Just as institutional legitimation is important for transformations, deinstitutionalization contributed to the decline and fall of the conglomerate form of business firm (Davis, Diekmann, and

Tinsley, 1994). Population ecology theory would emphasize that the loss of niche leads to death. Organizational death has multiple explanations, which operate simultaneously, just as our analysis of other organizational processes demonstrates.

INNOVATION IN ORGANIZATIONS

We will now narrow our focus and consider innovations in organizations. The focus is narrower here because an innovation may have an impact on only a small part of an organization. An innovation is a departure from existing practices or technologies and represents a significant departure from the state of the art at the time it appears (Kimberly, 1981). Innovations range from minor variations in current practices to radical departures that call for major reorientations (Pennings, 1987:6). The practice of organizational downsizing is a drastic form of innovation that has had repercussions that reach far beyond the downsized organization (Budros, 2001).

Most analyses of innovation have focused on the technological side, such as the patterns by which hospitals adopt new medical techniques or the patterns of computer utilization. Other forms of innovation involve organizational or administrative practices. In a study of administrative practices and technological innovations in libraries, Damanpour and Evan (1984) found that technological innovations were adopted at a faster rate than innovations involving administrative practices. At the same time, adoption of an administrative innovation tended to trigger the adoption of technological innovations more readily than the reverse.

The interplay between technological and administrative innovations is illustrated by analyses that study management information systems. As organizations bring information technology into increasing use (technological innovation), they are able to decrease the number of organizational levels and personnel needed to process information (administrative innovation) (Thach and Woodman, 1994). This interplay is graphically illustrated in Figure 8–3. The information technology (IT) industry develops new hardware and software, which organizations adopt to remain competitive and also because they copy one another. As these changes take place, organizations put pressure on the IT industry, which develops even newer hardware and software, and the cycle starts again.

Innovations within an organization are not random; innovation occurs in relation to the past and present conditions of the organization. Three forms of

FIGURE 8–3   IT Is Implemented as a Response Both to External Competition and to Institutional Influence

innovation can take place in organizations. The first is the programmed innovation that is planned through product or service research and development. Nonprogrammed innovations occur when there is "slack" in the organization; that is, more resources are available than are presently needed. Those resources are then used for innovative purposes. The innovations are nonprogrammed because the organization cannot really anticipate when extra resources will be available. Innovation is distressed when it is forced on the organization, such as when a crisis is perceived and new actions are taken. Innovations can develop within the organization or be imposed upon it by forces in the environment (Zaltman, Duncan, and Holbek, 1973).

The characteristics of the innovation itself are of critical importance in determining whether or not it will be adopted. Zaltman, Duncan, and Holbek note that the following characteristics of an innovation make it more or less attractive and thus more or less likely to be utilized by an organization:

1. *Cost.* Cost factors involve two elements, the economic and the social. Economic costs include the initial cost of adopting an innovation or a new program and the continuing costs of keeping it in operation. Social costs involve changed status arrangements within the organization as individuals and groups gain or lose power because of the new developments. Either type of cost is likely to be viewed as exorbitant by opponents and minimized by proponents of a proposed change.

2. *Return on Investment.* It is obvious that innovations will be selected that will yield high returns on investments. The situation is much more difficult when an innovation or a technological policy is in the nonbusiness sector.

3. *Efficiency.* The more efficient innovation will be selected over the less efficient status quo situation or alternative innovation.

4. *Risk and Uncertainty.* The less the risk and uncertainty, the greater the likelihood of adopting an innovation.

5. *Communicability.* The clarity of the results is associated with likelihood of innovation.

6. *Compatibility.* The more compatible the innovation is with the existing system, the more likely it is to be adopted. This, of course, implies that organizations are likely to be conservative in their innovations or technological policies, since what is compatible is unlikely to be radical.

7. *Complexity.* More complex innovations are less likely to be adapted. Again, this is a strain toward conservatism.

8. *Scientific Status.* If an innovation is perceived to have sound scientific status, it is more likely to be adopted.

9. *Perceived Relative Advantage.* The greater the advantage, the more likely that the innovation will be adopted.

10. *Point of Origin.* Innovations are more likely to be adopted if they originate within the organization. This is based at least partially on the perceived credibility of the source of the innovation.

11. *Terminality.* This involves the timing of the innovation. In some cases, an innovation is worthwhile only if it is adopted at a particular time or in a particular sequence in the organization's operations.

12. *Status Quo Ante.* This refers to whether or not the decision to innovate is reversible. Can there be a return to the previous state of the organization, or is the

decision irreversible? A related question is whether or not the innovation or technological policy is divisible. Can a little bit at a time be tried, or does a total package have to be adopted?

13. *Commitment.* This involves behaviors and attitudes toward the innovation. Participation in the decision to innovate tends to raise the commitment of organizational members toward the innovation. A higher level of commitment is associated with more successful innovation.

14. *Interpersonal Relations.* If an innovation or a technological policy is likely to be disruptive to interpersonal relationships, it is less likely to be adopted.

15. *Publicness versus Privateness.* If an innovation is likely to affect a large part of the public, it will typically involve a larger decision-making body than an innovation that is limited to a private party. The larger decision-making body will tend to impede adoption.

16. *Gatekeepers.* This refers to the number of steps of approval an innovation must pass through. Must it pass through several or only one or two? The greater the number of gatekeepers, the more likely that an innovation will be turned down.

17. *Susceptibility to Successive Modification.* If an innovation itself can be modified as conditions or the technology changes, it stands more chance of adoption. This is related to the idea of reversibility, since the organization is not "locked" into a path that might begin to move away from the original objective.

18. *Gateway Capacity.* The adoption of one innovation or the development of a technological policy is likely to lead to the capacity to involve the organization in additional such actions.

19. *Gateway Innovations.* This refers to the fact that some innovations, even small changes in an organization's structure, can pave the way for additional innovations. (pp. 33–45)

What these characteristics suggest, of course, is that the less radical innovations are the ones most likely to be adopted. Innovations do not arrive at an organization's doorstep with adoption automatic. Instead, innovation characteristics interact with organizational characteristics, and both innovation characteristics and organizational conditions are embedded in an environmental situation (Damanpour, 1991).

Organizational Characteristics.   The characteristics of the innovation interact with the characteristics of the innovating organization. Hage and Aiken (1970) have found that the following organizational characteristics are related to high levels of innovation:

1. High complexity in the professional training of organizational members.
2. High decentralization of power.
3. Low formalization.
4. Low stratification in the differential distribution of rewards (if high stratification is present, those with high rewards are likely to resist change).
5. A low emphasis on volume (as opposed to quality) of production.
6. A low emphasis on efficiency in the cost of production or service.
7. A high level of job satisfaction on the part of organizational members. (pp. 30–61)

In a continuation of this line of reasoning, it is argued that more radical innovations will occur when there is a high concentration of cosmopolitan professionals or specialists. A complex division of labor, with professional personnel, can lead to greater creative capacity in organizations, especially in the form of research departments (Hage, 1999). The values of the dominant coalition also are critical. If these values are prochange, then innovation is more likely (Hage, 1980:205–6).

Further research supplements the directions taken here. The adoption of innovations is related to organizational size, specialization, differentiation, and decentralization. The values of lower-level decision makers must also be considered, since their perspectives and interests must also be compatible with the innovation (Moch, 1976; Moch and Morse, 1977).

There is some controversy regarding the relative importance of organizational characteristics and the attitudes of organizational members. Baldridge and Burnham (1975), for example, have argued that organizational characteristics are more important to the innovation process than the attitudes of the members of the organization. Hage and Dewar (1973) argue the opposite, that the values of the elites in organizations are more important than structural characteristics. This is another example of the chicken–egg situation, since the interaction of elite values and organizational characteristics is undoubtedly what leads to high or low rates of change. For example, a highly specialized organization headed by a dominant coalition that favors change is much more likely to change than a nonspecialized organization headed by a coalition that values stability. Other combinations of organizational characteristics and elite values would yield different rates of change.

The role of elite values can perhaps be seen more clearly if the process of change and innovation is viewed as a political process within the organization. In a study of the Teacher Corps, a federal program of the 1960s, Corwin (1973) found that the training programs were affected by the political economy of the colleges and universities involved. The economic conditions and the internal politics of the organizations involved affected how the innovation was adopted. Organizations are characterized by power struggles. The outcome of these struggles, together with organizational characteristics, determines whether or not a particular change will be made.

Not surprisingly, the environment in which the innovation and the organization are found is an important consideration. A study done during a period of growth found that innovation increased as incentives for innovation increased, the efficiency of organizational mechanisms for developing innovative alternatives increased, and the presence of organizational characteristics enabling innovation increased (Daft and Becker, 1978). This was a study of schools during a period of relative affluence, when schools were being encouraged by federal policies and funds to try new programs.

An analysis of the rates of adoption of innovations among hospitals found that the better a hospital's linkages are with other hospitals, the higher are the rates of innovation (Goes and Park, 1997). Similarly, as study of the international chemical industry found, organizations with network linkages had increased levels of innovation (Ahuja, 2000). Networks among organizations will be discussed in detail in the next chapter.

Another study examined innovation in periods of adversity. Manns and March (1978) looked at university departments and found that under adversity, departments tended to increase the variety of course offerings, provide more attractive packaging, make courses more accessible, and increase course benefits, through such mechanisms as more credits and higher grades. A key finding of this study was that strong departments responded to adversity with fewer innovations than weaker ones. The point here is that in adversity the less successful programs had to innovate more, whereas the stronger programs were insulated from adversity. The stronger programs had access to alternative resources, such as federal grants.

The innovation process itself is not simple. Zaltman, Duncan, and Holbeck (1973) identified two stages in the innovation process—initiation and implementation. Hage (1980:209–10) expands the process to four stages—evaluation, initiation, implementation, and routinization. Regardless of the number of stages, there is agreement that successful innovation requires different organizational arrangements for each stage. Thus, decentralization might be more desirable in the initiation stage, whereas a more centralized approach might be more appropriate for the implementation stage.

As noted earlier, innovation can essentially be forced on an organization by other organizations. A study of hospitals and medical-device manufacturers documents this. The proliferation of performance standards for hospitals, based largely on federal regulations, has made the use of medical devices, such as body scanners, mandatory in hospitals. Because the quality and reliability of the devices is controlled by the manufacturers, not the hospitals, the hospitals are growing increasingly dependent on the medical-device manufacturers. Instead of deciding on their own to adopt medical devices, hospitals are being forced to do so (McNeil and Minihan, 1977).

There is an additional environmental influence on innovation. Governmental policies can encourage or discourage innovation (Hall, 1981). Japanese governmental policies—including tax, trade, tariff, and regulatory policies—were, at one time, much better coordinated and more conducive to innovation than those of the United States (Holden, 1980). The result was rapid and intense innovation by Japanese business firms.

We have now identified organizational characteristics, elite or dominant coalition values, and environmental conditions as critical factors in the adoption of innovations and in change itself. This has been largely a structural approach to change and innovation.

An alternative approach to these issues is provided by Weick (1979). He views organizations as constantly changing or "enacting" entities. He recognizes the importance of factors such as size and technology but places much greater emphasis on individual perception and interpretation than has been the case in this analysis. In Weick's approach, constantly shifting constructions of reality within the organization mean that the organization is fluid as the environment is interpreted and enacted. We view organizations as much less fluid, with both structural factors and power arrangements playing key roles in the inhibition of change and innovation. Organizations do tend toward conservatism.

SUMMARY AND CONCLUSIONS

This chapter has examined the sources and processes of change within organizations. We found that although it is useful to focus on environmental pressures as a source of change, it is impossible to ignore internal sources of organizational change. Organizations have varying potential for change. Both individual and organizational characteristics inhibit and encourage change. We have considered organizational change cycles. In this we borrowed heavily from the ecological approach to organizations, since, despite its limitations, it offers strong insights into the change process.

The chapter has also analyzed the innovation process from the perspective that there are innovation and organizational characteristics that resist and facilitate the process. From the research findings in regard to innovation, we concluded that organizational characteristics, the values of elites, and environmental pressures all contribute to change and innovation. Thus far in the book, the chapters have focused on organizational characteristics, including the interplay between power, leadership, and decision making with elite or dominant coalition values. Ever since the analysis of organizational structure, in Chapter 3 and particularly in this chapter, the environments of organizations have been seen as crucial for organizational structures and processes. The next chapter will be specifically focused on organizational environments.

In regard to innovation and change, we can conclude that these are critical processes for organizations. They are at the heart of our overall interest in effectiveness. They contribute to growth, survival, and death. The purpose here was not to do a life-cycle analysis but, rather, to demonstrate that these are not trivial processes for organizations. Again, if we could identify exactly what leads to growth or which changes or innovations are going to be successful, we would have the key to understanding and control of organizations. Although we do not have the key, we do have at least partial answers, which have been identified in the analysis thus far. Bringing in the environment will add another element to our understanding.

EXERCISES

1. Although you may not know too much about the history of your two organizations, describe what you know of their foundings. What changes have taken place in them? What factors led to the changes?
2. Describe any innovations that have taken place in your two organizations in terms of the individual, organizational, and environmental factors that were important in the innovation process.

Chapter 9

Organizational Environments and Interorganizational Relationships

•◆•

OVERVIEW

Organizational environments have been a prominent part of our analyses of organizations. In this chapter, environments are considered in several ways. First, we look at the environmental conditions that must be present for the formation of organizations. Organizations don't just happen. Earlier societies were not societies of organizations.

The chapter then discusses various ways in which organizational environments can be categorized and analyzed. Are environments turbulent or calm? Are we interested in the legal environment or the technological environment? Each environmental dimension has a different impact on an organization.

The last topic in the chapter is "interorganizational relationships." This topic is important for several reasons. First, the environment is experienced on an interorganizational basis—the legal environment is enforced by local, state, and federal agencies. Also, organizations attempt to influence the environment through interorganizational linkages, such as through memberships on boards of directors or the formation of strategic alliances. Interorganizational relationships are powerful weapons.

The critical importance of organizational environments has been emphasized throughout our analysis. Terms such as *global economy* and *core and peripheral markets* emphasize the fact that all organizations are affected by their surroundings. In this chapter we will deal specifically with the nature and impact of organizational environments. By environment we mean *"all phenomena that are external to and potentially or actually influence the population under study"* (Hawley, 1968:330; italics added). The population under study here, of course, is organizations.

This chapter has three purposes. The first purpose is to demonstrate how configurations of environmental conditions were necessary for the very formation of organizations in the first place. The second purpose is to develop categories by which organizational environments can be easily conceptualized. The third purpose is to examine how the environment "enters" organizations by means of interorganizational linkages through the use of networks, interlocking boards of directors, and other mechanisms.

THE ENVIRONMENT AND THE FORMATION OF ORGANIZATIONS

Organizational formation (or birth or founding) was considered in the last chapter from the perspective of the population ecology model. Here we move back in history to consider the environmental conditions necessary for the emergence of organizations as basically new forms of social interaction. Stinchcombe (1965) presented a seminal work on the interface between environments and the formation of organizations. He notes (p. 143) that special-purpose organizations took over various social functions, such as economic production, policing, education, political action, and military action, at different rates in different societies. These organizations have replaced or supplemented multipurpose groups such as the family or the community for these purposes.

If organizations take over such tasks, there must be an awareness of alternative ways of accomplishing these tasks. The alternative forms must be seen as having an attractive cost–benefit calculation, and the people involved must have sufficient wealth, legitimacy, and strength of numbers to get the new organization off the ground. These resources must be translated into power in order to overcome resistance from those interested in maintaining the older system.

These conditions have not been distributed randomly throughout history, but they have been present in sufficient degrees to allow new organizations and new organizational forms to emerge. Both new organizations and new organizational forms suffer the liability of newness that has been discussed. Stinchcombe notes that new organizations are more likely to survive than are new organizational forms.

Basic Environmental Conditions.   The conditions just discussed are actually intermediate variables between some more basic environmental characteristics and the rate of organizational formation. One of the basic characteristics necessary for organizational development is the general literacy and specialized advanced schooling of the population. The presence of literacy raises the likelihood that each of the intermediate variables will be sufficiently present for organizational development to occur. Stinchcombe states that

> [L]iteracy and schooling raise practically every variable which encourages the formation of organizations and increases the staying power of new organizations. It enables more alternatives to be posed to more people. It facilitates learning new roles with no nearby role model. It encourages impersonal contact with customers. It allows money and resources to be distributed more easily to strangers and over distances. It provides records of transactions so that they can be enforced later, making the future more predictable. It increases the predictability of the future environment of an organization by increasing the available information and by making possible a uniform body of law over a large area. (pp. 150–51)

In addition to the key variable of education and literacy, several other factors are crucial for the conditions permitting organizational formation. Urbanization is a second factor identified by Stinchcombe in this regard. He notes that the rate of urbanization should be slow enough to allow the rural migrants to learn and develop routines of urban living. At the same time, the development of urban life is associated with greater heterogeneity of lifestyle, thus providing more alternative working and living arrangements. The urban scene requires dealing with strangers, and this too assists organizational development, since ascriptive role relationships are likely to be minimized. Impersonal laws are necessary in urban areas just as they are in organizations. Urbanization, like education, increases the organizational capacity of populations, although not to the same degree, according to Stinchcombe.

A third important factor, and one that has long been identified, is the presence of a money economy. This sort of economy

> liberates resources so that they can be more easily recruited by new organizations, facilitates the formation of free markets so that customers can transfer loyalties, depersonalizes economic social relations, simplifies the calculation of the advantages of alternative ways of doing things, and allows more precise anticipation of the consequences of future conditions on the organization. (Stinchcombe, 1965:152)

A fourth condition is the political base of a society. For the creation of new organizations, political revolutions are held to be important because of their rearranging of vested interest groups and power systems. Resources are allocated on bases different from those in the past.

The final societal condition identified by Stinchcombe is the existing level of organizational density. The greater the density and the greater the range of organizational alternatives already available, the greater the likelihood that people will have had experience in organizations. This suggests that there is likely to be an exponential growth curve for organizations in a society—assuming, of course, that the other conditions are also present.

This analysis has been concerned with the conditions of the society that are important for the formation of new organizations and new organizational forms. Although the picture has been drawn in broad relief with historical data, the factors identified remain important for analyses at any time.

Technology and Organizational Form.   Stinchcombe's analysis contains an additional set of ideas that is relevant for our purposes. He maintains that the technological conditions available at the time of the formation of an organization set the limits for the form the organization can take.

> Organizations which have purposes that can be efficiently reached with the socially possible organizational forms tend to be founded during the period in which they become possible. Then, both because they can function effectively with those organizational forms and because the forms tend to become institutionalized, the basic structure of the organization tends to remain relatively stable. (p. 153)

The emphasis on technology is consistent with the argument here, with the addition that if the newly introduced organizational form is compatible with the technology of the times, it tends to persist over time regardless of gradual changes in technology.

The emphasis in this section has been on the formation of new organizations and new organizational forms. The implication is that the environment at the time of organizational formation is critical for the form that the organization takes and that this form persists over time. That may be an oversimplification. The conditions surrounding the origins of an organization do persist in their impact on the organization, but these conditions are constantly being confronted with ongoing environmental conditions (Meyer and Brown, 1977). The organizational–environmental relationship is dynamic.

ENVIRONMENTAL DIMENSIONS

Thus far, we have treated the environment in a rather undifferentiated manner. In the next two sections we will consider two ways in which aspects of the environment can be categorized into useful dimensions.

In this section we will examine the content of the environment, including technological and economic considerations. In the following section we will consider the environment from a more analytical perspective that includes factors such as the stability or the turbulence of the environment. We will then combine these sets of dimensions.

Technological Conditions

Technological conditions are a convenient starting point, since this topic and the research surrounding it have already been the subject of much attention and can set the stage for the less systematically researched topics that follow.

It will be remembered, following the works of Perrow, Lawrence and Lorsch, and others, that organizations operating in an uncertain and dynamic technological environment exhibit structures and internal processes different from those operating in a more certain and unchanging technological environment. At this point we need not review the direction of the relationships and the supporting evidence, but it is important to recognize that the organization responds to this aspect of its environment. In fact, in the business firms Lawrence and Lorsch studied, special organizational divisions were established (research and development) to keep the organization current. In other organizations, departments such as industrial engineering and management information systems are so designated.

Beyond their empirical evidence that technology is salient in the operation of organizations, these findings have implications vital to our understanding of organizational–environmental interactions. In the first place, technology and other environmental characteristics are something "out there." The organization does not exist in a vacuum. Technological developments in any sphere of activity have the potential to get to the organizations related to them. New ideas come into circulation and become part of the environment as soon as they cease being the private property of any one individual or organization. Since sciences have norms of distributing knowledge, scientific developments become part of the public domain as a matter of course. A development that can be patented is a different matter, but if it is thought to be significant, other organizations will seek to buy it, copy it, or further extend the previous development. In any case, an organization must keep up with such developments in the technological spheres crucial to its continued success.

More subtle forms of the technological environment are found outside the hard sciences and engineering. In management and administration, new ideas are introduced through research, serendipity, or practice. In service-oriented organizations, such as schools, social-work agencies, and hospitals, the same types of technological shifts can be seen.

Organizations do not respond to technological change through simple absorption. Instead, the organization's political process operates through the advocacy of change or stability. Organizations of every kind contain their own internal "radical" and "reactionary" responses to technological and all other environmental conditions. Since the rate of technological and other environmental changes is not constant for all organizations, the degree to which organizations must develop response mechanisms varies. For all, however, technology remains an important consideration.

Legal Conditions

Another environmental dimension that is critical for organizations is the legal conditions that are part of the organization's surroundings. At one extreme are organizations that operate outside the law and respond to the legal system by attempting to evade the law at all costs and remain underground. At another extreme are local voluntary organizations that have no involvement whatsoever with safety, health, or other kinds of local, state, and national laws and regulations.

The overwhelming majority of organizations must live with federal, state, and local laws and regulations as a major part of their environments. At the very least, legal mandates set many of the operating conditions of many organizations, ranging from specific prohibitions of certain kinds of behavior to regulations requiring the periodic reporting of income and staffing. The importance of laws is exemplified by the staffs of legal and other experts who are integral to many organizations and who are specifically charged with interpreting and protecting their organizations' positions. The trend toward lawyers serving as chief executive officers is indicative of the critical nature of legal conditions for organizations (Priest and Rothman, 1985).

When a major new law is passed or an interpretation modified, organizations must make some important changes if the law has relevance to them, as analyses of civil rights laws have demonstrated (Edelman, 1990). Relatively mundane matters such as tax and employment regulations are important for nearly all organizations. More striking are the cases of major shifts that affect organizations in the public and private sectors. For example, U.S. Supreme Court decisions regarding school desegregation have had tremendous impacts on the school organizations involved. Concern for the environment has resulted in laws and regulations regarding pollution that have affected many organizations as they utilize their resources in fighting or complying with the new statutes. It should be evident that legal conditions result from actions of legislative bodies, the judicial system, and the executive branches of government at all levels.

Organizations are not benign recipients of laws and regulations. Organizations in all sectors attempt to select the appropriate legal strategy aimed at the appropriate arm of government. Organizations are important actors in the development of laws and regulations through their lobbying efforts (Champagne, Neef, and Nagel, 1981).

The legal dimension is an important component of "coercive" forces identified by institutional theorists. These were discussed in Chapter 3.

Political Conditions

Laws are not passed without pressure for their enactment. The political conditions that bring about new laws also have their effects on organizations. Strong political pressures to reduce or increase military and aerospace spending have led to crises or opportunities for organizations in those areas. Police departments have been buffeted back and forth between support for "law and order" and condemnation of "police brutality." School systems have drastically altered parts or all of their curricula in the face of threats from groups concerned with such topics as sex education and "left-wing" textbooks. Some organizations are directly affected by the political process because their hierarchy can be drastically changed by election results. All government units face this possibility after every election as top officials are changed at the discretion of a new administration.

Organizations in the private sector are less directly affected than public ones, but they must still be attuned to the political climate. Since lobbying for legislation that will provide tax advantages or favorable international trade agreements is an accepted part of the legislative and administrative system of the United States, organizations must devote resources to the lobbying process.

Lobbying can be very successful. Corporate tax rates are lower in states in which large corporations control a large proportion of the assets. This does not happen by accident (Jacobs, 1987, 1988). As was indicated in the previous chapter, the business policies of states have had major implications for the development of transportation, fossil fuels, and other business activities (Prechel, 1997, 2000).

Once legislation is passed in the legal dimension, political pressures are still brought to bear in the implementation of regulations. An analysis of the early history of the Occupational Safety and Health Administration (OSHA) in the United States documents the strong political pressures that were placed on this organization (McCaffrey, 1982). Anecdotal evidence suggests that this agency remains under intense political pressures.

Well-documented illegal corporate contributions to domestic and foreign political parties and individuals are further evidence of the importance of the political factor for organizations. In a different arena, "institutional advertising" is designed to generate public support through its presentation of the advertising organization as a good corporate citizen.

Research on the formation (births) and mortality (deaths) of newspapers in Argentina and Ireland found that political turbulence was related to the founding of the newspapers (Carroll and Delacroix, 1982; Delacroix and Carroll, 1983). At the same time, newspapers founded during periods of turbulence are outlived by newspapers born under stable conditions. Additional research on political conditions and organizations would undoubtedly reveal more such patterns.

Politics plays a role at the local level as well as at the national or global level. A county in Texas decided to deny a tax break to Apple because that company provided health benefits for unmarried partners of employees (Verhovek, 1993). Local politics in that county affected Apple and county government organizations.

We have portrayed the political environment in a rather gentle way thus far. It is hardly gentle when something like a political revolution takes place. A political revolution is a form of "environmental jolt" (Meyer, 1982). The collapse of the former East Germany is a case in point. The changed political system had ramifications for almost all organizations. Even cultural organizations, such as symphony orchestras, were affected by this jolt (Allmendinger and Hackman, 1996). Interestingly, the onset of socialism in East Germany had less impact on orchestras than its collapse.

Another aspect of the political environment, also from a study of former East Germany, is the political system itself. This study found that branches of the Zeiss company in East Germany were unable to innovate as much as their partner branches in the West. Innovation by plan—the political environment—did not work (Kogut and Zander, 2000).

Economic Conditions

An environmental condition that is more obvious, but again strangely neglected by most sociologists, is the state of the economy in which the organization is operating. To most business leaders, this is the crucial variable. In universities and in government work, experience also shows the importance of economic conditions when budgets are being prepared, defended, and appropriated. The sheer availability of financial resources is one of the crucial environmental conditions for the birth of organizations (Pennings, 1982). Changing economic conditions serve as important constraints on any organization. The market structure in the United States has been very stable over time, even though there are major swings through large and small recessions, depressions, inflationary periods, and so on (Burt, 1988).

Economic changes do not affect all parts of an organization equally. In periods of economic distress, an organization is likely to cut back or eliminate those programs it feels are least important to its overall goals, except, of course, for those instances in which external political pressures preclude such "rational" decisions (Freeman, 1979). Economic affluence permits government agencies to engage in a wider range of programs. For example, a study of state employment agencies found that agencies in wealthier states provided unemployment insurance to a greater proportion of the unemployed than did the agencies in the poorer states (Klatzky, 1970b). Since these agencies were paying out more, they also received a disproportionately larger share of federal funds than their less affluent peers in other states. The rich agencies get richer as the poor agencies get poorer. Of course, political changes can bring about changed economic conditions for these governmental organizations. It is impossible to disentangle political and economic factors in many cases.

Changing economic conditions are, in fact, excellent indicators of the priorities of organizations. That organizational programs vary according to the economic conditions that are confronted contributes to a paradox for most organizations. Since total rationality is not an assumption of this analysis, it can be safely assumed that an organization cannot be sure of exactly what contribution each of its parts makes to the whole. For example, research and development can be viewed as one of the luxuries that should go when an organization faces some hard times. But by concentrating on the production and distribution of what R & D has done in the past, the organization may miss the development of a new product that would be of great long-run benefit. Periods of economic difficulty do force organizations to evaluate their priorities and trim areas that are viewed as being least vital. As in the case of the communication process, the criteria by which the evaluations are accomplished are the key variables, and there is no assumption being made here that the decision process is rational.

Economic conditions surrounding organizations improve and decline with the organizations responding to the situation. Competition is an important factor in their responses in any situation. Economic competition can be most easily seen among business organizations, where success is measured in the competitive marketplace. Although the competition is not "pure," it is still an evident part of the value system in a private-enterprise economy. Economic competition among organizations takes many forms. An analysis of the patterns of corporate philanthropy among a set of business firms concluded that corporate philanthropy was a co-optive relationship, akin to advertising (Burt, 1983). The reasoning behind this conclusion was that the proportion of net income that an organization gave to charity varied with the extent to which the firms were dependent upon consumption by people who were able to do something about uncertainty in the demand for their product. A supermarket chain might thus engage in widely publicized charitable efforts in an effort to try to ensure continued patronage in a local market by appearing to be a good citizen.

Less evident than competition between business firms, but equally real, is economic competition among and within organizations outside the business sphere. From repeated experiences in government agencies at several levels, it is clear that competition is fierce during budget season (Wildavsky, 1964). Government agencies are all competing for part of the tax revenues, which constitute a finite "pot." Organizations that rely on contributions from members, such as churches, are also affected by the general economic conditions, since the contributors have more or less income available. An interesting research question is the extent to which the severity of economic competition varies among organizations in all sectors of society. It appears almost equal, regardless of the organizations' major emphases.

Demographic Conditions

Demography is another frequently overlooked factor. The number of people served and their age and sex distributions make a great deal of difference to all organizations. As a general rule, an organization can predict its probable "market" for the future from information in census data, but population shifts, such as those resulting from migration, are less predictable and can make an organization vulnerable. In a society where race, religion, and ethnicity are important considerations, shifts in these aspects of the demographic condition must also be considered.

The most striking examples of the importance of demographic change have come from organizations located in the central cities of growing and declining metropolitan areas. Businesses, schools, and police departments have different clienteles from what they once had, even though the organizations themselves might not reflect this. At least in the short run, it is the urban poor and minority group members who suffer the consequences. The organizations themselves, however, eventually undergo transitions (often painful) as they begin to realize that their clienteles have become different and that they themselves must change.

Demographic distributions within an organization have important ramifications for a wide variety of organizationally important issues, such as performance, innovation and adaptability, turnover, and interorganizational linkages (Pfeffer, 1983). For organizations that use an external labor market, demographic conditions in the environment would thus be reflected within the organization. For example, fast-food restaurants experienced a shortage of younger workers in the late 1980s and turned to older workers for their counter staff.

Ecological Conditions

Related to the demography scene is the general ecological situation surrounding an organization. The number of organizations with which it has contacts and relationships and the environment in which it is located are components of the organization's social ecological system. An organization in an urban area is much more likely to have contacts with a myriad of other organizations than is one in a rural area. Since the density of other organizations around any particular organization varies widely, the potential for relationships also varies.

If we shift from social ecology to the physical environment, we find that the relationships between organizations and ecological conditions become even more evident because of the recent concerns about the total ecological system. Organizations have effects on the environment as is abundantly demonstrated by the various organizations that pollute and the others that fight pollution.

A more subtle point is that the environment affects organizations. Factors such as climate and geography set limits on how organizations allocate resources. Transportation and communication costs rise if an organization is distant from its markets or clients. Even such mundane items as heating and cooling expenses must be considered limits on an organization.

Some organizations are located to take advantage of physical environmental conditions. This is most easily seen in the case of organizations using physical raw materials, such as ore or petroleum, or those using particular characteristics of the environment, such as ski areas. More subtle is the fact that organizations such as national professional associations and trade associations tend to be located in just one place in the United States—Washington, D.C. That is where their action is. It is their social ecological environment. Although ecological factors are generally constants, since only in unusual circumstances are there significant changes, these conditions cannot be ignored in a total organizational analysis involving comparisons between organizations.

Cultural Conditions

The environmental conditions discussed thus far are fairly straightforward. The culture surrounding an organization is much harder to conceptualize. In Chapter 3 the importance of national cultures for organizational structure was discussed in detail, but there is more to culture than national culture.

Although the influence of national culture is now an accepted fact, it is not clear whether culture overrides other factors in determining how an organization is shaped and operates. There is evidence suggesting that organizations at an equivalent technological level—for example, at the same degree of automation of production—are quite similar in most respects, as was indicated in the chapters on structure. The basic problem is to sort out the influences of these various environmental factors as they impinge on the organization. Unfortunately, not enough is yet known for such fine distinctions to be made. The various factors discussed so far definitely interrelate in their organizational effects in a very complex interaction pattern. For example, it appears that the more routine and standardized the technology, the less the impact of cultural factors. The production of children's toy automobiles is probably carried out in similar organizational forms in Hong Kong, London, Japan, Switzerland, and Tonka, Minnesota. When one moves to less routinized technological operations, such as local government, the administration of justice, or highway construction, the impact of culture is likely to be higher. Culture is important for organizational structuring. It also has an important impact on the ways in which organizations formulate their strategies for the future (Schneider, 1989).

Culture is not a constant, even in a single local setting. Values and norms change as events affect the population involved. If they involve conditions relevant to the organization, these shifts are significant for it. Newspaper editorials, letters to the editor, and other colorations of reports in the mass media indicate how values can change in regard to particular organizations or types of organizations. These value shifts may precede or accompany political shifts, which would have a more direct impact. Changes in consumer tastes represent another way that cultural conditions can affect organizations. Examples of this are easily found; a dramatic one is that of the Ford Motor Company's contrasting experiences with the Edsel and Mustang cars. Tobacco companies are faced with major shifts in values and continue to scramble to reduce the damage caused by the anti-tobacco movement (Dunbar and Wasilewski, 1985).

The culture–organization relationship is not a one-way street. Organizations attempt to shape cultural values through their public relations efforts. Organizations also shape cultures as they expand into world markets. The movement of Japanese automobile firms into the U.S. manufacturing scene has shaped the behavior of their suppliers, who had to learn to supply on a "just-in-time" basis (Florida and Kenney, 1991). Powerful organizations are very capable of changing cultural values.

ANALYTICAL DIMENSIONS

Another way of categorizing aspects of the environment is by their analytical elements (Aldrich, 1979:53–70; see also Aldrich and Marsden, 1988). As we will see, it is possible to intertwine a variation of Aldrich's dimensions with those just outlined. Aldrich's list of dimensions is described below.

Environmental Capacity

The capacity of an environment is to its "richness" or "leanness," or the level of resources available to an organization. According to Aldrich:

> Organizations have access to more resources in rich environments, but such environments also attract other organizations. Stockpiling and hoarding of resources is probably not as prevalent in rich as in lean environments. Lean environments also promote cut-throat competitive practices, and apart from rewarding organizations capable of stockpiling and hoarding, lean environments reward efficiency in the use

of resources. Two alternatives are open to organizations in lean environments: move to a richer environment, or develop a more efficient structure. The latter alternative can be accomplished by improving operating practices, merging with other organizations, becoming more aggressive vis-à-vis other organizations, or moving to a protected subenvironment through specialization. (p. 53)

There are many examples of such organizational responses. American Airlines, for instance, moved its corporate headquarters from New York City to Dallas. Although the phrase "rich and lean environment" was not used, the reasons given for the move—access to qualified personnel and more modern facilities—essentially had that meaning. At times some of the responses that Aldrich suggests are not possible. Legal requirements, for example, may prevent merger because of the threat of monopoly. In such cases, as Pfeffer and Nowak (1976) point out, organizations may engage in joint ventures. Joint ventures involve the investment of resources from several organizations in a single large project, such as the Concorde airplane developed by France and England. Joint ventures such as this are a form of interorganizational relationship that will be considered shortly.

Environmental Homogeneity–Heterogeneity

This dimension refers to the degree of similarity or differentiation within the environment. A homogeneous environment is simpler for organizations, since standardized ways of responding can be developed. Many organizations attempt to make their environment more homogeneous by limiting the kinds of products made, clients served, markets entered, and so on. Social service organizations consistently attempt to make their environment homogeneous by referring clients that do not fit within their operations to other social service organizations. The result of this, of course, is that the most difficult clients are referred and referred and referred. This is yet another form of interorganizational linkage.

Environmental Stability–Instability

This term refers to the extent of turnover of elements or parts of the environment. Stability, like homogeneity, permits standardization. Instability leads to unpredictability, which organizations resist. Any aspect of an organization's environment can be stable or unstable, whether it be economic, legal, or technological conditions. An environment can be stable for a long time and then undergo a major upheaval (Gersick, 1991).

Environmental Concentration–Dispersion

Concentration or dispersion in the environment involves the distribution of the elements in the environment. Are they located in one place or are they scattered across a large area? It is easier for an organization to operate with a more concentrated environment, as in the case of customers or clients.

Domain Consensus–Dissensus

Organizations claim a domain or a market. This dimension refers to the degree to which those claims are recognized or disputed by other parties, such as government agencies. If the interested and relevant parties agree that a particular organization has the right and the obligation to operate in a particular way in a particular area, there is domain consensus. This dimension is thus concerned with organizational "turf."

Organizations attempt to achieve domain consensus by securing protective legislation or regulations, such as import quotas, tariffs, or exclusive rights to a sales territory. In the public sector, there are frequent consensus–dissensus debates about federal, state, or local responsibilities for programs in transportation, education, or social welfare. Disputes over domain are another way organizations relate to one another.

Environmental Turbulence

This is the most difficult of Aldrich's dimensions to understand, because turbulence seems a great deal like instability. Turbulence here means that there is a great deal of causal interconnection (tight coupling) among the elements in the environment. In a turbulent environment, there is a high rate of environmental interconnection. An economic shift has political and technological ramifications in a turbulent environment. The movement of business firms from the Northeast to the Sun Belt in the United States is an example of such turbulence. This movement has lowered the tax base in the Northeast, forcing increases in the tax rates to maintain essential and nonessential services, which in turn has led to additional decisions to move. These moves also affect other sectors, such as education, health, and social services.

On the basis of their research, Dess and Beard (1984) believe that the foregoing six dimensions can be reduced to three dimensions. They propose that the dimensions of munificence (capacity), complexity (homogeneity–heterogeneity and concentration–dispersion), and dynamism (stability–instability and turbulence) capture the essence of Aldrich's distinctions. On that basis, we can now intertwine the content dimensions with the analytical dimensions (see Figure 9–1). Each of the content dimensions can be characterized by its munificence, complexity, and dynamism.

Before turning to an analysis of how environments are perceived by the organizations, one other characteristic of environments, which is not included in these dimensions, must be considered. This is the degree to which the environment itself is organized (Jurkovich, 1974). This is crucial in regard to consumers, for example, since organized consumers can be much more threatening to an organization than nonorganized individuals. Most environmental pressures come from other organizations in the form of government agencies, competing organizations, cultural organizations, and the like. When we examine interorganizational relationships, the specific linkages between organizations and their counterparts will be analyzed in detail.

ANALYTICAL CATEGORIES

	MUNIFICENCE	COMPLEXITY	DYNAMISM
CONTENT CONDITIONS			
TECHNOLOGICAL			
LEGAL			
POLITICAL			
ECONOMIC			
DEMOGRAPHIC			
ECOLOGICAL			
CULTURAL			

FIGURE 9–1   Environmental Dimensions
Source: Andrew H. Van de Ven and Diane L. Ferry, *Measuring and Assessing Organizations* (New York: John Wiley, 1980), p. 298.

THE PERCEPTION OF THE ENVIRONMENT

We have been proceeding as though the environment is simply something "out there" beyond the organization, which anyone in the organization can readily spot and identify. It would be handy if that were the case, but it is not. The environment comes into the organization as information and, like all information, is subject to the communications and decision-making problems that have been identified. Environmental information is information to be processed.

People have different positions in organizations. Some people are identified as "gate keepers" (Nagi, 1974) or "boundary spanners," who are designated to admit certain information that is relevant to the organization. Their perceptions are influenced by their positions within the organization. Of course, it is difficult to determine where the organization stops and the environment begins. Different positions are at an organization's boundaries, depending on what the activity at the moment is. At times it can be the switchboard operator; at other times it is the president or the chief executive officer (Starbuck, 1976).

An organization selects those aspects of the environment with which it is going to deal (Starbuck, 1976:1078–80). The selection process is affected by the selection processes of other organizations with which it is in contact. At the same time, of course, interorganizational linkages are affected by environmental pressures. In this manner, organizations go about constructing or inventing their environments. The scope of the domain or environment claimed or selected by organizations has an impact on its operations. Narrow domain claims are associated with stability, broad and inconsistent claims with loss of functions. Broad claims coupled with technological capacity and newness lead to domain expansion (Meyer, 1975). Domain claims seldom contract.

Organizational theory has stressed the importance of perceived uncertainty in the environment (Duncan, 1973). It is equally important to stress that much of the environment that is perceived is actually quite certain, rather than uncertain. Colleges and universities, for example, face a certain demographic profile of the number and distribution of potential students. Business firms face a certain environment of governmental regulations. The environment thus contains elements of certainty and uncertainty. Even when an environment is certain, of course, there is no guarantee that it will be perceived as such (Milliken, 1990).

Just as the perceptions of individuals are shaped by their experiences, so are the perceptions of organizations. Organizations may actually be more realistic than individuals because of their constant comparisons with and sharing personnel among comparable organizations (Starbuck, 1976:1080–81), but it has not yet been clearly demonstrated that this is the case. It must be remembered that the perceivers of the environment are themselves individuals, all with idiosyncrasies in perception.

THE IMPACT OF THE ENVIRONMENT ON THE ORGANIZATION

What do all these environmental factors, however selected and perceived, do to organizations? There are several answers. In the first place, organizations vary in their vulnerability to environmental pressures (Jacobs, 1974). The more dependent an organization is on its environment, the more vulnerable it is. An organization with strong financial resources is less vulnerable to economic fluctuations than is one with no reserves. In the 1970s and early 1980s, petroleum manufacturers were highly dependent on and vulnerable to political shifts in their sources of raw materials and their markets. They attempted to manipulate their environment by stabilizing the political conditions. Tobacco companies attempted to manage, regulate, and reduce the damage of the antismoking movement (Dunbar and Wasilewski, 1985). It is interesting to note here that the antismoking movement is the environment for tobacco companies and that this environment includes government agencies, citizens' groups, airline workers, and numerous other factions. Tobacco smoke is an alien part of my personal environment.

When an organization is vulnerable, it reacts to the environment. Several studies have shown that strong environmental pressures are related to increased formalization and a general "tightening" of the organization (see Boddewyn, 1974; Freeman, 1973; Khandwalla, 1972; and Pfeffer and Leblebici, 1973). It is odd that the environmental pressures do this, since in many ways the loosely coupled organization is more adaptive to the environment and is more likely to develop innovations that might be beneficial over the long run (Weick, 1976). Organizations that are vulnerable to the environment, of course, face a greater risk of failure if an innovation happens not to be successful.

Every organization is dependent on its environment to some degree. Each adapts internal strategies to deal with the perceived pressures (Snow and Hrebiniak, 1980). Contingency theory strongly suggests that there is no best way to cope with environmental pressures. The specific stance that an organization takes derives from choices that are made within it. This decision-making process is a political one in the sense that different options are supported by different factions within the decision-making structure. The option finally selected is a consequence of the power of individuals and groups that support it. That environmental pressures often tighten the organization may be a consequence of the fact that this is the option that powerful segments of organizations have traditionally taken. It may not be the one most useful for the organization, of course.

Among the strategies that organizations develop for dealing with their environments, a critical one is to attempt to shape the environment itself. An analysis of pharmaceutical manufacturing firms found that they had been more successful than the typical firms in the phonograph-record industry largely because the pharmaceutical firms had been able to control relevant aspects of their environments. The pharmaceutical firms could exert control over pricing and distribution, patent and copyright laws, and external opinion leaders (Hirsch, 1975). This control of the environment was a source of greater profitability. Organizations attempt to gain and maintain power over environmental conditions that are of strategic importance to them.

It might appear that when resources are scarce, organizations might resort to illegal acts such as price fixing or other activities to restrain trade. Actually the opposite appears to be true. Counterintuitively, large firms in munificent environments were found to be more likely to commit illegal acts (Baureus and Near, 1991). Organizations compete with one another for technological, political, economic, legal, and other advantages. This competition takes place in overlapping dimensions of the environment. A political advantage can contribute to economic advantage and vice versa. For example, the interests of the financial and industrial core industries in the United States became vested interests in the U.S. State Department in the 1886 to 1905 period, whereas other interests were not as well protected in foreign policy (Roy, 1981; see also Carstensen and Werking, 1983; and Roy, 1983a,b). In the same vein, there is evidence that indicates that corporate elites in the United States and Great Britain have inclusive and diffusely structured economic and social relationships. These transcend individual firms and lead to interactions with government that promote policies favorable to these elites (Useem, 1982). Organizational environments are thus subject to actual, attempted, and perhaps even unintentional manipulation by the organizations within them.

INTERORGANIZATIONAL RELATIONSHIPS

At this point our analysis will move from a consideration of organizational environments in a broad, general sense to a consideration of the specific organizations in contact with one another through interorganizational relationships (IORs). The relationships of any single organization with its environment take place through the actions of other organizations—organizations affect organizations (Haunschild and Miner, 1997). The legal environment is experienced through the actions of government enforcement and regulative agencies; the economic environment through competing organizations, organizations that give donations, and so on. The cultural dimension of the environment has been identified as the basis of support for small family-run firms in the knitwear industry (Lazerson, 1995). Here cooperative IORs exist among knitwear firms in a community, rather than the competitive IORs that exist among other businesses.

Individuals as well as organizations are affected by IORs. For example, clients of social service organizations are vitally affected by IORs. A common practice is client referral. Theoretically, if one agency is unable to provide the needed services for a particular client, the individual is referred to an appropriate agency for service. What happens in practice is that clients who are easily treated or provided services are not referred, and the more difficult ones are referred, with the most difficult cases sometimes eventually "falling between the cracks" of the referring set of organizations.

At the societal level, there has been a long-standing concern with the actual and potential power of the "military-industrial complex." This refers to interorganizational patterns linking the military with industry into a powerful set of organizations that can dominate other spheres of life. Linkages among powerful organizations through interlocking boards of directors have become the focus of intense scrutiny by political and organizational sociologists.

Organizational theorists began paying attention to IORs when they started looking beyond organizational boundaries into organizational environments and when urban sociologists began to recognize urban communities as networks of organizations (Cook, 1977), particularly in regard to the delivery of social services (Litwak and Hylton, 1962; Warren, 1967). A consistent research finding is that integrated IORs contribute to improved health and social care at the community level (Alter and Hage, 1993; Goes and Park, 1997; Provan and Milward, 1995). To understand IORs, we will first examine the variety of forms of IORs that can be identified. We will also identify various levels of analysis that can be utilized in the understanding of IORs.

IOR: Forms and Levels

There is a general agreement that IORs have three basic forms. These are illustrated in Figure 9–2. The dyad or pairwise relationship is the simplest form of IOR and has probably received the most attention in empirical research. The interorganizational set idea was derived from analysis of role sets (Merton, 1957).

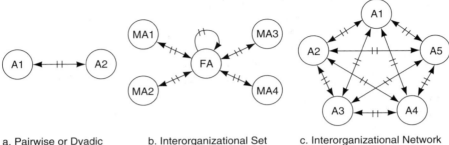

a. Pairwise or Dyadic   b. Interorganizational Set   c. Interorganizational Network
   Interorganizational
   Relationship

FIGURE 9–2   Forms of Interorganizational Relationships

Evan (1966) and Caplow (1964) introduced the organizational set idea into the literature. The emphasis is on a focal agency (FA in Figure 9–2) and its dyadic relationships with other organizations. It is very possible to trace the impact of changes in one dyadic relationship as they affect other pairwise relations within the set (Caplow, 1964; Evan, 1966).

The "action set" is a variation on the organizational set. The action set is composed of "a group of organizations formed in a temporary alliance for a limited purpose" (Aldrich, 1979:281). According to Aldrich, "Action sets may have their own formalized agreements, internal division of labor, behavioral norms vis-à-vis other organizations, and clearly defined principles for the recruitment of new members" (p. 281).

Interorganizational networks are more inclusive. They consist "of all organizations linked by a specified type of relation, and (are) constructed by finding the ties between all organizations in a population" (Aldrich, 1979:281). Networks are "the total pattern of interrelationships among a cluster of organizations that are meshed together in a social system to attain collective and self-interest goals or to resolve specific problems in a target population" (Van de Ven and Ferry, 1980:299). Analyses of business organizations are paying particular attention to networks. For example, when the knowledge base of an industry is both complex and expanding, the locus of innovation has been found to be in networks rather than individual firms (Powell, Koput, and Smith-Doerr, 1996). Networks have also been found to be the bases of integrative agreements that can transcend economic factors in decision making. This finding comes from an analysis of the New York garment industry (Uzzi, 1997). Embeddedness in social networks continues to be the basis of the corporate charitable contributions in the Twin Cities (Galaskiewicz, 1997) that were described in Chapter 1 and will also be considered here.

Networks of organizations can be incredibly complex. Figure 9–3 depicts the network of organizations involved in human organ transplantations. All of the organizations shown have a stake in the transplantation process. The individual recipient is faced with a bewildering array of organizations in the process of

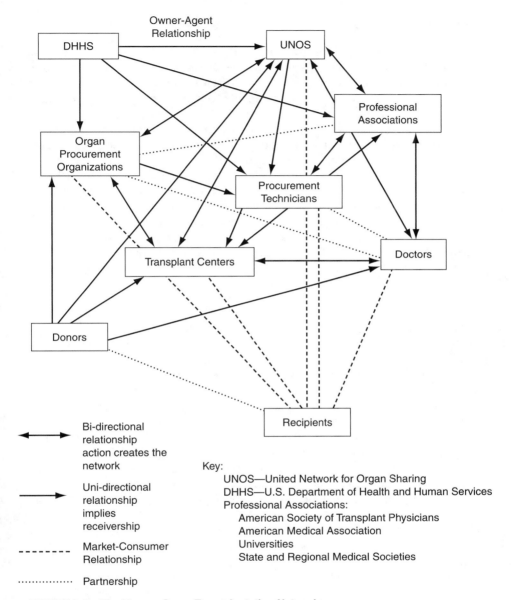

FIGURE 9–3   The Human Organ Transplantation Network
Source: Leslie A. Korb, *The Organ Transplantation Network: A Qualitative Examination of Power, Professionalism, Efficiency, Congruence and Compliance among Stakeholders* (unpublished Ph.D. dissertation, Albany, NY, University at Albany, 2000).

receiving a new heart or kidney. Each of the organizations involved is well meaning, but also self serving.

There is yet another form of IOR. This is the joint venture (Pfeffer and Nowak, 1976). It entails the creation of a new organizational entity by the joining of organizations in a partnership. The joint venture provides a way to avoid illegal mergers but still permits joint-capital investment on the part of the organizations involved. Pfeffer and Nowak note that joint ventures may occur in both profit and nonprofit sectors. Among profit-seeking organizations, oil and gas exploration efforts are a common form of joint venture, as the participating organizations, which have both competitive and symbiotic relationships among themselves, seek to reduce environmental uncertainty and reduce the risks for each participant. Joint ventures among nonprofit organizations are exemplified by alliances formed among private colleges. Through these alliances, they can achieve competitive advantages over independent colleges.

The joint venture is a good place to begin to examine the issue of level of analysis. In the case of the joint venture, one could focus attention on the newly created entity—the joint venture—or on the participating organizations, or on both. This is true for all forms of interorganizational interaction. In the case of the dyad, for example, the focus of interest could be on the organizations involved, on the relationship itself, or on the environment in which the dyadic relationship is based. The focus could also be on the individuals involved, such as boundary personnel. One of my very bright undergraduate students (Kristen) pointed out that it is individuals who carry out interorganizational relationships.

A major difficulty in interorganizational analyses is the ordering among the units of investigation. Using a simplified set of distinctions among the environment, the organizations involved, and the qualities of the relationships, we can identify the following alternatives as shown in Figure 9–4.

Each alternative represents a possible assumption about causal ordering. The possibility of feedback loops for each alternative complicates the situation further. Unfortunately, we do not have the answer regarding optimal ordering. The reason for this is that each component is interactive with the others. We probably have an extended example of the chicken-versus-egg argument here, with

FIGURE 9–4   Alternative Causal Orders
Source: Ronald S. Burt, Kenneth Christman, and Harold C. Kilburn Jr., "Testing a Structural Theory of Corporate Co-optation: Interorganizational Directorate Ties as a Strategy for Avoiding Market Constraints on Profits," *American Sociological Review*, Vol. 45, Figure 1, p. 827.

Environment ⟶	Organizations ⟶	Relationships
Organizations ⟶	Relationships ⟶	Environment
Relationships ⟶	Organizations ⟶	Environment
Organizations ⟶	Environment ⟶	Relationships
Environment ⟶	Relationships ⟶	Organizations
Relationships ⟶	Environment ⟶	Organizations

causal priority difficult to establish and probably not worth the effort, since each component does affect and is affected by the other.

Early analyses of IORs were overwhelmingly oriented to the delivery of human services such as health care, employment service, youth-serving organizations, and welfare organizations. The reason for this was the belief that interorganizational coordination would lead to improved service delivery and lower costs. Federal and state research support and programs reflected this emphasis, and researchers in the area responded to these emphases. The heavy emphasis on human-service IORs reflected aspects of the cultural dimension of the more general environment as the necessity of delivery of human services remains, thankfully, an ongoing cultural value. More recently, the focus has shifted to IORs in the business sector.

A FRAMEWORK FOR IOR ANALYSIS

This section focuses on IORs themselves, rather than on the participating organizations. We will consider characteristics of the general environment that appear to be important, specific situational factors affecting relationships, the bases of the relationships, resource flows in relationships, actual transactions, and finally outcomes of the relationships.

General Environmental Characteristics

We earlier identified dimensions of organizational environments. These same dimensions are critical for IORs. Thus, technological, legal, political, economic, demographic, ecological, and cultural conditions have been identified. For example, legal mandates have been shown to be an important basis for interaction (Hall et al., 1977). The cultural conditions in a community could support or repress IORs. Organizations in highly complex technological environments, such as nuclear-waste management, are known to each other and can rank each other's performance (Shrum and Wuthnow, 1988).

We can also analyze the environment along a different set of dimensions. As indicated in a previous section of this chapter, environmental capacity, homogeneity–heterogeneity, stability–instability, concentration–dispersion, consensus–dissensus, and turbulence are used as analytical environmental dimensions.

Turbulence has been identified as an important factor because it refers to the increasing causal interconnection among the elements in the environment. This means that there is a greater rate of interconnection among the organizations in a system (Emery and Trist, 1965; Terreberry, 1968). As turbulence increases, we would expect a higher rate of IORs.

Environmental complexity plays a similar role, as the number of activities and situations in the environment rise with increasing complexity. Organizations deal with complexity by specializing in a limited range of activities (Aldrich, 1979). This in turn leads to a loosely coupled system in which links among organizations are necessary for organizational survival. Aldrich's emphasis on survival suggests that organizations are not tightly bound to one another but only to the extent that they need one another for survival. This is too limited a view of the importance of the environment, since other characteristics, such as legal or economic situations, may lead to tighter binding than would simply be caused by complexity.

Homogeneity–heterogeneity has an impact on the range of organizations that have interactions, with a heterogeneous environment having the capability for a wider range of interactions. A heterogeneous environment leads to a proliferation of organizational programs, which may contribute to a higher level of interorganizational interaction (Aldrich, 1979).

Environmental capacity is similar to the economic dimension but also includes other resource bases. There are contradictory interpretations of the impact of environmental capacity. Galaskiewicz and Shatin (1981), on the one hand, report that poor neighborhoods draw fewer social service organizations and thus fewer interorganizational linkages. Aiken and Hage (1968), on the other hand, report that a shortage of resources draws organizations together. Turk (1973) found that the scale of municipal government was related to the development of interorganizational relationships. A rich environment may provide the organization with resources that permit it to engage in interorganizational relationships that it otherwise might not.

The stability–instability factor also appears to have mixed consequences. Galaskiewicz and Shatin report that stable clientele provides certainty for organizations and thus less need for interaction. Stability may also permit the development of formalized or routinized relationships (Aldrich, 1979).

The concentration–dispersion dimension is more straightforward. For example, concentration of manpower agencies contributes to interagency interactions (Aldrich, 1979). Similarly, the consensus–dissensus dimension appears to have a one-directional relationship with interorganizational interactions, with domain consensus contributing to more interactions.

Obviously, more research is needed to determine the patterns of relationships between the environment, IORs, and the organizations involved. Such research is difficult to accomplish, since environmental qualities have to be measured over time, as do IORs. The problem of causal ordering referred to earlier also presents severe analytical problems. Despite these problems, a full understanding of IORs is impossible without an adequate conceptualization and eventual measurement of these general environmental properties.

Situational Factors

There is agreement that the general environment is important as a setting for IORs. The specific situations in which IORs take place are also crucial. The situational factors that will be discussed represent preconditions for or antecedents of (Halpert, 1982) interactions. There are five factors that are important here.

1. Awareness. It has long been recognized that organizations operate in a "field" of other organizations (Warren, 1967). Less recognized is the fact that organizations vary in their awareness of the field around them. Awareness refers to both the recognition of other organizations and the recognition by organizational representatives that their organization is interdependent with other organizations in their field.

IORs do not occur automatically. A good part of interorganizational theory is predicated on the assumption that IORs will not occur unless there is awareness of potential or actual interdependence among the organizations involved (Levine, White, and Paul, 1963). There is a form of hierarchy of awareness (Klonglan et al., 1976). First is a general awareness of the existence of other organizations and their activities. The next level involves mutual acquaintance among the directors of the organizations. The focus on directors is probably too narrow, since acquaintances among staff members would be of great importance in some instances. The next levels of awareness involve specific interactions and joint board membership among directors. We will deal with these two issues separately, since they are a step beyond simple awareness.

An alternative approach suggests that there are two levels of awareness (Van de Ven and Ferry, 1980). At the more general level is the extent to which boundary spanners in organizations are knowledgeable about the goals, services, and resources present in other organizations. This awareness provides identification of alternative sources of services and resources. According to Van de Ven and Ferry, higher levels of awareness are likely to result in higher levels of interaction.

The second level of awareness involves interpersonal ties among organizational personnel (Boje and Whetten, 1981). These can involve "old school" ties, membership in common professional organizations, membership in common religious or fraternal organizations, simple friendships, or contacts that are based solely on work. Interpersonal ties are crucial for interorganizational relationships at periods of environmental turbulence (Galaskiewicz and Shatin, 1981). A higher level of interpersonal ties is seen to be linked to higher levels of interorganizational interaction.

The quality of ties is overlooked in most analyses. Obviously, friendships will yield a different form of interorganizational relationship than will animosity. A study of hotels in Sydney, Australia, revealed that friendship ties among hotel managers yielded enhanced collaboration and better information exchange. These friendships also mitigated competition (Ingram and Roberts, 2000). Other personal ties, such as those between auditors and their clients, reduce the likelihood of ties breaking (Seabright, Levinthal, and Fichman, 1992).

2. Domain Consensus–Dissensus. The domain issue has particular salience in interorganizational relationships. Unfortunately, several meanings are embedded in the usage that the concept has received.

One meaning has a simple spatial referent. The domain is the geographical area served by an organization, such as the "service area" or "catchment area" used by neighborhood health centers or the city as used by hotels. In these spatial cases, the issue of domain is usually settled in advance, and domain is not really an issue except for potential clients or customers who may straddle a border of two organizations' domains.

A more complex and important meaning of domain concerns the level of agreement about role or task differentiation among the organizations involved in human service IORs (Levine, White, and Paul, 1963). The roles organizations play relative to one another, in regard to their programs and services and clients to be served, are critical for the organizations involved and involve such issues as whether or not dyads of organizations serve common clients (Molnar, 1978). Domain consensus can also refer to the degree to which an organization's claim to a specific domain is disrupted or recognized by another organization (Aldrich, 1979).

Two issues are intertwined here. The first is the issue of consensus or agreement on domain; the second is that of the commonness of the domain. It is quite possible that organizations could claim the same domain with consensus or dissensus.

Another aspect of the domain issue involves ideological considerations. Ideological issues can include the compatibility of the goals of the organizations involved, conformity in treatment ideologies in social service organizations, or compatibility in understanding the nature of the issues faced (Benson et al., 1973; Boje and Whetten, 1981; Mulford, 1980). The ideological issue becomes important in practice. These differences, which can be severe or mild, affect the qualities of interactions among the organizations.

3. Geographical Proximity. The distribution of organizations in space has received relatively little attention in the literature on organizations in general. Geographical proximity refers to the spatial distance between organizations or their subunits. It has been noted that distance can facilitate or inhibit interactions (Broskowski, 1980). It is more difficult for both organizations and individuals to establish or maintain relationships across distances. It can also be noted that the type of unit involved in an IOR interacts with the spatial issue. Modern communication techniques permit the rapid flow of information across space, but clients or staff members are more difficult to transfer.

The decision to coordinate with another organization is easier if the organizations involved are physically close to each other. Proximity promotes familiarity of domains. In many communities several city or county agencies might be housed in the same building, such as a "public safety" facility. This proximity would facilitate interactions in comparison with organizations that are spread throughout some geographical area.

4. Localized Dependence. Related to geographical proximity is the degree to which organizations are dependent upon a local area for their resources (Galaskiewicz, 1979; Maas, 1979). Localized dependence refers to the extent to which needed resources are obtained only from a local area rather than from a more widely dispersed resource base. If organizations with localized dependence are successful in commanding localized resources, they are more powerful or central in the network of organizations in a community. If, on the other hand, there is high localized dependency with relatively weak access to resources, the organization is much more vulnerable to the power of other organizations.

5. Size. The final situational factor is the size of the actual or potential set or network of organizations. Most analyses have focused on the actual number of organizations in a network (Van de Ven and Ferry, 1980). Size is a situational factor in that at any given time there is a finite number of organizations available for interactions. In general, the number of organizations in a relationship is related to the complexity faced by any single organization. It is also likely that large numbers of relationships weaken the quality of the relationships (Caragonne, 1978; John, 1977). An increase in the number of organizations in a relationship affects dependencies, domains, and the potential rewards or resources for participating in the relationship. Again, the analogy with individuals is appropriate here. Many ties reduce the likelihood of each tie being strong, so that there would be a greater proportion of superficial linkages in a large network than in a smaller network. It appears that a large set or network would have the potential for dissipating resources and actions, but it could also provide many alternatives for an organization, in the areas of resource acquisition, client flows, and the like.

The number of relationships increases exponentially as group size increases (Caplow, 1964). The same thing would occur among organizations. The number of organizations in a relationship, or the number potentially available, thus is an important situational factor for interorganizational relationships.

Reasons for Interaction

IORs do not just happen. They occur in an environment and in a situational context. They also occur for reasons. There are three basic reasons for IORs (Galaskiewicz, 1985). The first is the procurement and allocation of resources such as facilities, materials, products, and revenues (Gulati and Gargiulo, 1999). These are crucial for organizational survival. The second is to form coalitions for political advocacy and advantage. The third is to achieve legitimacy or public approval. The last reason can be seen in instances of interlocking boards of directors among cultural organizations and corporations. On the basis of the study in the Minneapolis–St. Paul area, Galaskiewicz found that:

> . . . personnel from more influential companies tended to be recruited to more cultural boards and that companies tended to sit on the boards of more prestigious cultural organizations. One interpretation of these findings is that cultural organizations were striving to enhance their own reputations by aligning with the more influential companies in the area; and corporations were striving to enhance their legitimacy by aligning themselves with more prestigious cultural organizations. (pp. 296–97)

We will identify four specific reasons or bases for contact here. They range from ad hoc situations to those mandated by law or regulation. The outcome from each basis is likely to be different for the organizations involved and for the relationship itself.

1. Ad Hoc Bases. Relationships have an ad hoc basis when there is little or no previous patterning in the relationships among organizations. A specific need, problem, or issue may arise among two or more organizations. In the social service area, a client with an unusual problem may trigger one organization to call up another to get an opinion or to make a referral. Ad hoc bases are the least important for IORs, since they tend to be one-shot operations. If an ad hoc situation repeats itself or more elements enter the relationships among the agencies involved, other bases for a continued relationship will develop.

2. Exchange Bases. The exchange basis for IORs has been the dominant orientation toward such relationships since Levine and White's (1961) seminal paper. According to Levine and White, exchange is "any voluntary activity between two organizations which has consequences, actual or anticipated, for the realization of their respective goals or objectives" (p. 120). Cook (1977) has extended this formulation beyond the two-party implication of Levine and White. She examines exchange within networks of organizations and incorporates power differentials among organizations into her formulation. The exchange idea incorporates the notion that organizations must acquire resources and that exchange is the major mechanism by which this occurs.

The exchange basis can be seen as a form of bargaining in which each organization seeks to maximize its advantage in acquiring resources from another organization (Schmidt and Kochan, 1977). Although the exchange formulation seems to imply that this is bargaining among equals, modern exchange theory, as exemplified by Cook's work, does not make that assumption. Power differences among organizations are taken into account. Even when there is a great imbalance of power, the powerful organization that seeks to interact with a weaker organization can do so because of the power difference (Schmidt and Kochan, 1977). The exchange is unequal, but the participants do engage in resource exchange. The exchange basis emphasizes the importance of resource acquisition for the organizations involved. It also implies rationality, as the organizations seek to maximize their gains in interaction. All the problems associated with decision making in organizations must be considered in exchange interactions, since decisions here cannot be assumed to be any more rational than decisions made in other spheres of organizational actions.

Resource exchange has far-reaching consequences (Van de Ven and Walker, 1984). Perceptions of resource dependence are an important spur for IORs. Resource dependence is a powerful direct determinant of IOR communications, resource transactions, and consensus. Monetary transactions and client referrals involve different patterns of coordination.

Exchange is an important basis for interorganizational interactions. It becomes less of a factor, however, when the interactions among organizations become formalized. Formalization is likely if resource exchanges continue (Van de Ven and Walker, 1984).

3. Formalized Agreements. Formalization is the degree to which the interdependency among organizations is given official sanction by the parties involved (Marrett, 1971). This official sanction or recognition is typically written down and may be legally or contractually binding (Van de Ven and Ferry, 1980). A formal agreement is based on exchange. Once the agreement is signed or otherwise authorized, the relationship changes, since interactions are based on a specified pattern rather than ongoing through the exchange process at each interaction episode.

Another basis for interaction has a very different source from that of agreements among the organizations involved. In many instances, interactions among organizations are mandated from outside the interacting parties.

4. Mandatedness. This basis for IORs has received increasing attention in recent years. Mandatedness refers to the extent to which relationships are governed by laws or regulations. These laws or regulations are imposed on the relationship by legislative or administrative rulings—the legal environmental dimension. The organizational actors are brought together because of a legal-political mandate (Raelin, 1982). For example, laws regarding unemployment compensation may require a public employment agency to interact with a welfare department to determine client eligibility. Such interaction may or may not have occurred without a mandate present. A mandated relationship may place an organization in a contradictory position (Halpert, 1982). Compliance with the mandate may disrupt established procedures. At the same time, it may be necessary for the organization if it is to receive financial support. Mandated relationships may well lead to conflict, since organizations may be forced to interact even with domain dissensus, interpersonal animosities among members, and so on.

Mandated interactions do not guarantee that interactions will take place. Unless there is some sort of enforcement mechanism, organizations may ignore a mandate. Since mandates are typically associated with some type of resource flow and with monitoring, they usually do in fact serve as an important basis for interorganizational interactions. It is quite possible that an organization can receive contradictory mandates (Gardner and Snipe, 1970). This means that an organization will have to try to serve several mandates at one time along with its own orientations from an exchange perspective. It may seek to interact with one organization but be forced to interact with one or more other organizations. Again, this moves the analysis of interorganizational interactions still further from a basis of pure rationality.

Mandated interactions continue to receive attention in research and practice. Governmental regulatory agencies are mandated to interact with business firms. City and county government agencies are mandated to interact with state and federal agencies. Although exchange considerations enter into the passage of laws and regulations through the process of lobbying and the give-and-take of policy formulation, the presence of a strong and enforced mandate leads to IORs of a different form from those which evolve from ongoing exchanges. For example, a study found that mandated collective bargaining led to greater subunit power within organizations than was the case when mandated collective bargaining was not present (Schwochan, Fenilee, and Delaney, 1988). Another study found that the presence of mandates was related to greater frequency of interactions (Oliver, 1990). This would in turn lead to more intense interactions, and the relationship would tend to grow in many directions.

In this section we have examined ad hoc, exchange, formalized-agreement, and mandated bases of interorganizational interactions. Each basis has a different outcome. At the same time, all interorganizational interactions involve something passing between the organizations involved. We will now turn to a consideration of these resources that flow between organizations.

Resource Flows

Regardless of the environment, the situational factors, and the bases of interactions, interorganizational interactions have a content, and it is to this that we now turn. Exchange theory properly focuses on resource exchange, and we will examine resource interdependency among organizations. The flow of resources varies in intensity, so we will examine this quantitative aspect of interactions. We will then turn to the issue of joint programs, where organizations, in addition to exchanging resources, engage in activities together.

Resource Interdependence.   Situations in which two or more organizations are dependent upon one another for the resources each has access to or controls are the basis of resource interdependency. Resources take a variety of forms, such as inflows and outflows of information, money, and social support (Galaskiewicz and Marsden, 1978). There can be other resources for funds, facilities, and personnel. Organizations that have intersecting domains tend to be more interdependent. Equipment and meeting rooms can be added to the list of resources that could be exchanged; so can clients (Boje and Whetten, 1981; Mulford, 1980).

It has long been recognized that organizations are seldom capable of controlling all the resources they require (Levine and White, 1961; Litwak and Hylton, 1962). An interorganizational division of labor can develop in which the participating organizations specialize by providing a particular service in return for a particular resource they need (Aldrich, 1979). Each organization becomes dependent upon the other in this situation. Organizations tend to resist dependence and to attempt to make other organizations dependent upon them (Benson, 1975).

Intensity.   The level of resource investment required of the organizations involved in IORs determines the intensity of the relationship (Aldrich, 1979; Marrett, 1971). For service organizations, the higher the level of referrals, services provided, staff support, facilities and other resources, the greater the intensity of the relationship. Implicit in the consideration of intensity is the question of the relative proportion of an organization's resources that are invested in the relationship. The higher the proportion, the more intense the relationship and the greater the dependency (Baker, 1990).

The more intense the relationship, the more important it is for the organizations involved. The relationships that any organization has vary in their intensity from the casual to the all-consuming. The former makes little difference, whereas the latter has the potential to consume the organization if all its efforts involve interorganizational relationships and if those relationships use up all its resources.

Intensity is sometimes confused with or combined with the frequency of interactions. This is a bad mix, since frequent interactions can be casual but very intense interactions can be infrequent. For this reason, we will consider frequency in another context. Dyadic relationships, networks, and organizational sets can all vary in intensity. Interactions become most intense in crises. For example, the tragic disappearance of a female student at my university led to intense and prolonged interaction between the campus police and the state police. Research on disasters such as earthquakes and floods reveals similarly intense interactions (Drabek et al., 1981). When there is no crisis, relationships will be less intense. The impact of intensity is both networkwide and organization specific.

Joint Programs/Joint Ventures and Strategic Alliances.   There has been a rush of interest in what used to be known simply as joint programs. Joint programs are a special type of resource flow (Aiken and Hage, 1968; Mulford and Mulford, 1980). Here the emphasis is not simply on resource flows in the context of interdependency but also on substantial resource commitment and collaboration. Aiken and Hage found that joint programs were of particular importance to the welfare and health organizations that they studied. They were more salient than client, personnel, or financial support flows. Joint programs were not "minor incidents" in the lives of the organizations. Some had existed for more than twenty years (p. 919). Aiken and Hage also found that joint programs tended to foster other joint programs, since the IORs grew in scope and depth. Joint programs involve an investment of resources and an intense relationship. They also involve purposive actions in regard to some issue that is jointly confronted.

The concept of joint ventures and strategic alliances has become an important component in the literature on business organizations. The basic idea is that of joint ventures. Organizations come together for research and development purposes, such as in biotechnology. Participating organizations invest resources and pursue "enduring exchange relationships with one another" (Podolny and Page, 1998:59). The organizations can be traditional business firms, universities, e-commerce ventures, and government agencies. The hope is that these ventures and alliances will lead to new opportunities as new combinations of products and services are developed. The purpose of this interorganizational collaboration is innovation (Ahuja, 2000). This interaction is purposive and not just responsive to environmental pressures.

Transaction Forms

IORs are interaction processes between organizations and within networks and sets. These interactions can be structured in many ways. The forms of interaction are:

1. Interorganizational interactions can be *formalized* to varying degrees. Chambers of Commerce, Councils of Churches, and the National Collegiate Athletic Association (NCAA) all attempt to formalize interactions among members to some extent.

2. The relationships can be *standardized,* such as when community colleges and four-year colleges and universities have transfer agreements. When there is low standardization, each interaction is treated as unique.
3. Relationships vary in their *importance.* Important interactions are likely to be more frequent.
4. Frequency of interaction can be a two-edged sword. It can be related to both *cooperation and conflict* between organizations (Hall, Clark, and Giordano, 1978).
5. Relationships can vary in their *reciprocity or the symmetry* of the transactions between organizations. A small supplier might be entirely dependent on a large organizational customer. This large organizational customer is only minimally reliant on the small supplier.
6. This imbalance in dependency is a part of the *power differences* between organizations. In interorganizational networks, the centrality of organizations in the network give them their power.
7. Interorganizational relationships can take the forms of *cooperation or conflict.* The development of these forms is based on power differences and reciprocity in the interactions themselves. They are also based on differences in operating philosophies. When there is conflict, many transactions go through attempts at *conflict resolution.*
8. Finally, relationships can vary in the degree of *coordination* present. Coordination occurs when organizations adjust to one another in the pursuit of common goals.

INTERLOCKING BOARDS OF DIRECTORS

Interlocking boards of directors are an important and very different form of IOR. In this form a member or members of the board of directors (or board of trustees) of one organization also serve on boards of other organizations. Board interlocks take place in both the private and the public sectors.

Interlocking boards of directors have been the subject of commentary and research for a long time. In 1913, U.S. Supreme Court Justice Louis Brandeis warned that such interlocks contain many evils, such as the suppression of competition (Pennings, 1980b). Contemporary analyses of interlocks run the gamut from analyses of board interlocks as the means by which elites maintain their position and exercise societal control to scholarly analyses of the manner in which organizations attempt to control uncertainties by such interlocks. Interlocks serve as an invaluable source of information (Haunschild and Beckman, 1998).

In the basic form of director interlock, an officer or a director of one organization is a member of the board of directors of another organization. In another form of interlock, members of two organizations sit on the board of a third organization (Burt, Christman, and Kilburn, 1980). The interlocking organizations are not randomly selected. Since organizations cannot purchase or merge with all organizations in their environments because of limited resources and federal merger restrictions, interlocking boards of directors are a less direct way to link organizations. Interlocking directorates provide opportunities for collusion, co-optation, monitoring, legitimacy, career advancement, and social cohesion (Mizruchi, 1996).

In the world of interlocking directorates, financial institutions are the dominant actors (Keister, 1998). Commercial banks, investment banks, and insurance companies are the most likely organizations to have their members on the boards of other types of organizations (Pennings, 1980a,b). These relationships are quite stable over time. Some analysts go so far as to conclude that the corporate system is dominated by only a handful of New York commercial banks and financial institutions (Mintz and Schwartz, 1981). This has not always been the case. Railroads, along with the telegraph and coal industries, were at the core of interlocks for the period 1886 to 1905 in the United States (Roy, 1983a,b; see also Mizruchi and Bunting, 1981). Railroads were very powerful in that era as the nation industrialized and moved west.

Interlocks are a means by which organizations can attempt to manage uncertainty in their environments (Pennings, 1980a,b). Interlocks provide access to resources and can influence decisions. There are instances in which interlock occurs because an organization demands representation on another organization's board, thus lowering the autonomy of the latter organization (Aldrich, 1979).

It is imperative to note that interlocks are purposive. Purposiveness is evident for both parties. Organizations that are experiencing financial problems, such as declining solvency and declining rates of profit, seek out directors from financial institutions (Mizruchi and Stearns, 1988). At the same time, financial firms "infiltrate" the decision-making structure of firms with solvency problems. These interlocks would only take place in situations in which some hope for the future was perceived. Financial institutions would not interlock with lost causes. Interlocks tend to be reconstituted if they are broken. Breaks occur when a director dies or retires (Portugal, 1993; Stearns and Mizruchi, 1986).

Reconstitution of ties is linked to ongoing resource dependencies. These dependencies can take the form of local political and community support for state colleges (Portugal, 1993) or more general financial support for organizations as diverse as hospitals (Boeker and Goodstein, 1991) and airlines (Lang and Lockhart, 1990). Interlocking boards are also affected by local community ties through the interactions at upper class clubs or the presence of corporate headquarters (Kono et al., 1998). Pennings's (1980a,b) findings are helpful in understanding the operation of interlocks. Of the 797 largest American business firms, only 62 have no interlocks with the remaining 735 firms. Financial firms are disproportionately represented in the interlocks. Interlocks are most common in concentrated industries where monopolies almost exist in the first place. Financial firms avoid interlocks with firms that appear risky, instead seeking interlocks with those that are not risky. Well-interlocked firms were found to have greater economic effectiveness. This was particularly the case with firms that rely on equity financing and that are capital intensive. The relationships between interlocks and economic effectiveness were strongest for effective organizations. Financial firms do not want to get involved with operations that they perceive as performing poorly. Pennings views these patterns of interlocks as persuasive attempts by financial firms to enhance their position with solvent firms that will be reliable customers for loans, bonds, and other forms of debt. It is a technique by which financial firms acquire good customers and by which the customers have access to financial resources. Interlocks are thus a device for managing competition to control uncertainty in corporate profits (Burt, 1983). It has also been found that interlocks have been used to try to prevent hostile takeovers—a situation in which networks are used to spread the "poison pill" (Davis, 1991). The so-called poison pill is a device in which stockholders (other firms) are given the opportunity to buy a company's stock at an extremely low price on an option. This opportunity spreads through the network and prevents the hostile takeover.

These findings are hardly radical, but they are in keeping with what we understand about the ways in which organizations seek to acquire resources and enhance their position in their environment. It should be stressed that organizations in the public sector engage in the same kinds of activities through their boards of trustees, advisory boards, and the like. Research has demonstrated the importance of boards for organizations as diverse as the YMCA (Zald, 1970) and the United Way (Provan, Beyer, and Kruytbosch, 1980). An examination of the board of any college or university would reveal similar linkages into important segments of the organization's environments.

Evidence of a slightly different slant can be found in the research carried out in the Minneapolis–St. Paul metropolitan area (Galaskiewicz et al., 1985; Galaskiewicz, 1997). Contrary to some studies, this research has not found consistent patterns of interlock among firms that constrained one another across industries. Neither local sales patterns nor labor markets affected the patterns of interlock.

This research found that social status within the community was important for interlocks. Socially elite individuals who were associated with large corporations were disproportionately represented on boards of directors. Firms tended to interlock with those of equal social standing. According to Galaskiewicz et al., both "clout and grace" (1985:423) contributed to the densest interlocks. Economic clout and social grace made companies and people attractive to one another.

The Galaskiewicz studies dealt with interlocks and corporate philanthropy. There are interesting linkages at levels below the boards of directors. There are "corporate contributions officers" who hold staff positions well below the top executive level. People in these positions also have cohesion with one another, since they have similar-to-identical role relationships. This contributes to the "contagion" in philanthropy that was identified in the Minneapolis–St. Paul area (Galaskiewicz and Burt, 1991). The authors caution that there may be a regional influence on their findings.

Some analysts believe that the actual power of boards of directors is quite limited in that their power is to ratify or defeat what the chief executive officer and his or her administration propose to do. Quite frequently, the executive officer and the administration have greater knowledge than members of the board and can thus control the situation. At the same time, boards of directors can remove top administrative officers (James and Soref, 1981). The presence of external influences on a board of directors can have little effect on the behavior of managers in some cases (Fligstein and Brantley, 1992). At the same time, boards of directors are at the apex of power in organizations and there is a natural jousting for power. Powerful top managers want to maintain their power and prefer passive boards. Active boards want to maintain or increase their power (Zajac and Westphal, 1996).

Board interlocks have an additional basis, which is independent of organizational issues. Political sociologists have focused on social class and its relationship with interlocks. Based on Canadian evidence, Ornstein (1984) concluded that corporate imperatives and class solidarity factors operate in interlocks. Using data from a U.S. Senate committee, Kerbo and Della Fave (1983) found that there is an "intercorporate complex" of major corporations, with banks in a central coordinating position. They also found evidence for an inner group of the "corporate class" that provides the human linkages.

The social-class argument has persuasive evidence in its behalf at the local level (Galaskiewicz et al., 1985; Palmer, Friedland, and Singh, 1986) and at the national level (Domhoff and Dye, 1987; Mintz and Schwartz, 1981; Useem, 1979, 1982, 1984). An analysis of the 1980 congressional elections found that corporate contributions to political action committees (PACs) for these elections were based on ideological conservatism (Clawson and Neustadt, 1989). They conclude that interlocks are based on classwide rational actions. Although it is hard to comprehend how classes can be more rational than organizations, the class argument is persuasive.

The class argument is especially persuasive if it is used in conjunction with an organizational perspective on interlocks. Mizruchi (1989, 1992) provides just that perspective. He examined 1,596 dyads among 57 large manufacturing firms. He found that membership in the same primary industry or several similar industries, geographical proximity of corporate headquarters (but not plant locations), market constraints, and common relations with financial institutions (through stock ownership or directorate ties) were related to similarity of political behavior. He argues that resource dependency and social class explanations were both operative.

Director interlocks are a means by which the resources that are important to organizations and their relationships flow between organizations. They can give an organization a competitive advantage through access to financing, information, and other resources.

OUTCOMES OF IOR

As might be expected, the outcomes of IOR are complex and difficult to measure. In the human-services area, much of the research has been concerned with improved service delivery, which itself is difficult to conceptualize and measure. A study of health care delivery with a focus on two hospitals found that service delivery was quite well coordinated through a complex system of formal and informal arrangements (Milner, 1980). One of the hospitals provided high-quality care to affluent patients, and the other provided lower-quality care to the poor. The interorganizational arrangements served to maintain this differentiation. IORs were thus effective on the one hand but divisive on the other.

The outcome issue is both simple and complex. Its simplicity is that it lies in the eyes and minds of the beholders. The complexity of the outcome issue is that there are multiple eyes and minds that can make this assessment. This problem is identical to the issue of organizational effectiveness, which will be considered in the next chapter. The perceived effectiveness of interorganizational interactions can be assessed from the standpoint of participants within each organization, the organization as a whole, clients served or disserved, the community in which the interactions take place, or legislative or administrative decision makers who have jurisdiction over the particular dyads, sets, or networks in question. The outcome issue is thus one of political power, resource dependence, and moral choice. Outcomes that are good for one organization may be bad for another; clients may benefit, but the organizations may suffer; relationships may be cost-effective but damaging to organizations and clients. Analyses of IORs must keep these considerations in mind.

Much of the research on which this analysis has been based was carried out in social and human service organizations, with the exception of the materials on director interlocks. We clearly need an expanded database from a broader range of organizations. The analysis contained relatively little reference to the organizations involved in interactions. Little is actually known of this linkage. We also suffer from a shortage of information about the individuals involved in IOR interactions. There is some limited information on boundary spanners, but this role may actually be a peripheral one, with much greater importance found in the individuals who are on interlocking boards or those who interpret and decide upon the information brought by boundary spanners. There are important political and moral issues in regard to the power of interlocking directorates. The area of IORs is thus one of great research potential. There is a general belief that the relationships are important, even though this has not yet been fully demonstrated.

SUMMARY AND CONCLUSIONS

This chapter has been focused on organizational environments, a topic that has been stressed throughout our analysis of organizations. The more general content and analytical dimensions of the environment were considered. Attention was then focused on specific aspects of environments as they are played out through IORs.

There is always a danger of converting analyses of organizational environments into the primary focus of organizational analyses. That would be a huge mistake. Environments are an important component of organizational analysis, to be sure, but the real focus should be organizational effectiveness, to which we turn in the next chapter. Environments will not disappear in the consideration of effectiveness, but neither will they overwhelm the analysis.

EXERCISES

1. What are the most critical elements of the environments of your two organizations?
2. Describe the interorganizational linkages between your two organizations and their environments.

Chapter 10

Organizational Theory

•◆•

OVERVIEW

This chapter critically evaluates the major contemporary organizational theories that have been discussed throughout this book. Population ecology, resource dependence, rational contingency, and institutional theories are at the core of contemporary organizational analyses. The presentation is designed to build to the conclusion that organizational theories must be used in combination. Organizations are complex phenomena—the theoretical explanations must be adequate to explain this complexity and a combination approach is increasingly proving to be the most adequate.

The objective of this chapter is to examine contemporary theories about organizations. The various theories to be considered permit us to see and understand the different facets of organizations. The intent is not to advocate the superiority of any one theory but to argue that theoretical integration is necessary for full comprehension of organizational processes. There are interesting sets of debates surrounding some of the theories to be considered, and I will attempt to steer through these debates among the various "paradigm warriors" (Aldrich, 1988) involved.

In the sections that follow, we will consider four alternative schools of thought about organizations. These schools of thought can be labeled theories, models, or perspectives, depending on the analyst. Each school yields insights; none has been empirically verified as the explanation of organizational phenomena.

Before beginning the consideration of the alternative schools, we want to make it clear that the history of organizational theory will not be included in this analysis. Pugh (1966) and Clegg and Dunkerley (1980) are useful resources for people interested in tracing the historical roots of contemporary organizational theory.

The approach taken here is inductive. The inductive approach permits us to build on the empirical research that has been summarized in earlier chapters. Indeed, the theories themselves have already been identified and critically evaluated at many earlier points. The theories to be considered are grouped similarly to Pfeffer's (1982, 1997) and Donaldson's (1995) overviews and critiques of organizational theory. Our focus is the organizational level of analysis. Pfeffer bases his analysis of organizational theories on the perspectives on action that are taken. One such perspective sees organizational actions as externally constrained and controlled, and thus we will consider the population-ecology and resource-dependence models as Pfeffer does. At almost the opposite extreme are models of organizational action that see such actions as purposive and rational, with an emphasis on goal direction. Included in this category are the rational-contingency model, which includes the Marxist or class twist to the traditional model, and the transaction-cost model, which has developed out of the field of economics. A final perspective on action sees organizations as based on ideas contained in an organization's field or emergent from the values of organizational actors. This is the institutional approach to organizations.

THE POPULATION-ECOLOGY MODEL

The population-ecology model is associated with the works of Aldrich and Pfeffer (1976), Hannan and Freeman (1977b), Aldrich (1979), Kasarda and Bidwell (1984), Bidwell and Kasarda (1985), McKelvey (1982), McKelvey and Aldrich (1983), Carroll (1988), Carroll and Hannan (1989), and Hannan and Freeman (1989). This approach "posits that environmental factors select those organizational characteristics that best fit the environment" (Aldrich and Pfeffer, 1976:79).

The population-ecology approach (sometimes known as the natural-selection model) was a major orientation in our consideration of organizational change and transformation. According to Aldrich and Pfeffer, the model differs from Campbell's (1969) analysis of systemic evolution in that no assumption of progression is made. The natural-selection model does not assume that changes are necessarily in the direction of more complex or better organizations. The direction of change in organizations is simply toward a better fit with the environment.

According to Aldrich and Pfeffer, the population-ecology model does not deal with single organizational units but is concerned with forms or populations of organizations. Organizational forms that have the appropriate fit with the environment are selected over those that do not fit or fit less appropriately.

Following Campbell, Aldrich and Pfeffer suggest that there are three stages in the natural-selection model. In the first stage variations occur in organizational forms. These variations can be planned or unplanned. Once variations have occurred, the second stage, selection, is reached. The analogy here is with organic evolution, in which some mutations work and others do not. Organizational forms that fit are selected over those that do not. The final stage is retention. The forms that are selected are "preserved, duplicated, or reproduced" (p. 81). Retention is accomplished, in the contemporary situation, through devices such as business schools that train future organizational managers and executives (Aldrich, 1979). The training contains lessons learned from organizational forms that have been successful or selected.

Organizational forms fill niches in the environment. Niches are "distinct combinations of resources and other constraints that are sufficient to support an organizational form" (Aldrich, 1979:28). The notion of niches raises the fascinating possibility that there are unfilled niches "out there" just waiting for the right organizational form. Aldrich (p. 112) suggests that home video games and pocket electronic calculators were examples of unfilled niches being filled, but those are poor examples, since they are not organizational forms but simply consumer products. A better example of a once-unfilled but now-filled niche is the conglomerate corporation, in which a set of unrelated industries are brought together under a single ownership. This was a new organizational form that was selected by the environment as appropriate. This organizational form is now in decline (Davis, Diekmann, and Tinsley, 1994). Another example of a niche now filled is the fast-food restaurant form of organization.

Research on niches (Carroll, 1985; Freeman and Hannan, 1983) has shown that narrow niches tend to support organizations that are specialized, whereas wider niches support more generalist organizations. In Carroll's research, for example, he found that narrow niches in ethnic groups, neighborhoods, and religious and professional groups provided support for specialized newspapers. Freeman and Hannan's research involved restaurants with much the same result.

Aldrich and Pfeffer identify some problems with the population-ecology model. The sources of the original variations are not specified. Managerial processes within organizations are ignored. Inasmuch as only the successful organizational forms will survive in the long run, the processes by which the fit between the organization and the environment is achieved are ignored. The model also has the problem of being analogous to economic theories that assume perfect competition. In almost all instances, perfect competition does not exist.

Van de Ven (1979) provides some additional criticisms of this model. Van de Ven suggests that the notion of "fit" between the environment and organizations is unclear. According to Van de Ven, population ecologists appear to use fit as

> . . . either an unquestioned axiom or inductive generalization in a causal model that asserts that organizational environment determines structure because effective or

surviving organizations adopt structures that fit their environmental niches relatively better than those that do not survive. To avoid a tautology, the proposition
implicitly reduces to the hypothesis that organizational survival or effectiveness
moderates the relationship between environment and structure. (p. 323)

This is interesting, because effectiveness is scarcely mentioned in the
population-ecology modeling efforts. Van de Ven goes on to criticize the population-
ecology model for drawing too heavily on analogies with biological systems.
This biological analogy is ill founded, since it does not deal with human decisions
and motives. Ethical problems are ignored, and the whole process is viewed as
inevitable.

Young (1988, 1989) has also severely criticized the population-ecology
model, specifically the form presented by Hannan and Freeman, because of its reliance on biological theory. Freeman and Hannan (1989) believe that the population-
ecology approach is well suited for viewing organizations as complex systems
with limited flexibility, but Young argues that the approach may be suited for only
a narrow range of organizational phenomena.

Van de Ven also criticizes the model because of its downplaying of strategic choices made on behalf of organizations. The variations in forms that occur
have some source and, according to Van de Ven, that source is the strategic
choices made within organizations. The idea of strategic choice will be incorpo-
rated in the present analysis at a later point.

There is another aspect of choice that is not considered in the population-
ecology model. Some federal agencies have been created as last-resort responses
to socioeconomic or technological difficulties. These agencies fill a niche, to be
sure, but the niche is defined by governmental decision makers (Grafton, 1975).

There is an additional troublesome aspect of the population-ecology model.
Organizations are not inert masses, even though they seem so at times. Even
organizations that are seemingly inert have an impact by their very inertia, but
that is not the point. The point is that organizations do things. They transform inputs into outputs. Those outputs have an impact on the society. Individuals,
groups, and other organizations respond to organizational outputs. We are harmed
and benefited by organizational outputs. In this sense we are the environment of
organizations. Therefore, if we respond to organizations with support or opposition, and if we have power or can influence power holders, the environment responds to organizations. The population-ecology model tends to portray an
environment not as filled with human actors but, rather, as an unfeeling, uncaring
condition in which organizations must operate. The model removes power, conflict, disruption, and social-class variables from the analysis of social processes
(Perrow, 1979:243).

Carroll's (1988) anthology includes several papers that do in fact deal with
institutional, cultural, and political forces, which suggests that population ecologists are paying heed to the criticisms. Hannan and Carroll's (1992) own research
includes legitimation, which is a major consideration from institutional theory, as
a major variable. The population ecologists are thus responding to some of the
criticisms of their model.

These criticisms of the population-ecology model are not intended to suggest that it has no utility. The model has utility primarily in two areas. As some sort of "ultimate test" of effectiveness, survival is a positive indication and organizational death a negative indication. The natural-selection model can thus give a historical perspective that other approaches do not. It does not work well, however, with large contemporary private and public organizations that are almost guaranteed survival for a short time and even a medium length of time (Aldrich and Pfeffer, 1976:88). The natural-selection model is also useful as a sensitizing concept to the importance of environmental factors. If an organizational form is in a period of growth or decline, because of an expanding or a shrinking niche, any model must take that into consideration. Medical technology in developed countries has now permitted many people to live until old age, with all the attendant infirmities. The organizational form of the hospital is inappropriate for the aging and ill individual who is not faced with a life-threatening emergency. The organizational form of the hospice appears to be filling the niche that was created. Evaluations of hospices will have to take survival and the growth potential into account.

Population-ecology theorists are very careful to note that their approach is concerned with organizational populations rather than with individual organizations. Unfortunately, many of the examples provided by theorists in support of the population-ecology approach have tended to be focused on individual organizations. Part of the difficulty has been semantic and part has been due to insufficient specification of the level of analysis being used. Carroll (1984a) has provided a useful set of distinctions among levels of analysis. He notes that the organizational level can be used when referring to life-cycle processes among organizations. At the population-ecology level, the growth and decline of entire populations of organizations can be traced. Finally, there is the community-ecology level. At this level populations of organizations that exist together within the same region can be examined. According to Astley (1985), the community-population perspective permits an examination of similarities within a population of organizations and also permits analyses of between-population differences. Astley believes that a community-ecology perspective has the room to allow factors such as opportunism and choice to be included in organizational analyses.

THE RESOURCE-DEPENDENCE MODEL

The population-ecology model downplays the role of organizational actors in determining the fate of organizations. There is an alternative model, the resource-dependence model, which brings organizational decisions and actions back into consideration (Aldrich and Pfeffer, 1976; Pfeffer and Salancik, 1978). The discussion that follows relies heavily on Aldrich and Pfeffer's analysis, with some additions and extensions.

The resource-dependence model has strong ties to the political-economy model of organizations and the dependence-exchange approach. The basic premise of the resource-dependence model is that decisions are made within organizations. These decisions are made within the internal political context of the organization. The decisions deal with environmental conditions faced by the organization (Schreyogg, 1980). Another important aspect of the model is that organizations attempt to deal actively with the environment. Organizations will attempt to manipulate the environment to their own advantage. Rather than being passive recipients of environmental forces, as the population-ecology model implies, organizations will make strategic decisions about adapting to the environment. The role of management is vital in this process. The earlier analysis of IORs is based heavily on resource-dependence theory.

The resource-dependence model begins with the assumption that no organization is able to generate all the various resources that it needs. Similarly, not every possible activity can be performed within an organization to make it self-sustaining. Both of these conditions mean that organizations must be dependent on the environment for resources. Even seemingly self-sustaining organizations, such as isolated monasteries, must recruit new members or they will go out of existence. The resources that are needed can be in the form of raw materials, finances, personnel, or services or production operations that the organization cannot or does not perform for itself. Resources would also include technological innovations (Marple, 1982). The sources of resources in the environment are other organizations, the exception being farming and extractive industries that have the potential of owning the raw-material physical base. Even these organizations are dependent on other organizations for other resources. The fact that resources are obtained from other organizations means that the resource-dependence model can be thought of as an interorganizational resource-dependence model.

Since the resource-dependence model portrays the organization as an active participant in its relationship with the environment, it also contains the idea that the administrators of organizations "manage their environments as well as their organizations, and the former activity may be as important, or even more important, than the latter" (Aldrich and Pfeffer, 1976:83). This is the institutional level of operations, in which the organization is linked to the social structure by its top executives (Parsons, 1960). A key element of the resource-dependence model is strategic choice (Chandler, 1962; Child, 1972). This concept implies that a decision is made among a set of alternatives in regard to the strategy that the organization will utilize in its dealings with the environment. The assumption is that the environment does not force the organization into a situation in which no choice is possible. The organization is faced with a set of possible alternatives in dealing with the environment. Aldrich and Pfeffer note that the criteria by which choices are made and by which structures are determined are both important and problematic. There is not just one optimal structure or course of action.

The resource-dependence model stresses the importance of internal power arrangements in the determination of the choices made. Both internal power arrangements and the demands of external groups are central to the decision-making process. The resource-dependence model does not include the idea of goals as part of the decision-making process.

The resource-dependence model suggests that organizations are, or attempt to be, active in affecting their environment. This contributes to the variation among organizations, since variations are the result of conscious, planned responses to environmental contingencies. Organizations attempt to absorb interdependence and uncertainty, either completely, as through merger (Pfeffer, 1972b), or partially, as through cooperation (Allen, 1974; Pfeffer, 1972a) or the movement of personnel among organizations (Aldrich and Pfeffer, 1976:87; Pfeffer and Leblebici, 1973). The conglomerate corporation is a striking example of variation in organizational form brought about by strategic choice. It is also striking that the conglomerate form has recently been disappearing or selected out.

The resource-dependence model does deal with the selection process, which was central to the population-ecology model. Instead of viewing selection solely from the standpoint of the environment selecting appropriate organizational forms, the resource-dependence model considers the ways in which organizations interact with their environments to ensure that they survive and thrive. The environment is still the key factor, however. Aldrich and Pfeffer (1976:89) argue that the environment contains many of the constraints, uncertainties, and contingencies faced by organizations. Organizational units that have the capability of dealing with constraints, uncertainties, and contingencies are those that obtain the most power within the organization (Hickson et al., 1971). The power distribution within the organization is critical in determining the nature of the choices made, thus linking the environment to the choices made through the power process operating within the organization. The emphasis on power within the organization is a necessary one, since decisions are made in a political context. The resource-dependence model emphasizes interunit power differentials and tends to ignore hierarchical power differences. Hierarchical power differences must be considered in any analysis of strategic choice, since such differences can override interunit power struggles. It is quite possible that interunit power developments, as between marketing and production departments, have a crucial role in determining who rises in the hierarchy, but once the hierarchy is set, the power of the positions at the top of the organization would appear to be most central to the strategic decisions that are made. Regardless of the source of the power, of course, the strategic choices remain tied to environmental pressures. Again, the idea of goals, in the area of decision making, is not included in this model.

There are three ways in which strategic choices are made about the environment (Aldrich and Pfeffer, 1976). The first is that decision makers in organizations do have autonomy. This autonomy is much greater than would be suggested by a strict adherence to environmental determinism. The autonomy of the decision makers is reflected in the fact that more than one kind of decision can be made about the environmental niche being occupied—more than one kind of structure is suitable for given environments. In addition, organizations can enter or leave niches. This is illustrated by the fact that business firms can decide to try new markets or abandon old ones. Similarly, many colleges and universities are attempting to expand their niches, obviously in the face of decreasing demand by traditional students, by offering more and more courses and programs designed for nontraditional, older students.

The second way in which strategic choices are made about the environment involves attempts to manipulate the environment itself. Business firms attempt to create a demand for their products; they may also enter into arrangements with other firms to regulate competition, legally or illegally.

Operating through the political process, business firms may also secure the passage of tariffs or quotas to restrict competition from foreign firms. Organizations in the public sector do essentially the same thing when they expand or fight for the retention of their jurisdiction. Organizations seek to reduce their dependency on other organizations (Dunford, 1987). It is also to an organization's advantage to have other organizations dependent on it. Dunford notes that some organizations even suppress technological development, through manipulating patents, as a means of controlling resource dependence.

The third way in which the strategic choices are made about the environment is based on the fact that particular environmental conditions are perceived and evaluated differently by different people. This point is a crucial one and requires some elaboration. Organizational actors define reality in terms of their own background and values. A study documented the manner in which recruitment policies for executives in a large business firm resulted in the firm's having executives of very homogeneous backgrounds (Kanter, 1977). Kanter suggests that this permits the executives to have a great deal of trust in one another, since they will experience things in the same ways and, by implication, make the same kinds of decisions. The problem with such homogeneity, of course, is that the single point of view may be unable to detect errors.

The environment is perceived, interpreted, and evaluated by human actors within the organization. The perception becomes the reality, and environmental conditions are important only as they are perceived by organizational decision makers. Different actors can perceive the same phenomenon quite differently. The point is that the environment is acted upon by organizational decision makers on the basis of their perceptions, interpretations, and evaluations. Although there may be commonality because of homogeneity of background within an organization, and even this will not be perfect, there will not be commonality between organizations. Thus, different organizations will act differently toward the same environmental conditions, if the perceptions are different. In this regard, the critical question is the extent to which organizational perceptions vary from objective indicators of environmental conditions (Starbuck, 1976).

There are limitations on the range of choices that are available to organizational decision makers. There may be legal barriers that prevent an organization from moving into a particular area. Economic barriers also exist. Some projects may be too expensive. Markets can be so dominated by a few firms that it is impossible for a new, small firm to enter.

In addition to barriers that preclude certain decisions, decisions to attempt to alter the environment may not be possible for many organizations. Small organizations, for example, have much less power than large organizations to modify their environments. A small state college has much less impact on the educational environment than does Harvard University.

The final aspect of the resource-dependence model is the manner in which the retention of organizational forms takes place. Aldrich and Pfeffer suggest several mechanisms that organizations utilize to retain previously successful adaptations. In many ways, these retention mechanisms represent tactical decisions about how the organization is to operate once strategic decisions have been made.

One such retention device is bureaucratization. Organizations develop documentation and filing systems. Examples from the organizational past serve as precedents for the organizational present. The development of organizational policy serves the same function. Records and policies can provide the framework and content for decisions to be made. This provides continuity for the organization and ensures that the past forms are retained. Role specialization and standardization, with related job descriptions, also ensure that the policies are followed. Another important characteristic of bureaucracy, advancement based on performance, also aids in continuity. If people are advanced through the system, their experiences will be quite common and they will react in ways similar to the ways in which people have reacted in the past. Finally, the bureaucratic mechanism of a hierarchical structure also helps the retention process. The power of those at the top of the organization is viewed as legitimate. Authority is exercised, and each decision is not questioned. Bureaucratization is probably the most efficient form of administration, and all organizations will move toward this form if they seek efficiency (Perrow, 1979).

Another retention device is the socialization process. Persons entering an organization are continually socialized in formal and informal ways (Dornbusch, 1955), with the result that "the culture of the organization is transmitted to new members" (p. 97). Part of the culture of the organization involves folk wisdom and operating "rules of thumb" that persist over time.

Finally, the leadership structure of organizations tends to be consistent over time. As has been noted, people are screened and filtered as they move to the top of organizations. The screening and filtering is done by people already at the top of the organization, and they are very likely to select people who are like themselves. There are thus several mechanisms that ensure that organizational forms that have been successful will be retained. The emphasis of the resource-dependence model is on the manner in which organizations deal with environmental contingencies.

Resource acquisition is a major activity of organizations, and the resource-dependence model captures this, but it sidesteps the issue of goals. As will be seen shortly, I believe that this model must be augmented by a model that views organizational actions as being goal-based as well.

THE RATIONAL-CONTINGENCY MODEL

The resource-dependence model ignores goals, as does the population-ecology model. Both approaches appear to run counter to the reality of actual decision making. In the sections that follow, we will again consider the issue of goals and then turn to the theories linked to a goals-based perspective.

The goal-based approach does not make assumptions about the rationality involved in decision making, nor does it take the simplistic view that organizations are merely instruments designed to carry out goals. Rather, the approach adds goals back into the reasons that organizations act as they do. Goals are part of the culture of organizations and part of the mind-sets of decision makers. Organizations, like the individuals who compose them, are purposive creatures. The purposiveness can be overcome by external pressures, to be sure, and the organization may die or have to drastically alter its operations. The models that emphasize the environment are correct in pointing out the importance of the environment for the births and deaths of organizations. They err, however, in abandoning the consideration of goals.

It is now widely accepted that organizations have multiple and conflicting goals. This means that priorities among goals are problematic for organizations. Priorities are established by dominant coalitions within organizations. The dominant coalition is a direct or an indirect

> . . . representation or cross-section of horizontal constituencies (that is, subunits) and vertical constituencies (such as employees, management, owners, or stockholders) with different and possibly competing expectations. Consensus about the importance of the various criteria of effectiveness is hypothesized to be a function of the relative weights that the various constituencies carry in the negotiated order which we call organization. Consensus among members of the dominant coalition can be employed as a vehicle for obtaining effectiveness data. For example, how important is market share versus employee satisfaction? What should be the trade-off between research and development, between teaching and research, between patient care, medical research, and physicians' education? And so on. The consensus of the coalition allows the identification of such effectiveness criteria. These criteria may have different degrees of importance for the different constituencies in the dominant coalition; but somehow the preferences and expectations are aggregated, combined, modified, adjusted, and shared by the members of the dominant coalition. By invoking the concept of dominant coalition it is possible to preserve the notion of organizations as rational decision-making entities. (Pennings and Goodman, 1977:152)

Pennings and Goodman's term "effectiveness criteria" has the same meaning, for our purposes here, as goals. Their emphasis on rationality is correct but perhaps overstated. If we return for the moment to the environmental-based models, we can see that things happen around an organization that cannot be foreseen. And there may be competing external pressures or internal issues that cannot be rationally resolved because of their clearly contradictory nature. Nonetheless, the Pennings and Goodman approach is useful as a way of bringing goals back into the consideration of politics and decisions made by organizations.

Goals are constraints for organizational decision making. So too are the environmental constraints discussed in the earlier sections. As a way of combining important elements from the perspectives of multiple and conflicting goals and environmental constraints, many analysts advocate the rational-contingency model (Donaldson, 1995, 1996).

The rational-contingency idea has been developed from contingency theory that emerged from Lawrence and Lorsch's (1967) seminal work. The basic ideas have been developed further. Donaldson (1985) claims that contingency theory is a part of "normal science" (p. ix). His strong advocacy of contingency theory (see also Hinings, 1988) is based on his conclusion that empirical evidence strongly supports its utility—a point with which we agree.

Contingency theory can be summarized in the following manner: *"The best way to organize depends on the nature of the environment to which the organization must relate"* (Scott, 1981:114; italics added). Thus, in Lawrence and Lorsch's study, successful plastics firms were those that were differentiated to deal with an uncertain and changing environment, whereas beer bottle firms, with a less differentiated environment, were less differentiated internally. For our purposes, goals would be equally as important as the environment.

Contingency theory has been heavily criticized as being tautological. It has also been criticized as not being a theory, since it does not explain why or how a best way to organize develops (Schoonhoven, 1981; Tosi and Slocum, 1984). In addition, the idea of a best way to organize for a particular environment ignores political considerations, such as demands for collective bargaining, for a minimum wage, or for a union contract (Katz and Kahn, 1978:249). High efficiency could be the result of paying low wages or of inducing workers to work long hours (Wal-Mart has been accused of using these tactics) or to work harder. Consumers and regulators are also vital for organizational operations (Pfeffer and Salancik, 1978). Despite these problems, contingency theory has become an important part of the literature on organizations.

When the idea of contingency is added to the notion of rationality, we have the rational-contingency model. Organizations are viewed as attempting to attain goals and deal with their environments, with the realization that there is not one best way to do so. Findings as diverse as Burt's (1983) on corporate philanthropy and Langston's (1984) analysis of the British pottery industry are supportive of this approach. In the case of corporate philanthropy, it was found that the proportion of business firms' net incomes contributed to charity varied with the extent to which the firms were in sectors dependent upon consumption by individuals rather than other organizations. The organizations perceived charitable contributions as contributing to their profitability through their attempts to enhance their public relations image. In the British pottery example, bureaucratic elements were retained by the pottery firms because the bureaucratic elements increased profitability. Langston implies that this can be interpreted either in a rational-contingency manner or as a worker-control strategy.

THE INSTITUTIONAL MODEL

The final theoretical model to be considered is the institutional model. We first introduced this model in the discussion of organizational structure. It can best be appreciated by looking at the ways in which the model seeks to explain why organizations take the forms that they do. Much of the research here has been carried out in not-for-profit organizations with relatively indeterminate technologies.

DiMaggio and Powell (1983) argue that "institutional isomorphism" is now the dominant reason that such organizations assume the forms that they do. According to DiMaggio and Powell, Weber's original (1952, 1968) analysis of the driving force behind the move toward rationalization and bureaucratization was based on a capitalist market economy, with bureaucratization an "iron cage" in which humanity was bound, since the process of bureaucratization was irreversible.

DiMaggio and Powell believe that major social changes have altered this situation to such a large extent that an alternative explanation is needed. Their analysis is based on the assumption that organizations exist in "fields" of other, similar organizations. They define an organizational field as follows:

> By organizational field, we mean those organizations that, in the aggregate, constitute a recognized area of institutional life: key suppliers, resource and product consumers, regulatory agencies and other organizations that produce similar services and products. The virtue of this unit of analysis is that it directs our attention not simply to competing firms, as does the population approach of Hannan and Freeman (1977b), or to networks of organizations that actually interact, as does the interorganizational network approach of Laumann et al. (1978), but to the totality of relevant actors. (p. 148)

According to this perspective, organizations are increasingly homogeneous within fields. Thus, public universities acquire a sameness, as do department stores, airlines, professional football teams, motor vehicle bureaus, and so on. DiMaggio and Powell cite three reasons for this isomorphism among organizations in a field. First, coercive forces from the environment, such as government regulations and cultural expectations, can impose standardization on organizations. Government regulations, for example, force restaurants (we hope) to maintain minimum health standards. Organizations take forms that are institutionalized and legitimated by the state (Meyer and Rowan, 1977).

Second, DiMaggio and Powell also note that organizations mimic or model each other. This occurs as organizations face uncertainty and look for answers to their uncertainty in the ways in which other organizations in their field have faced similar uncertainties. Public schools add and subtract administrative positions to come into isomorphism with prevailing norms, values, and technical lore in their institutional environment (Rowan, 1982). DiMaggio and Powell argue that large organizations tend to use a relatively small number of consulting firms that, "like Johnny Appleseeds, spread a few organizational models throughout the land" (p. 152). A concrete example, noted by DiMaggio and Powell, is Japan's conscious modeling of its courts, postal system, military, banking, and art education programs on Western models in the late nineteenth century.

A *New York Times* article reported that business firms are establishing formal intelligence departments to keep tabs on competitors from home and abroad. One source is quoted as saying that "understanding your competitors' positions and how they might evolve is the essence of the strategic game" (Prokesh, 1985). In DiMaggio and Powell's conceptualization, the field is more than simply competitors. The establishment of intelligence departments reflects the strong mimetic tendencies within organizations.

Third, normative pressures push organizations toward isomorphism as the workforce, and especially management, becomes more professionalized. Both professional training and the growth and elaboration of professional networks within organizational fields lead to a situation in which the managerial personnel in organizations in the same field are barely indistinguishable from one another. As people participate in trade and professional associations, their ideas tend to homogenize.

The institutional perspective thus views organizational design not as a rational process but as one of both external and internal pressures that lead organizations in a field to resemble one another over time. In this perspective strategic choices or attempts at member control would be viewed as coming from the institutional order in which an organization is embedded.

Institutional theory also places a strong emphasis on symbols. We were given a strong symbol of the place of institutional theory when *Administrative Science Quarterly* placed Scott's (1987b) theoretical review of institutional theory as its lead article. These placements are hardly accidental.

The work of DiMaggio and Powell (DiMaggio, 1988; DiMaggio and Powell, 1983; Powell, 1985; Powell and DiMaggio, 1991) emphasizes the ways in which institutionalized practices are brought into organizations as noted above. Organizations in the same field develop isomorphism as they exchange professional personnel and face common exigencies such as governmental policies.

An alternative institutional approach is associated with the works of Meyer, Scott, and Zucker (Meyer and Scott, 1983; Scott, 1987b; Zucker, 1988). This approach contains a healthy dose of concern for environmental issues but basically turns our attention more inward. The focus is on ways in which practices and patterns are given values and how interaction patterns and structures are legitimated. It is a grand extension of Berger and Luckman's (1967) view that reality is socially constructed. Zucker's (1988) anthology provides an intellectually exciting view of organizations from this institutional perspective. In this set of papers individual actors are viewed as having feelings and meanings. They are not narrow, technocratic decision makers. Organizations are not shaped by the impersonal forces of technology or by the demands of a relentless environment.

Despite the attractiveness of the institutional formulations, we see four problems looming that raise serious issues for institutional theory (Hall, 1992; see also Hirsch, 1997).

The first problem is potential tautological reasoning. This form of reasoning was a major contributor to the demise of functional theory within sociology. "A tautology is circular reasoning in which variables are defined in terms of each other, thus making causes and effects obscure and difficult to assess" (Turner and Maryanski, 1979:124; see also Turner, 1979). This problem appears to creep into DiMaggio's (1988) analysis when he notes:

> Put simply, the argument of this section is that institutionalization is a product of the political efforts of actors to accomplish their ends and that the success of an institutionalization project and the form that the resulting institution takes depend on the relative power of actors who support, oppose, or otherwise strive to influence it.

> I refer to the politics of institutionalization as *structural* because they follow an internal logic of contradiction, such that the success of an institutionalization process creates new sets of legitimated actors who, in the course of pursuing distinct interests, tend to delegitimate and deinstitutionalize aspects of the organizational form to which they owe their own autonomy and legitimacy. Central to this line of argument is an apparent paradox rooted in the two senses in which the term *institutionalization* is used. Institutionalization as an outcome places organizational structures and practices beyond the reach of interest and politics. By contrast, institutionalization as a process is profoundly political and reflects the relative power of organized interests and the actors who mobilize around them. (p. 13; italics in original)

If that is not tautological reasoning, it is uncomfortably close to it. This quotation also contains the seeds of a problem that will be noted later—the tendency to bring all organizational phenomena under the institutional label. This problem also plagued the functionalists.

The second problem is that institutional theory has paid almost no attention to what is institutionalized and what is not. This can be seen in the weirdly ironic case of Talcott Parsons. Parsons wrote fairly extensively about organizations and even specified the institutional level of analysis (Parsons, 1960). This is not even mentioned in Scott's (1987b), DiMaggio's (1988), or Zucker's (1988) works, although Parsons does reappear in Scott (1995). This is not a call to go back to Parsons but, rather, empirical evidence that not everything that says institutional is institutionalized.

This is a critical problem. There is a tendency to apply institutional theory in an ex post facto manner. This can be done almost mystically. Ideas and practices come and go for no reason other than institutionalization. It would appear that, in reality, some performance criteria are applied in assessing the success of a practice. We will later argue that the adoption of structures or practices is much more than institutionalized whim.

The third problem is essentially ontological. The prime interest rate and changes in it are very real to borrowing organizations; the number of eighteen-year-olds is very real to college administrators; and the number of twenty-one-year-olds is very real to brewers. Institutional theory can be very useful at this point. Individual and collective organizational myths develop about the meanings of these realities. This point has been very well demonstrated. The danger, however, is in making the reality that was the source of the myth into the myth itself.

The fourth problem is overextension. There is a tendency, as noted above, to apply institutional theory to a vast array of situations and organizations. DiMaggio and Powell (1983) were careful to hypothesize that institutional effects were more likely in situations of indeterminate technology and ambiguous goals.

There are additional criticisms of institutional theory. It is seen as ignoring deinstitutionalization processes. Some ideas are rejected, and others are replaced (Oliver, 1992). There is also a strong tendency to overlook or downplay issues such as efficiency (Abbott, 1992). Institutional theory essentially captured organizational theory in the 1990s. It became "institutionalized" itself (Tolbert and Zucker, 1996). In so doing, it has almost become "authoritarian" as it has swept our theoretical landscape (Hirsch, 1997). Undoubtedly, a new perspective will emerge to sweep the institutional approach aside. Although such an exciting new perspective is not in sight at the moment, there is excitement in the form of attempts to combine the perspectives that we have been considering.

COMBINING THE PERSPECTIVES

As organizational research moved into the new millennium, there has been widespread acceptance of the need to apply these theories in combination, rather than as competing explanations. Fligstein's (1985) research is an exemplar here, as is that by Pfeffer and Davis-Blake (1987), Singh, Tucker, and House (1986), Mezias (1990), Palmer, Jennings, and Zhou (1993), Baum and Haveman (1997), and Haveman and Rao (1997). These researchers do not test theories against one another. Rather, they seek to explain the largest amount of variance that they can. No single set of combinations is dominant.

Fligstein and Mara-Drita (1996) examined rational and environmental factors in the emergence of a single market in the European Union. Goodstein (1994) combined institutional and rational-contingency approaches in an examination of the extent to which organizations get involved with work-family issues. A similar combination of perspectives is found in an analysis of the U.S. Government Accounting Office (Gupta, Dirsmith, and Fogarty, 1994).

Resource-dependence theory and institutional theory were combined in an analysis of the proportion of women in management (Blum, Fields, and Goodman, 1994). Gooderham, Nordhaug, and Ringdal (1999) combined rational and institutional theory in their analysis of human resource practices in a set of European firms. These are examples of a trend that is solidly growing.

SUMMARY AND CONCLUSIONS

It is almost common sense to realize that organizations must acquire resources as they simultaneously seek to achieve their goals and keep up with their competitors. There appears to be a strong sentiment among organizational theorists that the time has come to cease being paradigm warriors and instead seek fuller explanations through combining perspectives. As this is done, theoretical growth will be evident. We may even be able to move toward the elusive goal of specifying which theoretical explanations work in which settings and thus have truly meaningful explanations of organizations. This book has been an effort in that direction.

EXERCISES

1. Which theoretical perspective do you find most adequate? Why? Which do you find least adequate? Why?
2. Discuss reasons for using theoretical explanations in combination with one another.

Chapter 11

Organizational Effectiveness

———————— •◆• ————————

OVERVIEW

This chapter deals with the "independent variable" of all of the previous chapters. Organizational structures and processes are in place in order to achieve effectiveness. A new model of effectiveness, the contradiction model, is developed. The contradiction model contains the elements of multiple and conflicting goals, environments, stakeholders, and time frames. Most organizations cannot be effective in every way. They face constraints that are beyond their control. They also face constraints that they attempt to manipulate. Despite these constraints, organizations try to be effective.

This whole book has been about organizational effectiveness. We study organizations primarily to understand how and why they are effective or ineffective. We may want to make them more or less effective from an economic, political, or moral perspective. It is well recognized that the various parties concerned with any single organization can have contrasting and conflicting views on its effectiveness. We are not neutral about the organizations with which we deal as workers, clients, customers, or publics. We do not want to be abused by any organization, public or private. We also want the organizations in which we participate as a member to do well. To do well is to be effective. Our perspective on effectiveness, however, varies with our positions in the organization. We have different perspectives about the other organizations of which we are a part.

In this chapter our analysis comes full circle. We began this book by considering some of the outcomes of organizations. We then examined structural characteristics, processes within organizations, and organizational environments. In essence, the outcomes of structural arrangements, processes such as decision making and leadership, and dealing with the environment are designed to contribute to organizational effectiveness. Unfortunately, like many organizations, organizational effectiveness itself is highly complex.

There are several competing models or theories of effectiveness in the literature that have served as the bases for analyses of effectiveness. In the present chapter these models will be analyzed and their strengths and weaknesses highlighted. Inherent in the models and in the debates about the models is the idea that organizational effectiveness as a concept contains contradictions. With that in mind, we will develop a contradiction model of effectiveness, which is designed to encompass the insights that previous models have identified.

For practitioners and scholars who concentrate on organizational analysis, organizational effectiveness has been a dominant explicit and implicit point of departure. This reflects the administrative-technical orientation of many people who study organizations (Benson, 1977). They wish to find ways to adjust organizations to enhance effectiveness. Benson notes that although many studies deal with effectiveness in a direct and highly visible way, even those studies that do not focus on effectiveness tend to deal with it implicitly, as an underlying or background orientation.

Not everyone is concerned with organizational effectiveness in this manner. There are many important social issues that have generated attempts to prevent organizational effectiveness. Opponents of nuclear-energy development and generation and of abortion are essentially against the effectiveness of the organizations that provide electricity and abortions. Ironically, the success of these oppositional efforts depends upon the effectiveness of the oppositional organizations.

The present analysis is an attempt to decompose the concept of organizational effectiveness and to expose and examine the contradictions inherent in the concept and its applications. The purpose is to provide a sounder basis for research, theory, and practice. We hope that the analysis will be informative for individuals concerned with altering the directions that organizations take.

TOWARD A CONTRADICTION MODEL OF EFFECTIVENESS

Before we get into the specifics of the contradiction model of effectiveness that is to be introduced here, it should be made clear that the approach to be taken forces the analysis of effectiveness away from attempts to conceive of *overall* organizational effectiveness. A contradiction model requires the uncompromised acceptance of the fact that it is folly to try to conceptualize organizations as simply effective or ineffective (Campbell, 1977).

Although there is agreement that effectiveness as an overall concept has little or no utility, it would be a big mistake to simply ignore issues and findings that have been developed in regard to effectiveness. This seeming paradox can be resolved if a contradiction model of effectiveness is used. Put very simply, a contradiction model of effectiveness will consider organizations to be more or less effective in regard to the variety of goals that they pursue, the variety of environmental resources that they attempt to acquire, the variety of stakeholders inside and outside the organization, and the variety of time frames by which effectiveness is judged. The idea of variety in goals, environmental resources, and so on is key here, since it suggests that an organization can be very effective in some aspects of its operations and less so in others.

The contradiction idea has its roots in a research project that was discussed in an earlier chapter: the study of organizations that deal with problem youths. It was found that these organizations had multiple and conflicting goals. One set of organizations in the study were juvenile detention centers. These organizations had the goals, among others, of "maintaining secure custody" and "providing healthy living arrangements." On the face of it, those are incompatible goals, since secure custody would be optimized by simply locking the youths in cells, which is hardly a healthy living arrangement.

The example of contradictory goals just noted comes from the public sector. It is frequently believed that goals here are more amorphous and contradictory than those in the private sector. Unfortunately, the private-sector picture is also one of contradictions. For example, the goal idea seems simple in the case of profit-making organizations. Indeed, much of the research on effectiveness has used this type of organization because of assumed goal clarity. The seemingly readily quantifiable profit goal is not such a simple matter, however. It is confounded by such issues as the time perspective (long-run or short-run profits); the rate of profit (in the form of returns to investors); survival and growth in a turbulent and unpredictable environment that might in the short run preclude profit making; the intrusion of other values, such as providing quality products or services or benefiting humankind; and the firm's position compared with that of others in the same industry. Even the nature of profit itself is multifaceted. It can involve return on stockholders' equity, return on total capital, sales growth, earnings-per-share growth, debt-to-equity ratio, and net-profit margin. These are not well correlated (*Forbes*, 1973), which alone makes the idea of goals extremely complex.

The goal approach has another complication. We have already demonstrated that organizational decisions and actions cannot be viewed simply from a rational-model framework. Decisions that at first appear to be rational turn out to be disastrous because of events beyond organizational control.

In the pages that follow, we will present and evaluate the major models of effectiveness. Each makes a positive contribution to our understanding and contributes to the contradiction model.

MODELS OF ORGANIZATIONAL EFFECTIVENESS

The system-resource model is the first effectiveness model to be examined, because an extensive analysis of the environmental-organizational interface has just been presented. This model was developed by Yuchtman and Seashore (1967; Seashore and Yuchtman, 1967), who begin by noting that variables concerning organizational effectiveness could be ordered into a hierarchy. At the top of the hierarchy is some ultimate criterion that can only be assessed over time. An example of such an ultimate criterion would be the optimum use of opportunities and resources found in the environment. According to the natural-selection model, the ultimate criterion would be survival or death.

Next come penultimate criteria, which are performance measures, such as business volume and market penetration, for organizations in specific industries. Other penultimate criteria are more time specific, such as having a high proportion of new members. The utility of this approach was examined by use of a data set from insurance agencies. The data revealed that there were identifiable factors that were stable over time and that involved organizational-environmental linkages.

Seashore and Yuchtman conclude that their findings lead to a definition of effectiveness of an organization as the *"ability to exploit its environment in the acquisition of scarce and valued resources to sustain its functioning"* (p. 393; italics in original). Their reasoning is that whereas some of the penultimate criteria found, such as business volume and market penetration, could be construed as goals, others, such as a high proportion of new members, could not.

Seashore and Yuchtman also conclude that resource acquisition must be viewed as relative to the capacity of the environment. Some organizations operate in rich environments; others act in poorer ones. They also note that their definition stresses the ability to utilize the environment rather than maximum utilization of the environment, since maximum utilization could lead to the total depletion of resources.

The Seashore-Yuchtman argument is persuasive but contains some problem areas. For instance, it is actually a question of semantics whether growth in business volume is viewed as only one form of resource acquisition or as a goal. The relatively stable penultimate criteria discussed by Seashore and Yuchtman can easily be viewed as goals or as constraints on the decisions made by the insurance firms in question. The less stable criteria, such as youthfulness of members, could turn out to be predictor variables for these sorts of organizations. It is well known, for example, that young men and women who enter the life insurance sales occupation have good success at first, selling to relatives and friends. This would appear to be a means by which a goal, such as sales volume, could be achieved.

Resource acquisition does not just happen, but is based on what the organization is attempting to achieve—namely, its goals. This is in line with our earlier discussion of decision making, in which decisions are made on the basis of perceived environmental conditions and organizational goals. It is reasonable to argue that resources are seldom acquired just for their own sake; they are also acquired according to the paths selected by the power coalitions in the organization.

Seashore and Yuchtman implicitly recognize this point when they suggest that criteria for determining effectiveness must be identified.

The Goal Model

The goal model of effectiveness is both simple and complex. In the simple version, effectiveness has been defined as the degree to which "an organization realizes its goals" (Etzioni, 1964:8). The model becomes complex as soon as it is realized that most organizations have multiple and frequently conflicting goals. Structural differentiation in organizations is related to goal diversity and goal incompatibility (Kochan, Cummings, and Huber, 1976). Since most organizations do exhibit structural diversity, such multiplicity and incompatibility can almost be taken for granted in most organizations. This makes the goal model difficult to use but does not automatically destroy its utility.

Goals involve intents and outcomes and serve as constraints on decision making. Organizational goals are by definition creations of individuals, singly or collectively. At the same time, the determination of a goal for collective action becomes a standard by which the collective action is judged. The collectively determined, commonly based goal seldom remains constant over time. New considerations imposed from without or within deflect the organization from its original goal, not only changing the activities of the organization, but also becoming part of the overall goal structure. The important point is that the goal of any organization is an abstraction distilled from the desires of members and pressures from the environment and internal system.

Thinking of goals as abstract values has the utility of indicating the reason organizational members do not just act on their feelings or whims on a particular day. At the same time, it is a mistake to take as the abstraction the official goal statements of the organization. Perrow (1961) has analyzed this situation nicely. He notes that official goals are "the general purposes of the organization as put forth in the charter, annual reports, public statements by key executives and other authoritative pronouncements." Operative goals, on the other hand, "designate the ends sought through the actual operating policies of the organization; they tell us what the organization actually is trying to do, regardless of what the official goals say are the aims" (p. 855).

In one of the early studies in the tradition of modern organizational theory, Blau (1955) found that two employment agency units, which had the same official goals, were very different in what they really were attempting to accomplish. One unit was highly competitive, with members striving to outproduce each other in the numbers of individuals placed. In the other unit, cooperation and quality of placement was stressed. In discussing this point, Perrow (1961) notes:

> Where operative goals provide the specific content of official goals, they reflect choices among competing values. They may be justified on the basis of an official goal, even though they may subvert another official goal. In one sense they are a means to official goals, but since the latter are vague or of high abstraction, the "means" become ends in themselves when the organization is the object of analysis.

For example, where profit making is the announced goal, operative goals will specify whether quality or quantity is to be emphasized, whether profits are to be short run and risky or long run and stable, and will indicate the relative priority of diverse and somewhat conflicting ends of customer service, employee morale, competitive pricing, diversification, or liquidity. Decisions on all of these factors influence the nature of the organization and distinguish it from another with an identical official goal. (pp. 855–56)

Operative goals may be linked directly to official goals. At the same time, operative goals can develop that are unrelated to official goals. Perrow goes on to note:

Unofficial operative goals, on the other hand, are tied more directly to group interests, and while they may support, be irrelevant to, or subvert official goals, they bear no necessary connection with them. An interest in a major supplier may dictate the policies of a corporate executive. The prestige that attaches to utilizing elaborate high speed computers may dictate the reorganization of inventory and accounting departments. Racial prejudice may influence the selection procedures of an employment agency. The personal ambition of a hospital administrator may lead to community alliances and activities which bind the organization without enhancing its goal achievement. On the other hand, while the use of interns and residents as "cheap labor" may subvert the official goals of medical education, it may substantially further the official goal of providing a high quality of patient care. (p. 856)

Operative goals are thus a derivation of and a distillation from official goals. They are developed and modified through ongoing interaction patterns within organizations. They are more than just the results of interpersonal interactions, however. They persist beyond the life of a particular interaction and become the standards by which the organization's actions are judged and around which decisions are made. Even though operative goals are developed in concrete interactions, they, like official goals, are abstractions, since they become standards by which actions and decisions are judged.

The discussion of the development of operative goals suggests that goals change over time. There are three reasons for changes in the goals of organizations. First, organizations are in direct interaction with the environment through their IORs. Organizational goal setting is affected by competitive, bargaining, cooptative, and coalitional relationships with the environment (Thompson and McEwen, 1958). Competition occurs when the rivalry between two organizations is mediated by a third party, as in the case of business firms competing for the same customers. Competition also occurs in the public sector as government agencies compete for a share of the tax dollar (Wildavsky, 1964). Competition affects the goal structure as the organization shapes its actions to try to ensure continued support. In this regard, of course, the goal model can be seen to encompass at least some aspects of the system-resource model.

Bargaining also involves resources but in a different manner. The organization is in direct interaction with suppliers, customers, and other organizations. In a bargaining situation, an organization has to "give" a little to get what it desires. Thompson and McEwen note the example of a university that bargains the right to name a building for a substantial gift to build the building. If the donor attaches strings to the gift, the university might alter its operative goals to get the money.

Co-optation is "the process of absorbing new elements into the leadership or policy-determining structure of an organization as a means of averting threats to its stability or existence" (Thompson and McEwen, 1958:27). The classic study of co-optation is Selznick's (1966) analysis of the development of the Tennessee Valley Authority. The TVA shifted its emphases as segments of the community were brought into its decision-making system. Business firms engage in co-optation as they engage in board interlocks when there are market constraints (Burt, 1983; Burt, Christman, and Kilburn, 1980). Co-optation is a two-way street, of course: Both co-opters and co-optees are affected by the action.

Coalition is the actual combining of two or more organizations. This is the most extreme form "of environmental conditioning of organizational goals" (Thompson and McEwen, 1958:28). In this case, the organizations in the coalition cannot set goals unilaterally.

Shifts in organizational goals as a result of direct interactions with other organizations in a focal organization's environment emphasizes the importance of dealing with operative, rather than official, goals. A reliance only on official goals would miss these sometimes subtle, sometimes dramatic shifts. This kind of analysis also indicates the importance of looking at organizational effectiveness over time, since a cross-sectional analysis might be done just before a significant shift occurs and thus be essentially meaningless.

The second reason that goals change is that internal organizational changes may occur. We have already noted the importance of power coalitions within organizations. These power coalitions can shift, sometimes as a result of external pressures, but also because of internal dynamics. Michels's (1949) classic study of the development of oligarchy in political parties and labor unions is illustrative of this. The goals of the rank and file tend to give way to those of the elites. Organizations can be seen as "battlegrounds for stakeholders, both inside and outside, who compete to influence the criteria for effectiveness so as to advance their own interests" (Kanter and Brinkerhoff, 1981:322).

Organizations may begin to emphasize goals that are easily quantifiable, at the expense of those that are not so easily quantified. Universities look at the number of faculty publications rather than at the more-difficult-to-measure goal of classroom teaching; business firms look at output per worker rather than at "diligence, cooperation, punctuality, loyalty, and responsibility" (Gross, 1968:542). If organizations do begin to emphasize that which is easily quantifiable, then there is a shift of goals in that direction. Goal shifts are also possible when there is slack in the organization and it is secure. A study of the National Council of Churches found that staff interactions guided by a new professional ideology and strong purposive commitments contributed to major and radical goal shifts within the organization (Jenkins, 1977). This study also suggests that threats to the organization's domain would probably lead to a more conservative stance.

The final source of goal shifts lies outside the organization and involves indirect pressures from the general environment. Economic conditions can become altered. Technological developments must be accommodated. Values shift. Organizational goals are adjusted to these environmental conditions. The classic study of this form of goal shift is Sills's (1957) analysis of the March of Dimes organization, which had been oriented toward the treatment of individuals who suffered the crippling effects of polio. The development of safe vaccines, a technological development, essentially eliminated the need for the continued existence of the organization, until it shifted its goals to include other crippling diseases.

Another example of this form of goal shift can be seen among colleges and universities as the demographic composition of the population shifts. Higher-educational organizations are now including nontraditional students as major recruitment targets, with "seminars for seniors" and a wide array of continuing-education programs. The demographic shifts are beyond the control of the organizations involved, as are the other sources of indirect pressure from the environment. Although organizations can try to influence values, manipulate the economy to their advantage, and keep up with technological developments, many situations are simply beyond organizational control. At various times, the United States has faced shortages of gasoline. Organizations, even petroleum firms, have no control over the actions of oil-producing nations. Thus, the environment can have an indirect but still crucial role in the determination of goal shifts.

Thus far, the analysis has suggested that organizations have multiple goals, which may be contradictory and which may also shift. We will now turn to a consideration of how goals can be used in analyzing effectiveness.

Goals and Effectiveness

The simplest use of the goal model suggests that an organization is effective to the degree to which it achieves its goals. According to Campbell (1977):

> The goal-centered view makes a reasonably explicit assumption that the organization is in the hands of a rational set of decision makers who have in mind a set of goals that they wish to pursue. Further, these goals are few enough in number to be manageable and can be defined well enough to be understood. Given that goals can be thus identified, it should be possible to plan the best management strategies for attaining them. Within this orientation, the way to assess organizational effectiveness would be to develop criterion measures to assess how well the goals are being achieved. (p. 19)

Unfortunately, for organizations and those who analyze them, the matter is not that simple. Hannan and Freeman (1977a) have examined the goal model and have pinpointed some of the problems with its use. They begin their analysis by pointing out that it would be unsatisfactory to totally drop the goal concept, since goals are part of the defining characteristics of organizations. They go on to note, however, that a first and major difficulty with the goal approach is that there is likely to be a multiplicity of organizational goals. This occurs even among the publicly legitimated or official goals, as has already been noted. Hannan and Freeman comment: "Virtually all public agencies and bureaus have very many public goals. For example, the number and diversity of goals of agencies like the Department of Health, Education, and Welfare (HEW) and the Department of Commerce boggle the imagination" (pp. 111–12).

According to Hannan and Freeman, the second broad problem with goals involves their specificity (p. 113). Universities have the very general goals of advancing the store of useful knowledge; police agencies have the goal of protecting the public. These broad goals become much more specific in actual operations, with the more specific goals taking a variety of possible forms. For the police, for example, protecting the public could be approached from the standpoint of putting more officers on foot patrol, cracking down on prostitution, putting more officers in plainclothes operations, or making public relations statements. Within the organization, units can move in divergent directions that are consistent with the broader goal but that could interfere with one another's operations.

The third problem with goals involves the temporal dimension. Hannan and Freeman (1977a) note:

> Should we consider the short run or the long run or both? The many published empirical studies that employ cross-sectional data on samples of organizations (see, for example, Lawrence and Lorsch, 1967) tacitly take the short-run perspective. Whether or not this is appropriate depends on the nature of the goals function for each organization. To the extent that the goals function stresses quick return on investment (as in many business ventures, disaster relief organizations, military field units, and so on) the short-run outcomes should be given highest priority. For those organizations that orient toward continued production (for example, many other types of business ventures, universities, research and development organizations, and so on) the year-to-year fluctuations in performance should be discounted and the average performance over longer periods emphasized. (p. 113)

Hannan and Freeman note that different levels in the hierarchy can employ different time frames, making the situation even more complex. They do not deal with the fact that different units within the same organization can also have different time frames. Hannan and Freeman also deal with the second part of the goal model, which is organizational performance or output. Outcome assessment is difficult for several reasons. The first is the time perspective used. An outcome that is successful for the short run could be disastrous for the long run. Another problem in outcome assessment involves "bounding systems" (Hannan and Freeman, 1977a:116), or the problem in distinguishing the effects of events both inside and outside the organization. The issue here is that it is very difficult to determine what activity within an organization contributes to some outcome. It is equally difficult to specify if that outcome is a result of organizational actions or the result of some external force. This point is not lost on organizational management. Corporate annual reports tend to attribute unfavorable outcomes to external, unstable, and uncontrollable causes. Favorable outcomes are attributed to actions taken by management (Bettman and Weitz, 1983). Closely related findings are reported in an analysis of letters to shareholders. These letters tend to be self-serving and attribute corporate performance to the actions taken by management (Staw, McKechnie, and Puffer, 1983). Interestingly, these letters appear to be convincing, since they are related to stock price increases. They are also related to the sale of stock by corporate management.

The quality of the input of an organization affects the quality of the output. Many social service organizations, for example, select clients (inputs or external forces) who appear to have good chances of success in the treatment that the organization provides. More problematic clients are referred elsewhere or are simply passed around the social service system. This sort of situation makes the assessment of the outcome of the social service organization difficult, since it is difficult to disentangle organizational and input effects.

The problem is made even more complicated by the fact that although both input quality and the contribution of units within organizations can be understood as contributors to performance, so too can the ability of the organization to control the quality of inputs. Control of environmental factors is an outcome of organizational actions. Organizations attempt to build up demands for their outputs. Success here means higher performance.

Hannan and Freeman conclude:

> Once we acknowledge that all these factors are subject to organizational strategy and action, we are faced with a serious methodological problem. All of the variables that appear in the conventional analyses are endogenous, that is, causally dependent on other variables in the model. For example, the quality of inputs may be a function of the expenditure on inputs, which is a function of output performance. If none of these factors is causally prior, or exogeneous, it is extremely difficult to obtain unique estimates of any relevant causal effects in the system. In the technical language of econometrics, the system is underidentified. To remedy this situation one must make a considerable number of strong assumptions concerning the details of the causal structure. Unfortunately, the existing theories of organizational performance (and effectiveness) do not provide a basis for these assumptions. (p. 122)

Hannan and Freeman conclude their argument by suggesting that effectiveness be dropped as a scientific concept, since comparisons across organizations cannot be made to construct and test abstract theories of organizations. They then suggest that effectiveness considerations remain valid for engineering or social criticism. By this they mean that effectiveness can be used in the administrative-technical sense by individuals interested in engineering or in managing organizations toward public or private goals. Social criticism can be accomplished by demonstrating that organizations are not doing what they claim to be doing or that they are not doing it well enough. In the contradiction model that will be developed here, the intent will be to permit effectiveness considerations to remain at the scientific level.

The goal model as an engineering tool can be readily seen in analyses of performance among business organizations. Performance refers to achieving economic goals, usually with a short-term emphasis. "High-performing firms" are a sacred symbol among some business analysts, but as with many sacred symbols, many meanings can be applied to it. Indeed, there are entire industries that have been developed around measuring high performance, such as accountancy, compensation management, financial planning, and fund managing (Meyer, 1994). There is an interesting institutional twist to the engineering of performance measurement, since measures of performance can be adopted out of the fear that not to adopt particular measures would be "disadvantageous" (Meyer, 1994:576). Performance measures are adopted on faith rather than on evidence.

We have now moved into the issue of who or which parties are to judge the performance of organizations in regard to goals. The views of different organizational stakeholders can vary widely and must be considered, as they will be in the contradiction model. In the next section, we will deal specifically with attempts to conceptualize effectiveness in terms of the satisfaction of organizational participants. One approach that has been tried, based on the goal model, has been to ask persons in superordinate positions about the effectiveness of organizational units that are subordinate to them. This approach is quite useful for performance assessments of organizational subunits. It also could be used in situations where organizations within a single political jurisdiction, such as state, county, or city organizations, are being examined. In reality, such effectiveness judgments are made at the time of budget allocations, but that process contains more than effectiveness considerations.

The approach of asking superordinates about the effectiveness of subordinates has been used with success by Mahoney and Weitzel (1969) and Duncan (1973). This approach has revealed that even superordinates stress different goals. Mahoney and Weitzel note:

> General business managers tend to use productivity and efficient performance. These high-order criteria refer to measures of output, whereas lower-order criteria tend to refer to characteristics of the organization climate, supervisory style, and organizational capacity for performance. The research and development managers, on the other hand, use cooperative behavior, staff development, and reliable performance as high-order criteria; and efficiency, productivity, and output behavior as lower-order criteria. (p. 362)

Effectiveness thus lies in the eyes and minds of the beholders, with the important qualification that some beholders are more powerful than others.

Participant-Satisfaction Models

In this section we will examine models of effectiveness that, in various ways and at various levels, utilize individuals as the primary frame of reference. The emphasis in these models is not satisfaction as seen in morale or some other psychological state of the individual. This is frequently a component of the goal model, seeing morale as just one of several goals. Rather, in these models the emphasis is on individual or group judgments about the quality of the organization.

Barnard (1938) set the tone for participant-satisfaction models with his analysis of organizations as cooperative, incentive-distributing devices. "Individuals contributed their activities to organizations in return for incentives, the contribution of each in the pursuit of his particularistic ends being a contribution to the satisfaction of the ends of others. Barnard regarded the motives of the individuals participating in organizations as the critical determinants. Only if these were satisfied, could the organization continue to operate" (Georgiou, 1973:300). Organizational success was not viewed as the achievement of goals but rather as survival through the ability to gain enough contributions from the members by providing sufficient rewards or incentives. Georgiou (1973), building on the work of Barnard, has developed what he labels a "counter paradigm" to the goal model (see also Samuel, 1979).

According to Georgiou:

> Thus, the essential thrust of the counter paradigm is that the emergence of organizations, their structure of roles, division of labor, and distribution of power, as well as their maintenance, change, and dissolution can best be understood as outcomes of the complex exchanges between individuals pursuing a diversity of goals. Although the primary focus of interest lies in the behavior within organizations, and the impact of the environment on this, the reciprocal influence of the organization on the environment is also accommodated. Since not all of the incentives derived from the processes of organizational exchange are consumed within the interpersonal relations of the members, organizational contributors gain resources with which they can influence the environment. (p. 308)

The implication of Georgiou's argument for effectiveness is that incentives within organizations must be adequate for maintaining the contributions of organizational members and must also contain a surplus for developing power capabilities for dealing with the environment. A basic problem with this argument is that it does not disclose how the incentives are brought into the organization in the first place. If a major incentive is money, the money must be secured. To be sure, money is brought into the organization through exchanges with the environment, but it appears that the system-resource approach or a goal model dealing with profit is necessary before considering individual inducements.

Cummings (1977) approaches effectiveness from a slightly different perspective. He states:

> One possibly fruitful way to conceive of an organization and the processes that define it is as an instrument or an arena within which participants can engage in behavior they perceive as instrumental to their goals. From this perspective, an effective organization is one in which the greatest percentage of participants perceive themselves as free to use the organization and its subsystem as instruments for their own ends. It is also argued that the greater the degree of perceived organizational instrumentality by each participant, the more effective the organization. Thus, this definition of an effective organization is entirely psychological in perspective. It attempts to incorporate both the number of persons who see the organization as a key instrument in fulfilling their needs and, for each person, the degree to which the organization is so perceived. (pp. 59–60)

According to this approach, factors such as profitability, efficiency, and productivity are necessary conditions for organizational survival and are not ends in themselves. The organization must acquire enough resources to permit it to be instrumental for its members. A loosely related approach argues that more effective organizations are those in which the members agree with the goals of the organization and thus work more consistently to achieve them (Steers, 1977).

Approaching organizational effectiveness from the perspective of individuals and their instrumental gains or their goals has three major problems. The first problem, which is particularly the case for Steers's approach, is that individuals have varying forms of linkages to the organizations of which they are a part. People's involvement in organizations can be alienative, calculative, or moral (Etzioni, 1961, 1975). These different forms of involvement preclude the possibility of individual and goal congruence in many types of organizations. Continuing for a moment with a criticism of Steers's approach, it does not appear to be unfair to note that many personnel in most organizations are probably unaware of the organization's official or operative goals, so that agreement becomes a moot point.

A second, and more basic, problem in these psychological formulations is that their focus on instrumentality for individuals neglects the activities or operations of the organization as a whole or by subunits. Although the instrumentality approach is capable of being generalized across organizations, it misses the fact that organizational outputs do something in society. They are consumed, enjoyed, but could be environmentally harmful. They affect other organizations and people in and out of other organizations as much as people within a focal organization. The psychological approach also downplays the reality of conflicts among goals and decisions that must be made in the face of environmental pressures. The problem is basically one of overlooking a major part of organizational reality. For example, there is a positive relationship between workers' commitment to the organization and such effectiveness indicators as adaptability, turnover, and tardiness. No such relationship was found with the effectiveness indicators of operating costs and absenteeism (Angle and Perry, 1981). Reducing effectiveness considerations to the individual level misses the point that there can be conflicts between desirable outcomes, such as lowered operating costs and lowered turnover.

A third problem with this form of individualistic approach is that it misses the fact that individuals outside the organization are affected by what organizations do. A study of the juvenile justice system found that the "clients" of a juvenile justice system network had clearly different views of the effectiveness of organizations such as the police, courts, and probation departments from those of the members of those agencies (Giordano, 1976, 1977). That is hardly surprising, of course, since the clients in this case were juveniles who had been in trouble with the law. Nonetheless, a client perspective on effectiveness would seem to be a critical component of any comprehensive effectiveness analysis.

Keeley (1978, 1984) has tried to overcome the problems of focusing only on the reactions of internal organizational actors by proposing a "social justice" approach to effectiveness. Building on the work of Rawls (1971), Keeley suggests that a guiding principle for organizational evaluation might be "maximization of the least advantaged participants in a social system" (1978:285). Keeley then proposes that this approach could be operationalized by minimizing the regret that participants experience in their interactions with the organization. Keeley's later work (1984) shifts to the idea of organizational harm but retains the same flavor. He recognizes the difficulties associated with the actual application of the approach but claims that the approach actually contains an optimization principle that goal models do not contain. It is possible to specify the manner in which group regret or harm can be minimized across organizations. It is not possible to specify how goal attainment can be optimized across organizations, given the diversity of goals.

Keeley (1978) concludes:

> Finally, the social-justice model—specifically the minimization of regret principle—manages to balance participant interests in an ethical, yet pragmatic, fashion. It may seem perverse to focus on regretful organizational participants rather than on those, possibly more in number, who enjoy the outcomes of cooperative activity. But the point is that generally aversive system consequences ought not, and, in the long run, probably will not, be tolerated by some participants so that positive consequences can be produced for others. Systems that minimize the aversive consequences of interaction are, therefore, claimed to be more just as well as more stable in the long run. (p. 290)

One can disagree with the practicality of Keeley's approach from the standpoint of the difficulties in determining levels of regret or harm for all system participants, but the point on ethicality is one that should remain fixed in effectiveness modeling.

Constraints, Goals, and Participants

A very different approach to the role of participants is taken by Pennings and Goodman (1977), who make a major contribution to the literature on effectiveness. They approach participants by using the concept of the dominant coalition. To show how Pennings and Goodman bring participants into effectiveness determination, it is necessary to trace their theoretical argument. Their approach is very similar to the contradiction model used in the present analysis.

Pennings and Goodman begin their argument by defining effectiveness: "Organizations are effective if relevant constraints can be satisfied and if organizational results approximate or exceed a set of referents for multiple goals" (p. 160). The idea of constraints involves conditions or requirements that must be satisfied if an organization is to be effective. Constraints involve policies or procedures, set in advance. They guide decision making and behavior in the organizations. Examples of constraints are "maintaining market share at a certain percentage, maintaining quality at a certain level, and not doing business in foreign countries requiring political kickbacks" (p. 160).

Organizational goals, on the other hand, refer to desired end states or objectives specified by the dominant coalition. Pennings and Goodman are explicit in their inclusion of multiple goals. Both constraints and goals are used in the assessment of effectiveness, but there are important differences between the two concepts. Goals receive special attention and concern from the dominant coalition. They are closely related to the motivations of the dominant coalition. Interestingly, goals and constraints can be on the same dimension or area of activity, but the difference lies in the attention paid by the dominant coalition. Pennings and Goodman state:

> Whether achieving a particular quantity or quality level is a goal or constraint depends partially on which is more central to the organization's dominant coalition. For example, some U.S. universities emphasize the number of students enrolled as a constraint for quality of academic excellence, whereas other universities emphasize high enrollment but are constrained by the need of maintaining a minimum level of academic excellence. (p. 161)

A second difference between goals and constraints is that "goals may or may not approximate a referent, whereas constraints must be satisfied as a necessary condition of organizational effectiveness. Degrees (or the relative amount) of organizational effectiveness can be assessed by the degree to which a goal approximates or exceeds a referent" (p. 161). This is obviously a complicated set of ideas and requires some discussion. Referents are the standards by which constraints and goals are evaluated. They involve the dominant coalition's standards of evaluation. Constraints must be met if an organization is to be effective, but just meeting the constraint does not mean effectiveness. Achieving a goal on top of the constraint is effectiveness. Pennings and Goodman use the example of a business firm that wants to increase its profits (a goal) and at the same time maintain the quality of service (a constraint). A failure in maintaining quality of service would contribute to ineffectiveness, but exceeding the quality of service standard would not lead to effectiveness. Only by increasing its profitability and maintaining the quality of service would the organization be effective. Effectiveness is based on the degree to which the goal is achieved.

Interestingly, Pennings and Goodman do not bring in resources as constraints. The system-resource and goal models could actually be nicely joined in this constraint-goal terminology. Certainly, resources are required, and the resource level required for operations is a constraint on the organization. This may be the most appropriate usage of the system-resource model—for example, viewing resources as important constraints that must be satisfied before movements toward goals can be realized.

Pennings and Goodman recognize that there are multiple goals and constraints and that the time frame for these is not constant. They also recognize that for each constraint or goal there may be multiple referents. They do not note that different referents for a single goal or constraint may have contradictory elements. They recognize that effectiveness must always be measured after the fact.

An important contribution of the Pennings-Goodman formulation is the specification that organizations have internal and external stakeholders. These are the components of the dominant coalition that decide goals and determine constraints. Effectiveness criteria are defined by the dominant coalition on the basis of consensus agreements that are achieved. Consensus is achieved by negotiation among the parties involved. This is not a simple process, since the various constituencies themselves have differing and multidimensional preferences.

The process of achieving consensus has the effect of focusing attention on the goals, constraints, and referents. It also forces the dominant coalition to consider alternative arrangements among these elements, adjusting levels of constraints so that goals might be achieved, or altering goals in the face of constraints that cannot be adjusted. Pennings and Goodman view organizations as being made up of multiple constituencies that influence the setting of constraints, goals, and referents. The internal dominant coalition determines the forms and emphases that these take. According to Pennings and Goodman, "although constituencies may hold many referents and constraints with which to evaluate the organization, it is only to the extent that these constraints and referents can be imposed on the organization that they become useful tools for assessing effectiveness" (p. 171).

There is an additional element that is important. Goals, constraints, and referents are determined by the dominant coalition. As the dominant coalition experiences changes in its composition that accompany power shifts or top leadership succession, goals, constraints, and referents will change. Changes take place over time in the perceptions of effectiveness and in evolving constituent preferences (Cameron and Whetten, 1981; Zammuto, 1982). Goals, constraints, and referents are thus moving targets over time.

The approach to be taken in our contradiction model is quite similar to that of Pennings and Goodman. A major difference is the utilization of resources as constraints. Another important difference is that whereas the Pennings-Goodman formulation stresses consensus achieved in the dominant coalition, the contradiction model will not assume consensus. To be sure, decisions have to be made, but there may be times when the consensus that is achieved for a particular decision is so tenuous that it is very short-lived, and the decision is soon reversed. The contradiction model stresses that the various stakeholders of an organization may have irreconcilable differences and that effectiveness for one party may be the opposite for another.

The Pennings-Goodman formulation is much more comprehensive than the other participant-satisfaction models considered earlier. The importance they attribute to the consensus achieved through the dominant coalition led to its placement here. The placement here is also based on the importance given to the political process in effectiveness determination. Both system-resource and goal modeling tend to imply rational decision making, with strategies adopted on the basis of how best to acquire resources or survive to minimize goal attainment. The present approach also assumes that decisions will be made on the basis of some degree of rationality, but tempered with the political facts of organizational life.

Effectiveness for Whom?

Charles Perrow has been a consistently perceptive analyst of organizations. This perceptiveness is exemplified in his analysis of effectiveness studies (1977). He first notes that most studies of effectiveness are what he calls the "variable analysis" type (p. 96). This type of study involves trying to isolate those variables that are somehow related to measures of effectiveness. This is in the administrative-technical tradition. In place of this form of analysis, Perrow suggests that analysts engage in two other types of effectiveness studies—"gross-malfunctioning analysis" and "revelatory analysis." Both involve the question, Effectiveness for whom?

Gross-malfunctioning analysis is proposed as a method to isolate poorly operating organizations with an eye toward improving their services or products. This is proposed as an alternative to the common practice of looking at high-performance organizations and trying to find the correlates of this high performance. Revelatory analysis deals more precisely with the effectiveness-for-whom question. Perrow views organizations as

> ... intentional human constructions but not necessarily rational systems guided by official goals; as bargaining arenas, rather than cooperative systems; as systems of power rather than crescive institutions reflecting cultural norms; and as resources for other organizations and groups rather than closed systems. If we define organizations, then, as intentional human constructions wherein people and groups compete for outputs of interest to them under conditions of unequal power, we have posed the issue of effectiveness quite differently than in the other two perspectives. We now have to ask, what does the organization produce? (p. 101)

In answer to this question, Perrow notes that human-service organizations, such as hospitals, prisons, schools, and welfare organizations, have outputs that are more critical than the services provided to clients. Employment opportunities, segregation and control of people who are thought to be deviant or of the wrong age to be part of society, business opportunities for legitimate business, and markets for organized crime are some of the major outputs of such social service organizations. Perrow believes that revelatory analysis would

> ... reveal what most managers know but social scientists cannot afford to acknowledge, namely, that complex social systems are greatly influenced by sheer chance, accident, luck; that most decisions are very ambiguous, preference orderings are incoherent and unstable, efforts at communication and understanding are often ineffective, subsystems are very loosely connected, and most attempts at social control are clumsy and unpredictable. (p. 103)

Perrow is suggesting two things here. First, organizations should not be analyzed with preconceived notions about what the function of the organization is. He is calling for an explicit recognition of the parties involved in organizational operations and their stake in the survival of the organization. The fact that different groups have different stakes suggests that an approach to organizations that looks at decisions and actions as a simple ordering around goals or environmental pressures is naive.

The effectiveness-for-whom issue is crucial in any effectiveness formulation. That different parties are affected in different ways by organizational actions should be clear. Actions that are successful in one direction may be unrelated to actions in another direction. For example, corporate social responsibility may be unrelated to the stock market performance of corporations, even though a good financial performance may yield the reputation of social responsibility. Efforts in one arena may have little impact in another.

THE CONTRADICTION MODEL

There is growing evidence that most organizational analysts are now realizing that effectiveness is a truly multifaceted phenomenon. Research on colleges and universities found that effectiveness is a "multidomain" phenomenon and concludes:

> Effectiveness in one domain may not necessarily relate to effectiveness in another domain. For example, maximizing the satisfaction and growth of individuals in an organization . . . may be negatively related to high levels of subunit output and co-ordination. . . . Specifically, publishing a large number of research reports may be a goal indicating a high level of effectiveness to faculty members (on an individual level) while indicating low effectiveness at the subunit or organizational level (e.g., poor teaching quality, little time with students, little personal attention for students, graduate student teaching instead of professors) to legislators and parents of undergraduates. (Cameron, 1978:625)

This point has a great deal of substantive validity. It is also quite close to the contradiction model. It does not deal with power differences among stakeholders or with temporal shifts in environmental pressures as we will do here.

Based on the evidence presented throughout this book and on the effectiveness models considered, the contradiction model can now be presented in a relatively simple manner:

1. Organizations face multiple and conflicting environmental constraints. These constraints may be imposed on an organization; they may be bargained for; they may be discovered; or they may be self-imposed (Seashore, 1977). Imposed constraints are beyond organizational control. They involve our familiar environmental dimensions, such as legal or economic positions. To be sure, organizations lobby for legal and regulative advantage, but taxes and regulations are essentially imposed on organizations. This imposition is not just from government. A computer or software manufacturer, such as Microsoft, that develops new systems is imposing this environment on users, if those users must adopt the new system to stay "state of the art." Bargained constraints involve contractual agreements and competitive pressures in markets. Discovered constraints are environmental constraints that appear unexpectedly, as when a coal company finds that its vein of ore has run out. Self-imposed constraints involve the definitions of the environment that organizations utilize. For example, a study of newspaper coverage of an oil spill documented the fact that newspapers differed markedly in the amount of space given to the spill (Molotch and Lester, 1975). Organizational policy thus defines the importance of environmental elements.

Regardless of the source of the constraints, their conflicting nature must be stressed, since efforts to deal with one constraint may operate against the meeting of another. Indeed, organizational units facing multiple contingencies are more prone to face design misfit and lower performance than those in simpler situations (Gresov, 1989). As a general rule, the larger and more complex the organization, the greater the range and variety of constraints it will face. Organizations have to consider their environments, recognize and order the constraints that are confronted, and attempt to predict the consequences of their actions—all within the limitations on decision making and rationality we have considered.

2. Organizations have multiple and conflicting goals. This point has been beaten to death, but one more pass is necessary here. A case from The University at Albany is instructive. It involved a threatened budget cut, which is an annual event that sometimes results in real cuts and sometimes does not. In the case being described, the threatened cuts were severe. Each vice president had to make up a list of "target" positions in his or her area. We know that decisions that are made in such situations are the result of power coalitions. At the same time, goals do not just disappear. Issues such as the emphasis on research, needs for the continued recruitment and retention of high-quality students and faculty to achieve the goal of being a high-quality university, and reiterations of the importance of having a safe and attractive campus were voiced and were much more than rhetoric. When the cuts were made, they were based on goals and power coalitions. Both contained contradictions that were played out in actions.

3. Organizations have multiple and conflicting internal and external stakeholders. By stakeholders we mean those people affected by an organization (Marcus and Goodman, 1991; Tsui, 1990). They may be employees, members, customers, clients, or the public at large. Stakeholders can also be other organizations, such as suppliers and customers. Individual and organizational stakeholders obviously can have different and contradictory interests (Harrison and Freeman, 1999).

4. Organizations have multiple and conflicting time frames. The issue of time frames is closely intertwined with our consideration of goals. Consider the following:

> To the extent that the goals function stresses quick return on investment (as in many business ventures, disaster relief organizations, military field units, and so on) the short-run outcomes should be given the highest priority. For those organizations that orient toward continued production (for example, many other types of business ventures, universities, research and development organizations, and so on) the year-to-year fluctuations in performance should be discounted and the average performance over longer periods emphasized.
>
> The conceptual problem is that we do not know how organizations discount time. Two organizations with the same goals operating with the same structure in the same environment may place a very different emphasis on speed of return on investment. One organization may capitalize on some situations in a way that increases both the probability of quick favorable outcomes and the risk of long-term decline. The other may eschew the quick return in favor of the long term security. . . . [T]he analyst must also know the premium placed on speed of return. (Hannan and Freeman, 1977a:113–14)

There are also intraorganizational variations in the time frame that is used (Lawrence and Lorsch, 1967). These differences occur between units and across levels on the vertical dimension.

The degree and mix of environmental constraints also vary over time. Constraints that were critical at one point may disappear as threats. New problems arise. Time also plays a role in the history of an organization, since new organizations are more vulnerable.

The temporal dimension of effectiveness is essentially one of judgment. Decisions must be made with regard to the time frame of reference for analyzing goal attainment, the nature and phasing of environmental constraints, and the historical situation of the organization. Failing to recognize this can lead the analyst and the practitioner to real problems. For the analyst it is only a poor study; for the practitioner it is organizational decline or death.

We have considered contradictions in environmental constraints, goals, stakeholders, and time. These are the realities constructed in and for all organizations. They are the basis for judgment and action. They lead to the conclusion that no organization is effective. Rather, organizations can be viewed as effective (or ineffective) to some degree in specific constraints, goals, stakeholders, and time frames.

Some Applications

When considering the issue of applications from a contradiction model, the first conclusion we must reach is that efforts to be effective always involve less than total rationality. It is now a matter of faith in organizational theory that organizations do not optimize in their decision making, as shown in the discussion of decision making.

The analysis presented here goes beyond those considerations and has emphasized that there are compromises that must be made among pressing constraints, goals, stakeholders, and time frames. The ordering of the compromises is based on power relationships and coalitions within the organizations, coupled with external pressures. This is done with the knowledge that if once an action is selected, others are not possible, particularly with constant or diminishing resources. Before we consider these matters further, it is imperative that we address a relatively neglected topic—constraints over which organizations can have no control.

Constraints Beyond Organizational Control. Organizations attempt to control those constraints that they perceive to be central to them. Devices such as industrial vertical integration, utilization of boards of directors, political intervention, and advertising are all efforts to reduce environmental uncertainty or shape the environment to the benefit of the organization. At the same time, some events are uncontrollable.

A simple example of this is the weather. An organization may be dependent upon particular weather patterns, but it can do little about the forces of nature. Cloud seeding has yet to become truly feasible, and no device has been developed to control the external temperature. Agricultural organizations are thus subject to droughts, floods, and prolonged hot or cold spells. Winter recreational organizations, such as ski resorts, suffer when there is no snow and when warm temperatures prevent snowmaking. A bad weather year can cause the death of some areas.

Organizations that are weather dependent can engage in activities that minimize the influence of nature, such as stockpiling food or making snow (even this does not work if the temperature is above freezing), but these organizations face a basically uncontrollable constraint.

More complex examples come in the forms of world political and economic shifts. The collapse of the Soviet regime essentially destroyed many existing organizations. The old organizations are simply gone.

There are other, less dramatic forces than the sweep of world events that are important for organizations but that they cannot control. These include such things as demographic patterns and local or regional economic developments. When a major employer leaves a community or goes out of business, all of the other organizations in the community are affected.

Uncontrollable events and forces happen to organizations. They are part of the constraint package that is faced. What is important for the discussion here is that they cannot be manipulated. They are conditions to which organizations must adjust as they deal with other constraints, goals, stakeholders, and time frames.

Environmental Constraints That Are Potentially Manipulable.   Organizations attempt to manipulate their environment. A major task of top management is to enhance the position of their organization in the environment. Analyses of interlocking corporate boards of directors have suggested that such interlocking can serve four major external functions. The selection of directors can be a means by which financial, legal, or other information or expertise can be brought to the organization. Directors can also be selected with the intent of facilitating the organization's search for capital or other resources. This is the primary reason that bank officials are so heavily represented on the corporate boards across the array of business firms. Community leaders on the boards of hospitals or colleges serve to bring in the resource of legitimacy. Board composition can also serve a political function. The selection of the appropriate director can assist in coping with federal and state agencies, since the presence of politically powerful groups can serve to blunt vigorous governmental actions. Finally, board composition has been viewed as a means by which the interests of powerful external organizations, such as banks, insurance companies, or controlling blocks of family interests, are served (Aldrich, 1979:297). These interlocking directorates do not create certainty for the organizations involved.

That aspects of the environment are only potentially manipulable can be seen in an analysis of the pharmaceutical and popular-music industries (Hirsch, 1975). The pharmaceutical industry had great success in protecting itself from competition by securing the passage of state and federal legislation. It also was successful in getting organized medicine, through the American Medical Association, to permit the industry to advertise drugs by their brand names rather than by their generic names. Prescriptions were sold by brand rather than by compound. Hirsch found that the popular-music (recording) industry had a similar structure to begin with but was unable to obtain protective legislation and exclusive rights to the profits possible whenever a song was played on the radio. The popular-music industry lobbied and used other techniques to try to protect itself, but it failed and had severe problems as musical tastes, as well as many other cultural elements, changed in the 1960s. One industry was successful in manipulating its environment; the other was not.

This is an area of uncertainty for organizations. If someone were to come up with a sure technique for controlling the environment, as the early and later monopolists have, every organization would adopt it. Antimonopoly laws are specifically designed to prevent environmental control. Organizations attempt to control as much as they legally can or as much as they can without being caught.

The discussion thus far has focused on the private sector. Public organizations also seek to control their environment. The public budgetary process is one in which resources are sought for organizational maintenance and growth. Public organizations send messages to their stakeholders and others. These messages are designed to protect the organization and further its interests. This "propaganda" may be quite detrimental to the public in many instances (Altheide and Johnson, 1980).

In this section we have argued that organizations engage in a variety of activities designed to manipulate their environment in their favor. Whether through interlocking boards of directors, purchasing suppliers, seeking to have favorable legislation passed, or propaganda, the attempt is to manipulate the environment on behalf of the organization. These efforts have only the potential for success, since other organizations with other purposes are interacting with the same components of the environment. Organizations can be most sure of the consequences of their actions when the organization itself is considered.

Organizational Characteristics.   Organizations have the capability of being structured and restructured in accordance with the outcomes of decision making and political processes within their own boundaries. Much of the thinking that has emerged from the contingency model has dealt directly with this issue. The basic notion is that there are multiple organizational forms that are most likely to be successful, depending upon the situations the organization is confronting. One of the major tasks of top management is to determine what the most appropriate organizational form is for various situations. It is not uncommon to find business firms in rapidly changing technological fields with no formal tables of organization or organizational charts, because the organization is in a constant change mode. There is a reciprocal relationship between strategy and structure (Miller, 1987).

Organizations are not completely flexible. Union contracts, custom, and laws militate against total self-determination. Nonetheless, it is possible to structure or restructure organizations to bring about greater adaptability or rigidity or more or less participation in the decision-making process. The organizational form is more subject to organizational control than other factors regarding effectiveness that we have considered. Whether organizational form is most crucial for organizational effectiveness is unclear. It would appear that ultimate survival might well be a function of factors beyond organizational control. The more controllable a particular situation is, perhaps the less important it is. It is quite clear that controlling the relevant environment, over time and across conditions, and structuring the organization to acquire sufficient resources and to pursue and move to accomplish major goals is a key to any consideration of effectiveness.

SUMMARY AND CONCLUSIONS

This chapter attempts to make some sense of the critical area of organizational effectiveness. Conceptual and methodological contradictions in the analysis of effectiveness were presented, and a contradiction model was developed. The model contains key elements of the resource-acquisition and goals models and is an attempt to combine them in a manner that retains their key insights but adds the important factor of inherent contradictions. Organizational effectiveness will remain the major concern for organizational practitioners and analysts. Ignoring the contradictions will not advance knowledge or practice. Ignoring that there are factors beyond organizational control or that are only potentially manipulable will also not contribute to theory or practice. It is only when theorists and practitioners realize the limited range of options open to organizations, as they confront constraints and mandates and attempt to move toward goal achievement and cope with the issues of multiple stakeholders and conflicting time frames, that both usable and theoretically interesting developments will take place.

EXERCISES

1. Discuss the goals, environments, and stakeholders of your two organizations. To what degree are there contradictions present?
2. Using the contradiction model, discuss the effectiveness of your two organizations.

References

Abbott, Andrew. 1988. *The System of Professions*. Chicago: University of Chicago Press.

———. 1989. "The New Occupational Structure: What Are the Questions?" *Work and Occupations,* 16, 273–91.

———. 1992. "An Old Institutionalist Reads the New Institutionalism." *Contemporary Sociology,* 21, 754–56.

Acker, Joan. 1992. "The Future of Women and Work: Ending the Twentieth Century." *Sociological Perspectives,* 35, 139–58.

Adler, Nancy J. 1996. "Global Women Political Leaders: An Invisible History, an Increasingly Important Future." *Leadership Quarterly,* 7, 133–161.

Adler, Paul S., and Bryan Borys. 1996. "Two Faces of Bureaucracy: Enabling and Coercive." *Administrative Science Quarterly,* 41, 61–89.

Ahuja, Gautam. 2000. "Collaboration Networks, Structural Holes, and Innovation: A Longitudinal Study." *Administrative Science Quarterly,* 45, 425–55.

Aiken, Michael, and Jerald Hage. 1966. "Organizational Alienation: A Comparative Analysis." *American Sociological Review,* 31, 497–507.

———. 1968. "Organizational Interdependence and Interorganizational Structure." *American Sociological Review,* 33, 912–30.

Aldrich, Howard E. 1971. "Organizational Boundaries and Interorganizational Conflict." *Human Relations,* 24, 279–87.

———. 1972a. "Technology and Organizational Structure: A Reexamination of the Findings of the Aston Group." *Administrative Science Quarterly,* 17, 26–43.

———. 1972b. "Reply to Hilton: Seduced and Abandoned." *Administrative Science Quarterly,* 17, 55–57.

———. 1979. *Organizations and Environments.* Upper Saddle River, NJ: Prentice Hall.

———. 1988. "Paradigm Warriors: Donaldson versus the Critics of Organization Theory." *Organization Studies,* 9, 18–25.

Aldrich, Howard E., and Peter V. Marsden. 1988. "Environments and Organizations," in *Handbook of Sociology,* ed. Neil J. Smelser, 361–92. Newbury Park, CA: Sage.

Aldrich, Howard E., and Jeffrey Pfeffer. 1976. "Environments of Organizations." *Annual Review of Sociology,* Vol. 2. Palo Alto, CA: Annual Reviews, Inc.

Alexander, Ernest R. 1979. "The Design of Alternatives in Organizational Contexts." *Administrative Science Quarterly,* 24, 382–404.

Alexander, Jeffrey A. 1991. "Adaptive Change in Corporate Control Practices." *Academy of Management Journal,* 34, 162–93.

Alford, Fred. 2001. *Whistle Blowers: Broken Lives and Organizational Power.* Ithaca, NY: Cornell University Press.

Allen, Michael Patrick. 1974. "The Structure of Interorganizational Elite Cooptation: Interlocking Corporate Directorates." *American Sociological Review,* 39, 393–96.

———. 1976. "Management Control in the Large Corporation: Comment on Zeitlin." *American Journal of Sociology,* 81, 885–94.

Allen, Michael Patrick, and Sharon K. Panian. 1982. "Power, Performance, and Succession in the Large Corporation." *Administrative Science Quarterly,* 27, 538–47.

Allen, Michael Patrick, Sharon K. Panian, and Roy E. Lotz. 1979. "Managerial Succession and Organizational Performance: A Recalcitrant Problem Revisited." *Administrative Science Quarterly,* 24, 167–80.

Allison, Paul D., and J. Scott Long. 1990. "Departmental Effects on Scientific Productivity." *American Sociological Review,* 55, 469–78.

Allmendinger, Jutta, and J. Richard Hackman. 1996. "Organizations in Changing Environments: The Case of East German Symphony Orchestras." *Administrative Science Quarterly,* 41, 337–69.

Alter, Catherine, and Jerald Hage. 1993. *Organizations Working Together.* Newbury Park, CA: Sage.

Altheide, David L., and John M. Johnson. 1980. *Bureaucratic Propaganda.* Boston: Allyn & Bacon.

Alutto, Joseph, and James A. Belasco. 1972. "A Typology for Participation in Organizational Decision Making." *Administrative Science Quarterly,* 17, 117–25.

Alvesson, Mats and Hugh Willmott. 2002. "Identity Regulation as Organizational Control: Producing the Appropriate Individual." *Journal of Management Studies,* 39, 619–44.

Amburgey, Terry, Dawn Kelly, and William P. Barnett. 1993. "Resetting the Clock: The Dynamics of Organizational Change and Failure." *Administrative Science Quarterly,* 38, 51–73.

Angle, Harold L., and James L. Perry. 1981. "An Empirical Assessment of Organizational Commitment and Organizational Effectiveness." *Administrative Science Quarterly,* 26, 1–14.

Ansell, C. K., and John F. Padgett. 1993. "Robust Action and the Rise of the Medici, 1400–1434." *American Journal of Sociology,* 98, 1259–1319.

Antonio, Robert J. 1979. "Domination and Production in Bureaucracy." *American Sociological Review,* 44, 895–912.

Appold, Stephen J., Sununta Siengthai, and John D. Kasarda. 1998. "The Employment of Women Managers and Professionals in an Emerging Economy: Gender Inequality as Organizational Practice." *Administrative Science Quarterly,* 43, 538–65.

Argote, Linda. 1982. "Input Uncertainty and Organizational Coordination in Hospital Emergency Units." *Administrative Science Quarterly,* 27, 420–34.

Argyris, Chris. 1972. *The Applicability of Organizational Sociology.* London: Cambridge University Press.

Aronowitz, Stanley. 1973. *False Promises.* New York: McGraw-Hill.

Arum, Richard. 1996. "Do Private Schools Force Public Schools to Compete?" *American Sociological Review,* 61, 29–46.

Astley, W. Graham. 1985. "The Two Ecologies: Population and Community Perspectives on Organizational Evolution." *Administrative Science Quarterly,* 30, 224–41.

Athanassaides, John C. 1974. "On Investigation of Some Communication Patterns of Female Subordinates in Hierarchical Organizations." *Human Relations,* 27, 195–209.

At-Twarjri, Mohammad I., and John R. Montansani. 1987. "The Impact of Context and Choice on the Boundary Spanning Process: An Empirical Extension." *Human Relations,* 40, 783–98.

Azumi, Koya, and Charles J. McMillan. 1974. *Subjective and Objective Measures of Organizational Structure.* New York: American Sociological Association.

Bacharach, Samuel B., Peter Bamberger, and Walter Sonnenstuhl. 1996. "The Organizational Transformation Process: The Micropolitics of Dissonance Reduction and the Alignment of Logics of Action." *Administrative Science Quarterly,* 41, 477–506.

Bacharach, Samuel B., and Edward J. Lawler. 1980. *Power and Politics in Organizations.* San Francisco: Jossey-Bass.

Bachrach, Peter, and Morton S. Baratz. 1962. "The Two Faces of Power." *American Political Science Review,* 56, 947–52.

Baker, Wayne E. 1990. "Market Networks and Corporate Behavior." *American Journal of Sociology,* 96, no. 3, 589–625.

Baldridge, J. Victor, and Robert A. Burnham. 1975. "Organizational Innovation: Individual, Organizational, and Environmental Impacts." *Administrative Science Quarterly,* 20, 165–76.

Bales, Robert F. 1953. "The Equilibrium Problem in Small Groups," in *Working Paper in Theory of Action,* eds. Talcott Parsons, Robert F. Bales, and Edward Shils. New York: Free Press.

Bales, Robert F., and Philip E. Slater. 1955. "Role Differentiation in Small Decision Making Groups," in *Family Socialization and Interaction Processes,* eds. Talcott Parsons and Robert Bales. New York: Free Press.

Barley, Stephen R. 1990. "The Alignment of Technology and Structure through Roles and Networks." *Administrative Science Quarterly,* 35, 61–103.

———. 2004. "What Sociologists Know (and Mostly Don't Know) about Technical Work," pp. 376–403 in *Handbook of Work and Organizations,* eds. Stephen Ackroyd, Rose Batt, Paul Thompson, and Pamela Tolbert. Oxford: Oxford University Press.

Barnard, Chester I. 1938. *The Function of the Executive.* Cambridge, MA: Harvard University Press.

Baron, James N. 1984. "Organizational Perspectives on Stratification," in *Annual Review of Sociology,* ed. Ralph Turner. Palo Alto, CA: Annual Reviews, Inc.

Baron, James N., and William T. Bielby. 1980. "Bringing the Firms Back In: Stratification, Segmentation and the Organization of Work." *American Sociological Review,* 45, 737–65.

Baum, Joel A. C., and Heather Haveman. 1997. "Love Thy Neighbor? Differentiation and Agglomeration in the Manhattan Hotel Industry, 1998–1990." *Administrative Science Quarterly,* 42, 304–38.

Baum, Joel A. C., and Christine Oliver. 1991. "Institutional Linkages and Organizational Mortality." *Administrative Science Quarterly,* 36, 187–218.

———. 1992. "Institutional Embeddedness and the Dynamics of Organizational Populations." *American Sociological Review,* 57, 540–59.

Baum, Joel A. C., and Jitendra V. Singh. 1994. "Organizational Niches and the Dynamics of Organizational Mortality." *American Journal of Sociology,* 100, 346–80.

———. 1996. "Dynamics of Organizational Responses to Competition." *Social Forces,* 74, 1261–97.

Baureus, Melissa S., and Janet P. Near. 1991. "Can Illegal Corporate Behavior Be Predicted: An Event History Analysis." *Academy of Management Journal,* 34, 9–36.

Bavelas, Alex. 1950. "Communication Patterns in Task Oriented Groups." *Journal of the Acoustic Society of America,* 22, 725–30.

Beamish, Thomas D. 2000. "Accumulating Trouble: Complex Organization, a Culture of Silence and a Secret Spill." *Social Problems,* 47, 473–98.

Beckman, Christine M., and Haunschild, Pamela R. 2002. "Network Learning: The Effects of Partners' Heterogeneity of Experience on Corporate Acquisitions." *Administrative Science Quarterly,* 47, 92–124.

Benson, J. Kenneth. 1975. "The Interlocking Network as a Political Economy." *Administrative Science Quarterly,* 20, 229–49.

Benson, J. Kenneth, Joseph T. Kunce, Charles A. Thompson, and David L. Allen. 1973. *Coordinating Human Services.* Columbia, MO: Regional Rehabilitation Institute, University of Missouri.

Berger, Joseph, Murray Webster, Celia L. Ridgeway, and S. J. Rosenholtz. 1986. "Status Cues, Expectations, and Behaviors," in *Advances in Group Processes,* Vol. 3, ed. E. J. Lawler, 1–22. Greenwich, CT: JAI Press.

Berger, Peter, and Thomas Luckman. 1967. *The Social Construction of Reality.* Garden City, NY: Anchor.

Berle, Adolph A., and Gardiner C. Means. 1932. *The Modern Corporation and Private Property.* New York: Macmillan.

Bettman, James R., and Barton A. Weitz. 1983. "Attributions in the Board Room: Causal Reasoning in Corporate Annual Reports." *Administrative Science Quarterly,* 28, 165–83.

Beyer, Janice M., and Harrison M. Trice. 1979. "A Reexamination of the Relations between Size and Various Components of Organizational Complexity." *Administrative Science Quarterly,* No. 1 (March), 48–64.

Bidwell, Charles E., and John D. Kasarda. 1985. *The Organization and Its Ecosystem: A Theory of Structuring in Organizations.* Greenwich, CT: JAI Press.

Bierstedt, Robert. 1950. "An Analysis of Social Power." *American Sociological Review,* 15, 730–38.

Biggart, Nicole Woolsey. 1977. "The Creative-Destructive Process of Organizational Change: The Case of the Post Office." *Administrative Science Quarterly,* 22, 410–26.

———. 1989. *Charismatic Capitalism: Direct Selling Organizations in America.* Chicago: University of Chicago Press.

Birnbaum, Phillip H., and Gilbert Y. Y. Wong. 1985. "Organizational Structure of Multinational Banks from a Culture-Free Perspective." *Administrative Science Quarterly,* 30, 262–77.

Blake, R. R., and J. S. Mouton. 1964. *The Managerial Grid.* Houston, TX: Gulf Publishing.

Blau, Judith R., and Richard D. Alba. 1982. "Empowering Nets of Participation." *Administrative Science Quarterly,* 27, 363–79.

Blau, Judith R., and William McKinley. 1979. "Ideas, Complexity, and Innovation." *Administrative Science Quarterly,* 24, 200–19.

Blau, Peter M. 1955. *The Dynamics of Bureaucracy.* Chicago: University of Chicago Press.

———. 1964. *Exchange and Power in Social Life.* New York: John Wiley.

———. 1968. "The Hierarchy of Authority in Organizations." *American Journal of Sociology,* 73, 453–67.

———. 1970. "Decentralization in Bureaucracies," in *Power in Organizations,* ed. Mayer N. Zald. Nashville: Vanderbilt University Press.

———. 1972. "Interdependence and Hierarchy in Organizations." *Social Science Research,* 1, 1–24.

———. 1973. *The Organization of Academic Work.* New York: John Wiley.

———. 1974. *On the Nature of Organizations.* New York: John Wiley.

Blau, Peter M., Wolf Heydebrand, and Robert E. Stauffer. 1966. "The Structure of Small Bureaucracies." *American Sociological Review,* 31, 179–91.

Blau, Peter M., and Richard A. Schoenherr. 1971. *The Structure of Organizations.* New York: Basic Books.

Blau, Peter M., and W. Richard Scott. 1962. *Formal Organizations.* San Francisco: Chandler.

Blum, Terry C., David Fields, and Jodi Goodman. 1994. "Organizational-Level Determinants of Women in Management." *Academy of Management Journal,* 37, 241–68.

Boddewyn, John. 1974. "External Affairs: A Corporate Function in Search of Conceptualization and Theory." *Organization and Administrative Sciences,* 5, 67–106.

Boeker, Warren. 1989. "Strategic Change: The Effects of Founding and History." *Academy of Management Journal,* 32, 489–515.

———. 1992. "Power and Managerial Dismissal: Scapegoating at the Top." *Administrative Science Quarterly,* 37, 400–21.

———. 1997a. "Strategic Change: The Influence of Managerial Characteristics and Organizational Growth." *Academy of Management Journal,* 40, 152–70.

———. 1997b. "Executive Migration and Strategic Change: The Effect of Top Manager Movement on Product Market Entry." *Administrative Science Quarterly,* 42, 213–36.

Boeker, Warren, and Jerry Goodstein. 1991. "Organizational Performance and Adaptation: Effects of Environment and Performance on Changes in Board Composition." *Academy of Management Journal,* 34, 805–26.

Boeker, Warren, and Richard Karichalil. 2002. "Entrepreneurial Transitions: Factors Influencing Founder Departure." *Academy of Management Journal,* 45, 818–26.

Boje, David M., and David A. Whetten. 1981. "Effects of Organizational Strategies and Contextual Constraints on Centrality and Attributions of Influence in Interorganizational Networks." *Administrative Science Quarterly,* 26, 378–95.

Boraas, Stephanie, and William M. Rodgers. 2003. "How Does Gender Play a Role in the Earnings Gap? An Update." *Monthly Labor Review,* 126, No. 3, 9–15.

Borman, W. C., and D. H. Brush. 1993. "More Progress toward a Taxonomy of Managerial Performance Requirements." *Human Performance,* 6, 1–21.

Boulding, Kenneth E. 1964. "A Pure Theory of Conflict Applied to Organizations," in *Power and Conflict in Organizations,* eds. Robert L. Kahn and Elise Boulding. New York: Basic Books.

Bowman, Scott R. 1996. *The Modern Corporation and American Political Thought: Law, Power, and Ideology.* University Park: Penn State Press.

Brass, Daniel J. 1984. "Being in the Right Place: A Structural Analysis of Individual Influence in an Organization." *Administrative Science Quarterly,* 29, 518–39.

Brass, Daniel J., and Marlene E. Burkhardt. 1993. "Potential Power and Power Use: An Investigation of Structure and Behavior." *Academy of Management Journal,* 36, 441–70.

Brewer, John. 1971. "Flow of Communication, Expert Qualifications, and Organizational Authority Structure." *American Sociological Review,* 36, 475–84.

Broskowski, Anthony. 1980. "Literature Review on Interorganizational Relationships and Their Relevance to Health and Mental Health Coordination." Tampa, FL: Northside Community Mental Health Center (final report), NIMH Contract #278-00300P.

Brown, M. Craig. 1982. "Administrative Succession and Organizational Performance: The Succession Effect." *Administrative Science Quarterly,* 27, 1–16.

Brown, Richard Harvey. 1978. "Bureaucracy as Praxis: Toward a Political Phenomenology of Formal Organizations." *Administrative Science Quarterly,* 23, 365–82.

Browning, Larry D., Janice M. Beyer, and Judy C. Shetler. 1995. "Building Cooperation in a Competitive Industry: SEMATECH and the Semiconductor Industry." *Academy of Management Journal,* 38, 113–51.

Brunsson, Nils. 1989. *The Organization of Hypocrisy: Talk, Decisions, and Actions in Organizations.* New York: John Wiley.

Bucher, Rue. 1970. "Social Process and Power in a Medical School," in *Power in Organizations,* ed. Mayer N. Zald. Nashville, TN: Vanderbilt University Press.

———. 1993. "An Analysis of Organizational Birth Types: Organizational Start-up and Entry in the Nineteenth-Century Life Insurance Industry." *Social Forces,* 72, 199–221.

———. 2000. "Organizational Types and Organizational Innovation: Downsizing among Institutionalized Market, Market, and Institutionalized Firms." *Sociological Forum,* 15, 273–306.

———. 2002. "The Mean and Lean Firm and Downsizing: Causes of Involuntary and Voluntary Downsizing." *Sociological Forum,* 17, 307–42.

Bugùra, Ayse, and Behlül Üsdiken. 1997. "Introduction: State, Market and Organizational Form," in *State, Market and Organizational Form,* eds. Ayse Bugùra and Behlül Üsdiken. Berlin: Walter de Gruyter.

Burke, John P. 1986. *Bureaucratic Responsibility.* Baltimore: Johns Hopkins University Press.

Burns, Tom, and G. M. Stalker. 1961. *The Management of Innovation.* London: Tavistock Publications.

———. 1983. "Corporate Philanthropy as a Cooptive Process." *Social Forces,* 62, 419–49.

———. 1988. "The Stability of American Markets." *American Journal of Sociology,* 94, No. 2 (September), 356–95.

———. 1992. *Structural Holes.* Cambridge, MA: Harvard University Press.

Burt, Ronald S., Kenneth P. Christman, and Harold C. Kilburn, Jr. 1980. "Testing a Structural Theory of Corporate Cooptation: Interorganizational Directorate Ties as a Strategy for Avoiding Market Constraints on Projects." *American Sociological Review,* 45, 821–41.

Cameron, Kim. 1978. "Measuring Organizational Effectiveness in Institutions of Higher Education." *Administrative Science Quarterly,* 23, 604–32.

Cameron, Kim, Myung U. Kim, and David A. Whetten. 1987. "Organizational Effects of Decline and Turbulence." *Administrative Science Quarterly,* 32, 222–40.

Cameron, Kim, and David A. Whetten. 1981. "Perceptions of Organizational Effectiveness over Organizational Life Cycles." *Administrative Science Quarterly,* 26, 524–44.

Campbell, Donald. 1969. "Variation and Selective Retention in Socio-Cultural Evolution." *General Systems: Yearbook of the Society for General Systems Research,* 16, 69–85.

Campbell, John P. 1977. "On the Nature of Organizational Effectiveness," in *New Perspectives on Organizational Effectiveness,* eds. Paul S. Goodman and Johannes M. Pennings. San Francisco: Jossey-Bass.

Caplow, Theodore. 1964. *Principles of Organization.* New York: Harcourt Brace Jovanovich.

———. 1976. *How to Run Any Organization.* New York: Holt, Rinehart & Winston.

Caragonne, P. 1978. "Service Integration: Where Do We Stand?" Paper prepared for the 39th National Conference on Public Administration, April, in Phoenix, Arizona.

Carli, Linda, and Alice H. Eagly. 1999. "Gender Effects on Social Influence and Emergent Leadership," in *Handbook of Gender and Work,* ed. G. N. Powell. Thousand Oaks, CA: Sage.

Carroll, Glenn R. 1984a. "Organizational Ecology." *Annual Review of Sociology,* Vol. 18. Palo Alto, CA: Annual Reviews, Inc.

———. 1984b. "Dynamics of Publisher Succession in Newspaper Organizations." *Administrative Science Quarterly,* 29, 93–113.

———. 1985. "Concentration and Specialization: Dynamics of Niche Width in Populations of Organizations." *American Journal of Sociology,* 90, 1262–83.

———, ed. 1988. *Ecological Models of Organizations.* Cambridge, MA: Ballinger.

Carroll, Glenn R., and Jacques Delacroix. 1982. "Organizational Mortality in the Newspaper Industries of Argentina and Ireland: An Ecological Approach." *Administrative Science Quarterly,* 27, 169–98.

Carroll, Glenn R., and Michael T. Hannan. 1989. "Density Dependence in the Evolution of Populations of Newspaper Organizations." *American Sociological Review,* 54, 524–41.

———. 2000. *The Demography of Corporations and Industries.* Princeton, NJ: Princeton University Press.

Carroll, Glenn R., and Yangchung Paul Huo. 1986. "Organizational Task and Institutional Environments in Ecological Perspective: Findings from the Local Newspaper Industry." *American Journal of Sociology,* 91, 838–73.

Carroll, Glenn R., Peter Preisendoerfer, Anand Swaninathan, and Gabriele Wiedenmayer. 1993. "Brewery and Branerei: The Organizational Ecology of Brewing." *Organizational Studies,* 14, 155–88.

Carroll, Glenn R., and James Wade. 1991. "Density Dependence in the Organizational Evolution of the American Brewing Industry across Different Levels of Analysis." *Social Science Research,* 20, 271–302.

Carstensen, Fred V., and Richard Hume Werking. 1983. "The Process of Bureaucratization in the U.S. State Department and the Vesting of Economic Interests: Toward Clearer Thinking and Better History." *Administrative Science Quarterly,* 28, 56–60.

Champagne, Anthony, Marian Neef, and Stuart Nagel. 1981. "Laws, Organizations, and the Judiciary," in *Handbook of Organizational Design,* Vol. 1, eds. Paul C. Nystrom and William H. Starbuck. New York: Oxford University Press.

Chandler, A. D., Jr. 1962. *Strategy and Structure.* Cambridge, MA: MIT Press.

Chen, Ming-Jer, and Donald Hambrick. 1995. "Speed, Stealth, and Selective Attack: How Small Firms Differ from Large Firms in Competitive Behavior." *Academy of Management Journal,* 38, 453–82.

Child, John. 1972. "Organizational Structure, Environment, and Performance: The Role of Strategic Choice." *Sociology,* 6, 1–22.

———. 1973. "Strategies of Control and Organizational Behavior." *Administrative Science Quarterly,* 18, 1–17.

———. 1976. "Participation, Organization, and Social Cohesion." *Human Relations,* 29, 429–51.

Child, John, and Alfred Kieser. 1981. "Development of Organization over Time," in *Handbook of Organizational Design,* eds. Paul C. Nystrom and William H. Starbuck, Vol. 1, 169–98. New York: Oxford University Press.

Child, John, and Roger Mansfield. 1972. "Technology, Size and Organizational Structure." *Sociology,* 6, 369–93.

Christenson, James A., James G. Hougland, Jr., Thomas W. Ilvento, and Jon M. Shepard. 1988. "The 'Organization Man' and the Community: The Impact of Organizational Norms and Personal Values on Community Participation and Transfers." *Social Forces,* 66, 808–26.

Clarke, Lee B. 1989. *Acceptable Risk? Making Decisions in a Toxic Environment.* Berkeley, CA: University of California Press.

Clawson, Dan, and Alan Neustadt. 1989. "Interlocks, PACs and Corporate Conservatism." *American Journal of Sociology,* 94, 749–73.

Clegg, Stewart. 1981. "Organization and Control." *Administrative Science Quarterly,* 26, 545–62.

Clegg, Stewart, and David Dunkerley. 1980. *Organization, Class, and Control.* London: Routledge and Kegan Paul.

Clinard, Marshall B., and Peter Yeager. 1980. *Corporate Crime.* New York: Free Press.

Cohen, Michael D., James G. March, and Johan P. Olsen. 1972. "A Garbage Can Model of Organizational Choice." *Administrative Science Quarterly,* 17, 1–25.

Coleman, James S. 1974. *Power and the Structure of Society.* New York: W. W. Norton.

Colignon, Richard. 1997. *The New Deal and Intellectuals: The Institutionalization of the TVA.* Albany: State University of New York Press.

Comstock, Donald, and W. Richard Scott. 1977. "Technology and the Structure of Subunits: Distinguishing Individual and Work Group Effects." *Administrative Science Quarterly,* 22, 177–202.

Conaty, Joseph, Hoda Mahmoudi, and George A. Miller. 1983. "Social Structure and Bureaucracy: A Comparison of Organizations in the United States and Prerevolutionary Iran." *Organization Studies,* 4, 105–28.

Cook, Karen S. 1977. "Exchange and Power in Networks of Interorganizational Relations." *Sociological Quarterly,* 18, 62–82.

Cooper, David J., Bob Hinings, Royston Greenwood, and J. L. Brown. 1996. "Sedimentation and Transformation in Organizational Change: The Case of Canadian Law Firms." *Organization Studies,* 17, 623–47.

Corwin, Ronald. 1973. *Reform and Organizational Survival: The Teacher Corps as an Instrument of Educational Change.* New York: John Wiley.

Coser, Lewis. 1956. *The Functions of Social Conflict.* New York: Free Press.

———. 1967. *Continuities in the Study of Social Conflict.* New York: Free Press.

Covaleski, Mark A., Mark W. Dirsmith, James B. Heian, and Sajay Samuel. 1998. "The Calculated and the Avowed: Techniques of Discipline and Struggle over Identity in Big Six Accounting Firms." *Administrative Science Quarterly,* 43, 293–327.

Craig, John G., and Edward Gross. 1970. "The Forum Theory of Organizational Democracy: Structural Guarantee as Time Related Variables." *American Sociological Review,* 35, 19–33.

Crittenden, Ann. 1978. "Philanthropy, The Business of the Not-So-Idle Rich." *New York Times,* July 23, sec. F.

Crozier, Michael. 1964. *The Bureaucratic Phenomenon.* Chicago: University of Chicago Press.

———. 1973. *The Stalled Society,* trans. Rupert Sawyer. New York: Viking Press.

Cummings, Larry L. 1977. "The Emergence of the Instrumental Organization," in *New Perspectives on Organizational Effectiveness,* eds. Paul S. Goodman and Johannes M. Pennings. San Francisco: Jossey-Bass.

Cyert, Richard M., and James G. March. 1963. *A Behavioral Theory of the Firm.* Upper Saddle River, NJ: Prentice Hall.

Daft, Richard L., and Selwin W. Becker. 1978. *Innovation in Organizations: Innovation Adoption in School Organizations.* New York: Elsevier.

Daft, Richard L., and Patricia J. Bradshaw. 1980. "The Process of Horizontal Differentiation: Two Models." *Administrative Science Quarterly,* 25, 441–56.

Dahl, Robert. 1957. "The Concept of Power." *Behavioral Science,* 2, 201–15.

Dalin, M. Tina. 1997. "Isomorphism in Context: The Power and Prescription of Institutional Norms." *Academy of Management Journal,* 40, 46–81.

Dalton, Melville. 1959. *Men Who Manage.* New York: John Wiley.

Damanpour, Fariborz. 1991. "Organizational Innovation: A Meta-Analysis of Effects of Determinants and Moderators." *Academy of Management Journal,* 34, 555–90.

Damanpour, Fariborz, and William M. Evan. 1984. "Organizational Innovation and Performance: The Problems of 'Organizational Lag.'" *Administrative Science Quarterly,* 29, 392–409.

Danet, Barbara. 1981. "Client-Organization Relationships," in *Handbook of Organizational Design,* Vol. 2, eds. Paul C. Nystrom and William H. Starbuck. New York: Oxford University Press.

D'Aunno, Thomas D., Robert I. Sutton, and Richard H. Price. 1991. "Isomorphism and External Support in Conflicting Institutional Environments: A Study of Drug Abuse Treatment Units." *Academy of Management Journal,* 34, 636–61.

D'Aveni, Richard A., and Ian G. MacMillan. 1990. "Crisis and the Content of Managerial Communications: A Study of the Focus of Attention to Top Managers in Surviving and Failing Firms." *Administrative Science Quarterly,* 35, 634–57.

Davis, Gerald F. 1991. "Agents Without Principles? The Spread of the Poison Pill through the Intercorporate Network." *Administrative Science Quarterly,* 36, 583–613.

Davis, Gerald F., Kristina A. Diekmann, and Catherine H. Tinsley. 1994. "The Decline and Fall of the Conglomerate Firm in the 1980s: The Deinstitutionalization of an Organizational Form." *American Sociological Review,* 59, 547–70.

Davis, Gerald F., and Henrich R. Greve. 1997. "Corporate Elite Networks and Governance Change in the 1980s." *American Journal of Sociology,* 103, 1–37.

Davis-Blake, Allison, and Brian Uzzi. 1993. "Determinants of Employment Externalization: A Study of Temporary Workers and Independent Contractors." *Administrative Science Quarterly,* 38, 195–223.

Day, D. V., and R. G. Lord. 1988. "Executive Leadership and Organizational Performance: Suggestions for a New Theory and Methodology." *Journal of Management,* 14, 453–64.

Delacroix, Jacques, and Glenn R. Carroll. 1983. "Organizational Foundings: An Ecological Study of the Newspaper Industries of Argentina and Ireland." *Administrative Science Quarterly,* 28, 274–91.

Delacroix, Jacques, and Anand Swaminathan. 1991. "Cosmetic, Speculative, and Adaptive Organizational Change in the Wine Industry: A Longitudinal Study." *Administrative Science Quarterly,* 36, 631–61.

Dess, Gregory G., and Donald W. Beard. 1984. "Dimensions of Organizational Task Environment." *Administrative Science Quarterly,* 29, 52–73.

Dewar, Robert D., and Jerald Hage. 1978. "Size, Technology, Complexity and Structural Differentiation: Toward a Theoretical Synthesis." *Administrative Science Quarterly,* 23, 111–36.

Dewar, Robert D., David A. Whetten, and David Boje. 1980. "An Examination of the Reliability and Validity of the Aiken and Hage Scales of Utilization, Formalization, and Task Routineness." *Administrative Science Quarterly,* 25, 120–28.

Digman, J. M. 1990. "Personality Structure: Emergence of the Five-Factor Model." *Annual Review of Psychology,* 41, 417–40.

DiMaggio, Paul J. 1988. "Interest and Agency in Institutional Theory," in *Institutional Patterns and Organizations: Culture and Environment,* ed. Lynne G. Zucker. Cambridge, MA: Ballinger.

DiMaggio, Paul J., and Walter W. Powell. 1983. "The Iron Cage Revisited: Institutional Isomorphism and Collective Rationality in Organizational Fields." *American Sociological Review,* 48, 147–60.

Dobbin, Frank, and Terry Boychuk. 1999. "National Employment Systems and Job Autonomy: Why Job Autonomy is High in the Nordic Countries and Low in the United States, Canada, and Australia." *Organization Studies,* 20, 257–91.

Dobbin, Frank, and Timothy J. Dowd. 1997. "How Policy Shapes Competition: Early Railroad Foundings in Massachusetts." *Administrative Science Quarterly,* 42, 501–29.

Dobbin, Frank, John R. Sutton, John M. Meyer, and W. Richard Scott. 1993. "Equal Opportunity Law and the Construction of Internal Labor Markets." *American Journal of Sociology,* 99, 396–427.

Domhoff, G. William, and Thomas R. Dye, eds. 1987. *Power Elites and Organizations.* Newbury Park, CA: Sage.

Donaldson, Lex. 1985. *In Defense of Organizational Theory: A Reply to the Critics.* Cambridge: Cambridge University Press.

———. 1987. "Strategy and Structural Adjustment to Regain Fit and Performance: In Defense of Contingency Theory." *Journal of Management,* 24, 1–24.

———. 1995. *American Anti-Management Theories of Organization: A Critique of Paradigm Proliferation.* Cambridge: Cambridge University Press.

———. 1996. "The Normal Science of Structural Contingence Theory," in *Handbook of Organization Studies,* eds. Stewart R. Clegg, Cynthia Hardy, and Walter R. Nord. Thousand Oaks, CA: Sage.

Donaldson, Lex, and Malcolm Warner. 1974. "Bureaucratic and Electoral Control in Occupational Interest Associations." *Sociology,* 8, 47–59.

Dornbusch, Sanford M. 1955. "The Military Academy as an Assimilating Institution." *Social Forces,* 33, 316–21.

Dornbusch, Sanford M., and W. Richard Scott. 1975. *Evaluation and the Exercise of Authority.* New York: Basic Books.

Downs, Anthony. 1967. *Inside Bureaucracy.* Boston: Little, Brown.

Drabek, Thomas E., Harriet L. Tamminga, Thomas S. Kilijanek, and Christopher R. Adams. 1981. *Managing Multiorganizational Emergency Responses: Emergent Search and Rescue Networks in Natural Disaster and Remote Area Settings.* Boulder: Institute of Behavioral Science, University of Colorado.

Drazin, Robert, and Andrew H. Van de Ven. 1985. "Alternative Forms of Fit in Contingency Theory." *Administrative Science Quarterly,* 30, 514–39.

DuBick, Michael A. 1978. "The Organizational Structure of Newspapers in Relation to Their Metropolitan Environments." *Administrative Science Quarterly,* 23, 418–33.

Dunbar, Roger L. M., and Nikolai Wasilewski. 1985. "Regulating External Threats in the Cigarette Industry." *Administrative Science Quarterly,* 30, 540–59.

———. 1973. "Multiple Decision-Making Structures in Adapting to Environmental Uncertainty: The Impact on Organizational Effectiveness." *Human Relations,* 26, 273–91.

Dunford, Richard. 1987. "The Suppression of Technology as a Strategy for Controlling Resource Dependence." *Administrative Science Quarterly,* 32, 512–25.

Dyck, Bruno, and Frederick A. Starke. 1999. "The Formation of Breakaway Organizations: Observations and a Process Model." *Administrative Science Quarterly,* 44, 792–822.

Eagly, Alice H., and Steven J. Karau. 1991. "Gender and the Emergence of Leaders: A Meta-Analysis." *Journal of Personality and Social Psychology,* 60, 685–710.

Edelman, Lauren B. 1990. "Legal Environments and Organizational Governance: The Expansion of Due Process of the American Workplace." *American Journal of Sociology,* 95, 1401–40.

Egelhoff, William G. 1982. "Strategy and Structure in Multinational Corporations: An Information Processing Approach." *Administrative Science Quarterly,* 27, 435–58.

Eitzen, D. Stanley, and Norman R. Yetman. 1972. "Managerial Change, Longevity and Organizational Effectiveness." *Administrative Science Quarterly,* 17, 110–18.

Emerson, Richard M. 1962. "Power-Dependence Relations." *American Sociological Review,* 27, 31–40.

Emery, Fred E., and E. L. Trist. 1965. "The Causal Texture of Organizational Environments." *Human Relations,* 18, 21–32.

England, Paula. 1992. *Comparable Worth: Theories and Evidence.* New York: Aldine de Gruyter.

Enz, Cathy A. 1988. "The Role of Value Congruence in Intraorganizational Power." *Administrative Science Quarterly,* 33, 284–304.

Etzioni, Amitai. 1961. *A Comparative Analysis of Complex Organizations.* New York: Free Press.

———. 1964. *Modern Organizations.* Upper Saddle River, NJ: Prentice Hall.

———. 1965. "Dual Leadership in Complex Organizations." *American Sociological Review,* 30, 688–98.

———. 1968. *The Active Society: A Theory of Societal and Political Processes.* New York: Free Press.

———. 1975. *A Comparative Analysis of Complex Organizations,* rev. ed. New York: Free Press.

———. 1991. *A Responsive Society: Collected Essays on Guiding Deliberate Social Change.* San Francisco: Jossey-Bass.

———. 1993. *The Spirit of Community Rights, Responsibilities and the Communitarian.* New York: Crown Publishers.

Evan, William. 1966. "The Organization Set: Toward a Theory of Interorganizational Relations," in *Approaches to Organizational Design,* ed. James Thompson. Pittsburgh, PA: University of Pittsburgh Press.

Farberman, Harvey A. 1975. "A Criminogenic Market Structure: The Automobile Industry." *Sociological Quarterly,* 16, 438–57.

Feldman, Martha S., and James G. March. 1981. "Information in Organizations as Signal and Symbol." *Administrative Science Quarterly,* 26, 171–86.

Fennell, Mary C. 1980. "The Effects of Environmental Characteristics on the Structure of Hospital Clusters." *Administrative Science Quarterly,* 29, 489–510.

Fiedler, Fred E. 1967. *A Theory of Leadership Effectiveness.* New York: McGraw-Hill.

———. 1972. "The Effects of Leadership Training and Experience: A Contingency Model Explanation." *Administrative Science Quarterly,* 17, 453–70.

Fiedler, Fred E., and M. M. Chemers. 1982. *Improving Leader Effectiveness: The Leader Match Concept,* 2nd ed. New York: Wiley.

Fiedler, Fred E., and J. E. Garcia. 1987. *New Approaches to Leadership: Cognitive Resources and Organizational Performance.* New York: Wiley.

Filardo, E. K. 1996. "Gender Patterns in African American and White Adolescents' Social Interactions in Same-Race, Mixed-Gender Groups." *Journal of Personality and Social Psychology,* 71, 71–82.

Filley, Alan C., and Robert J. House. 1969. *Managerial Processes and Organizational Behavior.* Glenview, IL: Scott, Foresman.

Finkelstein, Sydney. 1992. "Power in Top Management Teams: Dimension, Measurement and Validation." *Academy of Management Journal,* 35, 505–38.

Fligstein, Neil. 1985. "The Spread of the Multidivisional Form among Large Firms." *American Sociological Review,* 50, 377–91.

———. 1987. "The Intraorganizational Power Struggle: Rise of Financial Personnel to Top Leadership in Large Corporations, 1919–1979." *American Sociological Review,* 52, 44–58.

———. 1990. *The Transformation of Corporate Control.* Cambridge, MA: Harvard University.

———. 1995. "Networks of Power or the Financial Conception of Control? Comment on Palmer, Barber, Zhou, and Soysal (1995)." *American Sociological Review,* 60, 500–03.

Fligstein, Neil, and Peter Brantley. 1992. "Bank Control, Owner Control, or Organizational Dynamics: Who Controls the Large Modern Corporation." *American Journal of Sociology,* 98, 280–307.

Fligstein, Neil, and Robert Freeland. 1995. "Theoretical and Comparative Perspectives on Corporate Organization," in *Annual Review of Sociology*, eds. John Hagan and Karen S. Cook. Palo Alto, CA: Annual Reviews, Inc.

Fligstein, Neil, and Iona Mara-Drita. 1996. "How to Make a Market: Reflections on the Attempt to Create a Single Market in the European Union." *American Journal of Sociology*, 102, 1–33.

Florida, Richard, and Martin Kenney. 1991. "Transplanted Organizations: The Transfer of Japanese Industrial Organization to the U.S." *American Sociological Review*, 56, 381–98.

Fombrun, Charles J. 1986. "Structural Dynamics within and between Organizations." *Administrative Science Quarterly*, 31, 403–21.

Forbes. 1973. "The Numbers Game: The Larger the Company, the More Understanding the Accountant?" 112, 33–35.

Freeland, Robert F. 1997. "The Myth of the M-Form? Governance, Consent, and Organizational Change." *American Journal of Sociology*, 102, 483–526.

Freeman, John H. 1973. "Environment, Technology, and the Administrative Intensity of Manufacturing Organizations." *American Sociological Review*, 38, 750–63.

———. 1979. "Going to the Well: School District Administrative Intensity and Environmental Constraints." *Administrative Science Quarterly*, 24, 119–33.

Freeman, John H., Glenn Carroll, and Michael Hannan. 1983. "The Liability of Newness: Age-Dependence in Organizational Death Rates." *American Sociological Review*, 48, 692–710.

Freeman, John H., and Michael T. Hannan. 1983. "Niche Width and the Dynamics of Organizational Populations." *American Journal of Sociology*, 88, 1116–45.

———. 1989. "Setting the Record Straight: Rebuttal to Young." *American Journal of Sociology*, 95, 425–39.

Freidson, Eliot. 1970. *Professional Dominance*. Chicago: Aldine de Gruyter.

———. 1994. *Professionalism Reborn: Theory, Prophecy and Policy*. Chicago: University of Chicago Press.

French, John R. P., and Bertram Raven. 1968. "The Bases of Social Power," in *Group Dynamics*, 3rd ed., eds. Dorwin Cartwright and Alvin Zander. New York: Harper and Row.

Frost, Peter J., Larry F. Moore, Meryl Reis Louis, Craig C. Lundberg, and Joanne Martin, eds. 1985. *Organizational Culture*. Beverly Hills, CA: Sage.

Fu, P. P., and Gary Yukl. 2000. "Perceived Effectiveness of Influence Tactics in the United States and China." *Leadership Quarterly*, 11, 251–66.

Galaskiewicz, Joseph. 1979. "The Structure of Community Organizational Networks." *Social Forces*, 57, 1346–64.

———. 1985. "Interorganizational Relations." *Annual Review of Sociology*, Vol. 11. Palo Alto, CA: Annual Reviews, Inc.

———. 1997. "An Urban Grants Economy Revisited: Corporate Charitable Contributions in the Twin Cities, 1979–81, 1987–89." *Administrative Science Quarterly*, 42, 445–71.

Galaskiewicz, Joseph, and Ronald S. Burt. 1991. "Interorganizational Contagion in Corporate Philanthropy." *Administrative Science Quarterly*, 36, 88–105.

Galaskiewicz, Joseph, and Karl R. Krohn. 1984. "Positions, Roles, and Dependencies in a Community Interorganizational System." *Sociological Quarterly*, 25, 527–50.

Galaskiewicz, Joseph, and Peter J. Marsden. 1978. "Interorganizational Resources Networks: Formal Patterns of Overlap." *Social Science Research*, 7, 89–107.

Galaskiewicz, Joseph, and Deborah Shatin. 1981. "Leadership and Networking among Neighborhood Human Service Organizations." *Administrative Science Quarterly*, 26, 434–48.

Galaskiewicz, Joseph, Stanley Wasserman, Barbara Rauschenbach, Wolfgang Bielefeld, and Patti Mullaney. 1985. "The Influence of Corporate Power, Social Status, and Market Position on Corporate Interlocks in a Regional Network." *Social Forces*, 64, 403–31.

Gamoran, Adam, and Robert Dreeben. 1986. "Coupling and Control in Educational Organizations." *Administrative Science Quarterly*, 31, 612–32.

Gamson, William, and Norman Scotch. 1964. "Scapegoating in Baseball." *American Journal of Sociology*, 70, 69–72.

Gardner, Elmer A., and James N. Snipe. 1970. "Toward the Coordination and Integration of Personal Health Services." *American Journal of Public Health*, 60, 2068–78.

Geeraerts, Guy. 1984. "The Effects of Ownership on the Organization Structure in Small Firms." *Administrative Science Quarterly*, 29, 232–37.

Georgiou, Petro. 1973. "The Goal Paradigm and Notes Toward a Counter Paradigm." *Administrative Science Quarterly*, 18, 291–310.

Gersick, Connie J. G. 1991. "Revolutionary Change Theories: A Multilevel Explanation of the Punctuated Equilibrium Paradigm." *Academy of Management Review*, 16, 10–36.

———. 1994. "Pacing Strategic Change: The Case of a New Venture." *Academy of Management Journal*, 37, 9–45.

Giordano, Peggy C. 1974. *The Juvenile Justice System: The Client Perspective*. Ph.D. diss., University of Minnesota.

———. 1976. "The Sense of Injustice: An Analysis of Juveniles' Reaction to the Justice System." *Criminology*, 14, 93–112.

———. 1977. "The Client's Perspective in Agency Evaluation." *Social Work*, 22, 34–39.

Glass, Jennifer. 2000. "Envisioning the Integration of Family and Work: Toward a Kinder, Gentler Workplace." *Contemporary Sociology*, 29, 129–37.

Glisson, Charles A. 1978. "Dependence of Technological Routinizations on Structural Variables in Human Service Organizations." *Administrative Science Quarterly*, 23, 383–95.

Goes, James B., and Seung Ho Park. 1997. "Interorganizational Linkages and Innovation: The Case of Hospital Services." *Academy of Management Journal*, 40, 673–96.

Gooderham, Paul N., Odd Nordhaug, and Kristen Ringdal. 1999. "Institutional and Rational Determinants of Organizational Practices: Human Resource Management in European Firms." *Administrative Science Quarterly*, 44, 507–31.

Goodman, Paul S., Terri L. Griffith, and Deborah B. Fenner. 1990. "Understanding Technology and the Individual in an Organizational Context," in *Technology and Organizations*, eds. Paul S. Goodman, Lee Sproul, and Edwin Amenta, 45–86. San Francisco: Jossey-Bass.

Goodstein, Jerry D. 1994. "Institutional Pressures and Strategic Responsiveness: Employer Involvement in Work-Family Issues." *Academy of Management Journal*, 37, 350–82.

Goodstein, Jerry, and Warren Boeker. 1991. "Turbulence at the Top: A New Perspective on Governance Structure Changes and Strategic Change." *Academy of Management Journal*, 34, 306–30.

Gould, Roger V., and Roberto M. Fernandez. 1994. "A Dilemma of State Power: Brokerage and Influence in the National Health Policy Domain." *American Journal of Sociology*, 99, 1455–91.

Gouldner, Alvin, ed. 1950. *Studies in Leadership*. New York: Harper and Row.

———. 1954. *Patterns of Industrial Bureaucracy*. New York: Free Press.

Grafton, Carl. 1975. "The Creation of Federal Agencies." *Administration and Society*, 7, 328–65.

Granovetter, Mark. 1985. "Economic Action and Social Structure: The Problem of Embeddedness." *American Journal of Sociology*, 91, 481–510.

Grant, Donald Sherman II, Andrew W. Jones, and Albert J. Bergesen. 2002. "Organizational Size and Pollution: the Case of the U.S. Chemical Industry." *American Sociological Review*, 67, 389–407.

Gresov, Christopher. 1989. "Exploring Fit and Misfit with Multiple Contingencies." *Administrative Science Quarterly*, 34, 431–53.

Gross, Edward. 1968. "Universities as Organizations: A Research Approach." *American Sociological Review*, 33, 518–43.

Grusky, Oscar. 1963. "Managerial Succession and Organizational Effectiveness." *American Journal of Sociology*, 69, 21–31.

———. 1964. "Reply." *American Journal of Sociology*, 70, 72–76.

Guest, Robert. 1962. "Managerial Succession in Complex Organizations." *American Journal of Sociology*, 68, 47–54.

Guetzkow, Harold. 1965. "Communications in Organizations," in *Handbook of Organizations*, ed. James G. March. Chicago: Rand McNally.

Gulati, Ranjay. 1995. "Does Familiarity Breed Trust? The Implications of Repeated Ties for Contractual Choices in Alliances." *Academy of Management Journal*, 38, 85–112.

Gulati, Ranjay, and Martin Gargiulo. 1999. "Where Do Interorganizational Networks Come From?" *American Journal of Sociology*, 104, 1439–93.

Guler, Isen, Mauro F. Guillen, and J. M. MacPherson. 2002. "Global Competition, Institutions and the Diffusion of Organizational Practices: The International Spread of ISO 9000 Quality Certificates." *Administrative Science Quarterly,* 47, 207–32.

Gupta, Anil, and Vjay Govindarajan. 1991. "Knowledge Flows and the Structure of Control within Multinational Corporations." *Academy of Management Review,* 16, 768–92.

Gupta, Parveen P., Mark W. Dirsmith, and Timothy J. Fogarty. 1994. "Coordination and Control in a Government Agency: Contingency and Institutional Theory Perspectives on GAO Audits." *Administrative Science Quarterly,* 39, 264–84.

Gusfield, Joseph R. 1955. "Social Structure and Moral Reform: A Study of the Women's Christian Temperance Union." *American Journal of Sociology,* 61, 221–32.

———. 1963. *Symbolic Crusade.* Urbana: University of Illinois Press.

Hage, Jerald. 1965. "An Axiomatic Theory of Organizations." *Administrative Science Quarterly,* 10, 289–320.

———. 1974. *Communications and Organizational Control.* New York: Wiley.

———. 1980. *Theories of Organizations.* New York: Wiley.

———. 1999. "Organizational Innovation and Organizational Change." *Annual Review of Sociology,* 25, 597–622. Palo Alto, CA: Annual Reviews.

Hage, Jerald, and Michael Aiken. 1967a. "Relationship of Centralization to Other Structural Properties." *Administrative Science Quarterly,* 12, 72–91.

———. 1967b. "Program Change and Organizational Properties." *American Journal of Sociology,* 72, 503–19.

———. 1969. "Routine Technology, Social Structure, and Organizational Goals." *Administrative Science Quarterly,* 14, 366–77.

———. 1970. *Social Change in Complex Organizations.* New York: Random House.

Hage, Jerald, Michael Aiken, and Cora Bagley Marrett. 1971. "Organizational Structure and Communications." *American Sociological Review,* 36, 860–71.

Hage, Jerald, and Robert Dewar. 1973. "Elite Values versus Organizational Structure in Predicting Innovation." *Administrative Science Quarterly,* 18, 279–90.

Halberstam, David. 1972. *The Best and the Brightest.* New York: Random House.

Hall, Richard H. 1962. "Intraorganizational Structural Variation: Application of the Bureaucratic Model." *Administrative Science Quarterly,* 7, 295–308.

———. 1963. "The Concept of Bureaucracy." *American Journal of Sociology,* 69, 32–40.

———. 1968. "Professionalization and Bureaucratization." *American Sociological Review,* 33, 92–104.

———. 1981. "Technological Policies and Their Consequences," in *Handbook of Organizational Design,* Vol. 2, eds. Paul C. Nystrom and William H. Starbuck, 320–35. New York: Oxford University Press.

———. 1992. "Taking Things a Bit Too Far: Some Problems with Emergent Institutional Theory," in *Issues, Theory, and Research in Industrial/Organizational Psychology,* ed. Kathryn Kelley. New York: Elsevier Science Publishers.

———. 1994. *Sociology of Work: Perspectives, Analyses, and Issues.* Thousand Oaks, CA: Pine Forge Press.

Hall, Richard H., John P. Clark, and Peggy C. Giordano. 1978. "Interorganizational Coordination in the Delivery of Human Services," in *Organization and Environment: Theory, Issues, and Reality,* ed. Lucien Karpik. Beverly Hills, CA: Sage.

Hall, Richard H., John P. Clark, Peggy Giordano, Paul Johnson, and Martha Van Roekel. 1977. "Patterns of Interorganizational Relationships." *Administrative Science Quarterly,* 22, 457–74.

———. 1967b. "Organizational Size, Complexity, and Formalization." *American Sociological Review,* 32, 903–12.

Hall, Richard H., Shanhe Jiang, Karyn A. Loscocco, and John K. Allen. 1993. "Ownership Patterns and Centralization: A China and U.S. Comparison." *Sociological Forum,* 8, 595–608.

Hall, Richard H., and Charles R. Tittle. 1966. "Bureaucracy and Its Correlates." *American Journal of Sociology,* 72, 267–72.

Hall, Richard H., and Weiman Xu. 1990. "Run Silent, Run Deep: A Note on the Ever Pervasive Influence of Cultural Differences on Organizations in the Far East." *Organization Studies,* 11, 569–76.

Halpert, Burton P. 1982. "Antecedents," in *Interorganizational Coordination: Theory, Research, and Implementation,* eds. David L. Rogers and David A. Whetten and Associates. Ames: Iowa State University Press.

Hambrick, Donald C. 1981. "Environment, Strategy and Power within Top Management Teams." *Administrative Science Quarterly,* 26, 253–76.

Hambrick, Donald C., and Richard A. D'Aveni. 1988. "Large Corporate Failures as Downward Spirals." *Administrative Science Quarterly,* 33, 1–23.

Hamilton, Gary L., and Nicole Woolsey Biggart. 1988. "Market, Culture, and Authority: A Comparative Analysis of Management and Organization in the Far East." *American Journal of Sociology,* 94, Supplement, S52–S94.

Hamner, W. Clay, and Dennis Organ. 1973. *Organizational Behavior: An Applied Psychological Approach.* Dallas, TX: Business Publications.

Han, Shin-Kap. 1994. "Mimetic Isomorphism and its Effect on the Audit Service Market." *Social Forces,* 73, 637–63.

Hannan, Michael T. 1998. "Rethinking Age Dependency in Organizational Mortality: Logical Formalizations." *American Journal of Sociology,* 104, 126–64.

Hannan, Michael T., and Glenn R. Carroll. 1992. *Dynamics of Organizational Population.* New York: Oxford University Press.

Hannan, Michael T., and John H. Freeman. 1977a. "Obstacles to Comparative Studies," in *New Perspective on Organizational Effectiveness,* eds. Paul S. Goodman and Johannes Pennings. San Francisco: Jossey-Bass.

———. 1977b. "The Population Ecology of Organizations." *American Journal of Sociology,* 82, 929–64.

———. 1984. "Structural Inertia and Organizational Change." *American Sociological Review,* 49, 149–64.

———. 1987. "The Ecology of Organizational Founding: American Labor Unions, 1836–1985." *American Journal of Sociology,* 92, 910–43.

———. 1989. *Organizational Ecology.* Cambridge, MA: Harvard University Press.

Hansen, Morten T., and Martine R. Haas. 2001. "Competing for Attention in Knowledge Markets: Electronic Document Dissemination in a Management Consulting Company." *Administrative Science Quarterly,* 46, 1–28.

Hardy, Cynthia, and Stewart R. Clegg. 1996. "Some Dare Call It Power," in *Handbook of Organization Studies,* eds. Stewart R. Clegg, Cynthia Hardy, and Walter R. Nord. Thousand Oaks, CA: Sage.

Harris, Stanley G., and Robert I. Sutton. 1986. "Functions of Parting Ceremonies in Dying Organizations." *Academy of Management Journal,* 29, 5–30.

Harrison, Jeffrey S., and R. Edward Freeman. 1999. "Stakeholders, Social Responsibility, and Performance: Empirical Evidence and Theoretical Perspectives." *Academy of Management Journal,* 42, 479–85.

Haunschild, Pamela R., and Christine M. Beckman. 1998. "When Do Interlocks Matter? Alternate Sources of Information and Interlock Influence." *Administrative Science Quarterly,* 43, 815–44.

Haunschild, Pamela R., and Anne S. Miner. 1997. "Modes of IOR Imitation: The Effect of Outcome Salience and Uncertainty." *Administrative Science Quarterly,* 42, 477–500.

Haveman, Heather. 1992. "Between a Rock and a Hard Place: Organizational Change under Conditions of Fundamental Environmental Transformation." *Administrative Science Quarterly,* 37, 48–75.

———. 1993. "Organizational Size and Change: Diversification in the Savings and Loan Industry after Deregulation." *Administrative Science Quarterly,* 38, 20–50.

Haveman, Heather A., and Hayagreeva Rao. 1997. "Structuring a Theory of Moral Sentiments: Institutional and Organizational Coevolution in the Early Thrift Industry." *American Journal of Sociology,* 102, 1606–51.

Hawley, Amos H. 1968. "Human Ecology," in *International Encyclopedia of the Social Sciences,* ed. D. L. Sills. New York: Macmillan.

Hawley, W. E., and L. D. Rogers. 1974. *Improving the Quality of Urban Management.* Beverly Hills, CA: Sage.

Hedberg, Bo. 1981. "How Organizations Learn and Unlearn," in *Handbook of Organizational Design,* Vol. 2, eds. Paul C. Nystrom and William H. Starbuck. New York: Oxford University Press.

Heilbroner, Robert. 1974. "Nobody Talks about Busting General Motors in 500 Companies." *Forbes,* 113, 61.

Heller, Frank A. 1973. "Leadership Decision Making and Contingency Theory." *Industrial Relations,* 12, 183–99.

Helmich, Donald, and Warren B. Brown. 1972. "Succession Type and Organizational Change in the Corporate Enterprise." *Administrative Science Quarterly,* 17, 371–81.

Heydebrand, Wolf V. 1973. *Comparative Organizations: The Results of Empirical Research.* Upper Saddle River, NJ: Prentice Hall.

———. 1977. "Organizational Contradictions in Public Bureaucracies: Toward a Marxian Theory of Organizations." *Sociological Quarterly,* 18, 83–107.

———. 1990. "The Technocratic Organization of Academic Work," in *Structures of Power and Constraint: Papers in Honor of Peter M. Blau,* eds. Craig Calhoun, Marshall W. Meyer, and W. Richard Scott, 271–320. New York: Cambridge University Press.

Hickson, David J., C. R. Hinings, C. A. Lee, R. E. Schneck, and J. M. Pennings. 1971. "A 'Strategic Contingencies' Theory of Interorganizational Power." *Administrative Science Quarterly,* 16, 216–29.

Hickson, David J., C. R. Hinings, C. J. McMillan, and J. P. Schwitter. 1974. "The Culture Free Context of Organizational Structure: A Tri-National Comparison." *Sociology,* 8, 59–80.

Hickson, David J., Derek S. Pugh, and Diana C. Pheysey. 1969. "Operational Technology and Organizational Structure: An Empirical Reappraisal." *Administrative Science Quarterly,* 14, 378–97.

Hills, Frederick S., and Thomas A. Mahoney. 1978. "University Budgets and Organizational Decision Making." *Administrative Science Quarterly,* 23, 454–65.

Hinings, C. R. 1988. "Defending Organizational Theory: A British View from North America." *Organization Studies,* 9, 2–7.

Hirsch, Paul M. 1975. "Organizational Effectiveness and the Institutional Environment." *Administrative Science Quarterly,* 20, 327–44.

———. 1997. "Sociology without Social Structure: Neo-Institutional Theory Meets Brave New World." *American Journal of Sociology,* 102, 1702–23.

Hirschhorn, Larry. 1985. "On Technological Catastrophe." *Science,* 28, 846–47.

Hirschman, Albert O. 1972. *Exit, Voice, and Loyalty.* Cambridge, MA: Harvard University Press.

Hochschild, Arlie Russell. 1983. *The Managed Heart: Commercialization of Human Feeling.* Berkeley and Los Angeles: University of California Press.

Hoff, Timothy. 1998. "Same Profession, Different People: Stratification, Structure, and Physicians' Employment Choices." *Sociological Forum,* 13, 133–56.

Hoff, Timothy, and David McCaffrey. 1996. "Resisting, Adapting, and Negotiating: How Physicians Cope with Organizational and Economic Change." *Work and Occupations,* 23, 165–89.

Hofstede, Geert H. 1972. *Budget Control and the Autonomy of Organizational Units.* Proceedings of the First International Sociological Conference on Participation and Self-Management, Zagreb, Yugoslavia.

———. 1993. "Intercultural Conflict and Synergy in Europe," in *Management in Western Europe,* ed. David J. Hickson, 1–8. Berlin: de Gruyter.

Hogan, Robert, Gordon J. Curphy, and Joyce Hogan. 1994. "What We Know about Leadership." *American Psychologist,* 49, 493–504.

Holden, Constance. 1980. "Innovation—Japan Races Ahead as U.S. Falters." *Science,* 210, 751–54.

Hollander, Edwin P., and James W. Julian. 1969. "Contemporary Trends in the Analysis of Leadership Processes." *Psychological Bulletin,* 71, 387–97.

Hougland, James G., Jon M. Shepard, and James R. Wood. 1979. "Discrepancies in Perceived Organizational Control: Their Decrease and Importance in Local Churches." *Sociological Quarterly,* 20, 63–76.

Hougland, James G., and James R. Wood. 1980. "Control in Organizations and Commitment of Members." *Social Forces,* 59, 85–105.

House, Robert J. 1971. "A Path-Goal Theory of Leader Effectiveness." *Administrative Science Quarterly,* 16, 321–38.

Huffington, Arianna. 2003. *Pigs at the Trough: How Corporate Greed and Political Corruption Are Undermining America.* New York: Crown.

Hyde, Cheryl. 1992. "The Ideational System of Social Movement Agencies: An Examination of Feminist Health Centers," in *Human Services as Complex Organizations,* ed. Yeheskel Hasenfeld. Thousand Oaks, CA: Sage.

Ingram, Paul, and Peter W. Roberts. 2000. "Friendships among Competitors in the Sydney Hotel Industry." *American Journal of Sociology,* 106, 387–423.

Inkson, J., Derek S. Pugh, and David J. Hickson. 1970. "Organizational Context and Structure: An Abbreviated Replication." *Administrative Science Quarterly,* 15, 318–29.

Isabella, Lynn A. 1990. "Evolving Interpretations as a Change Unfolds: How Managers Construe Key Organizational Events." *Academy of Management Review,* 33, 7–41.

Jackall, Robert. 1988. *Moral Mazes: The World of Corporate Managers.* New York: Oxford University Press.

Jacobs, David. 1974. "Dependency and Vulnerability: An Exchange Approach to the Control of Organizations." *Administrative Science Quarterly,* 19, 45–59.

———. 1987. "Business Resources and Taxation: A Cross-Sectional Examination of the Relationship between Economic Organization and Public Policy." *Sociological Quarterly,* 28, 437–54.

———. 1988. "Corporate Economic Power and the State: A Longitudinal Assessment of Two Explanations." *American Journal of Sociology,* 93, 852–81.

———. 2001. "Unnatural Extinction: The Rise and Fall of the Independent Local Union." *Industrial Relations,* 40, 377–404.

———. 2004. *Employing Bureaucracy: Managers, Unions and the Transformation of Work in the 20th Century.* Mahawah, NJ: Erlbaum.

James, David R., and Michael Soref. 1981. "Profit Constraints on Managerial Autonomy: Managerial Theory and the Unmaking of the Corporate President." *American Sociological Review,* 46, 1–18.

Jenkins, J. Craig. 1977. "Radical Transformation of Organizational Goals." *Administrative Science Quarterly,* 22, 568–86.

John, D. 1977. *Managing the Human Service System: What Have We Learned from Services Integration?* Project SHARE Monograph Series. Rockville, MD: National Institute of Mental Health.

Johnston, George P., III, and William Snizek. 1991. "Combining Head and Heart in Complex Organizations: A Test of Etzioni's Dual Compliance Structure Hypothesis." *Human Relations,* 44, 1255–72.

Jurkovich, Ray. 1974. "A Core Typology of Organizational Environments." *Administrative Science Quarterly,* 19, 380–89.

Kabanoff, Boris. 1991. "Equity, Equality, Power, and Conflict." *Academy of Management Review,* 16, 416–41.

Kalleberg, Arne. 1983. "Work and Stratification: Structural Perspectives." *Work and Occupations,* 10, 251–59.

Kalleberg, Arne L., David Knoke, Peter V. Marsden, and Joe L. Spaeth. 1996. "Organizational Properties and Practices," in *Organizations in America: Analyzing Their Structures and Human Resource Practices,* eds. Arne L. Kalleberg, David Knoke, Peter V. Marsden, and Joe L. Spaeth. Thousand Oaks, CA: Sage.

Kalleberg, Arne L., and Mark E. Van Buren. 1996. "Is Bigger Better? Explaining the Relationship between Organizational Size and Job Rewards." *American Sociological Review,* 61, 47–76.

Kanter, Rosabeth Moss. 1968. "Commitment and Social Organization: A Study of Commitment Mechanisms in Utopian Communities." *American Sociological Review,* 33, 499–517.

———. 1977. *Men and Women of the Corporation.* New York: Basic Books.

———. 1979. "Power Failure in Management Circuits." *Harvard Business Review,* 57, 65–75.

Kanter, Rosabeth, and Derick Brinkerhoff. 1981. "Organizational Performance: Recent Developments in Measurement." *Annual Review of Sociology,* 7, 321–49.

Kanter, Rosabeth, Barry A. Stein, and Todd D. Jick. 1992. *The Challenge of Organizational Change: How Companies Experience It and Leaders Guide It.* New York: Free Press.

Kaplan, Abraham. 1964. "Power in Perspective," in *Power and Conflict in Organizations,* eds. Robert L. Kahn and Elise Boulding. New York: Basic Books.

Kasarda, John D., and Charles E. Bidwell. 1984. "A Human Ecological Theory of Organizational Structuring," in *Sociological Human Ecology: Contemporary Issues and Applications,* eds. Michael Micklin and Harvey M. Choldin. Boulder, CO: Westview Press.

Katz, Daniel. 1964. "Approaches to Managing Conflict," in *Power and Conflict in Organizations,* eds. Robert L. Kahn and Elise Boulding. New York: Basic Books.

Katz, Daniel, Barbara A. Gutek, Robert L. Kahn, and Eugenia Barton. 1975. *Bureaucratic Encounters.* Ann Arbor, MI: Institute for Social Research.

Katz, Daniel, and Robert L. Kahn. 1966. *The Social Psychology of Organizations,* rev. ed. New York: Wiley.

————. 1978. *The Sociology Psychology of Organizations,* rev. ed. New York: Wiley.

Katz, Ralph. 1982. "The Effects of Group Longevity on Project Communication and Performance." *Administrative Science Quarterly,* 27, 81–104.

Kaufman, Herbert. 1971. *The Limits of Organizational Change.* Tuscaloosa: University of Alabama Press.

Keeley, Michael. 1978. "A Social Justice Approach to Organizational Evaluation." *Administrative Science Quarterly,* 23, 272–92.

————. 1984. "Impartiality and Participant-Interest Theories of Organizational Effectiveness." *Administrative Science Quarterly,* 29, 1–12.

Keister, Lisa A. 1998. "Engineering Growth: Business Group Structure and Firm Performance in China's Transition Economy." *American Journal of Sociology,* 104, 404–40.

Kerbo, Harold R., and L. Richard Della Fave. 1983. "Corporate Linkage and Control of the Corporate Economy: New Evidence and a Reinterpretation." *Sociological Quarterly,* 24, 201–18.

Khandwalla, Pradip N. 1972. "Environment and Its Impact on the Organization." *International Studies of Management and Organization,* 2, 297–313.

Kieser, Alfred. 1989. "Organizational, Institutional, and Societal Evolution: Medieval Craft Guilds and the Genesis of Formal Organizations." *Administrative Science Quarterly,* 34, 540–65.

————. 1976. "Organizational Size and the Structuralist Perspective: A Review, Critique, and Proposal." *Administrative Science Quarterly,* 21, 577–97.

————. 1979. "Issues in the Creation of Organizations: Initiation, Innovation, and Institutionalization." *Academy of Management Journal,* 22, 437–57.

————. 1981. "Managerial Innovation," in *Handbook of Organizational Design,* Vol. 1, eds. Paul C. Nystrom and William H. Starbuck. New York: Oxford University Press.

Kimberly, John R., and Robert A. Miles and Associates, eds. 1980. *The Organizational Life Cycle.* San Francisco: Jossey-Bass.

Kimberly, John R., and Robert E. Quinn. 1984. "The Challenge of Transition Management," in *Managing Organizational Transitions,* eds. John R. Kimberly and Robert E. Quinn. Homewood, IL: Richard D. Irwin.

Klatzky, Sheila. 1970a. "The Relationship of Organizational Size to Complexity and Coordination." *Administrative Science Quarterly,* 15, 428–38.

————. 1970b. "Organizational Inequality: The Case of Public Employment Agency." *American Journal of Sociology,* 76, No. 3 (November), 474–91.

Klauss, Rudi, and Bernard M. Bass. 1982. *Interpersonal Communication in Organizations.* New York: Academic Press.

Klonglan, Gerald E., Richard D. Warren, Judy M. Winkelpleck, and Steven K. Paulson. 1976. "Interorganizational Measurement in the Social Services Sector: Differences by Hierarchical Level." *Administrative Science Quarterly,* 21, 675–87.

Knoke, David, and David Prensky. 1984. "What Relevance Do Organizational Theories Have for Voluntary Organizations?" *Social Science Quarterly,* 65, No. 1 (March), 3–20.

Kochan, Thomas A., Larry C. Cummings, and George P. Huber. 1976. "Operationalizing the Concepts of Goals and Goal Incompatibility in Organizational Behavior Research." *Human Relations,* 29, 527–44.

Kochan, Thomas A., George P. Huber, and Larry C. Cummings. 1975. "Determinants of Interorganizational Conflict in Collective Bargaining in the Public Sector." *Administrative Science Quarterly,* 20, 10–23.

Kochan, Thomas A., and Michael Useem. 1992. *Transforming Organization.* New York: Oxford University Press.

Kogut, Bruce, and Udo Zander. 2000. "Did Socialism Fail to Innovate? A Natural Experiment of the Two Zeiss Companies." *American Sociological Review,* 65, 169–90.

Kohn, Melvin. 1971. "Bureaucratic Man: A Portrait and Interpretation." *American Sociological Review,* 36, 461–74.

Kohn, Melvin, and Carmi Schooler. 1978. "The Reciprocal Effects of Substantive Complexity of Work and Intellectual Flexibility: A Longitudinal Assessment." *American Journal of Sociology,* 84, 1–23.

———. 1982. "Job Conditions and Personality: A Longitudinal Assessment of the Reciprocal Effects." *American Journal of Sociology,* 87, 1257–86.

Kono, Clifford, Donald Palmer, Roger Friedland, and Matthew Zafonte. 1998. "Lost in Space: The Geography of Corporate Interlocking Directorates." *American Journal of Sociology,* 103, 862–911.

Kornhauser, William. 1963. *Scientists in Industry.* Berkeley and Los Angeles: University of California Press.

Kraatz, Matthew S., and Edward J. Zajac. 1996. "Exploring the Limits of the New Institutionalism: The Causes and Consequences of Illegitimate Organizational Change." *American Sociological Review,* 61, 812–36.

Kralewski, John E., Laura Pitt, and Deborah Shatin. 1985. "Structural Characteristics of Medical Practice Groups." *Administrative Science Quarterly,* 30, 34–45.

Kunda, Gideon. 1992. *Engineering Culture: Control and Commitment in a High-Tech Corporation.* Philadelphia: Temple University.

Kunda, Gideon, Stephen R. Barley, and James Evans. 2002. "Why Do Contractors Contract? The Experience of Highly Skilled Technical Professionals in a Contingent Labor Market." *Industrial and Labor Relations Review,* 55, 234–62.

Lachman, Ron. 1989. "Power from What? A Reexamination of Its Relationship with Structural Conditions." *Administrative Science Quarterly,* 34, 231–51.

Lammers, Cornelius J. 1967. "Power and Participation in Decision Making." *American Journal of Sociology,* 73, 201–16.

———. 1975. "Self-Management and Participation: Two Concepts of Democratization in Organizations." *Organization and Administrative Sciences,* 5, 35–53.

———. 1981. "Contributions of Organizational Sociology: Part II: Contributions to Organizational Theory and Practice—A Liberal View." *Organization Studies,* 2, 361–76.

Lang, James R., and Daniel E. Lockhart. 1990. "Increased Environmental Uncertainty and Changes in Board Linkage Patterns." *Academy of Management Journal,* 33, 106–28.

Langston, John. 1984. "The Ecological Theory of Bureaucracy: The Case of Josiah Wedgwood and the British Pottery Industry." *Administrative Science Quarterly,* 29, 330–54.

Laumann, Edward O., Joseph Galaskiewicz, and Peter Marsden. 1978. "Community Structure as Interorganizational Linkage." *Annual Review of Sociology,* 4, 455–84.

Laumann, Edward O., and David Knoke. 1987. *The Organizational State: Social Choice in National Policy Domains.* Madison: University of Wisconsin Press.

Laumann, Edward O., David Knoke, and Yong-Hak Kim. 1985. "An Organizational Approach to State Policy Formation: A Comparative Study of Energy and Health Domains." *American Sociological Review,* 50, 1–19.

Lawrence, Paul R., and Jay W. Lorsch. 1967. *Organization and Environment.* Cambridge, MA: Harvard University Press.

———. 1995. "A New Phoenix? Modern Putting-Out in the Modern Knitwear Industry." *Administrative Science Quarterly,* 34, 40–59.

Leavitt, Harold J. 1951. "The Effects of Certain Communications Patterns on Group Performance." *Journal of Abnormal and Social Psychology,* 46, 38–50.

Leicht, Kevin T., Toby L. Parcel, and Robert L. Kaufman. 1992. "Measuring the Same Concept across Diverse Organizations." *Social Science Research,* 21, 149–74.

Leventhal, Daniel A. 1991. "Random Walks and Organizational Mortality." *Administrative Science Quarterly,* 36, 397–420.

Levine, Adeline Gordon. 1982. *Love Canal: Science, Politics, and People.* Lexington, MA: D. C. Heath.

Levine, Sol, and Paul E. White. 1961. "Exchange as a Conceptual Framework for the Study of Interorganizational Relationships." *Administrative Science Quarterly,* 5, 583–610.

Levine, Sol, Paul E. White, and Benjamin D. Paul. 1963. "Community Interorganizational Problems in Providing Medical Care and Social Services." *American Journal of Public Health,* 52(8), 1183–95.

Levitt, Barbara, and Clifford Nuss. 1989. "The Lid on the Garbage Can: Institutional Constraints on Decision Making in the Technical Core of College-Text Publishers." *Administrative Science Quarterly,* 34, 190–207.

Lieberson, Stanley, and James F. O'Connor. 1972. "Leadership and Organizational Performance: A Study of Large Corporations." *American Sociological Review,* 37, 117–30.

Liedholm, Carl, and Donald Mead. 1993. *The Structure and Growth of Microenterprises in Southern and Eastern Africa: Evidence from Recent Surveys.* Unpublished manuscript, Department of Economics, Michigan State University.

Lin, Nan. 1999. "Social Networks and Status Attainment." *Annual Review of Sociology,* 25, 467–87.

Lincoln, James R., Mitsuyo Hanada, and Kerry McBride. 1986. "Organizational Structures in Japanese and U.S. Manufacturing." *Administrative Science Quarterly,* 31, 338–64.

Lincoln, James R., and Gerald Zeitz. 1980. "Organizational Properties from Aggregate Data." *American Sociological Review,* 45, 391–405.

Lipset, Seymour Martin. 1960. *Agrarian Socialism.* Berkeley and Los Angeles: University of California Press.

Lipset, Seymour Martin, Martin A. Trow, and James S. Coleman. 1956. *Union Democracy.* New York: Free Press.

Litwak, Eugene. 1961. "Models of Organizations Which Permit Conflict." *American Journal of Sociology,* 76, 177–84.

Litwak, Eugene, and Lydia Hylton. 1962. "Interorganizational Analysis: A Hypothesis on Coordinating Agencies." *Administrative Science Quarterly,* 6, 395–420.

Long, J. Scott, and Robert McGinnis. 1981. "Organizational Context and Scientific Productivity." *American Sociological Review,* 46, 422–42.

Lord, R. G., C. L. DeVader, and G. M. Alliger. 1986. "A Meta-Analysis of the Relations between Personality Traits and Leadership Perceptions: An Application of Validity Generalization Procedures." *Journal of Applied Psychology,* 71, 402–10.

Lorsch, Jay W., and John J. Morse. 1974. *Organizations and Their Members: A Contingency Approach.* New York: Harper and Row.

Lozano, Beverly. 1989. *The Invisible Work Force: Transforming American Business with Outside and Home-Based Workers.* New York: Free Press.

Maas, Meridean Leone. 1979. *A Formal Theory of Organizational Power.* Ph.D. diss., Department of Sociology, Iowa State University.

Mahoney, Thomas A., and William Weitzel. 1969. "Managerial Models of Organizational Effectiveness." *Administrative Science Quarterly,* 14, 357–65.

Malan, Leon. 1994. *Organizational Responses to Turbulent Environments.* Ph.D. diss., State University of New York at Albany.

Manning, Peter K. 1992. *Organizational Communication.* New York: Aldine de Gruyter.

Manns, Curtis L., and James G. March. 1978. "Financial Adversity, Internal Competition, and Curricular Change in a University." *Administrative Science Quarterly,* 23, 541–52.

Mansfield, Roger. 1973. "Bureaucracy and Centralization: An Examination of Organizational Structure." *Administrative Science Quarterly,* 18, 77–88.

March, James G. 1981. "Footnotes to Organizational Change." *Administrative Science Quarterly,* 26, 563–77.

March, James G., and Herbert A. Simon. 1958. *Organizations.* New York: John Wiley.

March, James G., and Lee S. Sproul. 1990. "Technology, Management, and Cooptative Advantage," in *Technology and Organizations,* eds. Paul S. Goodman, Lee Sproul, and Edwin Amenta, 144–73. San Francisco: Jossey-Bass.

Marcus, Alfred A., and Robert S. Goodman. 1991. "Victims and Shareholders: The Dilemmas of Presenting Corporate Policy during a Crisis." *Academy of Management Journal,* 34, 281–305.

Marglin, Stephen A. 1974. "What Do Bosses Do? The Origins and Functions of Hierarchy in Capitalist Production." *Review of Radical Political Economics,* 6, 60–112.

Marple, David. 1982. "Technological Innovation and Organizational Survival: A Population Ecology Study of Nineteenth Century American Railroads." *Sociological Quarterly,* 23, 107–16.

Marrett, Cora Bagley. 1971. "On the Specification of Interorganizational Dimensions." *Sociology and Social Research,* 56, 83–99.

———. 1980. "Influences on the Rise of New Organizations: The Formation of Women's Medical Societies." *Administrative Science Quarterly,* 25, 185–99.

Marsden, Peter V., Cynthia R. Cook, and David Knoke. 1996. "American Organizations and Their Environments: A Descriptive Overview," in *Organizations in America: Analyzing Their Structures and Human Resource Practices,* eds. Arne L. Kalleberg, David Knoke, Peter Marsden, and Joe L. Spaeth. Thousand Oaks, CA: Sage.

Marsh, Robert M., and Hiroshi Mannari. 1980. "Technological Implications Theory: A Japanese Test." *Organization Studies*, 1, 161–83.

Maurice, Marc, Arndt Sorge, and Malcolm Warner. 1980. "Societal Differences in Organizing Manufacturing Units: A Comparison of France, West Germany and Great Britain." *Organization Studies*, 1, 59–86.

McCaffrey, David P. 1982. *OSHA and the Politics of Health Regulation*. New York: Plenum.

McKelvey, Bill. 1982. *Organizational Systematics: Taxonomy, Evolution, Classification*. Berkeley and Los Angeles: University of California Press.

McKelvey, Bill, and Howard Aldrich. 1983. "Populations, Natural Selection, and Applied Organizational Science." *Administrative Science Quarterly*, 28, 101–28.

McKinley, William. 1987. "Complexity and Administrative Intensity: The Case of Declining Organizations." *Administrative Science Quarterly*, 32, 81–105.

McMillan, Charles J. 1973. "Corporations without Citizenship: The Emergence of Multinational Enterprise," in *People and Organizations*, eds. Graeme Soloman and Kenneth Thompsons. London: Longman Group Limited.

McNeil, Kenneth, and Edmond Minihan. 1977. "Regulation of Medical Devices and Organizational Behavior in Hospitals." *Administrative Science Quarterly*, 22, 47–90.

Mechanic, David. 1962. "Sources of Power of Lower Participants in Complex Organizations." *Administrative Science Quarterly*, 7, 349–64.

Meindl, James R., Sanford B. Ehrlich, and Janet M. Dukerich. 1985. "The Romance of Leadership." *Administrative Science Quarterly*, 30, 78–102.

Merton, Robert K. 1957. *Social Theory and Social Structure*. Glencoe, IL: Free Press.

Meyer, Alan D. 1982. "Adapting to Environmental Jolts." *Administrative Science Quarterly*, 27, 515–37.

Meyer, John W., and Brian Rowan. 1977. "Institutionalized Organizations: Formal Structure as Myth and Ceremony." *American Journal of Sociology*, 83, 340–63.

Meyer, John W., and W. Richard Scott. 1983. *Organizational Environments: Ritual and Rationality*. Beverly Hills, CA: Sage.

Meyer, Marshall W. 1968a. "Automation and Bureaucratic Structure." *American Journal of Sociology*, 74, 256–64.

———. 1968b. "Two Authority Structures of Bureaucratic Organization." *Administrative Science Quarterly*, 13, 211–18.

———. 1971. "Some Constraints in Analyzing Data on Organizational Structures." *American Sociological Review*, 36, 294–97.

———. 1975. "Leadership and Organizational Structure." *American Journal of Sociology*, 81, No. 3 (November), 514–42.

———. 1994. "Measuring Performance in Economic Organizations," in *The Handbook of Economic Sociology*, eds. Neil Smelser and Richard Swedberg. Princeton, NJ: Princeton University Press.

Meyer, Marshall W., and M. Craig Brown. 1977. "The Process of Bureaucratization." *American Journal of Sociology*, 83, 364–85.

Meyer, Marshall W., and Lynn G. Zucker. 1989. *Permanently Failing Organizations*. Newbury Park, CA: Sage.

Mezias, Stephen J. 1990. "An Institutional Model of Organizational Practice: Financial Reporting at the Fortune 200." *Administrative Science Quarterly*, 35, 431–57.

Michels, Robert. 1949. *Political Parties*. New York: Free Press.

Miles, Raymond E., Charles C. Snow, and Jeffrey Pfeffer. 1974. "Organization Environment: Concepts and Issues." *Industrial Relations*, 13, 244–64.

Miller, C. Chet, William H. Glick, Yau-de Wang, and George P. Huber. 1991. "Understanding Technology-Structure Relationships: Theory Developing and Meta-Analytic Theory Testing." *Academy of Management Journal*, 34, 370–99.

Miller, Danny. 1987. "Strategy Making on Structure: Analysis and Implications for Performance." *Academy of Management Journal*, 30, 7–32.

Miller, Danny, and Cornelia Droge. 1986. "Psychological and Traditional Determinants of Structure." *Administrative Science Quarterly*, 31, 539–60.

Miller, George A. 1967. "Professionals in Bureaucracy, Alienation among Industrial Scientists and Engineers." *American Sociological Review*, 32, 755–68.

Milliken, Frances J. 1990. "Perceiving and Interpreting Environmental Change: An Examination of College Administrators' Interpretation of Changing Demographics." *Academy of Management Journal*, 33, 42–63.

Milner, Murray Jr. 1980. *Unequal Care: A Case Study of Interorganizational Relations in Health Care.* New York: Columbia University Press.

Miner, Anne S. 1987. "Idiosyncratic Jobs in Formalized Organizations." *Administrative Science Quarterly*, 32, 327–51.

Miner, Anne S., Terry L. Amburgey, and Timothy M. Steams. 1990. "Interorganizational Linkages and Population Dynamics: Buffering and Transformational Skills." *Administrative Science Quarterly*, 35, 689–713.

Mintz, Beth, and Michael Schwartz. 1981. "Interlocking Directorates and Interest Group Formation." *American Sociological Review*, 46, 951–69.

———. 1983. *Power In and Around Organizations.* Upper Saddle River, NJ: Prentice Hall.

Mintzberg, Henry, and Jim Waters. 1990. "Does Decision Get in the Way?" *Organizational Studies*, 11, 1–6.

Mitroff, Ian I., and Ralph H. Kilmann. 1984. *Corporate Tragedies: Product Tampering, Sabotage, and Other Catastrophes.* New York: Praeger.

Mizruchi, Mark S. 1989. "Similarity of Political Behavior among Large American Corporations." *American Journal of Sociology*, 95, 401–24.

———. 1992. *The Structure of Corporate Political Action: Interfirm Relations and Their Consequences.* Cambridge: Harvard University Press.

———. 1996. "What Do Interlocks Do?" *Annual Review of Sociology*, 22, 271–98.

Mizruchi, Mark S., and David Bunting. 1981. "Influence in Corporate Networks: An Examination of Four Measures." *Administrative Science Quarterly*, 26, 475–89.

Mizruchi, Mark S., and Lisa C. Fein. 1999. "The Social Construction of Organizational Knowledge: A Study of the Uses of Coercive, Mimetic, and Normative Isomorphism." *Administrative Science Quarterly*, 44, 653–83.

Mizruchi, Mark S., and Linda Brewster Stearns. 1988. "A Longitudinal Study of the Formation of Interlocking Directorates." *Administrative Science Quarterly*, 33, 194–210.

———. 2001. "Getting Deals Done: The Use of Social Networks in Banks' Decision Making." *American Sociological Review*, 66, 647–71.

Moch, Michael K. 1976. "Structure and Organizational Resource Allocation." *Administrative Science Quarterly*, 21, 661–74.

Moch, Michael K., and Edward V. Morse. 1977. "Size, Centralization, and Organizational Adoption of Innovation." *American Sociological Review*, 43, 716–25.

Mohan, Mary Leslie. 1993. *Organizational Communication and Cultural Vision: Approaches for Analysis.* Albany: State University of New York Press.

Mohr, Lawrence B. 1971. "Organizational Technology and Organizational Structure." *Administrative Science Quarterly*, 16, 444–51.

Molnar, Joseph J. 1978. "Comparative Organizational Properties and Interorganizational Interdependence." *Sociology and Social Research*, 63, 24–48.

Molotch, Harvey, and Marilyn Lester. 1975. "Accidental News: The Great Oil Spill as Local Occurrence and National Event." *American Journal of Sociology*, 81, 235–60.

Morgan, Gareth. 1986. *Images of Organizations.* Beverly Hills, CA: Sage.

Morrill, Calvin. 1991. "Conflict Management, Honor, and Organizational Change." *American Journal of Sociology*, 97, 585–621.

Mulford, Charles L. 1980. "Dyadic Properties as Correlates of Exchange and Conflict between Organizations." Unpublished paper, Department of Sociology, Iowa State University.

Mulford, Charles L., and Mary Ann Mulford. 1980. "Interdependence and Intraorganizational Structure for Voluntary Organizations." *Journal of Voluntary Action Research*, 9, 20–34.

Nee, Victor. 1992. "Organizational Dynamics of Market Transition: Hybrid Forms, Property Rights, and Mixed Economy in China." *Administrative Science Quarterly*, 37, 1–27.

Needleman, Martin L., and Carolyn Needleman. 1979. "Organizational Crime: Two Models of Criminogenesis." *Sociological Quarterly*, 20, 517–28.

Negandhi, Anant R., and Bernard C. Reimann. 1972. "A Contingency Theory of Organization Re-examined in the Context of a Developing Country." *Academy of Management Journal,* 15, 137–46.

———. 1973a. "Correlates of Decentralization: Closed and Open System Perspectives." *Academy of Management Journal,* 16, 570–82.

———. 1973b. "Task Environment, Decentralization and Organizational Effectiveness." *Human Relations,* 26, 203–14.

New York Times. 1981. April 27, sec. A.

Noon, Mike, and Rick Delbridge. 1993. "News from Behind My Head." *Organization Studies,* 14, 23–36.

Oliver, Christine. 1990. "Determinants of Interorganizational Relationships: Integration and Future Directions." *Academy of Management Review,* 15, 241–65.

———. 1992. "The Antecedents of Deinstitutionalization." *Organization Studies,* 13, 563–88.

Ornstein, Michael. 1984. "Interlocking Directorates in Canada: Intercorporate or Class Alliance?" *Administrative Science Quarterly,* 29, 210–37.

Orton, J. Douglas, and Karl E. Weick. 1990. "Loosely Coupled System: A Reconceptualization." *Academy of Management Review,* 15, 203–23.

Ott, J. Steven. 1989. *The Organizational Culture Perspective.* Chicago: Dorsey.

Ouchi, William G. 1977. "The Relationship between Organizational Structure and Organizational Control." *Administrative Science Quarterly,* 22, 95–113.

Ouchi, William G., and Alfred M. Jaeger. 1978. "Social Structure and Organizational Type," in *Environments and Organizations,* eds. Marshall W. Meyer and Associates. San Francisco: Jossey-Bass.

Ouchi, William G., and Jerry B. Johnson. 1978. "Types of Organizational Control and Their Relation to Emotional Well-Being." *Administrative Science Quarterly,* 23, 293–317.

Ouchi, William G., and Mary Ann Maguire. 1975. "Organizational Control: Two Functions." *Administrative Science Quarterly,* 20, 559–69.

Padgett, John F. 1980. "Managing Garbage Can Hierarchies." *Administrative Science Quarterly,* 25, 583–604.

Palmer, Donald, Brad M. Barber, and Xueguang Zhou. 1995. "The Finance Conception of Control: The Theory That Ate New York?" *American Sociological Review,* 60, 504–08.

Palmer, Donald, Brad M. Barber, Xueguang Zhou, and Yasemin Soysal. 1995. "The Friendly and Predatory Acquisition of Large U.S. Corporations in the 1960s: The Other Contested Terrain." *American Sociological Review,* 60, 469–99.

Palmer, Donald A., Roger Friedland, P. Devereaux Jennings, and Melanie E. Powers. 1987. "The Economics and Politics of Structure: The Multidivisional Form and the Large U.S. Corporation." *Administrative Science Quarterly,* 32, 25–48.

Palmer, Donald A., Roger Friedland, and Jitendra V. Singh. 1986. "The Ties That Bind: Organizational and Class Bases of Stability in a Corporate Interlock Network." *American Sociological Review,* 51, 781–96.

Palmer, Donald A., P. Devereaux Jennings, and Xueguang Zhou. 1993. "Late Adoption of the Multidivision Form by Large U.S. Corporations: Institutional, Political, and Economic Accounts." *Administrative Science Quarterly,* 38, 100–31.

Parsons, Talcott. 1960. *Structure and Process in Modern Society.* New York: Free Press.

Pascale, Richard. 1985. "The Paradox of 'Corporate Culture': Reconciling Ourselves to Socialization." *California Management Review,* 27, 26–41.

Pennings, Johannes M. 1973. "Measures of Organizational Structure: A Methodological Note." *American Journal of Sociology,* 79, 686–704.

———. 1980a. "Environmental Influences on the Creation Process," in *The Organizational Life Cycle,* eds. John R. Kimberly and Robert H. Miles and Associates. San Francisco: Jossey-Bass.

———. 1980b. *Interlocking Directorates.* San Francisco: Jossey-Bass.

———. 1982. "Organizational Birth Frequencies: An Empirical Investigation." *Administrative Science Quarterly,* 27, 120–44.

———. 1987. "On the Nature of New Technology as Organizational Innovation," in *New Technology in Organizational Innovation: The Development and Diffusion of Microelectronics,* eds. Johannes M. Pennings and Arend Buitendam, 3–12. Cambridge, MA: Ballinger.

Pennings, Johannes M., and Paul S. Goodman. 1977. "Toward a Workable Framework," in *New Perspectives on Organizational Effectiveness*, eds. S. Goodman and Johannes M. Pennings. San Francisco: Jossey-Bass.

Perlow, Leslie A. 1998. "Boundary Control: The Social Ordering of Work and Family Time in a High-Tech Corporation." *Administrative Science Quarterly*, 43, 328–56.

Perrow, Charles. 1961. "The Analysis of Goals in Complex Organizations." *American Sociological Review*, 26, 688–99.

———. 1967. "A Framework for the Comparative Analysis of Organizations." *American Sociological Review*, 32, 194–208.

———. 1970a. "Departmental Power and Perspective in Industrial Firms," in *Power in Organizations*, ed. Mayer N. Zald. Nashville, TN: Vanderbilt University Press.

———. 1970b. *Organizational Analysis*. Belmont, CA: Wadsworth.

———. 1977. "Three Types of Effectiveness Studies," in *New Perspectives on Organizational Effectiveness*, eds. Paul S. Goodman and Johannes M. Pennings. San Francisco: Jossey-Bass.

———. 1979, 1986. *Complex Organizations: A Critical Essay*, 2nd ed. Glenview, IL: Scott, Foresman.

———. 1984. *Normal Accidents: Living with High-Risk Technologies*. New York: Basic Books.

———. 1986. *Complex Organizations: A Critical Essay*. New York: Random House.

———. 1991. "A Society of Organizations." *Theory and Society*, 20, 725–62.

Perrow, Charles, and Mauro F. Guillen. 1990. *The AIDS Disaster: The Failure of Organizations in New York and the Nation*. New Haven, CT: Yale University Press.

Perrucci, Robert, and Marc Pilisuk. 1970. "Leaders and Ruling Elites: The Interorganizational Bases of Community Power." *American Sociological Review*, 35, 1040–57.

Peter, Laurence J., and Raymond Hull. 1969. *The Peter Principle*. New York: William Brown.

Peters, Thomas J., and Robert H. Waterman, Jr. 1982. *In Search of Excellence: Lessons from America's Best-Run Companies*. New York: Harper and Row.

Peterson, Richard A. 1970. "Some Consequences of Differentiation," in *Power in Organizations*, ed. Mayer N. Zald. Nashville: Vanderbilt University Press.

———. 1981. "Entrepreneurship and Organization," in *Handbook of Organizational Design*, Vol. 1, eds. Paul C. Nystrom and William H. Starbuck. New York: Oxford University Press.

Pfeffer, Jeffrey. 1972a. "Merger as a Response to Organizational Interdependence." *Administrative Science Quarterly*, 17, 328–94.

———. 1972b. "Size and Composition of Corporate Boards of Directors." *Administrative Science Quarterly*, 17, 218–28.

———. 1978. "The Micropolitics of Organizations," in *Environments and Organizations*, eds. Marshall W. Meyer and Associates. San Francisco: Jossey-Bass.

———. 1981. *Power in Organizations*. Marshfield, MA: Pitman.

———. 1982. *Organizations and Organization Theory*. Boston: Pitman.

———. 1983. "Organizational Demography," in *Research in Organizational Behavior*, Vol. 5, eds. L. L. Cummings and Barry M. Staw. Greenwich, CT: JAI Press.

———. 1997. *New Directions for Organizational Theory: Problems and Prospects*. New York: Oxford University Press.

Pfeffer, Jeffrey, and Yinon Cohen. 1984. "Determinants of Internal Labor Markets in Organizations." *Administrative Science Quarterly*, 29, 550–72.

Pfeffer, Jeffrey, and Alison Davis-Blake. 1987. "The Effect of the Proportion of Women on Salaries: The Case of College Administrators." *Administrative Science Quarterly*, 32, 1–24.

Pfeffer, Jeffrey, and Huseyin Leblebici. 1973. "The Effect of Competition on Some Dimensions of Organizational Structure." *Social Forces*, 52, 268–79.

Pfeffer, Jeffrey, and Anthony Long. 1977. "Resource Allocation in United Funds: Examination of Power and Dependence." *Social Forces*, 55, 776–90.

Pfeffer, Jeffrey, and William L. Moore. 1980. "Average Tenure of Academic Department Heads: The Effects of Paradigm, Size, and Departmental Demography." *Administrative Science Quarterly*, 25, 387–406.

Pfeffer, Jeffrey, and Phillip Nowak. 1976. "Joint Ventures and Interorganizational Dependence." *Administrative Science Quarterly*, 21, 398–418.

Pfeffer, Jeffrey, and Gerald R. Salancik. 1974. "Organizational Decision Making as a Political Process: The Case of a University Budget." *Administrative Science Quarterly,* 19, 135–51.

———. 1978. *The External Control of Organizations: A Resource Dependence Perspective.* New York: Harper and Row.

Podolny, Joel M., and Karen L. Page. 1998. "Network Forms of Organizations." *Annual Review of Sociology,* 24, 57–76.

Pondy, Louis R. 1967. "Organizational Conflict: Concepts and Models." *Administrative Science Quarterly,* 12, 296–320.

———. 1969. "Varieties of Organizational Conflict." *Administrative Science Quarterly,* 14, 499–505.

———. 1970. "Toward a Theory of Internal Resource Allocation," in *Power in Organizations,* ed. Mayer N. Zald. Nashville, TN: Vanderbilt University Press.

Portugal, Ed. 1993. *Boards of Directors: Links, Breaks, and Reconstitutions.* Ph.D. diss., State University of New York at Albany.

Powell, Walter W. 1985. *Getting Into Print.* Chicago: University of Chicago Press.

Powell, Walter W., and Paul DiMaggio. 1991. *The New Institutionalism in Organizational Analysis.* Chicago: University of Chicago Press.

Powell, Walter W., Kenneth W. Koput, and Laurel Smith-Doerr. 1996. "Interorganizational Collaboration and the Locus of Innovation: Networks of Learning in Biotechnology." *Administrative Science Quarterly,* 41, 116–45.

Prechel, Harland. 1997. "Corporate Transformation to the Multilayered Subsidiary Form: Changing Economic Conditions and State Business Policy." *Sociological Forum,* 12, 405–39.

———. 2000. *Big Business and the State: Historical Transitions and Corporate Transformation, 1980s–1990s.* Albany: State University of New York Press.

Price, James L. 1968. *Organizational Effectiveness: An Inventory of Propositions.* Homewood, IL: Richard D. Irwin.

Price, James L., and Charles W. Mueller. 1986. *Handbook of Organizational Measurement.* Marshfield, MA: Pitman.

Priest, T. B., and Robert A. Rothman. 1985. "Lawyers in Corporate Chief Executive Positions: A Historical Analysis of Careers." *Work and Occupations,* 12, 131–46.

Prokesh, Steven E. 1985. *New York Times,* October 28, sec. D.

Provan, Keith G., Janice M. Beyer, and Carlos Kruytbosch. 1980. "Environmental Linkages and Power in Resource-Dependence Relations between Organizations." *Administrative Science Quarterly,* 25, 200–25.

Provan, Keith G., and H. Brinton Milward. 1995. "A Preliminary Theory of Interorganizational Network Effectiveness: A Comparative Study of Four Community Mental Health Systems." *Administrative Science Quarterly,* 40, 1–33.

Pugh, Derek S. 1966. "Modern Organization Theory: A Psychological and Sociological Study." *Psychological Bulletin,* 66, 235–51.

Pugh, Derek S., David J. Hickson, C. R. Hinings, K. M. Lupton, K. M. McDonald, C. Turner, and T. Lupton. 1963. "A Conceptual Scheme for Organizational Analysis." *Administrative Science Quarterly,* 8, 289–315.

Pugh, Derek S., D. J. Hickson, C. R. Hinings, and C. Turner. 1968. "Dimensions of Organizational Structure." *Administrative Science Quarterly,* 13, 65–105.

Quinn, Robert E. 1977. "Coping with Cupid: The Formation, Impact, and Management of Romantic Relationships in Organizations." *Administrative Science Quarterly,* 22, 30–45.

Raelin, Joseph A. 1982. "A Policy Output Model of Interorganizational Relations." *Organization Studies,* 3, 243–67.

Ragins, Belle R., Bickley Townsend, and Mary Mattis. 1998. "Gender Gap in the Executive Suite: CEPs and Female Executives Report on Breaking the Glass Ceiling." *Academy of Management Executive,* 12, 28–42.

Rahim, M. Afzahur. 1986. *Managing Conflict in Organizations.* New York: Praeger.

———. 1989. *Managing Conflict: An Interdisciplinary Approach.* New York: Praeger.

Rakowski, Cathy A. 1994. *Contrapunto: The Informal Sector Debate in Latin America.* Albany: State University of New York Press.

Ranson, Stewart, Bob Hinings, and Royster Greenwood. 1980. "The Structuring of Organizational Structures." *Administrative Science Quarterly*, 25, 1–17.

Rao, Hayagreeva, and Eric H. Neilsen. 1992. "An Ecology of Agency Arrangement: Mortality of Savings and Loan Associations." *Administrative Science Quarterly*, 37, 448–70.

Raphael, Edna. 1967. "The Andersen-Warton Hypothesis in Local Unions: A Comparative Study." *American Sociological Review*, 32, 768–76.

Rawls, J. 1971. *A Theory of Justice*. Cambridge, MA: Harvard University Press.

Reinganum, Marc R. 1985. "The Effect of Executive Succession on Stockholder Wealth." *Administrative Science Quarterly*, 30, 46–60.

Reskin, Barbara F. 1998. *The Realities of Affirmative Action in Employment*. Washington, D.C.: American Sociological Association.

Reskin, Barbara, and Irene Padevic. 1994. *Women and Men at Work*. Thousand Oaks, CA: Pine Forge.

Revkin, Andrew C. 1997. "Babbitt Assails GE Over Ridding Hudson of Chemicals." *New York Times*, September 26, sec. B.

Rifkin, Jeremy. 1995. *The End of Work: The Decline of the Global Labor Force and the Dawn of the Post-Market Era*. New York: Putnam.

Ritzer, George. 1989. "The Permanently New Economy: The Case for Reviving Economic Sociology." *Work and Occupations*, 16, 243–72.

———. 2000. *The McDonaldization of Society*. Thousand Oaks, CA: Pine Forge Press.

Ritzer, George, and David Walczak. 1986. *Working: Conflict and Change*. Upper Saddle River, NJ: Prentice Hall.

Romanelli, Elaine. 1989. "Environments and Strategies of Organization Startup: Effects on Early Survival." *Administrative Science Quarterly*, 34, 369–87.

Romanelli, Elaine, and Michael Tushman. 1994. "Organizational Transformation as Punctuated Equilibrium: An Empirical Test." *Academy of Management Journal*, 37, 1141–66.

Romo, Frank P., and Michael Schwartz. 1995. "The Structural Embeddedness of Business Decisions: The Migration of Manufacturing Plants in New York State, 1960 to 1985." *American Sociological Review*, 60, 874–907.

Rosenbaum, James E. 1979. "Organizational Career Mobility: Promotion Chances in a Corporation during Periods of Growth and Contraction." *American Journal of Sociology*, 85, 21–48.

Rosenweig, Philip M., and Jitendra V. Singh. 1991. "Organizational Environments and the Multinational Enterprise." *Academy of Management Review*, 16, No. 2, 340–61.

Rosow, Jerome M., ed. 1974. *The Worker and the Job: Coping with Change*. Upper Saddle River, NJ: Prentice Hall.

Ross, Jerry, and Barry M. Staw. 1993. "Organizational Escalation and Exit: Lessons from the Shoreham Nuclear Power Plant." *Academy of Management Journal*, 36, 701–32.

Rothschild, Joyce, and J. Allen Whitt. 1986. *The Cooperative Workplace: Potentials and Dilemmas of Organizational Democracy and Participation*. New York: Cambridge University Press.

Rowan, Brian. 1982. "Organizational Structure and the Institutional Environment: The Case of Public Schools." *Administrative Science Quarterly*, 27, 259–79.

Roy, William G. 1981. "The Process of Bureaucratization of the U.S. State Department and the Vesting of Economic Interests, 1886–1905." *Administrative Science Quarterly*, 26, 419–33.

———. 1983a. "Toward Clearer Thinking: A Reply." *Administrative Science Quarterly*, 28, 61–64.

———. 1983b. "The Unfolding of the Interlocking Directorate Structure of the United States." *American Sociological Review*, 48, 248–57.

Rubin, I. 1979. "Loose Structure, Retrenchment and Adaptability in the University." Paper presented at the Midwest Sociological Society meetings, Minneapolis.

Rus, Veljko. 1972. "The Limits of Organized Participation," in *Proceedings of the First International Conference on Participation and Self-Management*, Vol. 2. Zagreb, Yugoslavia.

Sabel, Charles F. 1982. *Work and Politics*. New York: Cambridge University Press.

Salancik, Gerald R., and James R. Mindl. 1984. "Corporate Attributions as Strategic Illusions of Management Control." *Administrative Science Quarterly*, 29, 238–54.

Salancik, Gerald R., and Jeffrey Pfeffer. 1974. "The Bases and Use of Power in Organizational Decision Making: The Case of a University." *Administrative Science Quarterly*, 19, 453–73.

———. 1977. "Constraints on Administrator Discretion: The Limited Influence of Mayors on City Budgets." *Urban Affairs Quarterly,* 12, 475–98.

Samuel, Yitzhak. 1979. "An Exchange and Power Approach to the Concept of Organizational Effectiveness." Unpublished paper. Department of Sociology and Anthropology, Tel Aviv University, Israel.

Sanford, R. Nevitt. 1964. "Individual Conflict and Organizational Interaction," in *Power and Conflict in Organizations,* eds. Robert L. Kahn and Elise Boulding. New York: Basic Books.

Satow, Roberta. 1975. "Value-Rational Authority and Professional Organizations: Weber's Missing Type." *Administrative Science Quarterly,* 20, 526–31.

Schein, Virginia E. 1973. "The Relationship between Sex-Role Stereotypes and Requisite Management Characteristics." *Journal of Applied Psychology,* 57, 95–100.

Schmidt, Stuart M., and Thomas A. Kochan. 1972. "Conflict: Toward Conceptual Clarity." *Administrative Science Quarterly,* 17, 371–81.

———. 1977. "Interorganizational Relationships: Patterns and Motivations." *Administrative Science Quarterly,* 22, 220–34.

Schneider, Susan C. 1989. "Strategy Formulation: The Impact of National Culture." *Organization Studies,* 10, 149–68.

Schollhammer, Hans. 1971. "Organization Structures of Multinational Corporations." *Academy of Management Journal,* 14, 345–65.

Schoonhoven, Claudia Bird. 1981. "Problems with Contingency Theory: Testing Assumptions Hidden within the Language of Contingency 'Theory.'" *Administrative Science Quarterly,* 26, 349–77.

Schreyogg, Georg. 1980. "Contingency and Choice in Organization Theory." *Organization Studies,* 1, 305–26.

Schwochan, Susan, Peter Fenilee, and John Thomas Delaney. 1988. "The Resource Allocation Effects of Mandated Relationships." *Administrative Science Quarterly,* 33, 418–37.

———. 1981. *Organizations: Rational, Natural, and Open Systems.* Upper Saddle River, NJ: Prentice Hall.

———. 1987b. "The Adolescence of Institutional Theory." *Administrative Science Quarterly,* 32, 493–511.

———. 1995. *Institutions and Organizations.* Thousand Oaks, CA: Sage.

———. 1996. "The Mandate Is Still Being Honored: In Defense of Weber's Disciples." *Administrative Science Quarterly,* 41, 163–71.

Scott, W. Richard, Martin Ruef, Peter J. Mendel, and Carol A. Caronna. 2000. *Institutional Change and Healthcare Organizations: From Professional Dominance to Managed Care.* Chicago: University of Chicago Press.

Seabright, Mark A., Daniel A. Levinthal, and Mark Fichman. 1992. "Role of Individual Attachments in the Dissolution of Interorganizational Relationships." *Academy of Management Journal,* 35, 122–60.

Seashore, Stanley E. 1977. "An Elastic and Expandable Viewpoint," in *New Perspectives on Organizational Effectiveness,* eds. Paul S. Goodman and J. M. Pennings. San Francisco: Jossey-Bass.

Seashore, Stanley E., and Ephraim Yuchtman. 1967. "Factorial Analysis of Organizational Performance." *Administrative Science Quarterly,* 12, 377–95.

Seiler, Lauren H., and Gene F. Summers. 1979. "Corporate Involvement in Community Affairs." *Sociological Quarterly,* 20, 375–86.

Selznick, Philip. 1957. *Leadership in Administration.* New York: Harper and Row.

———. 1960. *The Organizational Weapon.* New York: Free Press.

———. 1966. *TVA and the Grass Roots,* ed. Harper Torchbook. New York: Harper and Row.

Sewell, William H. 1992. "A Theory of Structure: Duality, Agency, and Transformation." *American Journal of Sociology,* 98, 1–29.

Shenkar, Oded. 1984. "Is Bureaucracy Inevitable: The Chinese Experience." *Organizational Studies,* 5, 289–308.

Shrum, Wesley, and Robert Wuthnow. 1988. "Reputational Status of Organizations in Technical Systems." *American Journal of Sociology,* 93, 882–912.

Sills, David L. 1957. *The Volunteers.* New York: Free Press.

Simon, Herbert A. 1957. *Administrative Behavior.* New York: Free Press.

———. 1964. "On the Concept of Organizational Goal." *Administrative Science Quarterly,* 9, 1–22.

Simpson, Richard L. 1969. "Vertical and Horizontal Communication in Formal Organizations." *Administrative Science Quarterly*, 14, 188–96.

Singh, Jitendra V., David J. Tucker, and Robert J. House. 1986. "Organizational Legitimacy and the Liability of Newness." *Administrative Science Quarterly*, 31, 171–93.

Smircich, Linda. 1985. "Is the Concept of Culture a Paradigm for Understanding Organizations and Ourselves?" in *Organizational Culture*, eds. Peter J. Frost, Larry F. Moore, Meryl Reis Louis, Craig C. Lundberg, and Joanne Martin, 55–72. Beverly Hills, CA: Sage.

Smith, Kenwyn. 1989. "The Movement of Conflict in Organizations: The Joint Dynamics of Splitting and Triangulation." *Administrative Science Quarterly*, 34, 1–20.

Snow, Charles C., and Lawrence G. Hrebiniak. 1980. "Strategy, Distinctive Competence and Organizational Performance." *Administrative Science Quarterly*, 25, 317–36.

Sorge, Arndt. 1991. "Strategic Fit and the Societal Effect: Interpreting Cross-National Comparisons of Technology, Organization, and Human Resources." *Organization Studies*, 12, 161–90.

Staber, Udo, and Howard Aldrich. 1983. "Trade Association Stability and Public Policy," in *Organizational Theory and Public Policy*, eds. Richard H. Hall and Robert E. Quinn. Beverly Hills, CA: Sage.

Starbuck, William H. 1976. "Organizations and Their Environments," in *Handbook of Industrial and Organizational Psychology*, ed. Marvin D. Dunnette. Chicago: Rand McNally.

———. 1983. "Organizations as Action Generators." *American Sociological Review*, 48, 91–102.

Starbuck, William H., and Paul C. Nystrom. 1981. "Designing and Understanding Organizations," in *Handbook of Organizational Design*, Vol. 1, eds. Paul C. Nystrom and William H. Starbuck. New York: Oxford University Press.

Staw, Barry M. 1982. "Counterforces to Change," in *Change in Organizations: New Perspectives on Theory, Research, and Practice*, eds. Paul S. Goodman and Associates. San Francisco: Jossey-Bass.

Staw, Barry M., Pamela McKechnie, and Sheila M. Puffer. 1983. "The Justification of Organizational Performance." *Administrative Science Quarterly*, 28, 582–600.

Staw, Barry M., and Jerry Ross. 1989. "Understanding Behavior in Escalation Situations." *Science*, 246, 216–20.

Stearns, Linda Brewster, and Mark S. Mizruchi. 1986. "Broken-Tie Reconstitution and the Functions of Interorganizational Interlocks: A Reexamination." *Administrative Science Quarterly*, 31, 522–38.

Steckmest, Francis W. 1982. *Corporate Performance: The Key to Public Trust*. New York: McGraw-Hill.

Steers, R. M. 1977. *Organizational Effectiveness: A Behavioral View*. Pacific Palisades, CA: Goodyear.

Stevenson, William B. 1990. "Formal Structure and Networks of Interaction within Organizations." *Social Science Research*, 19, 112–31.

Stevenson, William B., and Danna Greenberg. 2000. "Agency and Social Networks: Strategies of Action in a Social Structure of Position, Opposition and Opportunity." *Administrative Science Quarterly*, 45, 651–78.

Stinchcombe, Arthur L. 1959. "Bureaucratic and Craft Administration of Productions." *Administrative Science Quarterly*, 4, 168–87.

———. 1965. "Organizations and Social Structure," in *Handbook of Organizations*, ed. James G. March. Chicago: Rand McNally.

———. 1990. *Information and Organizations*. Berkeley and Los Angeles: University of California Press.

Stogdill, R. M. 1974. *Handbook of Leadership*. New York: Free Press.

Stolzenberg, Ross M. 1978. "Bringing the Boss Back In: Employer Size, Employee Schooling and Socioeconomic Achievement." *American Sociological Review*, 43, 813–28.

Storing, Herbert. 1962. "The Science of Administration: Herbert A. Simon," in *Essays on the Scientific Study of Politics*, ed. H. Storing. New York: Holt, Rinehart & Winston.

Strang, David, and James N. Baron. 1990. "Categorical Imperative: The Structure of Job Titles in California State Agencies." *American Sociological Review*, 55, 479–95.

———. 1949. *White Collar Crime*. New York: Holt, Rinehart & Winston.

Sutton, John R., and Frank Dobbin. 1996. "The Two Faces of Governance: Responses to Legal Uncertainty in U.S. Firms 1955–1985." *American Sociological Review*, 61, 794–811.

Sutton, John R., Frank Dobbin, John Meyer, and W. Richard Scott. 1994. "The Legalization of the Workplace." *American Journal of Sociology*, 99, 944–71.

Sutton, Robert I. 1987. "The Process of Organizational Death: Disbanding and Reconnecting." *Administrative Science Quarterly,* 32, 542–69.

Swigert, Victoria Lynn, and Ronald A. Farrell. 1980–81. "Corporate Homicide: Definitional Processes in the Creation of Deviance." *Law and Society Review,* 15, 163–82.

Tannenbaum, Arnold S., Bogdan Kovacic, Menochen Rosner, Mino Vianello, and George Wieser. 1974. *Hierarchy in Organizations.* San Francisco: Jossey-Bass.

Tannenbaum, Arnold S., and Tamas Rozgonyi. 1986. *Authority and Reward in Organizations: An International Research.* Ann Arbor, MI: Survey Research Center.

Tayeb, Monir. 1987. "Contingency Theory and Culture: A Study of Matched English and Indian Manufacturing Firms." *Organization Studies,* 8, 241–61.

Taylor, James C. 1971. "Some Effects of Technology in Organizational Change." *Human Relations,* 24, 105–23.

Terkel, Studs. 1974. *Working.* New York: Pantheon Books.

Terreberry, Shirley. 1968. "The Evolution of Organizational Environments." *Administrative Science Quarterly,* 12, 590–613.

Thach, Liz, and Richard Woodman. 1994. "Organizational Change and Information Technology: Managing on the Edge of Cyberspace." *Organizational Dynamics,* 23, 30–46.

Thomas, Alan Berkeley. 1988. "Does Leadership Make a Difference to Organizational Performance?" *Administrative Science Quarterly,* 33, 388–400.

Thompson, James D. 1967. *Organizations in Action.* New York: McGraw-Hill.

Thompson, James D., and William McEwen. 1958. "Organizational Goals and Environment: Goalsetting as an Interaction Process." *American Sociological Review,* 23, 23–31.

Thompson, Victor. 1961. *Modern Organizations.* New York: Knopf.

Tickner, Joseph A. 2002. "The Precautionary Principle and Public Health Trade-Offs: Case Study of West Nile Virus." *Annals of the American Academy of Political and Social Science,* 584, 69–79.

Tilly, Chris, and Charles Tilly. 1998. *Work Under Capitalism.* Boulder, CO: Westview Press.

Tolbert, Pamela S. 1985. "Institutional Environments and Resource Dependence: Sources of Administrative Structure in Institutions of Higher Education." *Administrative Science Quarterly,* 30, 1–13.

———. 2004. "Introduction." pp. 329–37 in *Handbook of Work and Organizations,* eds. Stephen Ackroyd, Rose Batt, Paul Thompson, and Pamela Tolbert. Oxford: Oxford University Press.

Tolbert, Pamela S., and Lynne G. Zucker. 1983. "Institutional Sources of Change in the Formal Structure of Organizations: The Diffusion of Civil Service Reforms, 1880–1935." *Administrative Science Quarterly,* 28, 22–39.

———. 1996. "The Institutionalization of Institutional Theory," in *Handbook of Organization Studies,* ed. Stewart R. Clegg, Cynthia Hardy, and Walter R. Nord. Thousand Oaks, CA: Sage.

Tonry, Michael, and Albert J. Reiss, Jr., eds. 1994. *Beyond the Law: Crime in Complex Organizations.* Chicago: University of Chicago Press.

Tosi, Henry L., Jr., and John W. Slocum, Jr. 1984. "Contingency Theory: Some Suggested Directions." *Journal of Management,* 10, 9–26.

Toynbee, Arnold. 1974. "As I See It." *Forbes,* 113, 68.

Trice, Harrison M., and Janice M. Beyer. 1993. *The Cultures of Work Organizations.* Upper Saddle River, NJ: Prentice Hall.

Tsui, Anne S. 1990. "A Multiple-Constituency Model of Effectiveness: An Empirical Examination at the Human Resources Subunit Level." *Administrative Science Quarterly,* 35, 458–83.

Turk, Herman. 1973. "Comparative Urban Structure from an Interorganizational Perspective." *Administrative Science Quarterly,* 18, 37–55.

Turner, Jonathan H. 1979. *The Structure of Social Theory,* rev. ed. Homewood, IL: Dorsey.

Turner, Jonathan H., and Alexandra Maryanski. 1979. *Functionalism.* Menlo Park, CA: Benjamin Cummings.

Tushman, Michael L., and Phillip Anderson. 1986. "Technological Discontinuities and Organizational Environments." *Administrative Science Quarterly,* 31, 439–65.

Tushman, Michael L., and Richard B. Nelson. 1990. "Introduction: Technology, Organizations, and Innovation." *Administrative Science Quarterly,* 35, 1–8.

Useem, Michael. 1979. "The Social Organization of the American Business Elite and Participation of Corporate Directors in the Governance of American Institutions." *American Sociological Review,* 44, 553–72.

———. 1982. "Classwide Rationality in the Politics of Managers and Directors of Large Corporations in the United States and Great Britain." *Administrative Science Quarterly,* 27, 199–226.

———. 1984. *The Inner Circle.* New York: Oxford University Press.

Uzzi, Brian. 1996. "The Sources and Consequences of Embeddedness for the Economic Performance of Organizations: The Network Effect." *American Sociological Review,* 60, 674–98.

———. 1997. "Social Structure and Competition in Interfirm Networks: The Paradox of Embeddedness." *Administrative Science Quarterly,* 42, 35–67.

Valcour, P. Monique. 2002. "Managerial Behavior in a Multiplex Role System." *Human Relations,* 55, 1163–88.

Van Buren, Mark E. 1992. "Organizational Size and the Use of Firm Internal Markets in High Growth Establishments." *Social Science Research,* 21, 311–27.

Van de Ven, Andrew H. 1979. "Howard E. Aldrich: Organizations and Environments." *Administrative Science Quarterly,* 24, 320–26.

———. 1983. "Review of Thomas B. Peters and Robert H. Waterman, Jr., In Search of Excellence: Lessons from America's Best-Run Companies" (New York: Harper and Row, 1982), in *Administrative Science Quarterly,* 28, No. 4, 621–22.

Van de Ven, Andrew H., Andre L. Delbecq, and Richard Koenig, Jr. 1976. "Determinants of Coordination Modes within Organizations." *American Sociological Review,* 41, 322–38.

Van de Ven, Andrew H., and Diane L. Ferry. 1980. *Measuring and Assessing Organizations.* New York: Wiley.

Van de Ven, Andrew H., and Gordon Walker. 1984. "The Dynamics of Interorganizational Coordination." *Administrative Science Quarterly,* 29, 598–621.

Van Houton, Donald R. 1987. "The Political Economy and Technical Control of Work Humanization in Sweden during the 1970s and 1980s." *Work and Occupations,* 14, 483–513.

Vaughan, Diane. 1983. *Controlling Unlawful Organizational Behavior: Social Structure and Corporate Misconduct.* Chicago: University of Chicago Press.

———. 1990. "Autonomy, Interdependence, and Social Control: NASA and the Space Shuttle *Challenger.*" *Administrative Science Quarterly,* 35, 225–57.

———. 1996. *The Challenger Launch Decision: Risky Technology, Culture, and Deviance at NASA.* Chicago: University of Chicago Press.

———. 1999. "The Dark Side of Organizations: Mistake, Misconduct, and Disaster." *Annual Review of Sociology,* 25, 271–305.

Verhovek, Sam Howe. 1993. "A Texas County Snubs Apple Over Unwed-Partner Policy." *New York Times,* December 2, A1, BII.

Vroom, Victor H., and Philip W. Yetton. 1973. *Leadership and Decision Making.* Pittsburgh, PA: University of Pittsburgh Press.

Waegel, William B., M. David Ermann, and Alan M. Horowitz. 1981. "Organizational Responses to Imputations of Deviance." *Sociological Quarterly,* 22, 43–55.

Walker, Henry A., Barbara C. Ilardi, Anne M. McMahon, and Mary L. Fennell. 1996. "Gender, Interaction and Leadership." *Social Psychology Quarterly,* 59, 255–72.

Warren, Roland. 1967. "The Interorganizational Field as a Focus for Investigation." *Administrative Science Quarterly,* 12, 396–419.

Weber, Max. 1947. *The Theory of Social and Economic Organization,* trans. A. M. Parsons and T. Parsons. New York: Free Press.

———. 1952. *The Protestant Ethic and the Spirit of Capitalism.* New York: Scribner.

———. 1968. *Economy and Society: An Outline of Interpretive Sociology.* New York: Bedminster.

Weick, Karl E. 1976. "Educational Organizations as Loosely Coupled Systems." *Administrative Science Quarterly,* 21, 1–19.

———. 1979. *The Social Psychology of Organizing,* 2nd ed. Reading, MA: Addison-Wesley.

———. 1990. "Technology as Equivoque: Sensemaking in New Technologies," in *Technology and Organizations,* eds. Paul S. Goodman, Lee Sproul, and Edwin Amenta, 1–44. San Francisco: Jossey-Bass.

Weick, Karl E., and Karlene H. Roberts. 1993. "Collective Mind in Organizations: Heedful Interrelations on Flight Decks." *Administrative Science Quarterly,* 38, 357–81.

Weiner, Nan. 1977. "Situational and Leadership Influence on Organizational Performance." Unpublished paper. Columbus: College of Administrative Science, Ohio State University.

Weitzel, William, and Ellen Jonsson. 1989. "Decline in Organizations: A Literature Integration and Extension." *Administrative Science Quarterly,* 34, 91–109.

Westphal, James D., Marc D. Seidel, and Katherine J. Stewart. 2001. "Second-order Imitation: Uncovering Latent Effects of Board Network Ties." *Administrative Science Quarterly,* 46, 717–47.

Whetten, David A. 1980. "Sources, Responses and Effects of Organizational Decline," in *The Organizational Life Cycle,* eds. John R. Kimberly and Robert H. Miles and Associates. San Francisco: Jossey-Bass.

Wholey, Douglas R., Jon B. Christianson, and Susan M. Sanchez. 1992. "Organizational Size and Failure among Health Maintenance Organizations." *American Sociological Review,* 57, 829–42.

Wiewel, Wim, and Albert Hunter. 1985. "The Interorganizational Network as a Resource: A Comparative Case Study on Organizational Genesis." *Administrative Science Quarterly,* 30, 482–96.

Wildavsky, Aaron. 1964. *The Politics of the Budgetary Process.* Boston: Little, Brown.

Wilensky, Harold. 1967. *Organizational Intelligence: Knowledge and Policy in Government and Industry.* New York: Basic Books.

Williamson, Oliver E. 1975. *Markets and Hierarchies: Analysis and Antitrust Implications.* New York: Free Press.

———. 1985. *The Economic Institutions of Capitalism.* New York: Free Press.

Withey, Michael, and William H. Cooper. 1989. "Predicting Exit, Voice, Loyalty, and Neglect." *Administrative Science Quarterly,* 34, 521–39.

Wood, James R. 1975. "Legitimate Control and Organizational Transcendance." *Social Forces,* 54, 199–211.

Woodward, Joan. 1958. *Management and Technology.* London: Her Majesty's Stationery Office.

———. 1965. *Industrial Organizations: Theory and Practice.* London: Oxford University Press.

Work in America. 1973. Prepared under auspices of W. E. Upjohn Institute. Cambridge, MA: MIT Press.

Yarmolinsky, Adam. 1975. "Institutional Paralysis." *Daedalus,* 104, 61–67.

Yeager, Peter C. 1982. "Review of Francis W. Steckmest, *Corporate Performance: The Key to Public Trust* (New York: McGraw-Hill)," in *Contemporary Sociology,* 11, 747–48.

Young, Ruth C. 1988. "Is Population Ecology a Useful Paradigm for the Study of Organizations?" *American Journal of Sociology,* 94, 1–24.

———. 1989. "Reply to Freeman and Hannan and Brittain and Wholey." *American Journal of Sociology,* 95, 445–46.

Yuchtman, Ephraim, and Stanley Seashore. 1967. "A System Resource Approach to Organizational Effectiveness." *American Sociological Review,* 32, 891–903.

Yukl, Gary A. 1989, 2002. *Leadership in Organizations,* 2nd ed. Upper Saddle River, NJ: Prentice Hall.

Yukl, G. A., S. Wall, and R. Lepsinger. 1990. "Preliminary Report on the Validation of the Management Practices Survey," in *Measures of Leadership,* eds. K. E. Clark and M. B. Clark. West Orange, NJ: Leadership Library of America.

Zajac, Edward J., and James D. Westphal. 1996. "Director Reputation, CEO-Board Power, and the Dynamics of Board Interlocks." *Administrative Science Quarterly,* 41, 507–29.

Zald, Mayer ed. 1970. *Organizational Change: The Political Economy of the YMCA.* Chicago: University of Chicago Press.

Zalkind, Sheldon, and Timothy W. Costello. 1962. "Perceptions: Some Recent Research and Implications for Administration." *Administrative Science Quarterly,* 7, 218–35.

Zaltman, Gerald, Robert Duncan, and Jonny Holbek. 1973. *Innovations and Organizations.* New York: Wiley Interscience.

Zammuto, Raymond F. 1982. *Assessing Organizational Effectiveness.* Albany: State University of New York Press.

Zanetich, John T. 2003. *Knowledge Management in the Public Sector: A Case Study of the West Nile Virus Epidemic in New York State.* Unpublished Ph.D. diss., Albany, NY. State University at Albany (SUNY).

Zeitlin, Maurice. 1974. "Corporate Ownership and Control: The Large Corporation and the Capitalist Class." *American Journal of Sociology,* 79, 1073–1119.

———. 1976. "In Class Theory of the Large Corporation: Response to Others." *American Journal of Sociology,* 81, 894–903.

Zenger, Todd R., and Barbara S. Lawrence. 1989. "Organizational Demography: The Differential Effects of Age and Tenure Distributions on Technical Communication." *Academy of Management Journal,* 32, 353–76.

Zey, Mary. 1992. "Criticisms of Rational Choice Models," in *Decision Making: Alternatives to Rational Choice Models,* ed. Mary Zey, 9–31. Newbury Park, CA: Sage.

Zhou, Xueguant. 1993. "The Dynamics of Organizational Rules." *American Journal of Sociology,* 98, 1134–66.

Zucker, Lynne G. 1977. "The Role of Institutionalization in Cultural Persistence." *American Sociological Review,* 42, 726–43.

Zucker, Lynne G. ed. 1988. *Institutional Patterns and Organizations: Culture and Environment.* Cambridge, MA: Ballinger.

Name Index

A

Abbott, A., 16, 99, 220
Acker, J., 9
Adams, C. R., 201
Adler, N. J., 13
Adler, P. S., 45
Ahuja, G., 170, 201
Aiken, M., 34–35, 43–44, 46–48, 52, 57, 69, 145, 169, 194, 201
Alba, R. D., 152
Aldrich, H. E., 12, 25, 58–59, 67, 103, 138, 160–61, 183–84, 190, 193–94, 196, 200, 203, 207–9, 211–13, 215, 242
Alexander, J. A., 59
Alford, F., 14
Allen, D. L., 196
Allen, J. K., 60, 76
Allen, M. P., 91, 121, 124, 213
Alliger, G. M., 113
Allison, P. D., 7
Allmendinger, J., 179
Alter, C., 189
Altheide, D. L., 243
Alutto, J., 136
Alvesson, M., 94
Amburgey, T. L., 162–63
Anderson, P., 161
Angle, H. L., 234
Ansell, C. K., 91
Antonio, R. J., 11
Appold, S. J., 72
Argote, L., 42
Argyris, C., 67
Aronowitz, S., 5
Arum, R., 3
Astley, W. G., 211

Athanassaides, J. C., 141
At-Twarjri, M. I., 76
Azumi, K., 29

B

Bacharach, S. B., 61, 90–91, 134, 136, 163
Baker, W. E., 200
Baldridge, J. V., 43, 170
Bales, R. F., 111
Bamberger, P., 163
Baratz, M. S., 134
Barber, B. M., 163
Barley, S. R., 72, 100–101
Barnard, C. I., 72, 89, 129, 138, 232–33
Barnett, W. P., 163
Baron, J. N., 8, 35, 98
Barton, E., 6–7
Bass, B. M., 138
Baum, J. A. C., 161, 163, 166, 221
Baureus, M. S., 15, 188
Bavelas, A., 148
Beamish, T. D., 132
Beard, D. W., 185
Becker, S. W., 170
Beckman, C. M., 4, 133, 202
Belasco, J. A., 136
Benson, J. K., 196, 200, 223
Berger, J., 113
Berger, P., 219
Bergesen, A. J., 13
Berle, A. A., 11, 124
Bettman, J. R., 230
Beyer, J. M., 71–72, 133, 204
Bidwell, C. E., 208
Bielby, W. T., 8
Bielefeld, W., 204–5

Bierstedt, R., 87
Biggart, N. W., 4, 76, 83, 158
Birnbaum, P. H., 75–76
Blake, R. R., 112
Blau, J. R., 71, 152
Blau, P. M., 29, 36, 42, 47, 51, 54–56, 66, 87, 91, 96, 145, 226
Blum, T. C., 83, 221
Boddewyn, J., 187
Boeker, W., 95, 121–22, 159, 162, 203
Boje, D. M., 29, 46, 195–96, 200
Boraas, S., 99
Borman, W. C., 109
Borys, B., 45
Boulding, K. E., 101–2
Bowman, S. R., 16
Boychuk, T., 84
Bradshaw, P. J., 71
Brandeis, L., 202
Brantley, P., 90, 204
Brass, D. J., 55, 90
Brewer, J., 145
Brinkerhoff, D., 228
Broskowski, A., 196
Brown, J. L., 101
Brown, M. C., 49, 74, 121, 176
Brown, R. H., 25
Brown, W. B., 122
Browning, L. D., 133
Brunsson, N., 139
Brush, D. H., 109
Bucher, R., 94
Budros, A., 167
Bugùra, A., 84
Bunting, D., 203
Burke, J. P., 26
Burkhardt, M. E., 90
Burnham, R. A., 43, 170
Burns, T., 31, 40, 58
Burt, R. S., 12, 91, 180–81, 192, 202–4, 217, 228

C

Cameron, K., 164, 237, 239
Campbell, D., 208–9
Campbell, J. P., 224, 229
Caplow, T., 77, 190, 197

Caragonne, P., 197
Carli, L., 114
Caronna, C. A., 94
Carroll, G. R., 76, 123, 156, 158–60, 162–63, 166, 179, 208–9, 210–11
Carstensen, F. V., 13, 188
Champagne, A., 12, 178
Chandler, A. D., Jr., 78–79, 132, 212
Chemers, M. M., 116
Chen, M.-J., 67
Child, J., 25, 53, 56, 66, 70, 78, 156, 161, 212
Christenson, J. A., 10
Christianson, J. B., 166
Christman, K. P., 12, 192, 202, 228
Clark, J. P., 105, 193, 202
Clarke, L. B., 132
Clawson, D., 205
Clegg, S. R., 24, 45, 49, 84, 87, 138, 208
Clinard, M. B., 14
Cohen, M. D., 129, 132
Cohen, Y., 8
Coleman, J. S., 15–16, 125
Colignon, R., 18
Comstock, D., 69
Conaty, J., 76
Cook, C. R., 3
Cook, K. S., 189, 198
Cooper, D. J., 101
Cooper, W. H., 7
Corwin, R., 170
Coser, L., 103
Costello, T. W., 140–41
Covaleski, M. A., 54
Craig, J. G., 96
Crittenden, A., 10
Crozier, M., 37–38, 49, 90, 92
Cummings, L. C., 99, 226, 233
Curphy, G. J., 111
Cyert, R. M., 129, 131–32

D

Daft, R. L., 71, 170
Dahl, R., 87
Dalin, M. T., 76
Dalton, M., 98
Damanpour, F., 167, 169

Danet, B., 3
D'Aunno, T. D., 74
D'Aveni, R. A., 164, 166
Davis, G. F., 133, 163, 166–67, 204, 209
Davis-Blake, A., 6, 221
Day, D. V., 123
Delacroix, J., 158–60, 163, 166, 179
Delaney, J. T., 199
Delbecq, A. L., 57, 71
Dess, G. G., 185
DeVader, C. L., 113
Dewar, R. D., 29, 35, 46, 170
Diekmann, K. A., 166–67, 209
Digman, J. M., 111
DiMaggio, P. J., 81–82, 218–20
Dirsmith, M. W., 54, 84, 221
Dobbin, F., 82, 84, 159
Dole, C., 4
Domhoff, G. W., 205
Donaldson, L., 66, 81, 84, 208, 216–17
Dornbusch, S. M., 49, 55–56, 89, 215
Dowd, T. J., 159
Downs, A., 152
Drabek, T. E., 201
Drazin, R., 83
Dreeben, R., 59
Droge, C., 79
DuBick, M. A., 74
Dukerich, J. M., 109
Dunbar, R. L. M., 183, 187
Duncan, R., 168, 171
Dunford, R., 214
Dunkerley, D., 24, 45, 49, 138, 208
Dyck, B., 159
Dye, T. R., 205

E

Eagly, A. H., 114
Edelman, L. B., 178
Egelhoff, W. G., 24
Ehrlich, S. B., 109
Eitzen, D. S., 121
Emerson, R. M., 89
Emery, F. E., 193
England, P., 99
Enz, C. A., 94
Ermann, M. D., 16

Etzioni, A., 25, 90–91, 96, 105, 109, 111, 226, 234
Evan, W. M., 167, 190
Evans, J., 101

F

Farberman, H. A., 14
Farrell, R. A., 16
Fave, L. R. D., 205
Fein, L. C., 82
Feldman, M. S., 139
Fenilee, P., 199
Fennell, M. C., 74
Fennell, M. L., 113
Fenner, D. B., 68
Fernandez, R. M., 91
Ferry, D. L., 54, 190, 195, 197–98
Fichman, M., 195
Fiedler, F. E., 113, 116
Fields, D., 83, 221
Filardo, E. K., 114
Filley, A. C., 114, 116
Finkelstein, S., 90
Fligstein, N., 83, 90, 92, 122, 163, 204, 221
Florida, R., 183
Fogarty, T. J., 84, 221
Fombrun, C. J., 30
Freeland, R., 122, 132
Freeman, J. H., 81, 156, 159–60, 180, 187, 208–10, 218, 229–31
Freeman, R. E., 240
Freidson, E., 99, 101
French, J. R. P., 91
Friedland, R., 80, 203, 205
Frost, P. J., 49
Fu, P. P., 114

G

Galaskiewicz, J., 10, 190, 194–97, 200, 204–5, 218
Gamoran, A., 59
Gamson, W., 120
Garcia, J. E., 116
Gardner, E. A., 199
Gargiulo, M., 197

Geeraerts, G., 67
Georgiou, P., 232–33
Gersick, C. J. G., 157, 184
Giordano, P. C., 6, 193, 202, 234
Glass, J., 8
Glisson, C. A., 49, 70
Goes, J. B., 170, 189
Gooderham, P. N., 84, 221
Goodman, J., 83, 221
Goodman, P. S., 16, 68, 79, 216,
    235–37, 240
Goodstein, J. D., 83, 162, 203, 221
Gould, R. V., 91
Gouldner, A., 110, 117–19
Govindarajan, V., 31, 76
Grafton, C., 210
Granovetter, M., 133
Grant, D. S., II, 13
Greenberg, D., 91
Greenwood, R., 30, 54, 79, 101
Gresov, C., 84, 239
Greve, H. R., 163
Griffith, T. L., 68
Gross, E., 96, 228
Grusky, O., 119–20, 122
Guest, R., 118
Guetzkow, H., 149–50
Guillen, M. F., 14, 133
Gulati, R., 133, 197
Guler, I., 133
Gupta, A., 31, 76, 221
Gupta, P. P., 84
Gusfield, J. R., 20
Gutek, B. A., 6–7

H

Haas, J. E., 36–37, 67
Haas, M. R., 136
Hackman, J. R., 179
Hage, J., 7, 31, 34–35, 43–44, 46–48, 52,
    54, 57, 69, 101, 145, 147, 155,
    169–71, 189, 194, 201
Halberstam, D., 144
Hall, R. H., 5, 13, 17, 30–31, 36–37,
    52–53, 60, 66–67, 76, 98, 101, 171,
    193, 202, 219
Halpert, B. P., 194, 199

Hambrick, D. C., 67, 92, 164, 166
Hamilton, G. L., 76, 83
Hamner, W. C., 116
Han, S.-K., 84
Hanada, M., 76
Hannan, M. T., 81, 136, 156, 159, 160,
    162, 208, 209, 210, 218, 229–31,
    240
Hardy, C., 87
Harris, S. G., 166
Harrison, J. S., 240
Haunschild, P. R., 4, 133, 189, 202
Haveman, H., 68, 84, 156, 163, 221
Hawley, A. H., 174
Hawley, W. E., 58
Hedberg, B., 156
Heian, J. B., 54
Heilbronner, R., 24
Heller, F. A., 136
Helmich, D., 122
Heydebrand, W. V., 29, 30, 61, 66
Hickson, D. J., 36, 46, 48, 66, 69, 91–92,
    213
Hills, F. S., 95
Hinings, B., 30, 54, 79, 101
Hinings, C. R., 36, 46, 48, 91, 213, 217
Hirsch, P. M., 83, 188, 219–20, 242
Hirschhorn, L., 13
Hirschman, A. O., 7, 97
Hochschild, A. R., 7
Hoff, T., 100
Hofstede, G. H., 57, 75
Hogan, J., 111
Hogan, R., 111
Holbek, J., 68, 171
Holden, C., 171
Hollander, E. P., 112
Horowitz, A. M., 16
Hougland, J. G., 96
Hougland, J. G., Jr., 10
House, R. J., 112–14, 116, 161, 221
Hrebiniak, L. G., 188
Huber, G. P., 99, 226
Huffington, A., 124
Hull, R., 145
Hunter, A., 159
Huo, Y. P., 159
Hyde, C., 72
Hylton, L., 189, 200

I

Ilardi, B. C., 113
Ilvento, T. W., 10
Ingram, P., 195
Inkson, J., 66
Isabella, L. A., 162

J

Jackall, R., 25, 134
Jacobs, D., 179, 187
Jaeger, A. M., 75
James, D. R., 124, 204
Jenkins, J. C., 228
Jennings, P. D., 80, 221
Jiang, S., 60, 76
Jick, T. D., 155
John, D., 197
Johnson, J. B., 75
Johnson, J. M., 243
Johnson, P., 36, 66, 193
Jones, A. W., 13
Jonsson, E., 164
Julian, J. W., 112
Jurkovich, R., 185

K

Kabanoff, B., 99
Kahn, R. L., 6–7, 78, 109, 139, 142–43,
    146, 217
Kalleberg, A. L., 8, 29, 68
Kanter, R. M., 91, 94, 96, 138, 155, 214,
    228
Kaplan, A., 87
Karau, S. J., 114
Karichalil, R., 121–22
Kasarda, J. D., 72, 208
Katz, D., 6–7, 78, 97–99, 109, 139,
    142–43, 146, 217
Katz, R., 152
Kaufman, H., 157
Kaufman, R. L., 29
Keeley, M., 234–35
Keister, L. A., 202
Kelly, D., 163

Kenney, M., 183
Kerbo, H. R., 205
Khandwalla, P. N., 58, 73, 187
Kieser, A., 15, 156, 161
Kilburn, H. C., Jr., 12, 192, 202, 228
Kilijanek, T. S., 201
Kilmann, R. H., 14
Kim, M. U., 164
Kim, Y.-H., 13
Kimberly, J. R., 65–66, 155, 159, 162, 167
Klatzky, S., 66, 180
Klauss, R., 138
Klonglan, G. E., 195
Knoke, D., 3, 13, 25–26, 29, 218
Kochan, T. A., 99, 155, 198, 226
Koenig, R., Jr., 57, 71
Kogut, B., 179
Kohn, M., 5, 51
Kono, C., 203
Koput, K. W., 190
Korb, L. A., 191
Kornhauser, W., 51
Kovacic, B., 60
Kraatz, M. S., 83
Kralewski, J. E., 56
Krohn, K. R., 10
Kruytbosch, C., 204
Kunce, J. T., 196
Kunda, G., 94, 101

L

Lachman, R., 95
Lammers, C. J., 26, 61, 95
Lang, J. R., 203
Langston, J., 217
Laumann, E. O., 13, 25, 81, 218
Lawler, E. J., 61, 90–91, 136
Lawrence, B. S., 141
Lawrence, P. R., 39–41, 58, 69, 81, 97,
    105, 176–77, 216, 240
Lazerson, M. H., 189
Leavitt, H. J., 148
Leblebici, H., 58, 73, 187, 213
Lee, C. A., 91, 213
Leicht, K. T., 29
Lepsinger, R., 109
Lester, M., 239

Leventhal, D. A., 166
Levine, A. G., 15, 26
Levine, S., 195–97, 200
Levinthal, D. A., 195
Levitt, B., 132
Lieberson, S., 123–24
Liedholm, C., 3
Lin, N., 91
Lincoln, J. R., 29, 57, 76
Lipset, S. M., 21–23, 125
Litwak, E., 30, 189, 200
Lockhart, D. E., 203
Long, A., 95
Long, J. S., 7
Lord, R. G., 113, 123
Lorsch, J. W., 5, 39–41, 58, 69, 81, 97,
    105, 176–77, 216, 240
Loscocco, K. A., 60, 76
Lotz, R. E., 121
Louis, M. R., 49
Lozano, B., 6
Luckman, T., 219
Lundberg, C. C., 49
Lupton, K. M., 66
Lupton, T., 66

M

Maas, M. L., 196
MacMillan, I. G., 166
MacPherson, J. M., 133
Maguire, M. A., 57
Mahmoudi, H., 76
Mahoney, T. A., 95, 232
Malan, L., 74
Mannari, H., 75–76
Manning, P. K., 139
Manns, C. L., 171
Mansfield, R., 56, 66, 70
Mara-Drita, I., 221
March, J. G., 129–32, 135, 139, 144, 163, 171
Marcus, A. A., 16, 240
Marglin, S. A., 61
Marple, D., 212
Marrett, C. B., 145, 198, 200
Marsden, P. J., 200
Marsden, P. V., 3, 29, 183, 218
Marsh, R. M., 75–76
Martin, J., 49

Maryanski, A., 219
Mattis, M., 113
Maurice, M., 76
McBride, K., 76
McCaffrey, D., 100
McCaffrey, D. P., 179
McEwen, W., 227–28
McGinnis, R., 7
McKechnie, P., 230
McKelvey, B., 160, 208
McKinley, W., 42, 71
McMahon, A. M., 113
McMillan, C. J., 24, 29, 66
McNeil, K., 171
Mead, D., 3
Means, G. C., 11, 124
Mechanic, D., 89, 91
Meindl, J. R., 109
Mendel, P. J., 94
Merton, R. K., 3, 50, 189
Meyer, A. D., 179
Meyer, J. W., 82, 158, 218, 219
Meyer, M. W., 49, 66, 70, 74, 80, 162, 176,
    187, 231–32
Mezias, S. J., 82, 221
Michels, R., 95, 125, 228
Miles, R. A., 155
Miles, R. E., 79
Miller, D., 79, 84, 243
Miller, G. A., 51, 69, 76
Milliken, F. J., 187
Milner, M., Jr., 205
Milward, H. B., 189
Mindl, J. R., 122
Miner, A. S., 6, 18, 162
Minihan, E., 171
Mintz, B., 203, 205
Mintzberg, H., 87
Mitroff, I. I., 14
Mizruchi, M. S., 82, 202–3, 205
Moch, M. K., 170
Mohan, M. L., 139
Mohr, L. B., 69
Molnar, J. J., 196
Molotch, H., 239
Montansani, J. R., 76
Moore, L. F., 49
Moore, W. L., 122
Morrill, C., 106, 166
Morse, E. V., 170

Morse, J. J., 5
Mouton, J. S., 112
Mueller, C. W., 29
Mulford, C. L., 196, 200–201
Mulford, M. A., 201
Mullaney, P., 204–5

N

Nagel, S., 12, 178
Nagi, S. Z., 186
Near, J. P., 15, 188
Nee, N., 60
Needleman, C., 14
Needleman, M. L., 14
Neef, M., 12, 178
Negandhi, A. R., 58
Neilsen, E. H., 162
Nelson, R. B., 72
Neustadt, A., 205
Nordhaug, O., 84, 221
Nowak, P., 184, 192
Nuss, C., 132
Nystrom, P. C., 67, 77–78, 160

O

O'Connor, J. F., 123–24
Oliver, C., 166, 199, 220
Olsen, J. P., 129, 132
Organ, D., 116
Ornstein, M., 205
Orton, J. D., 59
Ott, J. S., 72
Ouchi, W. G., 57, 71, 75

P

Padevic, I., 8–9
Padgett, J. F., 91
Page, K. L., 4, 201
Palmer, D., 163, 203
Palmer, D. A., 80, 205, 221
Panian, S. K., 91, 121
Parcel, T. L., 29
Park, S. H., 170, 189

Parsons, T., 100, 212, 220
Pascale, R., 142
Paul, B. D., 195–96
Paulson, S. K., 195
Pennings, J. M., 12, 29, 79, 91, 159, 167,
    180, 202–3, 213, 216, 235–37
Perlow, L. A., 54
Perrow, C., 1–2, 13–14, 21, 31, 45, 68–69,
    92–93, 129–31, 176, 210, 215,
    226–27, 237–38
Perrucci, R., 10
Perry, J. L., 234
Peter, L. J., 145
Peters, T. J., 72, 77
Peterson, R. A., 96, 162
Pfeffer, J., 8, 58, 61, 73, 79, 87, 91–92,
    95, 122–23, 135–36, 181, 184,
    187, 192, 208–9, 211–13, 215,
    217, 221
Pheysey, D. C., 66, 69, 92
Pilisuk, M., 10
Pitt, L., 56
Podolny, J. M., 4, 201
Pondy, L. R., 95, 103
Portugal, E., 203
Powell, W. W., 81–82, 190, 218–20
Powers, M. E., 80
Prechel, H., 163, 179
Preisendoerfer, P., 76
Prensky, D., 25–26
Price, J. L., 29, 34
Price, R. H., 74
Priest, T. B., 92, 178
Prokesh, S. E., 82, 218
Provan, K. G., 189, 204
Puffer, S. M., 230
Pugh, D. S., 36, 46, 48, 66, 69, 92, 208

Q

Quinn, R. E., 50, 162

R

Raelin, J. A., 199
Ragins, B. R., 113
Rahim, M. A., 104–5
Rakowski, C. A., 3

Ranson, S., 30, 54, 79
Rao, H., 84, 162, 221
Raphael, E., 37
Rauschenbach, B., 204–5
Raven, B., 91
Rawls, J., 234
Reimann, B. C., 58
Reinganum, M. R., 123
Reiss, A. J., Jr., 14
Reskin, B. F., 8–9, 99
Revkin, A. C., 13
Ridgeway, C. L., 113
Rifkin, J., 5
Ringdal, K., 84, 221
Ritzer, G., 3, 34
Roberts, K. H., 148
Roberts, P. W., 195
Rodgers, W. M., 99
Rogers, L. D., 58
Romanelli, E., 158–59
Romo, F. P., 134
Rosenbaum, J. E., 8
Rosenholtz, S. J., 113
Rosenweig, P. M., 76
Rosner, M., 60
Rosow, J. M., 5
Ross, J., 133
Rothman, R. A., 92, 178
Rothschild, J., 55
Rowan, B., 158, 218
Roy, W. G., 13, 188, 203
Rozgonyi, T., 60
Rubin, I., 58
Ruef, M., 94
Rus, V., 59

S

Sabel, C. F., 97
Salancik, G. R., 79, 91–92, 95, 122–23,
    211, 217
Samuel, S., 54
Samuel, Y., 233
Sanchez, S. M., 166
Sanford, R. N., 97
Satow, R., 100
Schein, V. E., 113
Schmidt, S. M., 99, 198

Schneck, R. E., 91, 213
Schneider, S. C., 77, 183
Schoenherr, R. A., 36, 42, 47, 55, 66, 71
Schollhammer, H., 75
Schooler, C., 5
Schoonhoven, C. B., 217
Schreyogg, G., 77, 212
Schwartz, M., 134, 203, 205
Schwitter, J. P., 66
Schwochan, S., 199
Scotch, N., 120
Scott, W. R., 49, 51, 55–56, 69, 82, 89, 94,
    145, 217, 219–20
Seabright, M. A., 195
Seashore, S. E., 225, 239
Seidel, M. D., 133
Seiler, L. H., 10
Selznick, P., 17–20, 59, 109, 228
Sewell, W. H., 30
Shatin, D., 56, 195
Shenkar, O., 16
Shepard, J. M., 10, 96
Shetler, J. C., 133
Shrum, W., 193
Siengthai, S., 72
Sills, D. L., 29
Simon, H. A., 78, 128–30, 135
Simpson, R. L., 146
Singh, J. V., 76, 161, 163, 205, 221
Slater, P. E., 111
Slocum, J. W., Jr., 217
Smircich, L., 72
Smith, K., 102
Smith-Doerr, L., 190
Snipe, J. N., 199
Snow, C. C., 79, 188
Sonnenstuhl, W., 163
Soref, M., 124, 204
Sorge, A., 76, 84
Soysal, Y., 163
Spaeth, J. L., 29
Sproul, L. S., 144
Staber, U., 161
Stalker, G. M., 31, 40, 58
Starbuck, W. H., 67, 77–78, 160,
    186–87, 214
Starke, F. A., 159
Stauffer, R. E., 66
Staw, B. M., 133, 156, 230

Steams, T. M., 162
Stearns, L. B., 203
Steckmest, F. W., 26
Steers, R. M., 233
Stein, B. A., 155
Stevenson, W. B., 36, 91
Stewart, K. J., 133
Stinchcombe, A. L., 30, 34, 138, 174–76
Stogdill, R. M., 111
Stolzenberg, R. M., 8
Storing, H., 129
Strang, D., 35
Summers, G. F., 10
Sutton, J. R., 82, 84
Sutton, R. I., 74, 166
Swaninathan, A., 76, 163
Swigert, V. L., 16

T

Tamminga, H. L., 201
Tannenbaum, A. S., 60
Tayeb, M., 76
Taylor, J. C., 57
Terkel, S., 5
Terreberry, S., 193
Thach, L., 167
Thomas, A. B., 123
Thompson, C. A., 196
Thompson, J. D., 79, 130–31, 227–28
Thompson, V., 51
Tickner, J. A., 132
Tilly, C., 6
Tinsley, C. H., 166–67, 209
Tittle, C. R., 66
Tolbert, P. S., 83, 100, 158, 220
Tonry, M., 14
Tosi, H. L., Jr., 217
Townsend, B., 113
Toynbee, A., 24
Trice, H. M., 71–72
Trist, E. L., 193
Trow, M. A., 125
Tsui, A. S., 240
Tucker, D. J., 161, 221
Turk, H., 194
Turner, C., 36, 46, 48, 66
Turner, J. H., 219

Tushman, M., 158
Tushman, M. L., 72, 161

U

Üsdiken, B., 84
Useem, M., 12, 155, 188, 205
Uzzi, B., 6, 8, 134, 190

V

Valcour, P. M., 96, 125
Van Buren, M. E., 8, 68
Van de Ven, A. H., 54, 57, 71, 78, 83, 190,
    195, 197–98, 209–10
Van Houton, D. R., 84
Vaughan, D., 14–15, 44, 127
Verhovek, S. H., 179
Vianello, M., 60
Vroom, V. H., 112–13

W

Wade, J., 162
Waegel, W. B., 16
Walczak, D., 34
Walker, G., 198
Walker, H. A., 113
Wall, S., 109
Warner, M., 66, 76
Warren, R., 189, 195
Wasilewski, N., 183, 187
Wasserman, S., 204–5
Waterman, R. H., Jr., 72, 77
Weber, M., 31, 81, 87–88, 218
Webster, M., 113
Weick, K. E., 59, 72, 148, 171, 188
Weiner, N., 123
Weitz, B. A., 230
Weitzel, W., 164, 232
Werking, R. H., 13, 188
Westphal, J. D., 133, 204
Whetten, D. A., 29, 46, 58–59, 164,
    195–96, 200, 237
White, P. E., 195–97, 200
Whitt, J. A., 55

Wholey, D. R., 166
Wiedenmayer, G., 76
Wieser, G., 60
Wiewel, W., 159
Wildavsky, A., 181, 227
Wilensky, H., 144
Williamson, O. E., 4
Willmott, H., 94
Winkelpleck, J. M., 195
Withey, M., 7
Wong, G. Y. Y., 75–76
Wood, J. R., 96
Woodman, R., 167
Woodward, J., 68–69
Wuthnow, R., 193

X

Xu, W., 76

Y

Yarmolinsky, A., 58
Yeager, P. C., 14, 26

Yetman, N. R., 121
Yetton, P. W., 112–13
Young, R. C., 210
Yuchtman, E., 225
Yukl, G., 114–15
Yukl, G. A., 108–10

Z

Zafonte, M., 203
Zajac, E. J., 83, 204
Zald, M., 93, 95, 204
Zalkind, S., 140–41
Zaltman, G., 168, 171
Zammuto, R. F., 237
Zander, U., 179
Zanetich, J. T., 4
Zeitlin, M., 11, 124
Zeitz, G., 29, 57
Zenger, T. R., 141
Zey, M., 128
Zhou, X., 49, 163, 221
Zucker, L. G., 83, 88, 158, 162,
    219–20